Maryland Aloft

A Celebration of Aviators, Airfields and Aerospace

Maryland Historical Trust Press
Crownsville, Maryland

Edmund Preston • Barry A. Lanman • John R. Breihan

Published by
THE MARYLAND HISTORICAL TRUST PRESS

COPYRIGHT © 2003
THE MARYLAND HISTORICAL TRUST PRESS

All rights reserved.

MARYLAND HISTORICAL TRUST PRESS
Department of Housing and Community Development
100 Community Place
Crownsville, MD 21032-2023

ISBN 1-878399-82-9

This publication has been financed in part with state funds from the Maryland Historical Trust, an agency of the Department of Housing and Community Development of the State of Maryland. However, the contents and opinions do not necessarily reflect the views or policies of the Maryland Historical Trust or the Department of Housing and Community Development.

Library of Congress Cataloging-in-Publication Data
Preston, Edmund, 1941 -
    Maryland aloft: a celebration of aviators, airfields, and aerospace / Edmund Preston,
    Barry A. Lanman, John R. Breihan.
      p. cm.
    Includes bibliographical references and index.
    ISBN 1-878399-82-9
      1. Aeronautics--Maryland--History. I. Lanman, Barry Allen. II. Breihan, John R. III.
    Title.
    TL522.M3P742 2003
    629.13'09752--dc22

Printed in the United States of America by
Victor Graphics, 1211 Bernard Avenue, Baltimore, Maryland 21223

Graphic Design and Production by
Words & Pictures, Inc., 27 South River Road South, Edgewater, Maryland 21037-1415

Table of Contents

Acknowledgements

This is a publication for aviation aficionados, history buffs and serious researchers alike, and can be used in many ways. While the core material documents individual historic sites and some aviation-related sites of more recent vintage, the volume also presents a historical overview highlighting Maryland's role in aerospace history, as well as the stories of some of the people who were part of Maryland's aviation experience. "Flying Fields," written by Dr. John Breihan, discusses the evolution of airfields and the types of structures that would typically be found on such a site. "From Balloons to Rockets," written by Dr. Edmund Preston, presents a historical overview of Maryland's role in the development of human flight. "Grass Fields, Factory Floors, Airparks and Missile Sites" highlights over one hundred aviation sites in Maryland arranged chronologically in four distinct periods of aerospace history. At the end of the book, these sites are cross indexed by county, for those who may be interested in how specific areas were impacted by the development of aviation technology. Throughout the book are "Oral History Files," oral history interviews collected by Dr. Barry A. Lanman and staff oral historians Jennifer Braithwait Darrow and John D. Willard at the Martha Ross Center for Oral History at the University of Maryland, Baltimore County, which relay first person accounts of aviation history. To aid future researchers, the volume includes endnotes, a bibliography, and a brief directory of materials and collections related to Maryland aviation history.

This volume's genesis arose from a lunchtable conversation at the Maryland Historical Trust in January 2001. Richard Hughes, an archeologist and general aviation pilot, mentioned that the one hundredth anniversary of the Wright Brothers' first flight in Kitty Hawk, North Carolina, would be coming up shortly. Realizing that the State of Maryland has played a crucial role in the development of modern aviation, with the support of the Trust's Director, J. Rodney Little, a group of staff formed the "Centennial of Flight Committee" to honor those aviation achievements in Maryland.

Because the Maryland Historical Trust is responsible as the State's Historic Preservation Office for researching, documenting, and interpreting historical and cultural resources, the Committee quickly realized it should focus its efforts on identifying historic and archeological resources in Maryland that were significant to aviation history. Because of the nature of the topic, the Trust chose to define "historic resources" broadly to include such places as civil airports, factories, technical centers, military airfields, and missile bases, and included many facilities that are relatively recent in origin. Recognizing that many of those people who experienced aviation history firsthand were still alive, the Trust decided that gathering their stories had to be an integral part of the project. To help identify these people and places that told Maryland's aerospace history, the Trust partnered with Cathy Allen and the College Park Aviation Museum to host "A Meeting of the Minds" on June 13, 2001, with individuals who were knowledgeable about Maryland aviation history. The primary purpose of the meeting was to solicit suggestions for places to be surveyed and inventoried, people to be interviewed and collections to be researched.

Armed with a mountain of suggestions from the meeting's attendees, the Trust developed a two-pronged project: an inventory of historical sites and a series of oral history interviews. Using an MHT Non-Capital Historic Preservation Grant, the College Park Aviation Museum hired Dr. Edmund Preston, a former historian at the Federal Aviation Administration, to complete an inventory of aviation-related sites as well as a contextual essay on Maryland's aerospace history. To complement this work, the Martha Ross Center for Oral History at the University of Maryland, Baltimore County, under the leadership of Dr. Barry A. Lanman, completed over twenty-five oral history interviews of Marylanders who were there on the ground (or in the air). Realizing the breadth and importance of the data collected under this project, the Trust hired Dr. John Breihan, from the History Department at Loyola College, to edit the data into a popular publication on Maryland's aviation history, resulting in the publication you see today.

This project would not have gotten off the ground without the assistance of those attendees at the June 2001 "Meeting of the Minds," including: Cathy Allen, Director, Anne Smallman, Collections Curator, and Jane Welsh, Education Curator, College Park Aviation Museum; Mark Allen; Mary Alexander, Suzanne Almalel, Steve Bilicki, Nicole Diehlmann, Elaine Eff, Elizabeth Hughes, Richard Hughes, Peter Kurtze, and Scott Whipple, Maryland Historical Trust; John D. Anderson, Curator for Aerodynamics, and Tom Crouch, Senior Curator, National Air and Space Museum; Henry Bonner, Executive Director, and Thomas H. Quinlan, Patuxent River Naval Air Museum; Dr. John Breihan, Loyola College; Bruce Bustard, National Archives; Sharon C. Foster, Executive Director, Centennial of Flight Commission; William F. Holton, National Historian, Tuskegee Airmen, Inc.; Dr. Randall Mason, Director, Historic Preservation Program, University of Maryland College Park; Harry Mettee; Roger G. Miller, AFHSO/HOP; Charlie Morse; Matt Neitzey and Carl Smith, Prince George's County Convention and Visitor's Bureau; Stan Piet, Executive Director, Glenn L. Martin Maryland Aviation Museum; Edmund Preston, Historian, Federal Aviation Administration; Ritch Stevenson; Joseph N. Tatarewicz, Department of History, University of Maryland Baltimore County; John Tegler; and Debi Wynne, Baltimore Museum of Industry.

Many thanks are also due to those who agreed to have their stories recorded as part of the oral history project: Betsey Weick, Mary Feik, Col. George Henry (Ret.), Herbert H. Jones, Bill Rinn, Allen Clopper, Jack King, Aubrey Patterson, Gustavus (Gus) McLeod, Bruce Mundie, Bill Morris, Joe Frichera, Col. Paul Butler (Ret.), Henry Rinn, Elaine Harmon, Bill Almquist, Wendy Carter, Jane Straughan, Henry Phipps, Charles O'Brien, Richard Whistler, Paul Lebert, Maynard Binge, Jesse Mitchell, Gary Ryan, Charles Greenslit, Ferne Virginia Toms, Gayle Barnes, Janet Lee Simpson, and Kathryn Hutchinson James.

The editor and authors of this book owe an enormous debt to John F.R. Scott, author of *Voyages to Airy Regions*, the first general history of aviation in Maryland, who died just short of the hundredth birthday of the airplane. Other debts are owed to: Cathy Allen of the College Park Aviation Museum; Stan Piet, Roger Mason, Charles Morse, and Gil Pascal of the Glenn L. Martin Maryland Aviation Museum; Kent Mitchell and Kurtis Meyer of Hagerstown; Bruce Mundie of the Maryland Aviation Administration; Mark Schatz of the Ann Arrundell County Historical Society; Debbie McCallum of NASA Goddard; Nicole Purdy of Colquitt Design; Technical Sergeant Kirk Clear of Andrews Air Force Base; Paul Freeman and Joe Tatarewicz of the Granite Historical Society; Elaine Eff and Scott Whipple of the Maryland Historical Trust; Roger Thiel and Mike Streiter; and many others too numerous to mention.

Nicole A. Diehlmann
Mary Alexander
Richard Hughes
Maryland Historical Trust
Crownsville 2003

Flying Fields:
Where the Sky Meets the Ground

By John R. Breihan

This is an unusual book on aviation history: it does not center on airplanes. Not that there are no historic aircraft in Maryland. A number of them are on display at the College Park Aviation Museum, still more are to be seen at the Glenn L. Martin Maryland Aviation Museum in Middle River. Others, in various stages of restoration, stand in individual hangars around the state. And of course the Smithsonian Institution's incomparable collection of aircraft is just across the border in the District of Columbia and (after December 2003) in Virginia.

This is a book about people and places. Its publisher, the Maryland Historical Trust, is the state agency responsible for the preservation of historic properties, archeological sites, and communities. As such, the Trust maintains an inventory of Maryland's significant historical and architectural landmarks. The Trust also maintains an active interest in Maryland folklife and folkways, most often studied in the form of oral histories. Both strands come together in this book, which contains Edmund Preston's inventory of 125 sites associated with Maryland aviation, and the oral histories of fourteen Marylanders also associated with aviation, collected and digested by the Martha Ross Center for Oral History at the University of Maryland Baltimore County. Edmund Preston also provides an historical introduction drawing together aviation sites and human experiences of them.

The subject of this book, then, is the interface of ground and sky: the places on the earth specially constructed or prepared to enable people to fly through the air. The airfield and the airport are the most common examples, along with their distinctive structures, the hangar, the terminal, the tower, the runway, and the taxiway. Besides historic airports, Maryland also contains some of the most significant aircraft factories in the country, and some of the most significant aircraft research centers as well. Finally, Maryland was the site of

important events in early aviation, from the Wright Brothers' flights at College Park to the great Baltimore Aviation Meet of 1910, to the Schneider Cup races of 1925.

Throughout all of these sites and recollections, certain types of buildings recur again and again. First and most basic is *the field*, the place where aircraft take off and alight. Although a skilled pilot can land a plane in the legendary cow pasture, repeated operations call for a special field. It should be well drained, providing a smooth but not muddy surface for aircraft wheels. It should be cleared of all obstructions on the landing ground itself, and, as far as possible, vertical obstructions like trees or towers on its periphery. The earliest flying fields were great round prairies of grass, allowing airplanes to land and take off into the wind whatever direction the windsock blew. "Airfields" thus preceded "airports," and the term remains in common use.

The first *airports*—fields adapted for the transportation of people or goods—added a second structure, *the terminal*. Borrowed from the dominant transportation

Baltimore's municipal airport during the 1930s, Logan Field, was just that—a vast plain of grass and dirt along Dundalk Avenue, Baltimore County. Photo courtesy of Dundalk-Patapsco Neck Historical Society.

A 110-foot control tower dominated the design of the original terminal at Friendship (now Baltimore/Washington International) Airport, Anne Arundel County, completed in 1950. Also shown in this photograph are brand-new Martin 2-O-2 and 4-O-4 airliners.
Photo courtesy of Glenn L. Martin Maryland Aviation Museum.

er aircraft, or more than one plane, hangars employ a variety of structures to extend a roof across a large interior space without any supporting columns. The roof, usually a hangar's most notable feature, may be vaulted, gabled, cantilevered, or suspended. A door, wide and tall enough to admit aircraft wings and tails, is a second, though no less important, feature.

As aircraft grew heavier and more numerous, another basic element was added: *the runway*. Defining, and eventually paving the most common landing strips allowed arrivals and departures on the airfield to be more regulated and more numerous. Initially, runways were laid out along several prevailing wind directions, resulting in "X," "V" or "A" patterns. More recent airport design has sought to avoid dangerous

system of aviation's early years, the railroads, terminals were supposed to organize air transportation—sorting out passengers for one destination from those for another, and passengers from those who were remaining on the ground. Airport terminals also represent the home community to the outside world, and, perhaps more importantly, the aviation world to the home community. Terminals, therefore, have often been showpieces, with prosaic functions like baggage check-in and ticket sales carried out in soaring spaces amidst memorable architectural decoration.

At the other end of the spectrum, but even more basic to aviation, appearing on all but the most minimal airfield, is *the hangar*. Named after the French word for "carriage shed," it is one of a cluster of words like "aileron" (the rear moveable portion of a wing), "nacelle" (a streamlined covering of an engine) and "fuselage," that demonstrate the important role in early aviation of French flyers and designers. The hangar's primary purpose is to allow airplanes to be moved out of the elements for service, repair, or simply the preservation of their delicate structures. Though graceful in the air, aircraft are ungainly on the ground. Their tail rudders rise high vertically, their wings stretch wide horizontally. The ubiquitous "T-hangar" serves small private aircraft by reproducing their structure, fitting the tall tail in a raised center section and the wings in two side extensions – from the air forming a letter "T." To house larg-

The simplest of hangars, built in the 1930s and now standing at Mexico Farms Airport, Allegany County. Photo courtesy of Maryland Historical Trust.

runway intersections in favor of widely spaced parallel runways aligned along the dominant wind directions and allowing for simultaneous landings and take-offs. Smaller airports have increasingly focused on a single runway, aligned if possible to minimize crosswinds. The capacity of runways is enhanced by narrower *taxiways* that allow aircraft to leave the runway soon after landing, freeing it up for the next take-off or landing. Airport terminals are surrounded by broad paved *aprons* for loading or unloading; smaller airports have extensive tie-down areas for aircraft parking.

Although more visible from the air than from the ground, runways, taxiways, and aprons are structures too. Larger and heavier aircraft soon outgrew simple cinder or blacktop pavements. Modern planes require reinforced concrete up to twenty-four inches thick, laid upon substrata of sand and gravel, carefully graded for adequate drainage into a network of basins and culverts and storm sewers, and fitted with lights and instrument landing systems. Drains, sewers, and electrical conduits constitute an underground infrastructure of every modern airport.

Airports include a myriad of other structures. Perhaps the most familiar is the *control tower*, a glassed-in observation post high above the runway that provides a perch for air-traffic controllers to manage close-in traffic and taxiing aircraft at the busiest airports. Even small airports have an *office*, usually the headquarters of the "fixed base operator" who provides fuel, repairs, and other services to pilots. With the encouragement of the Maryland Aviation Administration even the smallest possess a *"pilot shelter,"* where a pilot can sit or stand out of the rain and telephone for a fuel truck or taxi. Aircraft fueling and repairs require a variety of structures besides hangars. Some airports have a *snack bar*. Private pilots adopt the best of them as destinations, flying long distances for a "$100 hamburger" (or, in Maryland, crab cake).

The interface between aviation and the ground is not limited to the airport. Maryland is the home of important *research and testing institutions* that have

Runways and taxiways at Salisbury -Ocean City: Wicomico Regional Airport displays the classic "A" alignment. Photo courtesy of MAA.

Famed aviators like Charles Lindbergh, Jimmy Doolittle, and Wiley Post— along with generations of other hungry pilots—have passed through this door to the snack bar at Mexico Farms Airport, Allegany County. Photo courtesy of MAA.

shaped the last century of aviation, from the military testing at Patuxent River Naval Air Station and Aberdeen Proving Ground to basic research at the Naval Ordnance Laboratory at White Oak, the Carderock Naval Surface Warfare Center, or Goddard Space Flight Center. These research facilities required a variety of structures. Perhaps the best known is the *wind tunnel,* where model planes and missiles are subjected to effects arising from speed. Maryland is home to a number of wind tunnels, ranging from the basic to the hypersonic. The Goddard Space Flight Center even has a facility for testing future craft against the magnetic winds of outer space.

The most dramatic buildings associated with Maryland aviation are the great *aircraft factories* outside Baltimore, Washington, and Hagerstown. Besides the usual structures of a metalworking factory— receiving warehouses, machine shops, design lofts—aircraft factories have the same requirements as hangars, only more so. Instead of just a few ungainly aircraft they must house a whole production line of them, needing both vertical space for their

*Above: Buildings 139 and 141 (now demolished) housed the subsonic wind tunnel built in 1942 at the Carderock Division, Naval Surface Warfare Center, Montgomery County.
Photo courtesy of the Maryland Historical Trust.*

tails and no obstructions for their wings. America's premier factory designer of the twentieth century was Albert Kahn. Three of his masterworks stand in Maryland. At the two Glenn L. Martin plants in Middle River, Kahn used huge steel bridge trusses to carry factory roofs across wide unobstructed assembly floors. At Fairchild in Hagerstown he used tall arches of laminated wood. Kahn believed that workers should have the benefit of natural light, so the walls and ceilings of his steel factories are sixty percent glass. The Middle River factories helped inspired the steel-and-glass "international style" architecture of such postwar masters as Mies van der Rohe As they assembled the sleek Marauders and SeaMasters, PT-13 trainers and Flying Boxcars, Martin and Fairchild workers could look up and see the sky.

*Below: A sixteen-foot Sitka spruce fan powered by a 700-horsepower electric motor provided the wind.
Photo courtesy of the Maryland Historical Trust.*

Perhaps the strangest aviation-related structures in Maryland were formed in the two rings of *Nike anti-aircraft missile sites* that guarded Washington and Baltimore from possible Soviet attack during the Cold War. Instead of serving aircraft, these sites were designed to destroy them, fixing on their prey with radar arrays mounted on concrete monoliths, then raising sleek missiles from underground silos to be fired on a signal from a concrete command post. The radars, silos, and command centers scattered across the Maryland landscape thankfully were never used; their surviving fragments remain as monuments to an era of fear.

The sites described in this book are workaday jobsites for the thousands of Marylanders who make their living in the many industries associated with aviation, while seldom leaving the ground themselves. All of us move about and around these sites every day. They are part of the landscape. But, every so often, we hear an engine or see a shadow cross the ground. We glance into the sky to see a sleek flying machine defying gravity, soaring above Maryland's green fields, an apparent miracle of power and grace and human ingenuity. Even after a century, we look up with wonder and pride.

The huge glass monitors of Martin's 1937 B Building loom above the 1929 Administration Building at Plant No. 1 in Middle River, Baltimore County. Photo courtesy of Glenn L. Martin Maryland Aviation Museum.

Kahn used more conventional sawtooth roof monitors in the 1942 Fairchild Aircraft plant at Hagerstown Airport, Washington County. Photo courtesy of Kent A. Mitchell.

Maryland Aloft

A Celebration of Aviators, Airfields and Aerospace

From Balloons to Rockets:
Maryland Aviation in Context

By Edmund Preston

The airplane was born on a wintry stretch of North Carolina coastland on December 17, 1903, but Marylanders began making aviation history over a century before the Wright Brothers' momentous flight, when aviation technology involved hot air or hydrogen gas enclosed within carefully-stitched silk. From those early balloon flights, Marylanders have been involved in almost all aspects of aerospace history including notable ventures in the development of airplanes, rockets, and related electronic systems. Maryland's aviation story begins in the late eighteenth century in a town near the Anacostia River.

The Age of Aeronauts

The opening scene in the drama of human flight in the United States took place in Maryland in 1784, inspired by events in France during the previous year. In that country, a balloon built by the Montgolfier brothers had astounded the world by carrying aloft a group of animals, soon followed by human aeronauts. Accounts of these achievements led enthusiastic Americans to experiment with small balloons, or "aerostats." Prominent citizens in Philadelphia began raising funds to construct one large enough to carry a passenger. This effort was overtaken, however, by a lone and relatively obscure entrepreneur—Peter Carnes of Bladensburg, Maryland.[1]

A colorful figure with a reputation as a jokester, Carnes was a lawyer and the proprietor of a commercial complex centering on the Indian Queen Tavern. Guided by no more than reports of developments in France and his own experiments, he built his American Aerostatic Balloon, which stood 30 feet high when inflated. Carnes planned to make a profit on this venture by selling tickets for a close-up view of the balloon being launched from within an enclosure. He gave a public demonstration of the device in Bladensburg on June 19, 1784, and prepared for a much-advertised ascent near Baltimore five days later.[2]

On the morning of June 24, many Baltimore businesses closed shop and crowds streamed from the city to the exhibition site at Howard Park. Carnes successfully raised and lowered the balloon several times, but did not attempt the personal ascent that his announcements had implied would take place. This was probably because he had come to realize that the device would not lift his considerable weight of more than 230 pounds. During the afternoon, however, a thirteen-year-old named Edward Warren stepped from among the onlookers and volunteered to go aloft in the tethered aerostat. This bold impulse made the young Warren the first American to leave the earth's surface in a flying machine.[3]

Carnes determined to cap this success by making an ascent in Philadelphia. He made repairs to the now-tattered balloon, and improved the brazier system that supplied it with hot air. To save the expense of building an enclosure, he chose the walled yard of the city jail as his launch site. On July 19, 1784, Carnes began his ascent, perched on a scaffold that was suspended

Maryland's first flying field—Peter Carnes' hot-air balloon rises above Howard Park, Baltimore, June 24, 1784. Photo courtesy of the National Air and Space Museum (NASM A-4914-D), Smithsonian Institution.

The George Washington Parke Custis *on the Potomac.*
Photo courtesy of the National Air and Space Museum
(SL 2003-6573), Smithsonian Institution.

beneath the balloon and its brazier. A gust of wind caused the edge of the scaffold to strike a projection from the wall, however, breaking the suspension chain and dropping the aeronaut to earth. Carnes was uninjured, but the freed balloon sped upward and burst into flames. This abortive launch was the last venture in aerostation for the Bladensburg innkeeper, who soon fled his Maryland residence to avoid legal action for debt.[4]

Despite Carnes' failure at Philadelphia, his brief career in ballooning had been impressive for its time and place. No further manned flights occurred in the United States until nine years later, when the French aeronaut Jean Pierre Blanchard made his celebrated voyage from Philadelphia to New Jersey in January 1793. Experts from Europe dominated American ballooning during the succeeding quarter century. One of these, Louis Guille, made an ascent at Baltimore in April 1820. Meanwhile, a less benign forerunner of modern aerospace technology had appeared in the skies over the Old Line State.[5]

During the War of 1812, British forces frequently employed weapons known as Congreve Rockets.

Developed by a British general, these missiles could be fired from land or shipboard, and might carry either incendiaries or an anti-personnel explosive charge. Although highly inaccurate, the rockets could sometimes be terrifyingly effective, particularly against an enemy to whom they were a novelty. Maryland was the scene of the most significant and best-known instances of their use. At the battle of Bladensburg on August 24, 1814, the rockets helped to panic the inexperienced American troops, clearing the invaders' path to Washington. As the British advanced on Baltimore during the following month, their ship *Erebus* launched rockets as a part of the bombardment of Fort McHenry. The tactic proved a failure, primarily because the range of the missiles was less than that of the defenders' guns. The "rocket's red glare" served to illuminate the U.S. flag still waving above the fort, inspiring a famous line by Francis Scott Key.[6]

During the early 1830s, the foreign hold on exhibition ballooning in the United States was broken by Charles Durant, a citizen of Jersey City, New Jersey. Among the most successful of his ascents were two made in 1833 from Observatory Garden on Federal Hill in Baltimore. The first of these took the aeronaut to the town of Bel Air in Harford County, while the second ended conveniently on the deck of a ship that conveyed him back to Baltimore. Inspired by Durant, a number of Baltimoreans became professional aeronauts, beginning in 1834 with ascents from their city and nearby communities. Lacking Durant's training, these balloonists had somewhat mixed results; however, they made their city for a time the "undisputed capital of American aeronautics," according to aviation historian Tom Crouch. Among the most interesting of the Baltimore aeronauts was Jane Warren, who made several free flights in 1837, including one that deposited her in the Chesapeake Bay near Poole's Island. Mrs. Warren was not the earliest female balloonist to operate in America, but she may have been the first who was a U. S. citizen.[7]

For all the wonder that they provoked, balloons were an impractical means of transportation, particularly because their movements depended upon the winds. John H. Pennington, a Baltimore piano maker, set himself to correct this defect with his Steam Dolphin Balloon. This oblong aerostat was to be constructed around a hollow "spinal frame" made of wood. Its power was to be provided by a steel steam engine that turned a pair of beveled wheels. In 1842, Pennington petitioned Congress for $2,000 to help him build such a vehicle, later raising the requested sum fivefold with the assurance that the "project is not only a rational one, but clearly a practical one." He persisted in seeking both public and private funding for his project into the 1850s, but never received the backing to become more than a theoretical advocate of the powered airship.[8]

Whatever their limitations, balloons were pressed into service for the national emergency presented by the Civil War. Thaddeus Lowe managed to establish himself as the Union's chief aeronaut. He headed a civilian Balloon Corps that operated at multiple locations, including posts in Maryland on the flanks of the army guarding the Potomac. To achieve greater mobility for the balloon units along the river, Lowe created a water-borne base from a former coal barge, the 122-foot *George Washington Parke Custis*. This vessel was redesigned so that its deck became an unobstructed launching platform, and it was fitted with a portable gas generator. On November 10, 1861, the *Custis* was towed to Stump Neck at the mouth of Mattawoman Creek, some three miles upstream from the headquarters of General Joseph Hooker at Budd's Ferry, Maryland. During the following evening, Lowe and two assistants went aloft in the balloon *Constitution* to observe Confederate positions on the southern side of the Potomac. This was not the first time that an aerostat was flown from a naval vessel, since another Union balloonist had made similar use of a steam tugboat in Virginia waters. Nevertheless, Lowe's ascent at Stump Neck marked the first operational use of a vessel specifically configured for launching a passenger-carrying aerial device. The barge *Custis* may therefore be considered an early ancestor of the modern aircraft carrier.[9]

The balloon unit continued to operate in the Budd's Ferry area during the winter of 1861. General Hooker at times was exasperated by the aeronauts' inability to ascend during poor weather, or when supplies for generating gas were lacking. Nevertheless, he recognized the usefulness of information they provided, and eventually went aloft for a first-hand view. The Confederates' belief in the value of this aerial surveillance to their opponents was shown by their elaborate camouflage measures—as well as by their determined attempts to bring down the observers with artillery fire.[10]

The other end of the Union line was commanded by General Charles P. Stone, who proved quicker than Hooker to appreciate the value of the balloons. Balloon Corps aeronauts made tethered flights near Stone's Poolesville headquarters from December 1861 until March of the following year. A leveled area covered with straw was created as a launching place, and the barge *Custis* was also used to support some operations on the stretch of the upper Potomac near Edward's Ferry.[11]

Balloons were not present at the war's most important battle in Maryland, fought at Antietam in September 1862, but Lowe made observation flights in that area after the engagement. This may have been the last significant series of ascents in the state during the conflict. By June 1863, when Confederate troops crossed Maryland in the drive north that ended at Gettysburg, Lowe had resigned and the undervalued Balloon Corps was in the process of dissolution.[12]

For many decades following the Civil War, Americans continued to exploit the potential of balloons, particularly as a vehicle for showmanship. This form of outdoor entertainment had its ugly side, as thousands of Baltimore citizens witnessed on September 9, 1905. Performing on a bar suspended beneath a balloon adrift over the city, a young acrobat lost his grip and fell to his death. Almost as dangerous, but without the tragic ending, were the thrilling flights that Lincoln Beachey conducted in his primitive dirigible from the city's Electric Park in July 1908. In less extreme forms, meanwhile, venturing aloft in aerostats was becoming a widespread form of amateur aerial recreation. Promotion of sport ballooning was one focus of the aero clubs that sprang up in many cities, Baltimore included, in the early twentieth century. By this time, however, heavier-than-air devices were claiming their place as the leading inspiration for aviation enthusiasts. Technology had moved decisively beyond its status in 1865, when *Scientific American* published an imaginative Baltimorean's proposal for a personal flying machine: a "basket car" propelled by the exertions of ten harnessed eagles. In the first decade of the twentieth century, more practical minds made the airplane a reality, and their achievements soon affected Maryland history.[13]

Pioneering the Airplane

The month of December 1903 saw the climax of two determined attempts to achieve powered, heavier-than-air flight. One was conducted by Wilbur and Orville Wright, a pair of Ohio bicycle makers who chose North Carolina coastland as their experimental site. The other was a better-financed campaign by Professor Samuel P. Langley, the distinguished Secretary of the Smithsonian Institution in Washington. On May 5, 1896, Langley successfully flew his unmanned Aerodrome No. 5 from a research boat on the Potomac, a river which is legally part of Maryland, except where it runs past the city of Washington. His anchorage was on the Virginia side, and it appears that the flight was confined within a lagoon on that shore. Encouraged, Langley pressed on toward his goal of manned flight. By October 7, 1903, the professor's assistant, Charles M. Manley, was ready to try his luck at piloting the 730-pound Great Aerodrome; however, the craft merely plunged from the launch boat into the river. A second test on December 8 took place at the confluence of the Potomac and Anacostia rivers, and again Manley was pitched directly into cold water. Unlike the October 7 experiment, this final debacle for Langley's project probably took place in waters belonging to the District of Columbia rather than Maryland. In any case, the future lay

Wilbur Wright instructing Army Lt. Frederick Humphreys in the first Military Flyer, October, 1909, at the College Park Airfield, Prince George's County. Photo courtesy of the College Park Aviation Museum, Frederick Humphreys Collection.

Hubert Latham soars over the Phoenix Shot Tower in November 1910. Photo courtesy of the Ann Arrundell County Historical Society.

with the Wright Brothers, whose fragile airplane flew triumphantly at Kitty Hawk on December 17.[14]

The Wrights' breakthrough was not widely understood or acclaimed for several years, partly due to their attempts to protect their invention from imitators. In 1908, however, the brothers received a contract to supply a usable airplane to the U.S. Department of War. The Wrights proved the viability of their aircraft with a series of spectacular test flights from the parade ground at Fort Myer, Virginia; however, they needed more space for the second phase of the contract, which entailed the training of two pilots. Balloon flights by one of the selected students helped the Army to choose a location for this airfield at College Park, a small Maryland community convenient to the capital city. During October and November, 1909, Wilbur Wright trained the U.S. military's two earliest qualified pilots, and gave partial instruction to a third officer. During this series of flights, Wilbur for the first time successfully attempted takeoff without the weight-driven catapult device he normally used to assist his aircraft on takeoff. He also took aloft the United States' first female airplane passenger, who described the experience as "simply grand."[15]

The excitement unleashed by the Wright Brothers' demonstrations of the practicality of flight brought a ready response from adventurous Marylanders. A young Baltimorean named Charles F. Elvers built an aircraft from scratch, guided by the Wrights' example and by his own examination of a plane built by Glenn Curtiss of Hammondsport, New York, the Wrights' great rival. Elvers made his first brief hop at his father's Owings Mills farm on October 22, 1909, followed by a series of further flights. He later described his creation as a "maze of cloth-covered sticks, a confusion of wires, a forest of home-made gadgets." However inelegant its design, this was the first in what would become a long and diverse succession of airplanes built in Maryland. Under parental pressure, Elvers stopped flying in less than a year, but not before he and Tom Hildebrandt had helped Bill Southard to fabricate another plane. Despite a crash, the three friends brought this machine to the Baltimore Aero Meet of November 1910.[16]

Held at the nearby town of Halethorpe, the meet was one of the first large international aeronautical competitions in the United States. The event was organized by the president of the Aero Club of Baltimore, an action that may be interpreted as the first round in the city's long fight to make itself a leading center of aviation. (Underlying this ambition was doubtless recognition that Baltimore's role as a nexus of water and land transportation routes had been a key factor in its earlier growth.) Liberal prizes were offered to the competitors in a variety of categories at Halethorpe, which ensured entry by many of the celebrities of contemporary aviation. Public attendance was massive. Although interrupted for several days by a severe storm—damage included the destruction of Southhard's aircraft—the event amply satisfied expectations. Particularly memorable was a flight by French pilot Hubert Latham, who thrilled thousands by sailing over Baltimore in his Antoinette monoplane.[17]

Flag at half-staff at Army Aviation School, College Park, Prince George's County, in 1912, probably marking the death of Wilbur Wright that May in Dayton, Ohio. Photo courtesy of the College Park Aviation Museum, Jesse Ayer Collection.

At College Park Airfield, meanwhile, the site of Wilbur Wright's training work for the Army was becoming the scene of several private aeronautical enterprises. The first of these probably belonged to airplane builder Rexford M. Smith, who constructed a hangar at the airfield during 1910. In November of that year, Smith took his first workable plane up for a short hop that was a maiden flight for both machine and pilot. Another individual who made his first flight in the new aircraft that day was Tony Jannus, a young mechanic from Washington who had installed the plane's Emerson engine. Jannus became a frequent pilot for Smith, and quickly earned a reputation as a skilled aviator. In March 1911, he attempted a flight from College Park Airfield to the Washington Aero Show, but was forced down by strong winds. The aircraft was trucked to the exposition, however, where other Maryland products on display included a second plane made by Smith and one built by the Christmas Aeroplane Company. Paul Peck, a pilot trained by Jannus, eventually took over most of the Smith firm's flying. He drew wide attention in August 1911 by taking off from College Park Airfield, circling the Capitol dome, and venturing over Virginia before landing in Washington.[18]

Jannus served as a test pilot for another early Maryland aircraft manufacturer, Edward R. Brown. Assisted by Donovan Swann and Clyde Loose, Brown completed one of the first amphibious airplanes, dubbed *Lord Baltimore II*. On May 17, 1911, a large crowd watched Jannus conduct this aircraft's impressive maiden flight, which began and ended on land at the edge of the Patapsco River. On June 7, Don Swann was at the controls of *Lord Baltimore II* for its initial water takeoff from the Patapsco. The ascent was successful, but the landing was marred by a minor crash resulting from the inexperienced pilot's difficulty in banking. To remedy this problem, Swann later devised an innovative stick control system.[19]

In the spring of 1911, the Army returned to College Park Airfield and prepared there a more elaborate and permanent training facility than had served for Wilbur Wright's 1909 instruction program. Commanded by a captain and maintained by enlisted personnel quartered on the site, this flying school may be considered the first U.S. military base specifically created for airplane operations. Rex Smith moved his hangar to align with the row of new Army structures, and civilian business proceeded amid the military bustle. Flight operations at the Army school began in June or July of 1911 and continued, except for a winter break, until November 1912. In addition to training flights, activities included important early tests of aerial communications, night landings, and weapon systems, including the first testing of a bombsight in an airplane and the first firing of a machine gun designed to be used in an airplane. The Army fliers also attracted attention with notable exploits that included high altitude flights and a forty-two-mile flight to visit the National Guard encampment at Frederick. The extreme hazards of aviation during this early period exacted their

From the Oral History Files . . .

Maryland Enlisted Men Receive Aviation Training in France & the First Aeronautic Detachment in World War I

An interview with Charles "Pat" O'Brien and Richard Whistler
by Jennifer Braithwait Darrow

In early June of 1917, the First Aeronautic Detachment from the United States Navy arrived in France for aviation training. Led by Lieutenant Kenneth Whiting, the Detachment consisted of seven officers and 122 enlisted men, six of whom came from Maryland. Sent at the request of the French Government, the First Aeronautic Detachment was the first unit from the United States to arrive for service in Europe during World War I.

James Henry O'Brien, Jr. was working as a blacksmith at his own shop when war broke out in Europe. He enlisted in the Navy on March 28, 1917, nine days before the United States entered the war. According to his son, Charles "Pat" O'Brien, "*He wanted to fly and ...the Navy was looking for volunteers, so him and his buddy ...Charlie Boylan ...went down together and enlisted.*"

"*Although none of us who volunteered had ever seen a plane close up, we were eager to go to war as pilots,*" O'Brien explained in an article he wrote in the 1950s for a local newspaper. Pat O'Brien offered further insight into his father's interest in flying, despite a lack of aviation experience, "*well, he heard all the stories about the daring young men and their flying machines, and they were called 'Knights of the Air' and they were glorified...*"

Members of the First Aeronautic Detachment to France, summer 1917, pictured in Tours with Caudron G.III. biplane and French instructor. Maryland members of the First Aeronautic Detachment were James H. O'Brien, Charles H. Hammann, Charles Boylan, John Ganster, and Paul Gillespie. Photo courtesy of Charles "Pat" O'Brien.

Five other men from Maryland were among the members of the First Aeronautic Detachment, Charles Hazeltine Hamman, Charley Boylan, John Ganster, Paul Gillespie, and Leonard R. Bruton. Bruton was unable to complete the training for medical reasons. Later, four other men from Maryland, Cary Eichelberger, Charley Roberts, George Manley and William E. Mitchell joined the detachment.

The First Aeronautic Detachment "*was very significant from the standpoint of naval aviation history,*" according to historian Richard Whistler, "*We declared war in April and by May they were loading these guys on ship to go to Europe, and this was at the French government's request.*" Whistler further explained that at the time Congress declared war, "*there was only really one active* [Navy] *aeronautic station, in the whole United States,*" in Pensacola, Florida and there were only about fifty officers and 250 enlisted men with any aviation experience. In fact, aviation training had been suspended between June and December of 1916 because of the number of accidents. The importance of the French in American aviation history was noted by O'Brien in his newspaper article, "*The French taught us; the French taught most of America's flying men in World War I. Capt. Eddie Rickenbacker was a student at Tours when we went through...*"

After a few weeks of naval indoctrination in Pensacola, Florida, the First Aeronautic Detachment left for France on two ships, the USS *Jupiter* from

toll, however, and four of the aviators lost their lives in accidents during the school's operation.[21]

The Navy, meanwhile, had also entered the field of heavier-than-air aviation, and completed preparation of its first airplane base in September 1911. Located at Greenbury Point near Annapolis, this aviation camp operated until early 1914, except for winter breaks. Using aircraft built by Curtiss and by the Wrights, the early naval aviators accomplished feats that included a trip to and from Fort Monroe, Virginia. They also experimented with such techniques as spotting submarines from the air. Across the river at the Naval Academy, one of the fliers suffered a wetting when he failed to become airborne in the first test of a compressed-air catapult for launching aircraft from shipboard. More tragically, an aviation camp flight ended in the Navy's first fatal airplane accident, caused by an encounter with turbulence over the Chesapeake Bay. [21]

The late summer of 1914 witnessed the outbreak of World War I, in which the United States was initially a neutral. Leadership in aviation had already shifted away from the United States to Europe, and the embattled nations there lost little time in applying aerial technology to combat. Among those concerned about the situation was Spencer Heath, whose American Propeller Company in Baltimore was a leading propeller manufacturer. During that autumn, Heath urged citizens to write to Congress about what the U.S. lack of aeronautical preparedness might mean if the country were drawn into the war.[22]

Heath's partner in this informal campaign was Tony Jannus, who had moved to Baltimore after winning new fame in Florida as chief pilot of the world's first scheduled heavier-than-air airline. In November 1914, Jannus and a *Baltimore Sun* employee dropped simulated "bombs" of printed matter over the city in an apparent attempt to demonstrate the potential of aerial warfare. Meanwhile, Jannus and his brother Roger were trying to launch an aircraft building company in a shed rented from the American Propeller firm. They built the *Lark*, a sleek flying boat capable of carrying four persons, which made a successful debut flight in April 1915. The enterprise did not endure, however, and during the next year Tony Jannus died while test flying a Curtiss plane in Russia.[23]

In April 1917, the United States entered the war against Germany. Eight men from Maryland were among the first 100 wartime volunteers to sign up as aviators, and many others followed their example. Baltimore's George Manley was killed during flight training in France, reportedly the first American airman to die in that country during the war. Charles H. Hammann, also from Baltimore, won the Congressional Medal of Honor for his daring seaplane rescue of a comrade shot down in Italian waters. Another flier known for unusual bravery was Galloway G. Cheston of West River, whose plane lost altitude while returning from a raid across German lines and was overwhelmed by several enemy fighters. Engine trouble also cost the life of Crisfield's Stanley L. Cochrane, who was serving as gunner aboard a plane forced to drop out of formation. Cochrane shot down two pursuing planes and continued to fire despite his mortal wounds, enabling his pilot to escape. The Maryland flier credited with the most victories in the war was William D. Tipton, who downed four airplanes and one observation balloon.[24]

As part of its industrial mobilization, the nation rushed to expand its small aircraft manufacturing capacity in an attempt to produce the vast fleet of planes that it promised to provide. A key contributor to the war effort was American Propeller, which reportedly built about three-quarters of all the propellers used by United States and its allies in the conflict. By the end of the conflict, the firm was employing 900 workers in five Baltimore plants. Otherwise, Maryland manufacturers were barely involved in aeronautical work at this time. In Hagerstown, however, a brief venture by the Maryland Pressed Steel company gave a foretaste of that city's future prominence in airframe production. Giuseppe Bellanca, later a famed aeronautical engineer, designed two prototypes of light military planes. Although the prototypes were successfully flight tested, neither model entered production, and the company went

Hoboken, New Jersey and the USS *Neptune* from Baltimore, Maryland. Once in France, the detachment was divided into groups for training as pilots, mechanics, and observers. Through flight logs, Pat O'Brien learned that his father initially trained on a Caudron G.III in Tours, France before being sent to Hourtin, France for flying boat training on the Donnet-Denhaut or DD-8. Following the training in France, the detachment was sent to England and Scotland for training in gunnery and bombing.

O'Brien was stationed at Dunkirk in January of 1918, where he flew flying boats for submarine and mine patrol. O'Brien also qualified on a Hanriot or HD-II, which was used as an escort for the larger, slower flying boat. The pilots stationed at Dunkirk strove to avoid aerial combat with enemy forces but they did pursue and attack German submarines.

"By the end of the summer we were considered too combat-tired to fly any more." O'Brien wrote in 1956. With his service in Dunkirk complete, Pat O'Brien explained that his father, *"had done his job at Dunkirk, and they were . . . shipping him home, getting ready to ship him home anyway, so he went to England. From England he went to Italy, done a little instructing in Italy, flight instructing."* O'Brien arrived in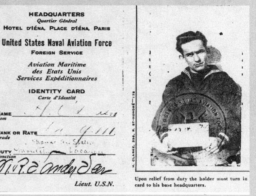

Identification card for James H. O'Brien issued by U.S. Naval Headquarters in Paris, France. Photo courtesy of Charles "Pat" O'Brien.

Italy in October of 1918. He stayed there until December. While in Italy, he qualified on a Macchi M-3.

O'Brien returned home on April 6, 1919 and was honorably discharged on September 30, 1921. O'Brien did not continue to fly once he returned from the war. According to Pat O'Brien, *"My father said, 'No, I'm not going to fly anymore.' He says, 'I got two reasons.' At that time he only had the two boys. And he says, 'And there they are standing there.' I remember him saying that ...he didn't want to fly anymore. I guess he saw too much."*

Several members of the First Aeronautic Detachment died while in service. George Manley was the first Maryland man to die, in a flying accident during training, in France. Cary Eichelberger was killed in a crash, as was Johnny Ganster. William Mitchell died of pneumonia. Charles Hazeltine Hammann won the Congressional Medal of Honor, for his rescue of a fellow pilot in enemy waters, the first for naval aviation, but died in a plane accident following the war in 1919. Charley Boylan died in a boating accident.

O'Brien said very little to anyone, including his family, about his service. Pat O'Brien learned of his father's experience from his mother and other relatives. He also discovered that his father had saved a number of items from his time in the military, which he stored in a trunk in his bedroom. As a child, Pat O'Brien would sneak in to his father's room and look inside. When his father passed away, Pat O'Brien inherited the trunk, which contained uniforms, photographs, flight logs, military orders, and a diary that several of the men from the detachment contributed to. This memorabilia, combined with extensive research by Richard Whistler, provided insight into the experiences of the men of the First Aeronautic Detachment who are no longer here to speak for themselves.

Charles "Pat" O'Brien, oral history interview, January 25, 2003
OHC-002 (MD-AVC) 020, 17 p.
Richard Whistler, oral history interview, January 25, 2003
MHT/OHC-002 (MD-AVC) 020, 47 p.

Mail being loaded aboard a DH-4 aircraft in front of the Air Mail Hangar at College Park Airport, Prince George's County, in 1920. Photo courtesy of the College Park Aviation Museum/NAEMC

out of business in the postwar period.[25]

The war effort in Maryland also included research and testing related to aerial combat. Some of this took place at the Naval Proving Ground at Indian Head, where the explosion of a bomb aboard an aircraft cost two lives. Testing of aerial bombs also occurred at the new Aberdeen Proving Ground, established by the Army in 1917. This facility was primarily devoted to surface weapons, but an air detachment soon arrived and set up a base for airplanes and dirigibles. The first bomb was dropped at the installation on September 2, 1918. On November 7, rocket pioneer Dr. Robert H. Goddard gave a demonstration at Aberdeen of small missiles that could be carried and fired by individual soldiers. This weapon was not developed for use in World War I, however, since an armistice was signed later that month.[26]

Despite the strains of the war, the federal government began building an air mail system. The program eventually yielded immense benefits by providing the first lighted airways and helping to develop the techniques of civil air transportation. The first regular air mail route connected Washington, Philadelphia, and New York. The Army initially provided the pilots for this service, which began with flights on May 15, 1918. After taking off from Washington's Polo Grounds under the eyes of President Woodrow Wilson, an inexperienced lieutenant lost his way and got no farther than Waldorf, Maryland. A simultaneous flight heading south from New York was more successful, however, and the military

fliers continued as mail carriers for three months. The postal authorities then began using their own pilots, and switched the southern terminus to College Park Airfield. On August 12, a northbound flight from that airport signaled the start of the Civilian Air Mail Service. Postal flights continued at the College Park field until May 1921. During the same period the Department of Commerce's Bureau of Standards also operated a laboratory at the airport that helped to develop radio marker beacons and direction-finding equipment. [27]

The Classic Era

The period between the two world wars was by some measures the classic age of U.S. aviation. For air minded enthusiasts, it was a thrilling time in which the airplane began to reveal much of its true potential, whether for transportation, practical tasks, or crowd-pleasing aerobatics. Many of those who had flown in the European conflict brought home a determination to keep and use their experience, often joining flying clubs that promoted aeronautics. In Baltimore, such a group took the initiative in establishing an airfield that eventually became the city's first municipal airport. This was Logan Field, named for a stunt pilot who failed to pull out of a tailspin during an air show there in 1920. Flying club members at Logan organized an observation squadron that in 1921 became one of the earliest National Guard flying units to receive federal recognition.[28]

Freelance pilots were also exploring the varied and often colorful possibilities of aviation. An example was Baltimore's Howard A. Kelly, Jr., who docked his Curtiss "hydroaeroplane" near the Hanover Street Bridge. Kelly liked to wave at the office workers who watched from windows as he flew among the tall buildings downtown. He scraped a living from jobs that included dropping free stage tickets and other promotional novelties, and sometimes indulged in airborne poaching of waterfowl, then a novel misdemeanor. Kelly's attempt to fly passengers to and from Norfolk during the summers of 1920-21 was not profitable, but he had better luck with shorter runs like ferrying doctors to an understaffed Eastern Shore hospital.[29]

One of Kelly's most profitable passenger destinations was Bay Shore Park, a popular amusement facility in eastern Baltimore County. In 1925, the park was the base for the annual Schneider Trophy Race, an international seaplane competition that was a showcase for cutting-edge aviation. In his Curtiss racer, Lt. James H. Doolittle rounded the corners of the triangular course with astounding skill, winning acclaim for the U.S. Army and the nation's aviation industry. In western Maryland, meanwhile, military efforts to develop aviation included the operation of an airfield near Cumberland as a sub-station along a model airway between Washington, DC, and Dayton, Ohio. This field later evolved into Mexico Farms Airport, still operating today as the state's second oldest airport. College Park Airport was again playing a role in the progress of aviation technology during this period. Between 1926 and 1934, the Bureau of Standards operated a facility at the field that made important advances in radio aides for landing and navigation.[30]

In addition to such technical development, the federal government began safety regulation of interstate aviation under the Air Commerce Act of 1926. Maryland passed its first general law on aeronautics in 1927, and created an aviation commission two years later. By 1935, the legislature had adopted nearly all the provisions of the uniform state aviation laws that federal authorities published as a suggested model. These measures helped to build a firm foundation for the growth of the young industry. In emotional terms, however, such governmental efforts were trivial compared to the feat of Charles A. Lindbergh on May 20-21, 1927. The young pilot's solo flight from New York to Paris electrified the nation and seemed to prove that the air age was truly at hand. In Baltimore, news of Lindbergh's successful landing was celebrated by a flyover in which six National Guard planes spelled out the initials of his name. In October, some 40,000 citizens braved drenching rain to greet the "Lone Eagle" when he visited the city.[31]

Baltimoreans had given solid proof of their commitment to aviation even before the enthusiasm triggered by Lindbergh's famous flight. On May 3, 1927, the city's voters had approved a $1.5 million loan to finance a new municipal airport. In 1928, the mayor announced the selection of a site at Dundalk, not far from the existing Logan Field. Most of the space was to be created by a landfill along the Patapsco River, but this seemed acceptable in order to create a major urban airport that could serve both seaplanes and landplanes. The first construction contract was awarded in February 1929.[32]

The aim of the airport project included making Baltimore a center of aviation manufacturing, not just of air transportation. The Doyle Aero Corporation was probably the city's first operator of a real airframe factory (as opposed to simple workshops such as those of Edward Brown or Tony Jannus). At its plant on Elm Avenue in the Hampden neighborhood, the Doyle firm in 1928 produced the Oriole, a high-

wing monoplane that seated two occupants.[33]

In May 1928, the Berliner-Joyce Aircraft Corporation began building a factory on a Dundalk site near both Logan Field and the new airport site. Henry A. Berliner was a brilliant engineer whose designs included an early helicopter that he had demonstrated at College Park Airport in 1924. Now refocused on conventional airplanes, Berliner had teamed with Temple N. Joyce and other executives to create the firm. "You can hit the top with men like that!" boasted a brochure claiming that the firm would "set new standards in aviation." A fly-over by thirty-five military aircraft celebrated the laying of the cornerstone of the Dundalk plant, which eventually included a wind tunnel. The company had moved in by June 1929, and work began on a compact fighter plane ordered by the Navy.[34]

The projected harbor-side airport seemed to be paying direct dividends in May 1929, when the Curtiss-Caproni Corporation selected it as the site for its plant, which was expected to employ up to 2,000 workers. Meanwhile, Baltimore's leaders had been angling for an

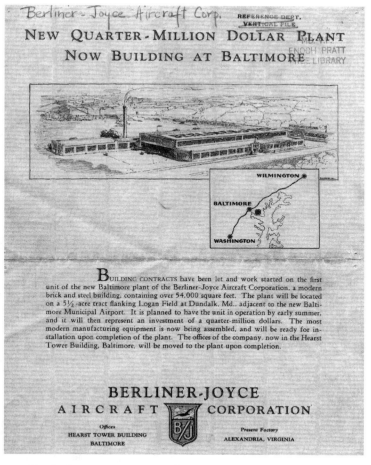

The Berliner-Joyce Factory along Broening Highway in Dundalk, Baltimore County, as it appeared in advertising copy in 1929. Photo courtesy of the Enoch Pratt Free Library.

even larger catch, Glenn L. Martin, a self-made aviation titan whose products included the first American-designed bomber. By the late 1920s, Martin was considering a move from his current plant in Cleveland, Ohio. Baltimore officials offered him fifty acres of land for free, but this was far below the scale at which Martin planned to operate. Quietly, he bought up 1,260 acres at nearby Middle River, and the company began its transfer east in early 1929. The company's first Maryland plane, the prototype of the Navy BM-1 dive bomber, rolled out that same year at a rented location in Baltimore. In October, employees began moving to the impressive new Middle River facility. Designed for the new era of all-metal aircraft, the plant was regarded as the most advanced aircraft factory of its time.[35]

Maryland's growing aeronautical sector got an important boost from another out-of-state mogul of aircraft production, Sherman Fairchild. In 1929, Fairchild was interested in diversifying his monoplane line and therefore open to a proposal from Kreider-Reisner Aircraft (KRA) of Hagerstown. Founded by Lewis E. Reisner and Ammon Kreider, this small but efficient firm had been producing its light Challenger biplanes since 1927. KRA wanted to make continued growth possible by constructing a modern factory, and it gained the resources to do this by becoming a Fairchild subsidiary. The alliance was formally announced on April 9, 1929, four days before Ammon Kreider died in a midair collision. Despite this loss, KRA speedily built the planned factory for its popular Challengers. Prospects seemed so encouraging in September 1929 that the company decided to make a substantial addition to the barely completed plant.[36]

In October 1929, panic selling on the New York stock exchange marked the start of the Great Depression, a severe economic downturn that quickly cut the demand for airplanes. In Baltimore, Doyle Aero folded after turning out its twelfth Oriole. Berliner-Joyce shelved plans to introduce a new commercial aircraft, and made do by continuing to work on military contracts. The company soon came under the control of North American Aviation, a Delaware corporation, and changed its name to B/J. Because of the hard times, the stillborn Curtiss-Caproni Corporation never had a chance to operate its new plant beside the harbor. In the autumn of 1931, the General Aviation Manufacturing Corporation leased the facility, where it turned out a handful of aircraft. In 1933, this company, too, was acquired by North American Aviation, which now had two Dundalk subsidiaries. North American concentrated the work of both organizations at the B/J plant for a time, but in November 1935 the company began moving its operations to a new factory in California.[37]

The Martin Aircraft Company seemed relatively unaffected by the depression, yet it suffered serious inter-

nal damage. Glenn Martin was forced to shelve plans for a public stock offering, and instead mortgaged the firm's assets as an expedient to stay in business. Fortunately, the company's principal customer was the federal government, which remained willing to buy at least a reasonable amount of aerial hardware. At the time of the stock market panic, Martin was working on a substantial Navy contract for its PM-1 flying boats. In October 1932, the company scored a crucial victory when the prototype of its B-10 bomber outclassed competitors. Early the next year, the Army placed an order for forty-eight of the B-10s, powerful offensive aircraft that were able to outrun contemporary pursuit planes. During this same period, Martin engineers were preparing the company for another kind of adventure, construction of some of the most memorable of the company's many flying boats. These streamlined M-130 clippers, the first of which made its maiden flight in 1934, had the range and lifting power that enabled Pan American Airways to pioneer airline service across the vastness of the Pacific.[38]

In Hagerstown, the onset of the depression nearly idled the new KRA/Fairchild plant. Its staff dwindled to some fifteen or twenty persons, who kept busy with minor projects. By 1931, however, the facility was turning out new aircraft, beginning with the Fairchild 22, an economically-priced light plane. Other distinctive products followed, ranging from cabin monoplanes to amphibious Jungle Clippers that were powered by a single massive engine atop the fuselage. The name Kreider-Reisner was discarded in 1934, and the Hagerstown establishment became known solely by the Fairchild name. Having survived depression, the factory was ready to help meet the challenges waiting at the end of the decade.[39]

The future of Maryland aviation was also aided by a crop of new airports that began to spring up in the late 1920s. One of these was Hagerstown Airport, established by KRA north of town in 1928, and later purchased and expanded by the city. Tred Avon Airport, probably the first commercial airport on Maryland's Eastern Shore, opened near Easton in the same year. At Frederick, an airway landing facility established by the U.S. Department of Commerce in 1929 became a summer camp for the state's National Guard fliers, who named it Detrick Field (after their medical officer) in 1931. Near the national capital, the first of several new commercial airfields to open during this period was Congressional Airport, which began a thirty-year period of operation in 1928. A new era for private flying at College Park Airport began in 1927, when management was assumed by George Brinckerhoff, a successful organizer of air shows and races. The state's most flamboyant center of such activity was Curtiss-Wright Airport, which opened on Baltimore's northern edge in 1930. Built in a theatrical Art Deco style, this facility was managed for much of its existence by the ace flier William D. Tipton, who had become a master promoter of both civil and National Guard aviation.[40]

Despite the vibrant atmosphere at Curtiss-Wright Airport, Logan Field remained Baltimore's premier airport for transportation during this period. In August 1930, Eastern Air Transport began flights there, becoming the first major airline to provide the city with scheduled passenger service. Nevertheless, Logan's modest size and oiled-cinder runways were beginning to make it obsolete as an air carrier facility. Baltimoreans remained well aware of this, but looked forward confidently to the opening of their new municipal airport on the Patapsco. In November 1930, they approved a second loan for the planned facility, this time in the amount of $2.5 million. By July 1931, however, the project's basic feasibility was in doubt because the filled earth at the site was not hardening as expected. Frustration mounted as engineers tried a series of ineffective remedies. Work on the airport limped on for more than ten additional years, exhausting funds from another major city loan as well as millions of dollars in federal assistance.[41]

While the airport construction faltered, the city pursued hopes of establishing another type of air transportation terminal, one that would involve a mooring tower rather than runways. To many, rigid dirigibles seemed to offer a proven form of long-distance transport that airplanes would have difficulty in matching. In 1928, Baltimoreans had marveled at a flyover by the giant *Graf Zeppelin*. Two years later, the city received a visit from Dr. Hugo Eckener, the celebrated German airship developer, who pronounced the locality ideal for a transatlantic zeppelin base. Although this prospect dimmed for a time, enthusiasm for it reemerged after the 811-feet-long *Hindenburg* made an aerial tour of Baltimore in 1936. Another visit by Eckener made the prize seem near, but during 1937 it was snatched away by the fiery destruction of the *Hindenburg* in a New Jersey accident. The vulnerability of hydrogen-filled airships was hardly a secret, and Baltimore itself had witnessed the 1919 explosion of a Navy dirigible in Dundalk. The *Hindenburg* disaster dramatized the danger, however, and scuttled the zeppelins as passenger carriers.[42]

Before the eclipse of the zeppelins, their strongest challengers in oceanic skies were the new breed of long-range seaplanes being built by Martin and other manufacturers. Baltimore dedicated a seaplane ramp at the municipal airport site in 1932, and fervently hoped that it would become the locus of a new Atlantic base being planned by Pan American Airways. The faltering landfill situation at the airport site was a major embarrassment for this campaign. In May 1936, Avery McBee wrote that two-thirds of the airport site was still "a great patch of slimy, undrained earth." Yet he believed that "in another eight

months or a year the city's dream of being the key port of air transportation in the East will be well on its way to realization." McBee was too optimistic about the pace of the landfill and the scope of Baltimore's future role; however, his confidence in the officials who were wooing Pan American was not misplaced. In November 1936, the airline accepted an agreement under which it would begin regular service within two years. In return, the city undertook to give Pan Am generous terms on a lease of ten acres, and to build there a base for the airline.[43]

Even before completion of the base, Pan American and Britain's Imperial Airways began offering service between Baltimore and Bermuda. On November 14, 1937, a harbor-side crowd broke into cheers as Pan Am's "Bermuda Clipper" was sighted arriving on the inaugural flight from the island. This was not the first such service for the nation, since Pan Am had already opened a New York-Bermuda route, but it brought well-heeled Baltimoreans within six hours of the subtropical resort. During the following year, such travelers were accommodated more gracefully by the new Pan American Seaplane Terminal. This striking building was the work of architect W. Watters Pagon, who successfully overcame the unstable nature of the site. Four massive piers supported the structure, which included hangar space, offices, a passenger concourse, lounge, and observation deck.[44]

As the construction of the new Baltimore Municipal Airport finally neared completion, other new buildings there included the Air Station, a handsome landplane terminal designed by Pagon in the Art Deco manner. Equally imposing, but very different in appearance, was a federally-funded building for use by the aviators of the Maryland National Guard. This structure housed offices, quarters, shops, and storage rooms behind two facades in Georgian/Federal Revival style, and its core was a large steel-frame hangar. After Baltimore Municipal's long-anticipated opening on November 16, 1941, three airlines served the airport. In May 1942, however, civilian traffic was suspended when the War Department took control of the facility. By that time, this takeover was only another step in the transformation of the Maryland aviation community by the necessities of war.[45]

The Impact of Global War

In the late 1930s, nationalistic regimes in both Europe and Asia were dragging a reluctant world toward war. By 1937, China was already resisting Japanese aggression, and the Dutch East Indies was preparing for a similar attack. The Martin Company was selling B-10 bombers to bolster the defenses of both regimes. Late in that year, the firm received a U.S. Navy order for PBM Mariners, and began work on what would eventually become a huge fleet of these patrol bombers. Yet America was still clinging hard to the dream of isolation

A swarm of construction workers races to complete C Building at Martin Plant No. 1, Middle River, Baltimore County. The 440,000-square-foot addition, designed by Albert Kahn, was completed in seventy-seven days during the spring of 1939. Martin workers called it the "French Building." Photo courtesy of Glenn L. Martin Maryland Aviation Museum.

from a quarrelsome world. At a congressional hearing in 1938, Glenn Martin found himself labeled a "merchant of death" for advocating the construction of long-range bombers. Soon, however, the quickening tempo of movement toward world war was galvanizing the Maryland aviation scene.[46]

In February 1939, France placed its first order for Martin M-167 attack bombers as part of a desperate bid to strengthen itself against the looming Nazi threat. The contract provided funds for further expansion of the Martin plant. During the summer, a trainer airplane for beginning pilots, designed by Fairchild's Armand Thieblot, won a U.S. Army competition, a success that would soon convert the company's Hagerstown establishment into a hive of urgent activity. On September 1, Germany's invasion of Poland triggered war in Europe. Meanwhile the French placed more large orders for the M-167s, which they called "Glenns" but are better remembered by the British designation "Marylands."[47]

Expansion of the Martin plant at Middle River to meet the French orders made it the nation's largest single aircraft factory, and yet its full potential had not been tapped. The years before and after American entry into the war in 1941 saw the production there of a range of aircraft that was remarkable in number and quality. The most extreme design was the Mars, an immense seaplane conceived as an aerial dreadnought but eventually used to haul cargo. Even more famous was the B-26 Marauder,

produced in a separate nearby plant erected in 1940-41. Typical of Martin design in its then-ultramodern appearance, the B-26 sported a plastic nose cone and mechanized gun turrets. The swift medium bomber was not the easiest plane to fly, but its destructive power and amazing ability to absorb punishment made it a formidable weapon.[48]

Fairchild's wartime contribution included a vast and varied swarm of trainers, and the company also began building the heavy transport aircraft that would become one of its signature products. To speed production, Fairchild adopted the influential "Hagerstown system," under which existing buildings throughout the city were converted to supplement work at the existing plant and at the large new facility constructed at the airport north of town. Fairchild and Martin were far from the only Maryland suppliers of wartime aviation products. In Baltimore, Allied Aviation used the former Berliner-Joyce plant to make aircraft parts and prototypes of Navy gliders. A large General Motors plant in the city switched from making automobile bodies to fabricating the tail sections of Grumman TBM Avengers.[49]

The war forced the Engineering and Research Corporation (ERCO) to suspend production of its popular personal plane, the Ercoupe, after rolling out only 112 of them at Riverdale, Maryland. ERCO turned to the grimmer task of making such items as gun turrets for the duration of the conflict; however, one Ercoupe had already earned a starring role as an Army test plane. In California during March 1941, the small aircraft achieved the world's first Jet-Assisted Takeoff (JATO). At the Engineering Experiment Station near Annapolis, Dr. Robert H. Goddard worked to develop a version of the JATO system that would enable a seaplane to rise from water. The result was the Navy's first such lift-off, made from the Severn River in September 1942. Goddard then turned to other aspects of rocket research, doggedly pursuing his work despite the illness that led to his death in a Baltimore hospital four days before V-J Day.[50]

Superiority in electronics was vital to victory in World War II, and Maryland was a center of progress in this field. The newly-created Bendix Radio Division began operations in Baltimore in 1937, and added a large Towson plant in 1941. It is claimed that the division produced seventy-five percent of the electronic equipment aboard U.S. aircraft flying in World War II. Bendix Radio was also active in the new field of radio detecting and ranging (known as radar), manufacturing Navy radar systems used as landing aids. Another key leader in electronics was the Westinghouse Corporation's Radio Division, which moved to Baltimore in 1938 and soon expanded to cope with defense-related orders. In 1940, Westinghouse management decided that the Baltimore group would become primarily a research and development center for radio-based equipment to be built both in Maryland and elsewhere. The division's broad range of wartime products included several types of radar systems. The most famous were the SC-270 and SC-271s, the Army's first long-range radars designed to warn of approaching enemy aircraft. These were initially produced in Baltimore during 1941, and later turned out at a Pennsylvania plant. Deployed in Hawaii, one of these systems detected large formations of Japanese aircraft moving toward Pearl Harbor on December 7, 1941. Misinterpreting the data, military authorities failed to alert the defending forces, a catastrophic error, but one that dramatized radar's value.[51]

In addition to producing radar detection systems, Westinghouse was among the organizations involved in another important wartime field of development, proximity fuses. The most challenging of these fuse projects was undertaken by Johns Hopkins University's Applied Physics Laboratory. Established in 1942 at a makeshift location in Silver Spring, this new laboratory created the variable time (VT) proximity fuse for use in spinning projectiles such as artillery shells. The fuses made anti-aircraft artillery shells more deadly by equipping them with devices that detected nearby aircraft and exploded the shells close by. Direct hits were no longer necessary. First tried in combat in the Pacific in early 1943, the VT fuses greatly improved anti-aircraft defenses, and their overall enhancement of artillery effectiveness made them one of the key advances of the war. Guided by Westinghouse SCR-584 radars, proximity fuses also compiled an excellent record in shooting down German V-1 flying bombs aimed at southern England. Other Maryland activities in the field of aviation-related munitions included testing at the Army proving grounds at Aberdeen and Edgewood, as well as production of bombs and anti-aircraft shells by Triumph Industries of Elkton.[52]

The contribution of Marylanders to victory in the air went far beyond their roles in science and industry. On the home front, air raid wardens made up about half of the state's civilian defense volunteers, who numbered some 165,000 at their peak. Other volunteers served as aircraft spotters in the early years of the conflict. The Maryland National Guard's 104th Observation Squadron was activated in February 1941. After the United States entered the war, the unit moved to New Jersey, where its pilots flew anti-submarine patrols in their O-47s. The squadron was later deactivated for the balance of the war, and its members joined other units. Among these personnel was Joe Maisch, a P-51 Mustang pilot awarded the Silver Star for his single-handed attack on a formation of German fighters, three of which he destroyed. Another former member of the 104th was John F. R. Scott, Jr., later a historian of Maryland aviation. Scott flew 100 combat hours in P-51s, and survived being shot down over Japan. Other Maryland fliers who served in the Pacific included Robert R. Ayres, who piloted a Douglas SBD dive bomber. In a dangerously low pass over a Japanese destroyer, Ayres delivered a bomb that sank the vessel. The last air combat victory of the war was credited to Clarence "Bill" Moore of Baltimore, a fighter pilot who downed a kamikaze plane on August 15, 1945.[53]

The war had a major impact on Maryland's aviation infrastructure. Many airports were taken over by the military, or closed for security reasons during the conflict. In the Frederick area, the Army converted Detrick Field to non-aviation purposes, and its replacement by a new municipal airport was slow. The war also delayed completion of another federally-backed project, construction of the new Cumberland Airport. The long-term effect of the conflict, however, was an increase in both civil and military airfields. Defense planning prompted the construction of large new airports at Easton and Salisbury on the Eastern Shore. At Westminster, enthusiastic members of the Civil Air Patrol established a base that later became a county airport. The most significant develop-

Building 3835 at Andrews Air Force Base, Prince George's County, is a classic vaulted hangar design, with extensive use of glass. It dates from the construction of the base in 1943-44. Photo courtesy of the Maryland Historical Trust.

From the Oral History Files...

Fred Weick and the Ercoupe

An interview with Betsey Weick
by Dr. Barry A. Lanman

Fred Weick was born on July 14, 1899 and saw his first airplane at the age of eleven. From that watershed event, his life-course was set. Weick's daughter, Betsey Weick, shared her reminiscences about how her father became involved in aviation.

"He talked his parents into taking him across Chicago to go to an air show...and when he was 90, he was telling me he was still surprised that he convinced his parents to do that"!

After high school, he attended Armour Institute of Technology and the University of Illinois. He specialized in mechanical and aeronautical engineering. Weick learned to fly and soloed circa 1923 and gained aviation experience by helping to convert old World War I airplanes to mail planes. His experience with airplanes continued when he came to Washington D.C. to design propellers. Following that brief endeavor, he took on a job at Hamilton Standard in California where he designed a propeller for Lindberg's West Coast to East Coast flight. During the same year, 1929, he developed a text on propeller design that remained the standard for thirty years and is considered a classic publication of its era.

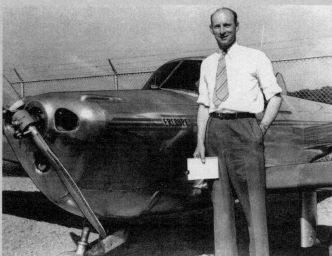

Fred Weick stands with clipboard in front of a sleek new Ercoupe.
Photo courtesy of Betsy Weick.

In 1929, Weick also received the prestigious Collier Trophy for the NACA cowling [engine cover] that increased speeds on airplanes. "It was the first cowling that...covered the engine completely instead of having the pistons and the cylinders out, it smoothed the air flow and then used the air to cool the engine. It was baffled inside to use the air flow to cool the engines which it also needed."

Developing His Own Airplane: the W-1

"He had this dream. He wanted to design an 'everyman's plane.' He wanted the plane that would take the place of the Ford...He pic-

tured...that it would be turned in every fifteen years or so for the new model...He paid close attention to the problems that people had with flying, the things that caused accidents...spinning, stalling and ground-looping when the plane was taxiing." Weick set out to design a plane that would resist all three.

He built the prototype W-1 in the family garage. "I think he completed it by the end of '34 and they were testing it. It was made of sticks and fabric and the wings... Mother sewed the fabric for the wings, and the master bedroom... The master bedroom, which was not very big, was where they doped [varnished] the wings, and my brother remembers the smell...

"The government bought it from him...eventually, it was 'surplused.' Unfortunately, it was much too expensive...It was a pusher prop with a tricycle landing gear and a twin tail and they built about nine of them...but it was too expensive and it died."

Association with Henry Berliner and the Development of the Ercoupe

"He had worked with Henry Berliner and he'd known him, I think, since the 1920s. He had known Dad's work on propellers and had been very interested in it. His father was Emile Berliner...He was an inventor in his own right and very interested in aviation... So when Henry knew about the W-1 he invited Dad to come up to the Washington area and to design a plane...to be produced commercially...So Dad came. He came up in late '35 or early '36 and started work on the plane."

Weick was brought to ERCO (Engineering and Research Corporation) as the chief engineer and the vice president in charge of the Ercoupe. Taking his knowledge and experience from the W-1, he designed Ercoupe: a low wing monoplane with twin boom and tricycle landing gear, and coordinated rudder and aileron control. "It looked ahead of its time. It did not have rudder pedals because the coordination was in the steering wheel, which it had instead of a stick."

Not only did the Ercoupe have to be developed and produced, Weick and Berliner had to design and build a factory. The location of the plant only a few blocks from the College Park Airport was selected because it was convenient to rail transportation and close in proximity to the airport. By 1938, the first prototype was built and had a single tail and a single vertical stabilizer. The orange and blue plane was known as the "Jeep."

An Ercoupe parked in front of the art-moderne ERCO factory in Riverdale, Prince George's County. Photo courtesy of Betsey Weick.

"Ted Waggy was a test pilot. Lester Wells was the president and Henry Berliner was chairman of the board. And Bob Sanders ran Sanders Aviation who eventually handled all the sales. . .In 1939, '40 and '41. . .They produced 110 Ercoupes before World War II. . .Late '39 and '40 they had done a run of a hundred and then they did ten more. . .That was the first light plane manufacturer that had a true assembly line. . . and they had machines that stretched metal and machines that shrank metals. . . they [also] had dies. . .It was quite effectively done. . . Then the war came and there were no materials, so Dad tried to get a wooden plane built, going back a decade. . .but there was too much going to the war, so that ended production until after the war."

During World War II, ERCO produced aviation materials such as propellers and turrets for the war effort. While Weick was engaged in the development and the testing of these war materials, he continued to work on his Ercoupe designs, such as a four-place Ercoupe and a twin-engine pusher-prop, high-wing, twin-boom plane that was designated the "Air Coach" and intended as a business plane. After the war, and due to the economic boom, production of the existing design for the two-place Ercoupe increased dramatically. *"I mean they built Ercoupes madly. They were building ten a day and then they put on a second shift and they were building twenty a day and then they put on a third shift and they were building thirty a day!"* Unfortunately, as quickly as the production expanded, the economic downturn of 1946 and 1947 reduced demand. *"Suddenly the demand was filled and they had ordered the materials for the next six months and they just could not make it past that. It came up too suddenly for them. . . so Henry Berliner just went out of the airplane business."*

When production of the Ercoupe ceased, Weick went to Texas A&M to work on an agricultural airplane. He became associated with the Piper Aircraft Co. over the next decade and designed the Cherokee. At the age of seventy, he retired but stayed active in aviation-related issues.

Along with the Collier Award, Weick received several honors including an honorary doctorate, the Guggenheim Award, the Albert Reed Award and the W.H. Fawcett Award, presented by Captain Eddie Rickenbacker, for the Ercoupe and the tricycle landing gear. However, what meant the most to him was hearing from World War II veterans and private pilots that told stories how the tricycle landing gear saved so many lives and was so much more stable.

Betsey Weick believes that her father saw himself as an aviation pioneer and enjoyed participating in various Ercoupe conventions and fly-in's such as the Experimental Aircraft Association's at Oshkosh, Wisconsin. *"He was proud of making the light plane safer and available to people who are handicapped."* Weick also understood the impact that ERCO had on the economics of Prince George's County. *"ERCO was the largest manufacturing facility in Price George's County. . .ERCO was followed by ACF and Link Singer. . .so Prince George's County had a supply of jobs and finances for maybe twenty-five years!"* Betsey herself learned to fly at College Park Airport. She currently works as a volunteer at the College Park Air Museum.

Betsey Weick, oral history interview, June 12, 2002,
MHT/OHC 002 (MD-AVC) 001, 49 p.

ment was the completion of two huge new military complexes in the spring of 1943. In southern Maryland, a hastily assembled work force built Naval Air Station Patuxent River and its auxiliary Webster Field, filling a pressing need for a modern and spacious venue for aviation testing. At Camp Springs, a similar rush project created the facility now known as Andrews Air Force Base, which provided an air defense and training center near the national capital.[54]

The wartime aviation building projects brought rapid changes to the Maryland environment, ranging from then-unrecognized ground pollution by chemicals to drastic alterations of the landscape. The creation of the Camp Springs and Patuxent bases, for example, spelled the end of two small communities and permanently transformed their rural surroundings. The construction and expansion of factories and military facilities was accompanied a surging influx of personnel. For example, Fairchild reported a jump in its Maryland staff from 200 in 1940 to a wartime peak of 8,000, while comparable figures for Martin Aircraft rose from 3,500 to 53,000. Many such workers and troops lived in barracks, trailers, or rented bedrooms, but others occupied houses built to accommodate them. The most distinctive of these housing projects were probably Aero Acres near Martin's Middle River plant, and the "flat-top" dwellings at Lexington Park near Patuxent.[55]

Among the nationwide social changes that accompanied the war was a broadening of the roles filled by women. Maryland aviation was no exception to this, although women were hardly a novelty in the state's skies. Female pilots had been flying airplanes in Maryland since at least 1912, when Bernetta Miller demonstrated a monoplane before officials at College Park Airfield. The worldwide emergency, however, expanded opportunities. In 1937, Congress authorized a Civilian Pilot Training Program (CPTP) in an effort to overtake a perceived German lead in flying skills. Many women took advantage of this program, under which twelve Maryland schools and other organizations offered flight training. CPTP graduates were often among those who joined the Women's Airforce Service Pilots (WASPs) during the war. They served as instructors and test pilots, and ferried military aircraft to destinations around the world. Elaine Harmon, for example, learned to fly in the CPTP, gave instrument flight training as a WASP, and was later a wartime air traffic controller. Another WASP flight instructor was Velta Benn, who learned to fly at College Park Airfield. Benn's busy postwar career in aviation included work for the Navy, and she is believed to be the first woman to make an arrested landing on an aircraft carrier. Still another Maryland WASP was Janet Lee Hutchinson, one of the three daughters of the Flying Hutchinson family, whose well-publicized aerial tours

From the Oral History Files...

Women Fly for the United States Military in World War II

An interview with Jane Straughan and Elaine Danforth Harmon
by Jennifer Braithwait Darrow

D ue to an increasing demand for pilots during World War II, the United States enlisted the help of Nancy Harkness Love and Jacqueline Cochran. Both women had approached the government, individually, when war began in Europe, with proposals to have women fly for the military. Later, the Women's Auxiliary Ferrying Squadron (WAFS), led by Love, and the Women's Flying Training Detachment (WFTD), headed by Cochran, were combined to create the Women Airforce Service Pilots or "WASP." The program was designed to decrease the need for male pilots at home by training female pilots to fly military aircraft for non-combat, domestic missions.

Jane Straughan, however, *"couldn't believe that anybody wanted me to fly anything that the Army had, because I didn't feel qualified."*

Straughan earned her pilot's license in 1938 after her husband encouraged her to take flying lessons at the Queen's Chapel Airport in Hyattsville. Straughan then made use of her aviation skills demonstrating the Ercoupe as an assistant to the sales manager at the Engineering and Research Corporation (ERCO) in Riverdale. It was while working for ERCO that Straughan attended a party for The Ninety-Nines, an organization of women aviators, and learned about the

Elaine Harmon, photographed in her flying gear in 1944, the same year she completed WASP training.
Photo courtesy of Elaine Harmon.

WASP program from Cochran. Straughan volunteered, and, much to her surprise, received a wire ordering her to report to Houston Municipal Airport in Texas with her flying gear and enough money to last for thirty days. Straughan, like all of the WASPs, was responsible for the expense of traveling to Texas. The first training class began on November 16, 1942 in Houston, Texas. When Straughan and the other trainees arrived, they were told, *"not to tell anyone who we were, because it was a secret."* According to Straughan, *"Nobody knew what to do with us, really. Cochran wasn't there when we got there. And they told us that, it was war time so we would have to find some place to live ... later ...they did move us ...into motor courts which were horrible. And they used to transport us back and forth to the field in what ...had been a cattle*

truck. At least it smelled like it." Training classes were later moved to Avenger Field in Sweetwater, Texas where the Army Air Forces had been training male cadets.

Elaine Harmon was raised in Baltimore, where, as a young girl, she watched a parade honoring Charles Lindbergh. As she recalled, she watched him, *"go down 33rd Street sitting ... up on the back of a convertible."* She later learned to fly at College Park Airport through the Civilian Pilot Training Program as a student at the University of Maryland. One woman was allowed into the program for every ten men enrolled. Harmon asked her father for permission to participate in the program because she knew that her mother would not approve. When she later joined the WASP, she said her mother, *"didn't write to me, didn't call me, nothing. She was really angry about my doing that."*

A typical day for WASP trainees, according to Harmon, began at 6 a.m. with Reveille and then breakfast. After breakfast, the trainees split into groups for flight training or ground school. Ground school classes included the study of engines, theory of flight, Morse code, and flight simulation in the "link trainer." After lunch, the trainees would continue with their training before cleaning up and attending dinner. While Straughan remembered occasionally attending the movies or going bowling while in training, Harmon didn't *"remember doing anything in particular,"* for entertainment, *"just studying."* While in training, the WASP were paid $150 a month but had to cover the cost of their room and board. After graduation, they received $250 a month, which was less than male pilots were making, but Harmon was not upset because, *"that was the most money I'd ever made. Before I went in, I made forty dollars a month, working as a bacteriologist, forty dollars a month."*

"When the program first started out," Harmon explained, *"it was supposed to be just for ferrying planes ... from the place of manufacture to ports where they would be sent overseas, or to bases where they would be used. And as the program went on, they found out that the women could do everything that the men did ...eventually, we were doing everything that was required."* Following their training, the WASP were assigned to bases around the country where their responsibilities were varied and included ferrying planes, testing planes, piloting transports, towing targets, instructing male pilots and flying planes for student navigators and bombardiers.

Jane Straughan was *"sent to New Castle Army Air Base at Wilmington, Delaware ...We could get orders to go most anywhere in the United States to pick up planes and take them someplace else."* Elaine Harmon *"was sent to Ellis Air Force Base in Las Vegas. And there, my job was to take the men up who wanted to practice their instrument flying in a BT-13. I would take the plane off and land it, but while they were up in the air, they would go under the hood and fly it, and I would just be there to make sure they didn't get into trouble."*

In 1944, Congress considered militarizing the WASP, but the measure failed. On December 20, 1944 the WASP were deactivated, more than six months before the war ended. As Straughan recalled, *"It was sad when they decided suddenly to let us go, because it was being made as a play that they didn't need us ... as far as my own feelings, I feel that they should have kept us until the end."* Elaine Harmon remembered Jacqueline Cochran coming to talk to her class on the day they graduated from training, *"Of course, she knew the program was being closed down at that point, she got to crying. She was so upset about the whole thing ... the war was winding down at that time, and they had plenty, plenty of pilots available."*

Following their service during the war, the WASP were offered commissions with the Air Force but they were no longer permitted to fly. Elaine Harmon *"was given a lieutenant commission. But when I went in, I had two young children. And after I got in, I had a third child. Shortly after that, I got this notice with the statement from rules and regulations that 'No woman could be in the reserves if she had a child under the age of eighteen' ... Now why they took me in, in the first place, I don't know."* Straughan also received a commission, as a captain, but following the birth of her twin

Jane Straughan and North America AT-6 at New Castle Army Base in Wilmington, Delaware, where she was stationed after completing WASP training. Photo courtesy of Jane Straughan.

sons, was informed that she could no longer remain in the reserves. Straughan continued to fly, with her husband, recreationally. They kept their plane in Frederick. Harmon, however, did not continue flying, but she remains an active member of the flying community through public speaking engagements and her membership in the Silver Wings Organization.

When asked what she enjoyed the most about being a WASP, Harmon replied, *"Well, two things really, of course, the flying was fun and the women ...just great, great women, I just enjoyed them so much ..."* More than 25,000 women applied to the WASP program. Fewer than 1,900 were accepted. When asked if she realized, at the time, the significance of becoming a WASP, Elaine Harmon said, *"Oh, I realized that it was a, you know, kind of pioneering experience, because aviation was still relatively new, and you know, women just didn't do things like this."*

The WASP served in a civilian capacity and were, therefore, not entitled to government benefits, such as insurance, or the honors of military personnel. More than 1,000 women served with the WASP during the war and thirty-eight died either in training or in the line of duty. After extensive lobbying efforts by the WASP, Senator Barry Goldwater introduced legislation in 1977 to honor the WASP as veterans. On November 23, 1977 President Carter signed the bill that finally gave the WASP veteran status.

Jane Straughan, oral history interview, October 16, 2002, MHT/OHC 002 (MD-AVC) 018, 31p.

Elaine Danforth Harmon, oral history interview, October 23, 2002, MHT/OHC 002 (MD-AVC) 015, 43 p.

had promoted air mindedness in the thirties.[56]

One of the most significant social trends of the war was the great rise in female industrial employment. The Martin Company hired its first nineteen women for factory jobs in October 1941, and the percentage of female workers climbed as high as thirty-five. Fairchild was somewhat slower to take on large numbers of women, but female representation in the company's workforce had reached a peak of thirty-six percent by February 1944. Although such percentages declined with the return of peace, the wartime experience affected future employment patterns. [57]

Like women, African Americans benefited from the war-induced labor shortage and from new federal government pressure on businesses to open long-closed doors. African American workers came to represent five percent of the Martin workforce, and two percent among the Fairchild employees at Hagerstown, a city where their share of the general population was relatively small. Although these workers were still segregated from their white counterparts on the job, they gained entry into a well-paid industrial employment. African Americans also took advantage of the CPTP program, in which racial discrimination against applicants was prohibited. Students

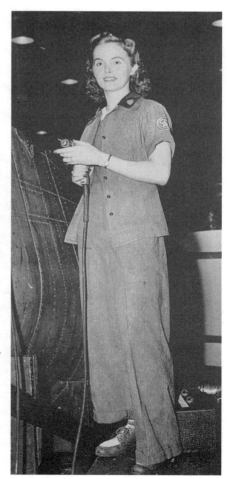

Glamorous "Martinette" works on Martin A-30 Baltimore light bomber at Martin's Middle River plant, Baltimore County, 1943 or 1944. She is wearing her stylish "Martinalls" work outfit. Photo courtesy of Glenn L. Martin Maryland Aviation Museum.

from Washington's Howard University took their flight training at Riverside Field (later Columbia Air Center), an African American-operated airport established during 1941 at Croom, Maryland. Managed by John Greene, who had been flying since 1922, the field gave African American fliers a welcome that was then typically denied to them at other airports in the state. At least 18 Marylanders were members of the Army's famed Tuskegee Airmen, whose wartime combat record exploded myths about African Americans' unsuitability for aviation. Among them, for example, were Robert Smith, who shot down a Messerschmitt in 1944, and Wendell Lucas, who became commander of the 99th Fighter Squadron in 1945. [58]

Postwar and Cold War

Following World War II, America faced economic adjustments and an uncertain peace that was soon over-shadowed by a tense standoff with the Soviet Union.

Baltimore emerged from the war determined to build the truly first-class airport that Harbor Field had failed to become. In May 1946, a municipal aviation commission produced a plan for establishing such a facility on a 32,000-acre site south of the city, near Friendship Church. President Harry S. Truman was the keynote speaker at the June 1950 dedication of the resulting airport. With its handsome terminal and long, heavy-duty runways, the new Friendship International was considered one of the nation's most advanced airports. Nevertheless, traffic there did not rise quickly, and by August 1953 the new airport was handling only five percent more flights than Harbor Field. The unimpressive start gave comfort to short-sighted critics who claimed that the vast, out-of-town facility was a useless "white elephant." The late fifties, however, witnessed an upward spurt of traffic at Friendship, which was the region's only civil airport capable of accepting the recently-introduced jet transports.

From the Oral History Files...

Building Airplanes at Fairchild

An Interview with Ferne Virginia Toms and Gayle Barnes

by Dr. Barry A. Lanman

Hired on April 10, 1942, Ferne Virginia Toms realized a dream: a job with the highest-paying employer in the Hagerstown area. Throughout her forty-year career with Fairchild Aircraft, a division of Fairchild Engine and Airplane Corporation, Toms used everything from rivets to Kevlar in the assembly of countless airplanes.

Ferne Virginia Toms and her husband Arthur Toms in the 1940s.
Photo courtesy of Ferne Virginia Toms.

In the true sense of the term, Toms was a "Rosie the Riveter." Her first job, an entry-level position, was "shooting" and "bucking" rivets. An oral history interview captured her thoughts and her experiences in the early days of World War II: *"I was hired, went to work and got the experience on the job. . .there was no time for training. . . Bucking rivets inside [a wing] was a noisy and hot job. . .You would have noise in your ear all day long. . .there would be six or more teams of riveters working on a wing at one*

time. . .I climbed all over the plane and did what needed to be done."

Mr. Gayle Barnes, who was interviewed in the same setting, interjected that *"riveting was an art. . .They seemed to have a sense of where the person was [you couldn't see the person on the other side of the sheet metal]. . .It was almost orchestrated. . .It was a team."* Toms estimated that an average day's work accounted for several thousand rivets during the average eight to ten hour shift.

A unique situation for this "Rosie" was that Toms' husband joined Fairchild Aircraft two months after she was hired and they ultimately became riveting buddies. He "shot" the rivets and she "bucked" them.

While the work was demanding, repetitive and physically strenuous, the workers generally got along well. However, Toms did state that *"A lot of men didn't want to work with women. . .we got the same wages as they did, and they didn't like that. . .We had a strong union. . . The UAW-CIO #842."*

Not all women at Fairchild worked on the assembly line. One unique job was a position called a "Guardette." The Guardettes, dressed in navy blue police-style uniforms, protected the plant at the gates and conducted internal security. Because Fairchild was a high security facility, this job produced a great deal of stress and it is theorized that this may have been a factor that caused a high rate of suicide among the females employed in this capacity. Toms was quite clear that she had no interest in being a Guardette due to the type of work and the lack of advancement in that field. In fact, she repeatedly made the point that she sought promotions and had the drive to earn more money. She knew that she didn't want to stay a "Rosie" her entire career. *"When I saw a job change [a job announcement] I put in for it. . .advancement was usually related to what you could do."*

As a result of this motivation, Toms moved from her original status as a "Rosie the Riveter" to time-keeper by the end of the World War II. As the years progressed and her experience increased, she helped assemble airplanes in a variety of ways. She became a tool and jig template layout worker and as a plastics fabricator. In the later part of her career, she also worked with composite materials like

This advantage ended in 1962 with the opening of Washington's Dulles International Airport. A disheartening dip followed before Friendship's patronage began to climb once again.[59]

By the late sixties, Friendship needed renovation and improvements that the city could not easily afford. The solution came as part of a general reshaping of the state government's role in transportation affairs. In 1970, the legislature at Annapolis authorized the creation of a Department of Transportation. The Maryland Aviation Commission became part of the new department, and was re-designated the Maryland Aviation Administration (MAA). The MAA assumed operation of Friendship after the state purchased the facility for $36 million in 1972. The following year, state authorities gave the airport a new name, Baltimore/Washington Inter-

Two "Rosies" riveting and bucking on a B-26 tail gun position. Photo courtesy of Glenn L. Martin Maryland Aviation Museum.

Kevlar in the construction of jet engine housings.

Gayle Barnes joined Fairchild in 1977 and started his aviation career in the same manner as Toms. He was employed in the sheet metal department. As Toms and Barnes became acquainted at work, they decided to car pool during a "gas crisis" in the late 1970s. The long drive from Boonsboro to Hagerstown and back became a daily social event and made work all the more enjoyable. This extended commute was common because workers came from all the surrounding small towns in the area.

Throughout her career, Toms helped build PT-19 Trainers, C-119s and C-123s. She also assisted the production of wing parts and control surfaces for 747s and 757s, and fins and rudders for the F-14. However, when she speaks of airplanes, the A-10 seems to be her favorite. Her preference for this airplane may relate to the fact that the A-10 was the "life-blood" of Fairchild for an extended period of time and that she helped build over 700 of these airplanes.

Barnes also enjoyed his expanding career with Fairchild and had hopes of staying with the company for his entire career, however, his employment ended with the downsizing and eventual closing of the Hagerstown plant by the mid-1980s While some workers were bitter about the closing, Barnes had fond memories of his Fairchild days and said that *"folks that went there [Fairchild Aircraft] tried to give them a good days work and they gave us a good days pay."* Barnes assesses what he took away with him after the factory ceased production. *"I learned to work with procedures, specifications and drawings . . . and people . . . These skills helped me . . . Fairchild equipped a lot of people to go somewhere else."*

Barnes ultimately obtained a job with OAO Corporation, a Beltsville, Maryland sub-contractor for Goddard Space Flight Center. However, he is now employed by Swales Aerospace and has worked on contracts for RCA, direct band television dishes and myriad communications satellites. His more recent endeavors have involved him in the development of crew aides and tools for the International Space Station and assembly and servicing tools for the Hubble Telescope.

When Fairchild Aircraft closed and other manufacturing plants left the state, some experts claimed that Maryland's "Glory Days" of aerospace production were past. Mr. Barnes sees the situation in a different light. *"The Baltimore-Washington area has become a technology corridor. I think they are drawing a lot of skilled workers that have a significant amount to contribute."*

In the final analysis, Toms characterized the complex relationship between the aviation manufacturer and Western Maryland. *"We were good to Fairchild. . .and Fairchild was good to us."*

Gayle Barnes and Ferne Virginia Toms, oral history interview, May 20, 2003. Interview not transcribed.

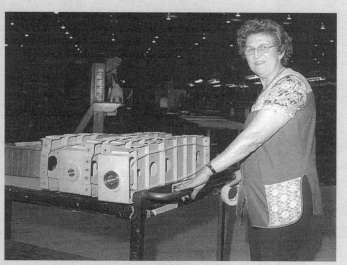

A riveter in the 1940s, Ferne Virginia Toms in the 1970s working in the parts control department at Fairchild Aircraft, Hagerstown, Washington County. Photo courtesy of Ferne Virginia Toms.

Chesapeake Airlines offered DC-3 service to Salisbury in 1948. Photo courtesy of the Ann Arrundell County Historical Society.

level of demand was relatively low. [61]

One aviator-entrepreneur who successfully adapted to conditions at a mid-sized airport was William S. D. "Bill" Newnam, a Marine pilot during the war. Newnam was a long-time manager of Easton Municipal Airport, who also operated Maryland Airlines during 1949-88. Using aircraft with modest seating capacity, he shuttled well-heeled commuters between Talbot County and destinations such as Washington National. While Newnam kept his airport viable through difficult times, another well-known Maryland aviator used somewhat similar tactics on a broader scale. Richard A. "Dick" Henson was a Fairchild test pilot who had operated a flying service at Hagerstown since 1932. Henson's career took a decisive turn in 1962, when he challenged the local dominance of Allegheny Airlines by beginning one of the nation's

national (BWI), and announced an ambitious plan aimed at drawing more passengers from the combined metropolitan areas. The rest of the decade saw a major upgrading of both the airfield and landside facilities, including a new terminal whose design emphasized convenience and efficiency. In 1980, the opening of an Amtrak rail station on the airport's grounds made BWI a leader in the national effort to create a more inter-modal transportation system.[60]

In the aftermath of the world war, the cities of Cumberland, Hagerstown, Easton, and Salisbury possessed mid-sized civil airports with the potential to offer air carrier service. The opening of Frederick Municipal in 1949 added a fifth such facility. Speaking at the dedication in May, the mayor noted that the airport had been built in the belief that it was necessary for Frederick's growth, and invited citizens to respect and use its facilities. All American Airways, which had been flying into the field since March, began daily stops with DC-3s on the day after the ceremony. A variety of carriers tried such service at the mid-sized airports during this period, but generally found it difficult to maintain. In 1961, the state established a commission to study the problem. The resulting report labeled Maryland's air service as substandard, and even called the situation a threat to economic stability. The study laid much of the blame on the currently dominant carrier, Allegheny Airlines, and urged the governor to insist that the airline be "hauled on the carpet" by federal regulators. The underlying problem, however, was probably the high cost of operating transport-category aircraft to and from communities where the

Dick Henson with his Beech King Air executive aircraft. Photo courtesy of the Ann Arrundell County Historical Society.

earliest scheduled air taxi operations. Using ten-seat Twin Beech aircraft, with even smaller planes as backups, he offered service that was tailored to the local market. Observing the success of its upstart rival, Allegheny in 1967 offered Henson an alliance that enabled him to expand beyond Hagerstown. Shifting his base to Salisbury in the 1980s, he eventually sold his thriving business to Piedmont Airlines, finally retiring in 1989 as a respected pioneer in regional air travel. [62]

In the field of private flying, the postwar era began briskly. A December 1946 news story called the preceding twelve months "the biggest year for aviation in Maryland's history." Nine new commercial airports had opened, the number of Maryland-owned planes had climbed from 386 to 720, and the roster of pilots had more than doubled, reaching 2,300. A major factor in this boom was the "GI bill of rights," which provided educational benefits that veterans could spend on flight training. A broader section of the population now experienced the advantages and pleasures of personal flight. The epitome of this lifestyle was represented by Kentmorr Airpark, an aeronautical community that opened on Kent Island soon after the war. This residential airpark, possibly the nation's first, offered "hangar bungalows" for vacationers, as well as home sites for those who wished to settle beside the runway. [63]

In August 1948, Maryland had thirty-four public-use airports, including twenty-eight of the smallest "Class 1" category that typically catered to private pilots. By early in the next decade, concern was growing about an airport decline, with the total down to thirty by 1952. Two years later, a journalist complained that the legislature was doing little to combat the continuing trend, while the State Aviation Commission was desperately trying to prevent Annapolis' Lee Airport from being converted into a drive-in movie theater. The beleaguered facility was able to reopen after a period of closure, but remained threatened. Despite such alarms, or perhaps in part because of the concern that they engendered, Maryland's total number of airports did not decline further during the next three decades. A state directory issued in April 1981, for example, listed thirty-nine public-use facilities. Some of the newer airports, like Montgomery County Airpark, successfully tied their fortunes to the new trend toward development of "industrial parks." Nevertheless, the smaller privately-owned commercial facilities remained very vulnerable. In addition to the usual business uncertainties, such operators faced the ever-increasing pressures of encroaching land development and rising real estate values. Maryland's population grew by 132 percent between 1940 and 1980, while the percentage of suburban dwellers rose from twenty-three to sixty-three. A new tool for helping the smaller airports appeared in 1982, when Congress authorized the Airport Improvement Program, a broadened scheme of federal aid that permitted grants to privately-owned facilities in the commercial category. [64]

Maryland's aircraft manufacturers adjusted with varying success to postwar conditions. "There's A Plane in Your Future," proclaimed the title of a 1946 *Baltimore* magazine article that touted the boom in private flying. The range of personal aircraft available included the city's own Winglet, which designer Cheston L. Eshelman produced for a time at Pimlico Airport. In this hopeful atmosphere, ERCO returned eagerly to building its Ercoupe, pushing sales hard with a campaign that included displays of the aircraft at Macy's and other department stores. Unfortunately, the depth of the demand for small planes had been greatly overestimated, and the national market went through a period of saturation. Production of the Ercoupe at Riverdale did not survive the glut, and the last one to be fabricated there was completed in early 1952. Devotees of the easy-to-fly plane could still obtain them from other companies, but ERCO exited from the field of airframe production. [65]

In contrast to ERCO's disappointing postwar experience, the Fairchild establishment at Hagerstown went through only a relatively brief period of adjustment, then entered a sustained era of aircraft manufacturing that included many notable models. The company's C-82 Packet cargo planes were not ready in time to see service against Japan, but their logistical value was obvious, and 224 were built by the end of production in 1948. The Packet was followed by the C-119 Flying Boxcar, a design that was similar but even more powerful and capacious. The C-119s performed well in the Korean War, and Fairchild supplied military forces with more than 1,100 of the durable planes before production ceased in 1955. Other products included the company's response to the challenge of building a replacement for

ERCO Plant operating at capacity, circa 1946-48, in Riverdale, Prince George's County. Photo courtesy of the College Park Aviation Museum, Lester Wells Collection.

the ubiquitous DC-3. Fairchild secured a share of that market with its high-wing F-27 turboprop transport and its stretched version, the FH-227, both developed in cooperation with Fokker Aircraft, B.V., of the Netherlands. One of the company's most distinctive aircraft was the A-10 Thunderbolt II, which made its first flight in 1972. With its outsized twin engines perched just behind the wings, this "Warthog" failed to match popular ideals of a beautiful airplane; however, it pleased military leaders interested in providing close air support for ground forces. The A-10's long production run ended in March 1984, when one of the planes became the last Fairchild aircraft produced in Hagerstown.[66]

At Martin's Middle River complex, the unexpectedly sudden surrender of Japan in August 1945 meant a drastic reduction in military orders and a slide in employment. Part of the company's response was to speed up its plans to enter the market for DC-3 replacements. The Martin 2-O-2 became the first new airliner available after the war, but soon encountered problems. A fatal crash in

The sprawling campus of the Goddard Space Flight Center in Greenbelt, Prince George's County. Photo courtesy of the Goddard Space Flight Center.

1948 revealed a design flaw that required extensive modifications and destroyed buyer interest. The 2-O-2 also lacked the pressurization that airlines were beginning to desire, and Martin was slow in producing a pressurized successor, the 4-O-4. The venture into airliners was a net loss, and contributed to Glenn Martin's retirement from leadership in 1952. Production of a variety of military planes continued, however, and the company pursued one last imaginative design that might have restored its status as a major aircraft producer. The SeaMaster, the world's first seaplane with multiple jet engines, was intended to fill the Navy's need for a nuclear bomber. A handful of SeaMasters were built, but in 1959 the Navy

cancelled the contract due to changes in its strategic planning. In December of the following year, aircraft production at Middle River came to an end with a final P5M Marlin. In 1961, the company merged with a large manufacturer of such materials as paint and cement, becoming Martin Marietta. The merger was part of a move toward diversification that had already involved the Middle River plant in a field that was becoming a key component of Maryland's aerospace industry—missiles.[67]

Rocketry research in Maryland did not cease with the end of World War II. Several weeks after V-J Day, for example, a group of German scientists arrived at Aberdeen Proving Ground and began helping their new employers by sorting through a mass of captured documents relating to the Germans' V-2 ballistic missile, used to bombard London and Antwerp in World War II. The Applied Physics Laboratory continued its interest in rocket research, designing instruments that soared one hundred miles upward aboard a V-2, and then helping to develop the Aerobee rocket as a vehicle for further high-altitude research. During the 1940s and 1950s, the Martin plant became involved in such projects as building the Gorgon, Oriole, Matador, and Viking systems. Fairchild's missile ventures included the SM-73 Goose, a pilotless decoy designed to fool Soviet defenses by mimicking manned bombers. Twenty SM-73s were built at Hagerstown, but the program was cancelled in 1958 because military authorities realized that they would be unable to recall the decoys if a war were averted at the last minute.[68]

During the Cold War, Maryland acquired an expanding network of research facilities whose scope included aerospace matters. The Naval Ordnance Laboratory, for example, opened in 1948 at White Oak. The growing Applied Physics Laboratory began its move to a much larger new campus in Howard County in 1954. The best-known of these scientific institutions was Greenbelt's Goddard Space Flight Center, dedicated by the National Aeronautics and Space Administration (NASA) in 1961. This spacious complex of laboratories and testing facilities became an important link in the chain of NASA centers that made possible the subsequent U.S. achievements in satellites and space exploration. Private enterprises in Maryland also found roles in the multifaceted space program. At Middle River in the sixties, for example, Martin Marietta assembled Titan launch vehicles and operated a simulation facility where Project Gemini astronauts trained. Later, the Baltimore division of Westinghouse supplied the television camera that captured the first Apollo moon walk, and Black and Decker provided a cordless Lunar Surface Drill.[69]

Space-related projects continued to be a part of the very diverse range of Maryland aerospace enterprises described by William Hallstead in a 1980 article. Fairchild was the only major company still manufacturing complete airplanes. A shrunken staff at Martin Marietta's Middle River establishment was turning out jet thrust reversers (although the plant was soon to experience an upturn as the producer of a launching system for naval missiles). In Glen Arm, a small Grumman Aerospace factory was fabricating components for a variety of aircraft. At a center near BWI Airport, Westinghouse employed 13,000 workers on projects that included radar systems and hardware for communications satellites. Other examples included Amecon of College Park, which had some 1,000 personnel working on aviation-related electronics, while the AIA Corporation was building equipment for loading cruise missiles into B-52 bombers.[70]

A missile widely deployed on Maryland soil during the Cold War was the Nike anti-aircraft weapon. Intended to protect against attack by Soviet nuclear bombers, Nike bases were established in rings around targets that included Baltimore and Washington. The first such site in the nation, located on the grounds of Fort Meade, became operational in 1954. During the following year, an accidental launch by this unit showered debris along the Baltimore-Washington Parkway. Although this incident increased public fears about the safety of the system, the number of Nike sites in Maryland grew to a peak of about nineteen in 1960. The Army's emphasis on the Nikes waned as the perception of the chief Soviet threat shifted from bombers to ballistic missiles, and all the sites were closed by the end of 1974.[71]

The evolution of military air bases in Maryland during the Cold War included the closure of Naval Air Facility Annapolis in 1962 after twenty-five years of operation, because the all-seaplane facility was no longer able to provide realistic training for the Academy. The Navy's large airfield at Patuxent River served a variety of purposes, including the basing of anti-submarine aircraft units in the sixties and seventies. Generally, however, the station developed in accordance with its original mission of aviation testing, and a series of enhancements kept it on the leading edge in that demanding field. The state's other major military airfield, Andrews Air Force Base, became something of a government airport for the

Nike Ajax (above) and Nike Hercules anti-aircraft missiles (left). Photos courtesy of the Granite Historical Society.

national capital. As such, Andrews was the televised background for news events both joyous and tragic, including the final return of assassinated President John F. Kennedy to Washington in 1963. Maryland's Air National Guard aviators, meanwhile, pursued a quest for a suitable base. Although their hangar at Harbor Field was impressive, the spongy runways had not improved and were useless for the jet age. In 1975, an agreement with Martin Marietta permitted a Guard unit to begin using part of the company's airport at Middle River, which became Martin State Airport after its purchase by the Maryland government during the following year. In 1982, new Guard facilities at Martin State were dedicated as Warfield Air National Guard Base, memorializing Major General Edwin Warfield III, who had helped to build Maryland's Air Guard into a truly modern force.[72]

Toward a Changing Horizon

The Cold War waned during the late eighties, and by the end of 1991 the long-feared Soviet Union had been formally dissolved. The lessening of international tension was followed by consolidation within the U.S.

defense industry. Among those embracing the trend was Martin Marietta, which in 1995 merged with Lockheed, historically one of America's great aircraft manufacturers. The giant Lockheed Martin Corporation that resulted was headquartered in Bethesda, although only a fraction of its employees worked within the state. Another merger that affected Maryland was the 1996 acquisition of Westinghouse's defense and electronics sector by California-based Northrop Grumman. Even when they remained separate, aerospace firms often collaborated on the era's highly complex projects. In October 2001, for example, it was announced that Northrop Grumman's unit near BWI Airport would provide the airborne radar and other electronics for a Joint Strike Fighter to be built by Lockheed Martin in Texas.[73]

According to a report by state authorities, Maryland's aerospace industry in 1998 consisted of forty-two core business establishments, with an additional thirty establishments closely supporting the sector. The core businesses had some 13,000 employees. This figure was estimated to be on the rise, but it was obviously a long way from the peak era during the forties. Nevertheless, the aerospace companies formed an influential and lucrative element of the state's economy. Not included in the employment figure were the nonprofit and governmental scientific organizations involved in the field, most of which usually labored outside the limelight. An exception to this anonymity was NASA's high-profile Goddard Space Flight Center. Achievements there during this period included a key role in orbiting the Hubble Space Telescope, which was roughly ten times more powerful than any earth-based observatory. An operations center at Goddard controlled Hubble after its launch in 1990, relaying the data that it yielded to a special scientific institute on the Baltimore campus of Johns Hopkins University.[74]

For military aviation, the end of the Cold War brought some retrenchment and a greater emphasis on preparedness for small-scale conflicts and humanitarian missions. Fairchild A-10s, the last Maryland-made combat planes, proved their worth in helping to reverse the 1991 Iraqi invasion of Kuwait. Some five years later, pilots of the state's Air National Guard flew A-10s in support of peacekeeping operations in Bosnia, one of several call-ups to participate in the varied overseas operations of the nineties. A wave of base closures and conversions mandated by a 1988 congressional act and subsequent legislation had less negative impact in Maryland than in some sections of the country. The Navy's Patuxent River station actually grew as a result of the policy, because the facility received functions from bases shut down elsewhere. The closure review authorities gave close scrutiny to Patuxent's auxiliary, Webster Field; however, the facility survived to pursue a future that included support for development of unmanned aerial vehicles. One casualty of the consolidation trend was the former Engineering Experiment Station, a venerable research center at Annapolis that had tested the engines of early naval aircraft. Another was the Army airfield named for Col. William D. Tipton, who had died in a postwar crash. In 1999, however, this facility on the edge of Fort Meade was reborn as the state's newest civil airport.[75]

Despite the addition of Tipton Airport, concern remained about the loss of general aviation facilities such as Baltimore Airpark, which closed in 2001 after the land was sold to a housing developer. The pressure on the smallest airports reflected the continued swelling of the state's population, which rose from 4.2 million to 5.3

Interstate 81 and U.S. Route 11 bend around the 5,461-foot runway 9-27 at Hagerstown Regional Airport/Richard A. Henson Field, Washington County. Photo courtesy of Maryland Aviation Administration.

million in the last two decades of the twentieth century. On the other hand, a number of outlying communities were successfully upgrading their airports as a means of attracting a larger share of new jobs and economic growth. In a December 2002 interview, Bruce Mundie of the Maryland Aviation Administration (MAA) discussed airport trends with historian Barry Lanman. Pointing to the spread of population northwest of the national capital, Mundie noted that Hagerstown Regional Airport had the highway links and improved on-site facilities to take advantage of the growth. He speculated that the airport might one day become a hub of the magnitude of Washington's Reagan National.[76]

Runway 6-24 at Potomac Airfield, Friendly, Prince George's County, runs directly into Featherstone Drive, a suburban street, in a dramatic example of the conflict between aviation and urban sprawl. Photo courtesy of Maryland Aviation Administration.

Government aid was essential to the health and future of airports ranging from BWI down to the modest commercial airfields that were beneficiaries of Maryland Aid to Private Airports (MAPA). Begun in late 1988, the MAPA program awarded more than nine million dollars in State assistance over the next fifteen-and-a-half years. Overall, however, the federal government was by far the greatest benefactor of Maryland's airports. Federal dollars made up about seventy-three percent of the $201 million in assistance that the facilities received from 1978 through late June 2003.[77]

Like many aspects of American life, aviation in Maryland was strongly affected by the September 2001 terrorist attacks on targets in New York and Washington. In the aftermath, fighters from Andrews Air Force Base helped to patrol the skies over the capital, while many nearby Maryland airports were shut down or sharply restricted. The tightest restrictions were enforced at the trio of airports within a fifteen-mile radius of the Washington Monument: College Park, Washington Executive/Hyde, and Potomac. Washington Executive/Hyde did not reopen for a year after the attacks, and strict security regulations continued to apply at all three facilities. Airports farther from Washington suffered too, although the effects of the crisis were not always wholly negative. Some facilities received new patronage as pilots shifted away from the capital, while others benefited from a boom in business jet travel by executives seeking to avoid airlines. Although named the fastest growing of North America's top thirty airports in 2001, BWI was naturally affected by the air carrier downturn. The facility continued its aggressive improvement program, however, and also became a test site for techniques and technology being tried by the new Federal Transportation Security Agency.[78]

Despite the lingering shadow of the terrorist episode, the mood in Maryland aviation circles seemed upbeat as the centennial of the Wright Brothers' 1903 flight approached. Numerous projects across the state were upgrading the infrastructure for both light planes and sophisticated jets. In his December 2002 interview, the MAA's Bruce Mundie was asked to identify the strongest periods in Maryland aviation history. His reply was unhesitating: "Right now." While optimistic about current prospects, air minded Marylanders remained proud of their aeronautical past, a heritage that is ably interpreted by several of the state's museums. On an apron at Martin State Airport, the restoration crew of the Glenn L. Martin Maryland Aviation Museum worked to restore a big Republic F-105 "Thunderchief" salvaged from Aberdeen Proving Ground. The goal was to recreate its appearance when flown as a "Wild Weasel" over North Vietnam by a now-senior executive at Lockheed Martin in Bethesda. The museum was also raising money to build a hangar for their collection. Meanwhile, at the College Park Aviation Museum, restoration was completed on a Boeing PT-17 "Stearman" that had belonged to Gustavus McLeod of Laytonsville. During 2000, McLeod had used the antique plane to become the first pilot to reach the North Pole in an open-cockpit aircraft. Unveiled at the two museums during 2003, the F-105 and PT-17 offered tangible proof that the spirit of aerial adventure remained alive in contemporary Maryland.[79]

Grass Fields, Factory Floors, Airparks and Missile Sites:

An Inventory of Aviation-Related Sites

By Edmund Preston

Chapter One: Pioneers

[Editor's note] *Marylanders began experimenting with aviation long before the Wright Brothers. Peter Carnes' initial balloon flights were a combination of science and showmanship, but by the Civil War balloons were put to military use. The airplane followed the same pattern, with the nearly simultaneous debut of the great Baltimore Aero Meet and the adaptation of airplanes to military service. Both the Army and the Navy had to evaluate the Wright Flyers, which were controlled by warping their fabric wings, against planes built by the brothers' archrival Glenn Curtiss, who used the French invention, the aileron. Pilots who learned to manipulate the levers that controlled Wright aircraft could not fly the wheel-and-shoulder-harness operated Curtiss machines—and vice versa. Parallel testing went on at College Park Airfield for the Army and along the Severn for the Navy. Eventually military aviation research was sent to the established research centers. Three of these—at Indian Head, Aberdeen, and Annapolis—were in Maryland. With America's entry into World War I, a Hagerstown steel company made an abortive bid to become the State's first supplier of factory-built aircraft. [When relevant, a MHT Maryland Inventory of Historic Properties (MIHP) number is shown. Numbers for properties that have multiple MIHP numbers, such as Aberdeen Proving Ground, are not shown.]*

GEORGE WASHINGTON HOUSE

originally INDIAN QUEEN TAVERN
Bladensburg, Prince George's
County (PG: 69-2) c. 1774-84

The George Washington House is located in Bladensburg at 4302 Baltimore Avenue. It is a two-and-a-half story brick structure, five bays wide, with a two-story porch covering its façade and a wooden addition at the rear. The structure was built circa 1760 by Jacob Wirt as part of a commercial complex that included a store, tavern/inn, billiard hall, and blacksmith shop.

The present name derives from a tradition that George Washington lodged at the hostelry. The structure's pertinence to aviation history lies in its association with pioneer balloonist Peter Carnes.[1]

Following the death of Wirt in 1774, Carnes became the operator of the Indian Queen Tavern. In 1784, he became the first American known to have built a balloon capable of carrying a passenger. According to the historian Tom D. Crouch, Carnes "had undoubtedly begun by launching small paper or silk balloons from one of the lots surrounding the Indian Queen Tavern. . ." Carnes gave a public demonstration of his full-scale balloon with a tethered, unmanned ascent near Bladensburg on June 19. This was followed by a similar demonstration at Howard Park near Baltimore on June 24. On that occasion, thirteen-year-old Edward Warren entered the tethered balloon to become the first person to leave the surface of the United

The George Washington House, formerly the Indian Queen Tavern, in Bladensburg was the site of early experiments by Peter Carnes, who made the first American manned balloon. Photo courtesy of the Maryland Historical Trust.

States in a flying machine. Carnes himself attempted to go aloft at Philadelphia on July 19, but abandoned ballooning after this failure. At about this same time, he left Maryland to avoid arrest as the result of legal action concerning rent due for the Indian Queen Tavern.[2]

In 1973, a historic sites survey by Christopher Owens found the George Washington House to be in altered and deteriorated condition, but noted that restoration was planned. "Transportation" was listed as the site's area of significance in the report, which was followed by its entry upon the National Register of Historic Places.[3]

Significance for Maryland air/space history: An historic structure associated with the life of an important figure in the history of American lighter-than-air flight.
Relevant years: c. 1774 – 1784, c. *Lat/Long*: 38-57N 76-57W
Map: ADC Md/Del 2000 *Num*: 20 *Grid*: A1 *Shows*: town

BALTIMORE AVIATION FIELD, HALETHORPE
Halethorpe, Baltimore County, 1910

The Baltimore Aero Meet [also referred to as the Baltimore Aviation Meet and the Baltimore Air Show of 1910], held at the nearby town of Halethorpe in November 1910, was one of the first large international aeronautical competitions in the United States. Organized by Col. Jerome H. Joyce, president of the Aero Club of Baltimore, the meet was an early example of the city's efforts to become a leading center of aviation. Besides demonstration flights, the events included competitions designed to test such performance factors as distance, speed, altitude, and duration of flight. A total of $50,400 in prize money was awarded. Participants included some of the era's most celebrated aviators from Britain, France, and the United States. Archibold Hoxsey flew the Wright Brothers' "baby grand" model, escaping injury when it crashed. Eugene Ely and Charles F. Willard flew planes built by Glenn Curtiss, who attended the event and had selected its site.[4]

The location of the meet met the basic requirement of level topography. Steam rollers further smoothed the surface of the airfield, which was reported to be 300 feet wide and a mile long. Another prime advantage of the field was ready access from the Baltimore and Ohio railway that bordered it on the northwest. The vicinity could also be reached by a Pennsylvania Railroad line, or by street car. A parking area for automobiles and horse-drawn vehicles was provided on the northwest side of the B&O tracks. A temporary footbridge allowed ticket holders to pass over the railway tracks and reach the spectator stands and private boxes. These elaborate preparations for the crowds proved justified by a massive attendance. Structures at the airfield itself included score-

boards and six twenty-five-foot pylons to mark the inner course. Two large tents served as hangars when the meet opened on November 2, but were replaced by a wooden structure following a severe storm on the following day. Damage caused by the storm interrupted the meet for several days and prolonged it until November 12.[5]

By far the most celebrated achievement of the meet was the flight over Baltimore by Hubert Latham. Many thousands of excited citizens watched as the French pilot's graceful Antoinette monoplane soared over pre-announced points that included Druid Lake, Patterson Park, and the offices of the *Sun* newspaper, sponsor of the flight. To follow such a prescribed course over a metropolis was hailed as a new and risky venture. Besides helping to demonstrate the basic practicality of aviation, the Halethorpe meet raised awareness of the airplane's potential as a weapon. One of the events was a bomb throwing competition that may have been one of the earliest public demonstrations of its kind.[6]

In 2003, the site of the Baltimore Aviation Field is largely occupied by industrial warehouses. The B&O raised track bed still remains along the northwest side of the former airfield. Two modern streets, Hollins Ferry Road and Trident Court, now parallel the railway and run through the area of the former airfield. The spectator stands erected for the 1910 event were located approximately along Hollins Ferry Road, northeast of its intersection with Halethorpe Farms Road.[7]

Significance for Maryland air/space history: The state's first large public demonstration of heavier-than-air flight and one of the earliest such events in the nation.
Relevant years: 1910 *Lat/Long*: 39-14N 76-42W
Map: ADC Md/Del 2000 Num: 15 Grid: D4 Shows: area

COLLEGE PARK AIRPORT
College Park, Prince George's County (PG:66-4)
1909-present

College Park Airport occupies a seventy-acre site about one mile east of the town of College Park and some four miles northeast of the District of Columbia. The site is east of the Metrorail/Baltimore and Ohio railway line, and south of the Anacostia River's Paint Branch. The entrance is on Corporal Frank S. Scott Drive, north of Paint Branch Parkway.[8]

The origins of College Park Airport date from the early years of powered, heavier-than-air flight. In 1908, Wilbur and Orville Wright entered into a contract with the U.S. Department of War to provide a usable airplane and to train two pilots. The Wrights proved the viability of their aircraft at Ft. Meyer, Virginia, but a more spacious area was desirable for the training phase of the contract. Balloon flights by Lt. Frank Lahm helped to identify a suitable site at College Park, conveniently connected to the capital by rail. The Army leased 160 acres and erected a temporary hangar at the field.[9]

Instruction at College Park was conducted by Wilbur Wright, who made fifty-five flights there between October 8 and November 2, 1909. Wright fulfilled his contract by qualifying the Army's two earliest pilots, Lt. Frederick E. Humphreys, followed shortly by Lahm. He also gave three hours of training to Lt. Benjamin Foulois, a future Air Corps commander. In late October, Mrs. Sarah Van Deman went aloft as Wright's passenger, making her the first woman to fly in an airplane in the United States. Lt. George C. Sweet became the Navy's first officer to make such a flight when Lahm took him up as a passenger on November 3. Two days later, an accident damaged the field's single aircraft, and the Army soon decided to shift its nascent flight program to Texas.[10]

In 1910, Rexford M. Smith formed a partnership with the aim of building aircraft. He constructed a hangar at the College Park field, and made his first flight in November. The National Aviation Company is reported to have held air meets at the field in 1910, and to have located there in the following year. Other organizations that established themselves at College Park Airfield during this era included the Christmas Aeroplane Company and the Washington Aeroplane Company, maker of the Columbia biplane. Famed pilots Tony Jannus and Paul Peck were among those who flew test flights at the field. Some of this activity continued at the College Park Airfield into 1917 or 1918, and other civilian enterprises were to follow.[11]

In the spring of 1911, meanwhile, the Army returned to establish a more elaborate flying school at College Park Airfield. Leasing greater acreage at the same location, the military cleared a larger field and, parallel to the railway, they set up a line of structures that included a headquarters building, a medical tent, and several hangars—initially four, with three added later. Rex Smith moved his hangar to align with this row, and the civilian activities continued beside the military ones.[12]

Flights at the Army school began in the summer and continued, except for a winter break in Georgia, until November 1912. Operations went beyond training to include spectacular flights over Washington and other feats that generated popular excitement. Lt. Henry H. "Hap" Arnold made a series of high altitude flights,

eventually climbing more than one mile. Arnold and another officer made an unusually long flight to visit the National Guard encampment at Frederick, which was forty-two miles distant. Three planes from the school landed at the Chevy Chase Golf Club in what has been called the Army's first group cross-country flight. Important tests were made with air-to-ground radio, the

The Army evaluated both Wright airplanes, controlled by wing-warping, and Curtiss planes, controlled by ailerons mounted between the wings. In this photograph, Wright aircraft occupy the two hangars on the left, Curtiss machines the two on the right. In the foreground is the grass airfield at College Park. Photo courtesy of the National Archives.

use of smoke for coded communications, and night landings assisted by acetylene lights. The Army made its first trials of a bomb sight, using practice bombs, and of firing a machine gun from an airplane.[13]

The achievements of the Army's College Park school were not without tragic cost. Two accidents during 1912 were fatal to four aviators: civilian test pilot Arthur L. Welch and Lt. Leighton Hazelhurst, on June 11; then Lt. Lewis Rockwell and Cpl. Frank Scott, on September 28. Hazelhurst and Rockwell were the Army's third and fourth officers to die in airplane crashes, while Scott was the first such casualty among its enlisted personnel.[14]

College Park Airport gained a new sort of prominence in 1918, when the Post Office began its first regular air mail route, which connected Washington, Philadelphia, and New York. This service was launched initially by Army pilots from Washington's polo field. After three months, the postal authorities began using their own pilots and switched the southern terminus to College Park. On August 12, Max Miller took off northbound as the civilian Air Mail Service began operations. Postal flights continued at College Park Airfield until the

continued on page 34

From the Oral History Files...

The Baltimore Aero Meet of 1910 and Hubert Latham's Flight Over Baltimore City

An Interview with Henry Rinn
by Dr. Barry A. Lanman

Note: In 1976, Henry Rinn was interviewed about early events in Maryland aviation history; he passed away shortly afterwards. His highly detailed account of the events has been verified by a variety of other sources and was included in the current research for the Maryland Centennial of Flight Celebration because it is believed that no eyewitnesses are still alive in 2003.

For almost five years after their first flight, the Wright Brothers experimented in private. Not until September 3, 1908, at Fort Myer, Virginia, did they give the public their first demonstration of powered flight. The military trials of the Wright Flyer finally gave witness to the actuality of man leaving the earth with the assistance of a powered machine. From that date, interest and elation over man's ability to fly grew exponentially.

In 1909, Louis Bleriot's flight across the English Channel and the first international air meet at Reims, France, only fueled the gathering storm of excitement. Now more than ever, people wanted to see this phenomenon for themselves. Building on this interest, cities in all parts of the United States and abroad wanted

Crowds gaze upwards at Farman and Curtiss biplanes at the Baltimore Aero Meet at Halethorpe, Baltimore County, November 1910. While more than one aviator flew at a time in some contests, this was probably a composite photograph. Photo courtesy of Barry A. Lanman.

to host an aviation event. Baltimore's civic leaders, not willing to be left out, urged the Aero Club of America to hold the next air meet in their city. Unfortunately, New York won the bid and the air show took place at Belmont Park. While small exhibitions occurred in the interim, Baltimore continued its quest for a major meet and eventually won out over six western cities vying for the same privilege. After the initial acceptance of Baltimore's proposal, the meet

was scheduled for November of 1910.

Col. Jerome Joyce, President of the Aero Club of Maryland, was appointed to organize the show. A large field in Halethorpe was selected because it made a natural airfield and it was only sixteen miles south of Baltimore City along Washington Boulevard. In addition to these features, the B&O and the Pennsylvania railroads provided excellent transportation to and from the location. With little work, the Baltimore Aviation Company developed an airfield and exhibit area that was a mile long and 300 yards wide. Seventeen years later the same site was to be used for the B&O's centennial of railroading, the "Festival of the Iron Horse." Although today it is the site of an industrial park, the sound of airplanes is still heard from Baltimore/Washington International Airport, only four miles away.

A good field and excellent transportation were only two of the three main components necessary in planning an endeavor of this type, however. The actual success of the meet depended on the ability of its promoters to attract a significant number of prominent names in aviation. To accomplish their goal, a large amount of prize money was needed.

It was to the credit of Col. Joyce and his committee that $50,400 was quickly raised for the contests. Thus, the financial inducements produced a list of participants that read like a "Who's Who" of aviation. Among the flyers competing for prizes and giving demonstrations were Charles Foster Willard, Count Jacques de Lesseps, Hubert Latham, James Radley, J. Armstrong Drexel, Clifford Harmon, Eugene Ely, and Glenn Curtiss.

A notable absence was the Wright Brothers. However, Archibald (Arch) Hoxsey, who was employed by the Wrights, flew a Wright Flyer and represented the company at the meet. By 1910, Hoxsey was well known as a "dare-devil" aviator and gained notoriety when he took Theodore Roosevelt for his first airplane ride. To demonstrate the practicality of the airplane, Hoxsey assembled his aircraft after it was delivered in a boxcar at the Pennsylvania Railroad station near Halethorpe. He then proceeded to fly the airplane to the field, which was about one mile in distance. This grand entrance served as a prelude to the stunts he would perform at the show, which included tight turns, twists and dives, not usually performed by other aviators of that era. Less than two months after leaving Baltimore, Hoxsey died in a crash at the second great Los Angeles Air Meet.

The meet was originally scheduled to run from November 2 to November 8, 1910. Twenty-one flights were planned each day, but weather conditions greatly altered the actual activities. Even a freak snowstorm intervened, causing the organizers to extend the meet for two days.

Spectators got to witness some of the most advanced aircraft of the time including Bleriot and Antoinette monoplanes, and Curtiss, Farman, and Wright biplanes. Visitors were treated to the spectacle of planes flying at sixty miles an hour, rising to 5,000 feet, and remaining aloft for almost an hour. For their efforts, cash prizes were awarded to the aviators who won contests for altitude, speed, endurance and distance, while the Michelin Cup was the prize for the best overall record at the meet.

Unique competitions were also conducted. One example was the bomb throwing competition. Targets were painted on the ground and sacks of flour were thrown at shapes by the aviators in flight. Hubert Latham won the Barry Cup for this contest, which is believed to be one of the earliest demonstrations of the airplane as a potential combat weapon. An eighteen-mile cross-country race, from the Halethorpe field to Fort Carroll and back, also attracted attention.

Henry Rinn attended the show at age thirteen. Sixty-nine years later, he described what he had observed. *". . . it was really overwhelming to me. . .I can't quite explain my reaction to seeing these planes come down the runway and go up in the air. . .Some performed various different acrobatics. Not what we know of today [as acrobatics], however, they had various contests of the speed and the altitude that they were flying. This really showed me what airplanes were capable of doing, particularly after the flight of Latham over Baltimore City."*

The First Flight over a City by a Planned Route

While all of the contests and exhibits at the Baltimore Aero Meet of 1910 were highly successful and well received, one flight stood apart from the rest: a flight over Baltimore City by a planned route. To that date, no one had deliberately embarked over extended areas of a major populated metropolis, although a few aviators had flown over small sections of cities such as Paris, Rome and Washington. Flying over crowded streets of a major city had not been attempted during the first seven years of powered flight because it was believed that the heated air currents from houses and streets made over-city flying exceedingly dangerous—not to mention the unreliability of the pre-1910 aircraft.

Capitalizing on this concept, the Baltimore *Sun* newspaper devised a promotional plan to have an aviator from the Aero Meet attempt an extended flight over the city using a prescribed flight plan. By doing so, it would give the maximum amount of citizens an opportunity to witness this great exploit and see their first airplane in flight. At the same time, it would increase the circulation

STORY OF LATHAM'S FLIGHT
FOR THE SUN'S $5,000 PRIZE, BEFORE AN
AUDIENCE OF HALF A MILLION PEOPLE

The Sun's breathless coverage of Latham's flight over Baltimore, November 7, 1910. Photo courtesy of the Baltimore Sun.

of the *Sun* papers. The $5,000 prize was a significant sum of money considering it represented ten years wages earned by the average worker. Several flyers were considered for this attraction, however, it quickly became clear that the logical selection was the Frenchman Hubert Latham. At twenty-seven years of age, Latham was already a noted aviator and adventurer. He had a successfully made a balloon trip from London to Paris, helped develop the Antoinette monoplane, participated in previous aviation contests

Hubert Latham takes off from Halethorpe field in his 50hp, 16-cylinder Antionette monoplane on November 7, 1910, for his timed circuit of Baltimore. Photo courtesy of Barry A. Lanman.

and attempted twice to cross the English Channel.

After several days of negotiations, Latham was contracted to make a flight that would demonstrate the practicality of the airplane. On the morning of November 7, 1910, Latham took off from the Halethorpe field and flew a prescribed course twenty-two and a half miles long that took him over such local landmarks as Fort McHenry, the Sun Building, Patterson and Druid Hill parks, North and Mt. Royal avenues, and the Winans residence at 1217 St. Paul Street, ending in a final lap down Charles Street.

Decades later, Rinn gave a crystal clear account of what he witnessed. *"They let us out of school to see Latham fly. . .I was at the location of Fayette and Green streets. Well, we were anticipating seeing him come into view and he was almost directly overhead when we saw him, and we just thought it was something fantastic. I just can't describe it any better way!"* When asked about the crowd's reaction, Rinn stated that *"most of the people were quiet and they were just dumbfounded at the feat. There was no applause or any other reaction outside of that."*

Hubert Latham's own personal oral account of the flight was printed in the *The Sun* on November 8, 1910. Excerpts from that account give us an understanding of the thoughts that were going through his mind during the flight and how he viewed the significance of this historic first in aviation. *"Thanks to the enterprise of* The Sun *and* The Evening Sun *in offering an inducement for the flight, the first trip in the air on a scheduled course over a city has been accomplished . . . From my own viewpoint as an aviator my flight over Baltimore was an unqualified success and I sincerely trust that it may have proved so to the people from their viewpoint as spectators . . .*

"As to my sensations in the air, my brain principally was busy in calculating the strength and direction of the wind and inspiring the hands to instant and accurate action as each wind current struck me. At the same time, I found opportunity to enjoy the great flight and the view of the great city and its great crowds.

"In a word, as you Americans put it, it was 'great'."

Henry Rinn, oral history interview, July 28, 1976,
MHT/OHC 002 (MD-AVC) 014, 46 p.

Emile and Henry Berliner's No. 5, based on an old French Nieuport aircraft fuselage, in front of the Post Office Hangar at College Park.
Photo courtesy of the College Park Aviation Museum, Berliner Family Collection.

ity to maneuver for ninety seconds at an altitude of about fifteen feet. This flight has been cited as the first controlled helicopter flight, although other writers do not share this assessment. In any case, Berliner's remarkable craft was represented the furthest advance that any American had then achieved on the path toward a truly practical helicopter.[16]

In 1927, College Park again began to play an important role in the application of radio technology to aeronautics. Between that year and 1934, the Bureau of Standards operated a facility at the field that included a seventy-foot wooden tower with attached wire antennas. Experiments helped to develop a radio range navigation system for the nation's airways, including a visual indicator for pilots, and also to develop an instrument landing capability. A key achievement came on September 5, 1931, when Marshall S. Boggs touched down at the field in the first blind landing using a complete radio landing beam system. (In contrast, Lt. James H. Doolittle had relied partly on instruments such as an altimeter for his famous hooded landing at Mitchell Field in 1929). Another historic flight occurred on March 20, 1933, when pilot James S. Kinney and scientist Harry Diamond flew from College Park Airport to Newark (Delaware) Municipal Airport in the first cross-country test of the use of radio systems for both navigation and landing.[17]

Washington-New York route was discontinued in May 1921. The Post Office Department added a hangar during this time, and also operated a laboratory that helped to develop radio marker beacons and direction finding equipment.[15]

In 1920, Henry A. Berliner began using College Park Airport as the site of experiments in vertical flight, an interest that he had been pursuing with his father, the inventor Emile Berliner. The younger Berliner evolved a triplane craft with two lifting rotors mounted on the wings, and a third rotor toward the rear of the fuselage. On February 23, 1924, the Berliner No. 5 showed its abil-

George Brinckerhoff assumed management of the airport in the same year that the Bureau of Standards began its scientific work there. Brinckerhoff organized popular air shows and races, and in 1936 gained acclaim for flying medical supplies to ice-bound islanders in the Chesapeake Bay. With the exception of a period of flight restriction at College Park Airport during World War II, he continued to run the facility and to conduct a flight school there until 1959. Available directories from the postwar period show that the airport had two turf runways. One of these, which ran roughly north-south in parallel to the railway, was closed in about 1967. The remaining strip, with a northwest heading, had been paved by 1969.[18]

A period of decline began at the

A Fairchild FC-2W equipped with early instrument landing system parked outside the Bureau of Standards radio tower and buildings at College Park.
Photo courtesy of the College Park Aviation Museum, NBS Collection.

airport in the 1950s, but concerned citizens achieved its preservation. The facility was acquired by the Maryland-National Capital Park and Planning Commission in 1973, and subsequently rehabilitated. The historical importance of the airport was recognized by its inclusion in the National Register of Historic Places in 1977, and in 1998 the College Park Aviation Museum opened to interpret its past to the public. A hangar and compass rose from the Air Mail Service days are extant, and the foundations of other historical structures are visible. The airport has a lighted runway 2,607 feet long, with a parallel taxiway. As of October 2001, the facility provided a base for seventy-three aircraft. The terrorist attacks in September of that year resulted in restrictions that severely hampered flight operations; nevertheless, the nation's oldest airport continues to serve aviation.[19]

Significance for Maryland air/ space history: The nation's oldest currently operating airport, site of the Army's earliest school for heavier-than-air flight, and the scene of many notable milestones in the development of both military and civil aviation.
Relevant years: 1909 - present
Lat/Long: 38-58-50N 76-55-22W
Map: ADC Md/Del 2000 *Num*: 20 *Grid*: A1
Shows: airport

UNITED STATES NAVAL ACADEMY
Annapolis, Anne Arundel County (AA-359)
1910-present

The United States Naval Academy is located in Annapolis on the south bank of the Severn River, north of Spa Creek. Its grounds occupy 329 acres of land that are divided into two sections by College Creek. Most of the main campus was designated a National Historic Landmark in 1961. Since its founding in 1845, the Academy has provided higher education and military training for the Navy's regular officer corps. This fundamental function has made it an important influence on many of the leaders of U.S. naval aviation. In addition, the Academy has specific associations with the history of flight in Maryland.[20]

The first involvement of the Academy with heavier-than-air aviation was probably its role in testing a kite-like airplane designed by Representative Butler Ames, an aviation enthusiast who funded the experiment himself. Ames' machine was assembled at the Academy in 1910 and placed aboard a torpedo boat that was based there. The ship steamed into the wind to test the aircraft's lifting power, with results that showed it

incapable of true flight.[21]

The Academy received a far more impressive introduction to the airplane in September 1911 with the arrival of Wright biplane B-1 and Lt. John Rodgers. As the Navy's second officer to become a qualified pilot, Rodgers is known to history as Naval Aviator No. 2. Both plane and pilot were slated for service at the Aviation Camp across the Severn (see separate entry on page 36), but that facil-

Dressed in an immaculate white uniform, Lt. Theodore Ellyson prepares his Curtiss for an attempted catapult launch from the Naval Academy dock in 1912. Photo courtesy of the Ann Arrundell County Historical Society.

ity was still incomplete. On September 7, Rogers took off from Farragut Field, a parade ground behind Bancroft Hall, for a thrilling demonstration flight. He capped this by taking off again and flying to Washington, D.C.[22]

On July 31, 1912, the Navy's first attempted launch of an airplane by catapult took place at the Academy dock where the frigate *Santee* had been moored. The compressed air device was designed to propel the Curtiss A-1 hydroplane along a pair of rails. The pilot was Lt. Theodore G. Ellyson, Naval Aviator No. 1. The plane pitched up during the launch, stalled, and hit the water at an angle. The experiment provided basic lessons on launching equipment and techniques, and Ellyson suffered no more than a ducking. He went on to make the first successful naval catapult flight, which took place that autumn at the Washington Navy Yard. (Ellyson was interred at the Academy following his death in an air crash in 1928).[23]

The Academy began to include aspects of aeronautical science in its course work as early as 1920. A revision in 1925 made aviation an integral part of the curriculum, including provisions for some flight training for recent graduates, and later for midshipmen. This flight instruction was at first provided by temporary duty personnel. In January 1927, the function was assumed by a Naval Air Detail, which consisted of four sailors, two officers, and one OU-1 seaplane. Two years later, the detail was succeeded by a squadron designated VN8-D5. As of 1930, the squadron had four assigned aircraft, as well as a plane shelter and crane at the *Santee* dock. To replace this inadequate facility, construction of a seaplane base across the Severn River began in 1937 (see entry on Naval Air Facility Annapolis). The opening of that installation marked the end of flight operations at the Academy itself.[24]

Significance for Maryland air/space history: In addition to its great educational influence, the Academy has been the scene of flight training and of several notable events in the history of early naval flight.
Relevant years: 1910 - present *Lat/Long*: 38-59N 76-29W
Map: ADC Md/Del 2000 *Num*: 21 *Grid*: A1 *Shows*: facility

NAVAL AVIATION CAMP, GREENBURY POINT
Annapolis, Anne Arundel County
1911-14

By mid-1911, the U. S. Navy had taken important early steps in the field of heavier-than-air aviation. These included: flights to and from ships; training of the first naval aviators at schools operated by the Wright Brothers and by Glenn Curtiss; and acquisition of the first naval aircraft. On July 6, Capt. Washington I. Chambers was ordered to Annapolis to oversee establishment of the Navy's first aviation base. The site selected occupied about sixty acres on Greenbury Point, a peninsula that projects into the Chesapeake Bay, north of the Severn River and south of Mill Creek. The Point is itself divided by Carr Creek, which flows into the Severn. Upstream from Carr Creek is the David Taylor Research Center, which in 1911 was the site of the Navy's Engineering Experiment Station (see separate entry). The Center faces the U.S. Naval Academy on the opposite side of the river.[25]

During September, 1911, the Navy completed preparation of the Aviation Camp on the Chesapeake (north) side of Greenbury Point. Near the shore, a thirty-six-by-ninety-foot wooden hangar was built to protect the aircraft, which included one Wright and two Curtiss biplanes. These were housed in three equal bays, each with a gabled roof. Attached to the hangar was an eighteen-by-forty-five-foot wing for office space, workshop, and barracks. Since one of the Curtiss craft was a hydroplane, a ramp was constructed nearby. The hangar and ramp appear to have been situated roughly midway between the mouth of Mill Creek and the tip of Greenbury Point. The airfield stretched south from the hangar to about the present location of Helix Road.[26]

Advantages of this installation included the proximity of the Engineering Experiment Station, which assisted in engine development and served as a place to make some of the many needed repairs. The camp's site also had serious drawbacks, including the small size of the airfield, shallow water at the ramp, and the stray bullets from the nearby rifle range. Nevertheless, the small group of naval aviators assigned to the Aviation Camp pressed forward with training and experimentation, including an inconclusive test of airborne radio. A notable flight occurred on October 25, when lieutenants Theodore G. Ellyson and John H. Towers flew an unbroken 122 miles in the hydroplane as part of a trip to Ft. Monroe, Virginia. During the next month, Towers was injured in an accident that wrecked this aircraft. He recovered, however, and the plane was repaired. One of the Wright aircraft was converted to a hydroplane, but was quickly damaged in another crash on December 11. By this time, winter cold was limiting operations at the camp. The aviators were ordered to California on December 29, and by January 3 the packed aircraft had been shipped west.[27]

In the spring of 1912, the Annapolis aviation camp reopened at a new location, this time on the Severn side of Greenbury Point. The site was a privately-owned beach, just upriver from the Engineering Experiment Station. No landplanes were used at this location, which lacked an airfield, and tents served to shelter the aircraft. The camp was divided by a dock, with Wright aviators on one side and the Curtiss contingent on the other.[28]

Operations in 1912 included experiments with air-surface radio communication, this time successful, and tests of spotting a submerged submarine from the air. One memorable flight took Ellyson and Towers across the bay to Centreville, where large crowds greeted the first fliers to visit the town. After a winter break in Cuba, the camp reopened in the spring of 1913. A Curtiss hydroplane flew to 7,200 feet, a record-breaking altitude for an American seaplane. On June 20, 1913, the Navy's first fatal airplane crash occurred. Ensign William D. Billingsley was piloting a Wright plane with Lieutenant Towers as passenger when they encountered rough turbulence over the Chesapeake. Billingsley fell to his death, but Towers survived by clinging to the aircraft. The tragedy demonstrated the value of safety belts and led to their introduction.[29]

In August 1913, a storm blew down the tents for the second time that year, damaging all the aircraft except for a newly-arrived Burgess flying boat. Despite this, Captain Chambers rejected proposals that the tents be replaced by a hangar. In November, a board headed by Chambers recommended creation of a permanent air station at Pensacola. In January 1914, the Aviation Camp was closed and its personnel transferred to this new location.[30]

Greenbury Point was not to be the site of aircraft

operations again until after 1937 (see entry on Naval Air Facility, Annapolis). Meanwhile, the hangar at the original bayside Aviation Camp was threatened by erosion. In 1923, it was dismantled and its lumber used to build shelters for hogs at the Naval Academy's farm. The site of that hangar and the associated airfield is now part of Naval Station Annapolis. The location of the 1912-14 riverside camp appears to lie near the border between the Naval Station and the grounds of the David Taylor Research Center.[31]

Significance for Maryland air/space history: Although short-lived, the original camp was the Navy's first aerodrome, and the later site also served as a center of naval aviation during its formative era.

Relevant years: 1911-1914 *Lat/Long*: 38-59N 76-28W
Map: ADC Md/Del 2000 *Num*: 21 *Grid*: A1 *Shows*: area

DAVID TAYLOR RESEARCH CENTER
formerly NAVY ENGINEERING EXPERIMENT STATION
Annapolis, Anne Arundel County (AA-2176)
1911-present

The Navy's Engineering Experiment Station (EES) was commissioned in 1908 as a testing facility for naval engines, materials, and equipment. It initially occupied ten acres on Greenbury Point at the edge of the Severn River, opposite the Naval Academy. Designed by architect Ernest Flagg, who also designed the Academy, the main building was constructed of brick, concrete, and steel. It was twenty-nine feet high to the eaves, and had a monitor roof. In plan it formed a long rectangle, 316 by about sixty-six feet, that was set at right angles to the river. Just downstream was a second, smaller structure, possibly connected to the main building by an ell.[32]

In 1911, the Navy's first air station was established near the EES, which assumed its earliest aviation-related function by testing the engines of the aircraft and providing a place for repair and conversion work. This aviation camp was at first located on the opposite side of Greenbury Point. During 1912-14, however, the aviators moved to the shore just upriver from the EES, where a row of tents served as hangars (see separate entry on page 36). The EES continued to grow during and after World War I. By 1925, it had doubled in area, and some of its buildings were located on filled land along the river.[33]

During World War II, Dr. Robert H. Goddard developed a Jet-Assisted Takeoff (JATO) system for the Navy at the EES. On September 23, 1942, testing of the system by a PBY flying boat on the Severn resulted in the Navy's first JATO takeoff, but also in a fire that caused an emergency landing. Goddard's focus subsequently shifted to variable-thrust rocket motors, and he continued to work

at the EES until shortly before his final illness in 1945.[24]

In the postwar era, the EES continued to grow, adding area by purchase of 8.1 acres west of Old Fort Road and by further landfill. In 1954-69, the Army used the facility's twenty-four-acre Bay Head Road Annex as part of Nike missile site W-26 (see separate entry on page 111). In 1963, the EES was renamed the Marine Engineering Laboratory. By 1967, the facility had twenty-four buildings used for research and development, as well as numerous others used for support functions. In that year, it was merged into a new Naval Ship Research and Development Center. The headquarters of this new organization was located at its other major component, the David Taylor Model Basin at Carderock. Further name changes followed for this combined organization: 1974-87, David Taylor Naval Ship R&D Center; 1987-1992, David Taylor Research Center; and subsequently, Carderock Division, Naval Surface Warfare Center (see separate entry on page 36).[25]

In 1996, the Naval Academy acquired 14.2 acres of the Annapolis laboratory's land for housing. The laboratory itself was decommissioned in 1999 as a result of base realignment legislation. In July 1998, meanwhile, Anne Arundel County had signed a lease for the 46.5-acre property. County authorities planned to redevelop the facility for defense-related use by the private sector. This new facility was designated the David Taylor Research Center. (As noted above, this same name had been used during 1987-92 for the combined organization of which the Annapolis laboratory was a part).[36]

Significance for Maryland air/space history: A Navy research and testing facility that operated for over eight decades, at times performing work relating to aviation and rocketry.

Relevant Years: 1911 – Current *Lat/Long*: 38-59N 76-28W
Map: ADC Md/Del 2000 *Num*: 21 *Grid*: A1 *Shows*: facility

INDIAN HEAD DIVISION, NAVAL SURFACE WARFARE CENTER
originally INDIAN HEAD PROVING GROUND
Indian Head, Charles County (CH-492)
1912-present

The Indian Head Division of the Naval Surface Warfare Center is just east of the town of Indian Head on a 3,500-acre peninsula between the north shore of Mattawoman Creek and the Potomac River. The facility's Stump Neck Annex occupies a similar, but smaller, peninsula south of the creek. Established in 1890 as a Naval Proving Ground, the station has served evolving purposes that include testing, research, and chemical production. Early aviation-related events at the facility included initial testing in 1912 of a recoilless gun designed to be fired from aircraft. Bombing tests occurred here as early as 1914, and the explosion of a bomb aboard an aircraft claimed two lives on November 8, 1916. Between 1920 and 1923, Dr. Robert H. Goddard used the site for developing rockets to propel depth charges and armor-piercing warheads.[37]

Meanwhile, a shift in mission for the station was reflected in its renaming as the Naval Powder Factory in 1921. In World War II, the facility began development and production of propellants for rockets, including jet-assisted takeoff (JATO) systems. Work in this field continued after the war, and the facility's name changed to Naval Propellant Plant in 1958. During 1959, twenty-three new buildings were constructed to support production of fuel for Polaris missiles. In January of that year, a successful test at Indian Head of a moveable nozzle for the Polaris represented an advance in missile directional control. During the following decade, the station produced fuel for the Scout, Zuni, Poseidon, and Anti-submarine (ASROC) rockets. Indian Head's redesignation as a Naval Ordnance Station in 1966 reflected a shift toward a more diverse role.[38] Rocket propellants, however, remained one of the major areas of work at the facility, which received its current name in 1991.

Significance for Maryland air/space history: A technical facility that has played a significant role in the development of rocketry, and has also been the site of testing aircraft-related systems.

Relevant years: 1912-present *Lat/Long*: 38-35N 77-10W
Map: ADC Md/Del 2000 *Num*: 19 *Grid*: D5-6 *Shows*: facility

ABERDEEN PROVING GROUND and PHILLIPS ARMY AIRFIELD
Aberdeen, Harford County
1917-present

Aberdeen Proving Ground (APG) occupies more than 72,500 acres that are east and south of the town of Aberdeen, bordering the Chesapeake Bay south of Swann Creek. In October 1917, the government acquired the original portion of the land in order to establish a facility for testing ordnance needed for World War I. Most of the installation's work involved surface weapons, and the first gun was fired there on January 2, 1918. Aerial warfare was included in its scope, however, and the first bomb was dropped on September 2 of the same year.[39]

Soon after the opening of the proving ground, an air detachment arrived and set up a base for airplanes and dirigibles at a location described as "behind the automotive test course." A report dated in March 1919 stated that by the previous midsummer a landing field, shops, and hangars worth more than a million dollars

had been built halfway between headquarters and the water range, and a bombing field had been chosen near the Bush River. Since an airfield of this scale was unlikely to be temporary, it was probably the same field shown in an aeronautical bulletin issued by the Army in May 1923. The facility was located a mile southeast of the main portion of the proving ground, just west of a railway line and close to the narrows separating the mainland from Spesutie Island. The irregularly-shaped airfield offered 2,000 feet for landing from four directions.[40]

Much of the early bomb testing was done from balloons and dirigibles, but these had been entirely replaced by airplanes by 1926. The work included the creation of bombing tables to improve the effectiveness of aerial bombardment. In September 1921, a Hadley Page Bomber at APG dropped a bomb of 4,000 pounds, then a world record. On June 6, 1923, the crash on takeoff of another Hadley Page claimed the life of Lt. Wendell D. Phillips, in whose honor the field was soon named. It has been reported that the technique of dive bombing was first tried at APG, and that a 75-mm aircraft cannon was first fired here during a B-18 flight in 1939.[41]

By the late 1930s, increased artillery testing nearby was presenting a hazard to operations at the airfield, which was also becoming too small for modern aircraft. On Feb. 5, 1943, the facility was replaced by a new Phillips Army Airfield, located at its present site about three miles west of the earlier field. Testing of aerial bombs continued at APG during World War II, but was increasingly shifted to bases in less populated areas. After its creation as a separate service in 1947, the Air Force began to take over this work from the Army.[42]

APG also has significant associations with the history of rocketry. On Nov 7, 1918, Dr. Robert H. Goddard gave a demonstration there of small rockets that were forerunners of the weapon later used by infantry against tanks in World War II. In 1942, one of the early tests of this shoulder-fired weapon took place at APG, and it was here that a chance remark led to its designation as the "Bazooka." During the war, advanced wind tunnels became part of the facility's technological armory. The Bomb Tunnel was first operated at supersonic speed in December 1944, while the Flexible Throat Wind Tunnel first attained Mach 4 speed in April 1948. Although built with the original intent of testing shells and bombs, the tunnels were ultimately used mainly for research on missiles and supersonic aircraft.[43]

On July 1, 1971, APG was greatly enlarged by an administrative merger with Edgewood Arsenal, although the functions of the two installations remained separate. This change brought a second airfield within APG's boundaries (see entry on Weide Army Heliport on page 42), but Phillips Army Airfield has remained the larger. Phillips today has an 8,000-foot lighted runway, as well as two 5,000-foot runways used in daylight only. North of the airfield is a control tower, fire station, hangars, and other support structures.[44]

Significance for Maryland air/space history: A military testing facility and airfield that has operated since World War I.
Relevant years: 1917 - present *Lat/Long*: 35-28N 76-10W
Map: ADC Md/Del 2000 *Num*: 16 *Grid*: E1 *Shows*: facility

MARYLAND PRESSED STEEL COMPANY PLANT
Hagerstown, Washington County
1917-1918

The former Maryland Pressed Steel Company plant is a complex of brick buildings occupying a 3.8-acre property on the west side of Pope Avenue, at number 901. The plant is reported to have been built in 1891 for the Crawford Bicycle Company, and was subsequently used by other manufacturers, including the Melrose casket company. During the era of World War I, the plant was occupied by the Maryland Pressed Steel company, which manufactured military products.[45]

During the war, Maryland Pressed Steel hired Giuseppe Bellanca to design an aircraft to be used as a trainer or scout plane. Working at the Pope Avenue facility, Bellanca in September 1917 completed the prototype of his CD Tractor Biplane. The plane used wing-warping for lateral control, was powered by a radial Anzani engine, and was able to achieve a speed of eighty-five miles per hour. Bellanca followed this with his model CE, which dispensed with wing-warping in favor of ailerons. This second model also had a more powerful engine, built by the same manufacturer. The CE was able to carry an additional 135 pounds, and had a reported top speed of 102 mph. The two prototypes were flight tested at nearby Doub's Meadow field (see separate entry on page 39). Neither of them entered production, however, and Maryland Pressed Steel went out of business in the aftermath of the war. After leaving Hagerstown, Bellanca continued his distinguished career as an aircraft designer and producer. Examples of his work included the "Columbia," used by Clarence Chamberlain and Charles Levine for their 1927 transatlantic flight, and the "Miss Veedol," in which Clyde Pangborne flew across the Pacific in 1931.[46]

The later history of the Pope Avenue plant included service as the Moller Motor Car Company works from 1927 to 1937. In 1987, Jeff Crampton acquired the property, where he operates the Pope Avenue Tire Company and also leases space to other businesses. The front of the complex has a distinctive central tower that is two bays wide and three stories high. An arch at the base of

the tower affords access to the main entrance area. The tower projects forward from a two-story section that flanks it with seven full bays on either side. An ell behind this section connects to a further group of contiguous buildings, most of them three stories high, behind which is a railway line. Comparison with two available earlier images suggests that the complex has received some wooden additions, and has undergone other alterations since the time of its use by Maryland Pressed Steel. Features no longer extant include a water tower that stood near the south end of the property, and dormers that once projected from the roof of the main front section. The central tower appears to have lost some of its original height, and is now topped by crenellation rather than the tall roof that gave the effect of a spire.[47]

Significance for Maryland air/space history: An industrial plant where a renowned aircraft designer produced two of his early prototypes.
Relevant years: 1917 – c. 1918 *Lat/Long*: 39-37N 77-43W
Map: ADC Md/Del 2000 *Num*: 36 *Grid*: N/A *Shows*: area

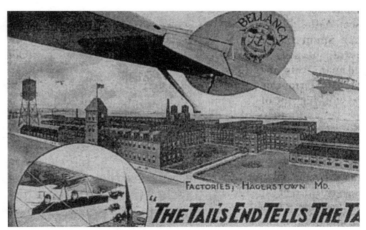

Advertising illustration, 1918, showing the Maryland Pressed Steel factory in Hagerstown being buzzed by Bellanca-designed biplanes. The multistory factory seems poorly suited to aircraft manufacture—and so it proved. Photo courtesy of Kent A. Mitchell.

DOUB'S MEADOW
Hagerstown, Washington County
1917-c. 1918

Doub's Meadow occupied the site of the present athletic field of South Hagerstown High School, located at 1101 South Potomac Street. The field itself is north of the school, west of South Potomac Street, south of Downsville Road, and east of Maryland Avenue. In the era of World War I, it was a farm field about two blocks southwest of the Maryland Pressed Steel Company plant on Pope Avenue, where Giuseppe Bellanca designed two light military aircraft. These were the CD Tractor

Biplane, completed in September 1917, and the later model CE. Prototypes of both these aircraft were flight tested at Doub's Meadow. The company did not produce aircraft based on either prototype, however, and it went out of business in the era following the war. (See entry on Maryland Pressed Steel for further information on the plant, the aircraft, and the designer).[48]

As mayor of Hagerstown, Charles E. Bowman later proposed that Doub's Meadow be developed as a municipal airport, but the project was never approved. The field may have continued to see some degree of flight activity as an emergency landing site. In September 1923, Lewis E. Reisner reported data on several Hagerstown-area emergency fields for publication in aeronautical bulletins. Of these, field No. 5 may have been Doub's Meadow, since it was located just south of the city along Sharpsburg Pike (Potomac Street). Measuring 850 by 1,021 feet, the field was described as "rather rolling, but solid and smooth."[49]

Today, the former Doub's Meadow remains an open space, although altered to accommodate athletic events and their spectators. Still standing along Downsville Road to the north are residences that appear in the background of a photograph of a Bellanca aircraft at the field about 1917.[50]

Significance for Maryland air/space history: The site of flight testing of early prototypes by an important aircraft designer.

Relevant years: 1917 - 1918, circa. *Lat/Long*: 39-37N 77-43W *Map*: ADC Md/Del 2000 *Num*: 36 *Grid*: N/A *Shows*: bordering streets

Chapter Two:
The Classic Era

[Editor's note] As the world emerged from the carnage of World War I, the future of aviation looked bright. The war had brought about great technical improvement in aircraft and engines, and produced thousands of pilots. War-surplus planes and pilots looked for new fields to conquer. A group of veterans formed the Maryland Air Guard. Other pilots joined the new government-sponsored air mail service. Still more flew for personal enjoyment, or raced or barnstormed for public entertainment. More than a dozen small airfields were established across Maryland between 1919 and 1937, and an important international air race took place at Bay Shore Park in 1925.

Aviation visionaries looked forward to transporting large numbers of passengers over long distances on "airlines." Charles A. Lindbergh's flight from New York to Paris in 1927 made this the world's dream. Lindbergh himself extended it by his flights around the country and his work for TWA and Pan Am. In October 1927, he flew "The Spirit of St. Louis" to Baltimore. After a parade to the Municipal Stadium, the Lone Eagle declared Baltimore's first municipal airport, Logan Field, to be inadequate. Within months work began on a new airport to be built on fill dredged from Baltimore Harbor. Its waterside location would serve not only landplanes but intercontinental flying boats.

Maryland has a tradition of manufacturing, and after 1927 investors and civic leaders were quick to promote aviation as a new manufacturing industry. A half-dozen important aircraft companies built factories in Maryland and, despite the onset of the Great Depression, built a succession of famous airplane models, while employing thousands of Marylanders in the new industry.

LOGAN FIELD
(BALTIMORE MUNICIPAL AIRPORT)
Dundalk, Baltimore County
1919-1945

Logan Field, Baltimore's first municipal airport, was just east of the city in Dundalk. It lay within an irregular area that is roughly bounded by Dundalk Avenue on the west and south, Sollers Point Road on the west, and Belclare Road on the north.[1]

The airfield was originally established by flying club members, who in 1919 gained permission to use the land from the "air-minded" manager of a Bethlehem Steel Company subsidiary. The facility was initially known as Dundalk Flying Field. On July 5, 1920, the American Flying Club sponsored an air show at the field that featured Lt. Patrick Logan, a noted stunt pilot. Logan

Maryland's first airport terminal, at Logan Field, Dundalk. Photo courtesy of the Ann Arrundell County Historical Society.

The Maryland Air National Guard, originally equipped with Curtiss Jennies, was organized at Logan Field in 1921.
Photo courtesy of Dundalk-Patapsco Neck Historical Society.

suffered fatal injuries when his plane failed to pull out of a tailspin, and the facility was subsequently renamed in his honor. It was evidently later in that same year that the City of Baltimore agreed to lease the property as a municipal airport.[2]

In 1921, a group of American Flying Club members based at the airfield received recognition as the 1st (later the 104th) Observation Squadron, the Maryland National Guard's first flying unit and one of the earliest such organizations in the nation. Shortly thereafter, an agreement was reached under which the federal government would assume oversight of Logan as an Air Service Field, but allow private and commercial operations to continue. This arrangement was reported in effect as late as May 1925. Lighting for night flying was introduced during the 1920s, helping to give Logan a period of repute as an advanced facility. Events at the field during 1929 included: the opening of a Department of Commerce aviation office; the beginning of regular air mail service for Baltimore; a spectacular air meet with reported attendance of 30,000; and an early midair refueling flight.[3]

On August 18, 1930, Eastern Air Transport service at Logan marked the start of Baltimore's first scheduled passenger flights by a major carrier.[4] By this time, the city was already planning a new airport with longer runways and seaplane access, but this project moved at an extremely slow pace. In the meantime, the quality of airline service to Baltimore was limited by Logan's inadequacies, which were only partly solved by a variety of improvements that included a radio control tower. In 1941, the year in which

the new harbor-side airport finally opened, a Civil Aeronautics Bulletin described Logan as possessing five hangars, three of which were military. The airfield had three oiled-cinder runways, the longest of which measured 3,230 feet.[5]

Wartime requirements led the Army to take over Logan between December 1943 and August 1945, after which the airport closed. By 1947, Bethlehem Steel was constructing 400 federally-funded houses on its share of the property, and the city soon sold its forty-seven acres. The resulting neighborhood recalls the airport through its name, Logan Village, although it is also known as Dundalk Village.[6]

Significance for Maryland air/space history: Baltimore's first municipal airport and Maryland's earliest base for its National Guard aviators.
Relevant years: 1919 – 1945

Lat/Long: 39-15N 76-31W *Map:* ADC Md/Del 2000 *Num:* 16
Grid: F4 *Shows:* area

WEIDE ARMY HELIPORT
formerly EDGEWOOD ARSENAL FIELD,
WEIDE ARMY AIRFIELD
Edgewood, Harford County
c. 1922-present

Weide Army Heliport is about two miles south of the town of Edgewood, on a peninsula that projects into the Chesapeake Bay between the Gunpowder and Bush rivers. Since 1971, this area has been part of Aberdeen Proving Ground (see separate entry on page 38), but it had earlier been a separate Army installation, Edgewood Arsenal. Established in 1917, the Arsenal was devoted to preparedness in the field of chemical, toxin, and biological warfare.[7]

Edgewood Arsenal's annual report for fiscal year 1922 contained, under the heading "Aviation Field," the following brief information: "Thirty-five acres of ground were plowed, leveled and seeded, and over 2000 feet of tile pipe laid underground for drainage." The absence of known earlier references makes it appear that this work marked the initial establishment of Edgewood Arsenal Field, rather than an improvement to it. Since the federal fiscal year ended on June 30 at that time, the airfield would presumably have been ready for use before the end of calendar year 1922.[8]

An Army aeronautical bulletin of September 1923

described the Arsenal's landing facility as a long, narrow field that was "situated in the 'L' of the concrete road opposite the corrals and between the high trees and the road." Another bulletin, issued in May 1925, recommended that the field be used for emergency landing only. During fiscal 1926, however, the Army did further grading and cleared fifteen acres of woodland to facilitate landing approach. A 100-by-100 foot hangar, which is still extant, was also constructed during these months. A bulletin published in September 1931 described the airfield as sixty-two acres, irregular in shape, with two sod runways, 2,500 feet east-west and 2,000 feet north-south. There were blinkers at the runway ends, a rotating beacon and facilities for servicing aircraft.[9]

A May 1941 publication showed that the north-south runway was now the longer, at 3,340 feet, while the east-west strip was 2,500 feet long. The airfield was described as restricted to light planes, but the approach of war soon brought change. By October 1941, the north-south runway was receiving a layer of concrete thick enough to accommodate heavy bombers. Presumably, it was also lengthened to its present 5,000 feet. The unpaved east-west landing strip, now abandoned, may well have been taken out of service at this time.[10]

In September 1955, the airfield was named in honor of Maj. Edward J. Weide, who commanded the chemical test squadron there during 1951-52. Maj. Weide's outstanding performance led to his appointment to the command of a larger unit before his early retirement and untimely death in 1954.[11]

The mission of the squadron stationed at the facility involved the testing of such weapons as aerial sprayers and chemical bombs. Some napalm testing took place during the era of the Vietnam conflict, but such operations waned in the 1960s. The Army National Guard, long a tenant at the field, became its primary user after the testing squadron's departure. A guide issued in 1972 described the field as the home of an Aviation Support Facility used by the Guard for both pilot training and maintenance of aircraft and associated equipment. During 2000, the usable length of the 5,000-foot runway was reduced 1,800 feet, and flight operations were restricted to rotorcraft.[12]

Significance for Maryland air/space history:
A military airfield that has operated since the era immediately following World War I.
Relevant years: c. 1922 - present
Lat/Long: 39-23N 76-17W
Map: ADC Md/Del 2000 *Num*: 16 *Grid*: C2
Shows: facility

MEXICO FARMS AIRPORT
Cumberland, Allegany County (AL-111-A-153)
1923-present

Mexico Farms Airport occupies a fifty-acre property that is three miles south of Cumberland, on the Maryland side of the Potomac River's North Branch. The facility is generally considered the state's second oldest continuously operating airport. The U.S. Army selected the site as a substation on the model airway that it operated between Washington and Dayton, Ohio. The Army leased the property, part of land known as Mexico Farm, in July 1923. (One account states that the field had already been in use by both government and local pilots for several years before this event.)[13]

In September 1923, an aeronautical bulletin showed the field as roughly triangular, affording up to 2,000 feet for operations east-west and 1,600 feet north-south. During the following year, a wooden barracks was built on concrete piers. An addition in 1928 doubled the size of the barracks. The barracks also served as a communications center for the field, which had two eighty-foot radio towers from which weather observations were broadcast. The military's need for the airway substation began to decline, however, in part because of the establishment of weather stations on higher ground. The Army reduced the staff at the facility to a caretaker in 1931, eventually removed its buildings and equipment, and terminated its lease in 1934.[14]

Civilian flying had been flourishing at Mexico Farms even before the Army's role declined. A separate civil airfield was established in 1928 on adjoining property owned by Jerome Johnson. Department of Commerce bulletins, however, listed only a single facility, designated Cumberland Airport. This was described as both commercial and military in September 1931, and simply as commercial by 1933. Allegany County's first

Cables support the roof of this hangar at Mexico Farms, constructed by the U.S. Army Air Corps circa 1928. Photo courtesy of the Maryland Historical Trust.

regular passenger flights began at the airport in that year, when the Johnson Airlines Company began a period of service. The City of Cumberland leased the airfield in 1934, and constructed a new runway. During the following year, an air show in celebration of the city's sesquicentennial featured a visit by the Goodyear Blimp, stunt flying, aircraft rides, and a military demonstration. In the view of one pair of authors, however, the golden era of aviation at Mexico Farms was already over. The capabilities of modern aircraft had reduced its value as a haven for long-range fliers facing difficulties.[15]

In 1941, the city of Cumberland began building a new airport at Wiley Ford, West Virginia, although its opening was delayed until after World War II (see separate entry on Greater Cumberland Regional Airport on page 93). In 1945, a commercial directory included Mexico Farms Airport under its current name, listing the owner and operator as J. J. Johnson. A more detailed state directory described the airport as it was in July 1946. Mexico Farms then had six hangars, the largest forty-six by sixty feet, as well as a building with offices and a lounge. The airport operated in the daytime only, offering student flying, charter service, and minor repairs. A sketch showed two intersecting turf runways measuring 2,100 feet (east-west) and 1,900 feet (northwest-southeast).[16]

In 1980, a historic sites survey report on Mexico Farms noted that nothing remained from the Army airfield era except some concrete foundation pads. The report described two other airfields dating from the later evolution of the facility. Extant structures included seven hangars pre-dating 1948 and exhibiting a variety of designs. Probably the earliest of them was a rectangular frame structure covered with corrugated metal, built about 1928. It was one of several hangars at the airport that used cables extending from tall posts to support a beam over the sliding doors. The report found Mexico Farms to be historically significant due to its role in the development of transportation, and as a community airport.[17]

In recent decades, Mexico Farms Airport has continued to provide a resource for local aviators. The September 2001 state directory showed an east-west turf runway at Mexico Farms measuring 2,120 feet. The northwest-southeast runway was closed indefinitely. Nine aircraft were based at the facility as of July 2001, and operations for the preceding twelve months totaled 1,261.[18]

Significance for Maryland air/space history: A facility that assisted airway development in the 1920s, was its county's only airport for a time, and has continued to serve general aviation.
Relevant years: 1923 - present
Lat/Long: 39-36-17N 78-45-39W
Map: ADC Md/Del 2000 *Num*: 2 *Grid*: C5 *Shows*: airport

BAY SHORE PARK
Edgemere, Baltimore County (BA-2361)
1925

Built in 1906, Bay Shore Park was an amusement park at the edge of the Chesapeake Bay, east of Baltimore between the Patapsco and Back rivers. In 1925, the park served as the base for that year's Schneider Trophy Race, an international hydroplane contest sponsored by French industrialist and aviator Jacques P. Schneider. The Baltimore Flying Club prepared the base by dredging and by construction of a slipway for moving the planes in and out of the water. Tents on wooden floors served as hangars. The 50-kilometer course was a triangular one whose three corners were: the end of the Bay Shore pier, north of Shallow Creek; the southern tip of Gibson's Island, and Huntington Point on the far side of the bay. Competitors each flew seven laps. The United States military participated in major air races during this era as a means of gaining prestige and stimulating aviation progress, and both the Army and Navy entered the Baltimore event. The British team's Henri Biard lost his life in a crash during preliminary trials. The race itself was held on October 24. The

Jimmy Doolittle and his Curtiss racer won the Schneider Cup in 1925 at Bay Shore Park with an average speed of 232.57 mph. Photo courtesy of the Ann Arrundell County Historical Society.

winner was the U.S. Army's Lt. James H. Doolittle, later an important leader in World War II. The victory was credited to the extraordinary skill of Doolittle, who attained the status of national hero, and to the excellent design of his Curtiss racing hydroplane. Bay Shore Park continued to operate for many years, but was demolished after its purchase by the Bethlehem Steel Company in the 1940s. Still

Kreider and Reisner built their first Challenger biplane in this shed, originally on Pennsylvania Avenue in Hagerstown (above).
As of 2003 it was still standing (left).
Photos courtesy of Kent A. Mitchell and Edmund Preston.

extant, however, is the pier that supported the judges' stand and spectator seating for the 1925 race. The area was acquired by the state in 1987, and is now part of North Point State Park.[19]

Significance for Maryland air/ space history: The base for one of the most famous contests of the classic age of aerial racing.
Relevant years: 1925 *Lat/Long*: 39-12N 76-25W
Map: ADC Md/Del 2000 *Num*: 16 *Grid*: A4 *Shows*: area

KREIDER-REISNER AIRCRAFT COMPANY
ORIGINAL PLANT AND AIRFIELD
Hagerstown, Washington County
c. 1925-1929

The "little green shed" originally stood on Hagerstown's Walnut Street, where it housed the Middlekauf shoe shop. In 1925, the modest wooden structure was reportedly moved to its present location on the west side of Pennsylvania Avenue, north of that street's intersection with Bellevue Avenue. There it played a key role in an enterprise formed during that same year, the Kreider-Reisner Aircraft Company, known as KRA.[20]

One of KRA's two founders was Lewis E. Reisner. With his brother Henry, Reisner had been dealing in aircraft parts and surplus planes, and had apparently also built a small number of aircraft patterned after the Waco design. The other founder was Ammon Kreider, a shoe manufacturer whose financial resources evidently helped the business to expand. In addition to becoming a Waco dealership, KRA now offered aircraft repair work that was carried on at the Pennsylvania Avenue shed.[21]

Spurred by the success of a midget racing plane built for them in Philadelphia, Kreider and Reisner decided to begin regular aircraft production. Their first aircraft, the Challenger, was completed at the Pennsylvania Avenue shed in time for a promotional tour in May 1927. The second aircraft of the Challenger series, designated the C-2, won production approval from federal regulators in December of the same year. A three-place biplane powered by an OX-5 engine, the C-2 successfully launched KRA as an aircraft manufacturer.[22]

The floor space of KRA's original shed has been estimated (perhaps generously) at 1,500 feet. Since this was clearly inadequate, the company quickly expanded into a cluster of nearby buildings, attaining a combined floor space of 27,000 feet by May 1928. Some of the work, however, continued to be performed in the original shed, as well as outside of its doors during fine summer weather.[23]

The growing company's requirement for more plant space was matched by a need to replace its tiny airfield, which was located behind the shed, between Pennsylvania Avenue and the present Burhams Boulevard. No more than about 600 feet in length, the field was bordered on the north by power lines and on the south by a quarry. In April 1928, KRA bought sixty acres north of town upon which to build a better airfield, a facility that eventually became the nucleus of Hagerstown's current airport (see separate entry on page 48).[24]

KRA's efficiency set the stage for company's acquisition by Sherman Fairchild, a major industrialist, and its subsequent expansion as an important center of aircraft production. The deal that made KRA a Fairchild subsidiary was formally announced in April 1929. In that same month, seventeen acres northeast of KRA's existing buildings were purchased as the site of a large new plant (see separate entry on page 52). Hastily constructed during the same year, this new facility occupied much of the space of the former KRA flying field.[25]

Today, the "little green shed" survives in altered and deteriorated condition. The structure has lost the additions that existed at its rear in the 1920s, as well as the "lean-to" section that extended along one side. The missing wooden siding has been replaced by metal sheets. The shed is the property of the owner of the house just to its north, at 851 Pennsylvania Avenue.[26]

Significance for Maryland air/space history: The original plant and airfield of a small enterprise that evolved into one of Maryland's largest aircraft manufacturing centers.
Relevant years: c. 1925 – 1929 *Lat/Long*: 34-40N; 77-43W
Map: ADC Md/Del 2000 *Num*: 36 *Grid*: N/A (city map)
Shows: area

DEPARTMENT OF COMMERCE SITE 11, NORFOLK-WASHINGTON AIRWAY
Shiloh, Charles County
c. 1927-c. 1932

In 1927, Washington, D.C., was included in an intercontinental air mail route, and began receiving regular air mail service after a lapse of six years.[27] As part of the Norfolk-Washington section of this route, the Department of Commerce operated Site 11, an intermediate airfield for use by pilots who might need to land between airports. On September 1, 1931, the Department published the first issue of Airway Bulletin No. 2, a directory of U.S. airports and landing fields. In its section on Maryland, the bulletin included Site 11. The facility was described as comprising sixty-five acres, and offering a sod landing field that measured 2,280 by 1,200 feet. To the northwest were a river and a tower supporting a light beacon that flashed the

numeral "1" in code. The description of Site 11 was headed "Rock Point," and included the sentence "Seven miles W." The meaning seems to be that the field was seven miles west of the community of Rock Point, which is near the point of a peninsula between the Wicomico and Potomac rivers. This description appears to have been an error, however, since it would have placed the field on the Virginia bank of the Potomac. Site 11 was also included in the second issue of Bulletin No. 2, published one year later. The facility was described in almost identical terms, although its shape was now called rectangular rather than irregular. In the 1932 publication, however, the entry on Site 11 was headed "Stodderts Point." Again, the sentence "Seven miles W." was used; this also seems an error, since it would have placed the field in the waters of the Potomac. It appears probable that the actual location was that indicated on the first Washington, D.C., aeronautical section chart, which was dated May 1932. The chart showed the field at Stoddard Point (to use a contemporary spelling), which is a projection of land on the west side of the Wicomico River. The point is about six miles north of Rock Point and some three miles east of Shiloh. Site 11 was not shown on the next chart in the series available at the National Archives, which is dated October 1933. The absence of Site 11 from subsequent charts or bulletins seems to indicate that it closed in about 1932. [28]

Significance for Maryland air/space history: An intermediate landing field and light beacon site that was part of the nation's early airway system.
Name: Department of Commerce Site 11, Norfolk-Washington Airway.
Relevant years: c.1927 – c. 1932 *Lat/Long*: 38-22N 76-52W
Map: ADC Md/Del 2000 *Num*: 25 *Grid*: B1 *Shows*: area

HEBRON AIRPORT
(DEL-MAR-VA AIRPORT)
Hebron, Wicomico County
1928-c. 1930

Hebron Airport was established in 1928 by Starlighters, Inc., a group whose president was Major Charles S. Bayer. Its opening was celebrated on Labor Day of that year, with exercises that included a well-attended air show. The program for the event explained that the new facility would exploit the Eastern Shore as a "Flyer's Paradise," offering such services as passenger flights, instruction, and aerial surveys. The operators announced a strong stand for safety, stating that pilots who offered passenger rides should be referred to them for evaluation. The airport boasted assets that included a hangar, an Aero-Club building, a club house for field personnel, and "one of the longest runways to be founding in any aviation field, a runway a mile and three eighths in length . . . ."[29] Although identified as Hebron Airport by lettering on a barn roof, the facility was also known by the name of Del-Mar-Va Airport and by variants on that designation. It was located directly north of Hebron, and five and one-half miles northwest of Salisbury.[30] John F. R. Scott, Jr., reported that the airport's closing on March 8, 1930, was followed by a legal dispute among its founders. Airport directories continued to list Del-Mar-Va as late as 1933; however, most listings after 1931 described it as an auxiliary facility rather than a commercial one.[31]

Significance for Maryland air/space history: An early effort to establish a commercial airport on the Eastern Shore.
Relevant years: 1928 - c.1930
Lat/Long: 38-26N 75-41W
Map: ADC Md/Del 2000 *Num*: 27 *Grid*: D1
Shows: area

Keystone bombers and tented camp of the Army Air Corps 59th Bomb Group at the Hebron Airport, June 1932. Photo courtesy of the Dundalk-Patapsco Neck Historical Society.

TRED AVON AIRPORT
Easton, Talbot County
1928-32

The original Tred Avon Airport was on the northwest shore of the Tred Avon River, one-and-one-half miles southwest of Easton. Beginning in June 1928, Malcolm and Stephen Hathaway established the facility as a base for their Tred Avon Flying Service.

The new airport was built on pastureland at the Hathway family's estate, Ratcliffe Manor. The property already had aviation associations dating back to 1917, when an off-duty Army pilot had landed his plane there, sparking the aviation interest of the youthful Hathaway brothers. Their cousin, H. Robbin Hollyday, rode aloft with the pilot, taking a picture that launched his career as a pioneer aerial photographer.[32]

Tred Avon Airport proved a popular success, drawing large crowds to air shows during 1929. Stephen Hathaway moved away from the area due to ill health, but Malcolm continued the business, offering charter flights, pilot training, aerial photography, fuel, and repairs. A sketch in an Airway Bulletin of May 1930 showed that the "L" shaped airfield had two sod landing strips measuring 1,700 and 1,900 feet. The longer of these, which had a north-southwest orientation, was described as having a "runway thereon" that was 100 feet wide. Three hangars stood in a row near the northeast corner of the "L."

This modest facility had its drawbacks, including frequent fog in the winter and a line of wire-bearing poles along the driveway bordering the longer landing strip. Hathaway soon moved his flying service to a new airport east of Easton, a transfer that probably took place in 1932. Confusingly, directories before World War II listed this new facility as Tred Avon Airport; however, it was popularly known as Webb Airport (see separate entry under that name on page 66). The site of the original Tred Avon Airport is now part of the Ratcliffe Farms housing development, located south of St. Michaels Road on Ratcliffe Manor Road.[33]

Significance for Maryland air/space history: Talbot County's first airport and an early center of Eastern Shore aviation.
Relevant years: 1928-1932 *Lat/Long*: 36-48-18N 76-06-00W
Map: ADC Md/Del 2000 *Num*: 41 *Grid*: E3 *Shows*: area

SCHROM AIRPORT
Greenbelt, Prince George's County
c. 1928-c. 1952

Schrom Airport was located at the edge of Greenbelt, a planned model community first settled in 1937. According to local historian Mary Lou Williamson, the airport predated the town. Frederick "Fritz" Schrom, described as a "flight-crazy farm boy," established the facility on his father's property in 1928. The airport began appearing on aeronautical section charts in April 1940. University of Maryland students took government-sponsored flight training there in the period before World War II. The earliest directory found to list the airport, a Civil Aeronautics Administration bulletin issued in May 1941, described it as one fourth of a mile southwest of the town. The 60-acre facility had three hangars and two gravel-and-dirt landing strips, 2,400 feet and 1,900 feet long. It offered fuel and major repairs. Williamson reported that the airport was closed due to wartime security restrictions in September 1942. She wrote that Fritz Schrom was still serving with the Army Ferrying Command in 1944, when the easing of restrictions allowed his wife to reopen the airport. The Civil Air Patrol used the facility for training during this period. Airport directories show construction underway at the airport in 1946, and by June 1950 there was a single paved runway 5,000 feet long. As described in a paper by Karin Thiessen, Schrom's desire to improve the airport conflicted with his neighbors' wish to maintain their town's "green belt." Residents objected to his ambitious plans, including an air freight depot, which they saw as promoting unwanted noise and road construction. This opposition may have contributed to the closing of the airport in about 1952; however, Thiessen cites other possible factors. These included concerns about coming airspace restrictions in the Washington area, or Fritz Schrom's reported shift toward the construction business rather than aviation. The airport site is now the Greenway Center shopping area, which is located south of Greenbelt Road, and east of the junction of Interstate 495 with the Baltimore-Washington Parkway. [34]

Significance for Maryland air/space history: One of several former general aviation airports in the Washington area.

Relevant years: c. 1928 – c. 1952   *Lat/Long*: 39-02N 76-54W

Map: ADC Metro Washington, 1998 *Num*: 6 *Grid*: C10

Shows: former site

CONGRESSIONAL AIRPORT
Rockville, Montgomery County (M: 26-21-62)
1928-1958

Congressional Airport was located on the west side of Rockville Pike at what is currently the 1601 block. In 1928, the Congressional School of Aeronautics leased 275 acres from the Wagner family with the aim of establishing a training facility and airport. This arrangement changed in the following year, when Congressional Airport, Inc., purchased 269 acres of the land from the Wagner family.[35] According to some accounts, the airport's founder was Maj. Harry Horton, a noted aviator. Horton's reputation helped to ensure the success of the facility, which became the scene of popular aerial demonstrations. A directory issued in September 1931 described Congressional Airport as a rolling sod field, rectangular in shape and measuring 2,500 by 2,000 feet. The airport was identified by lettering on the hangar roof, and by a rotating beacon operated by the Department of Commerce. The facility was closed for a time during World War II, then reopened. By 1947, its assets included ten hangars and an office building with a lounge. The landing area,

however, was still an unpaved field. That remained true as late as 1950, and probably throughout the facility's existence. By the 1950s, rapid residential and commercial development in the area was making the airport an anomaly. In March 1958, the facility was closed by its owner, Arthur C. Hyde, whose other properties included the Prince George's County airport bearing his name. Hyde converted the land occupied by Congressional Airport into the existing Congressional Plaza shopping center. One of the hangars continued to function as a roller skating rink until the year before its demolition in 1984. Two years later, a historical survey of Congressional Plaza found only one architectural element that remained from the airport, although its original function was unknown. This surviving element, a barrel-roofed structure being used as office space, was in the Congressional North section of the shopping center. It was located at the rear of a furniture store whose front faced south on Congressional Lane. A site visit in December 2002 showed that this structure was no longer extant.[36]

Significance for Maryland air/space history: A general aviation airport that operated from the late 1920s to the late 1950s.

Relevant years: 1928 – 1958   *Lat/Long*: 39-05N 77-10W

Map: ADC Md/Del 2000 *Num*: 14 *Grid*: D6 *Shows*: area

HAGERSTOWN REGIONAL AIRPORT-RICHARD A. HENSON FIELD
Hagerstown, Washington County
1928-present

Hagerstown Regional Airport-Richard A. Henson Field occupies a 680-acre site, four miles north of Hagerstown. The facility is east of Interstate Highway 81, north of Showalter Road, and west of U.S. Route 11.[37]

The airport's origin reflected the need of the Kreider-Reisner Aircraft Company (KRA) to replace the tiny landing strip at its factory complex in Hagerstown (see separate entry on page 45). KRA remedied this by establishing a Hagerstown Airport on sixty acres of farmland that it bought on April 7, 1928. During that same year, the company built a wooden hangar, some sixty feet square, on the north side of the property. Newly-produced aircraft were trucked from the factory to the airfield, where workers installed their wings and prepared them for flight testing. An October 1930 bulletin showed the airport as a rectangle measuring 1,360 by 1,950 feet; however, the field was effectively reduced to an "L" by a rocky area at its southwest corner.[38]

In 1934, KRA became the Fairchild Aircraft Corporation, a name that reflected its status as a Fairchild subsidiary since 1929. Also during 1934, the company struck

Right: A Fairchild C-119 Flying Boxcar flying over a changing Hagerstown Airport in the early 1950s: Municipal Hangar and grass field at the bottom of the photo; paved runway and Fairchild factory at top. Photo courtesy of Kent A. Mitchell. Below: A Fairchild 22 coming in to land on the grass field at Hagerstown in the mid-1930s. To the left, "The Always" lunch counter, ancestor of today's Airport Inn restaurant; to the right, the one-room office of the Henson Flying Service, ancestor of numerous Henson enterprises. Photo courtesy of Kent A. Mitchell.

a bargain that altered the future of the airport. The city of Hagerstown purchased the facility, except for Fairchild's hangar, and also added another twenty-one acres to the property. In return, the company agreed to lease rights at the airport, and to drop its plans for a move to Florida.[39]

During the year following its acquisition of the airport, the city launched a major improvement plan. In addition to two paved runways, this upgrade included a large brick hangar with an attached office and waiting room. (Neither this hangar nor the 1928 Fairchild hangar that stood near it are extant.) The federal government provided more than seventy percent of the $220,000 required for this project. On June 19, 1938, the resulting Hagerstown Municipal Airport was dedicated with observances that included parachute jumps and an air show involving sixty planes.[40]

A figure closely associated with the airport from its early days was Richard A. Henson, who in 1932 became the operator of a flying service there. In 1940, he established a flight school under the Civilian Pilot Training Program. Henson also served as a test pilot for Fairchild, whose increased production at this time added to the number of testing and delivery flights at the facility. The World War II period also saw the construction of a massive Fairchild complex at the southeast corner of the airport (see separate entry on page 80).[41]

In October 1945, Columbia Airlines began scheduled service at Hagerstown, using Boeing 247s. By the 1960s, the scheduled carrier was Allegheny Airlines. Richard Henson decided to challenge Allegheny, which was using transport planes with too many seats for the passenger demand. In April 1962, Henson launched his Hagerstown Commuter Airline, using Beech aircraft to link the town with metropolitan Washington. The popularity of this venture led to a 1967 agreement under which Henson teamed with his former rival. Operating as Allegheny Commuter Airlines, his fleet of modestly-sized planes served routes where transport-class aircraft were unprofitable. This successful arrangement had helped to set a national pattern, although Henson later moved his operation to Salisbury.[42]

In 1981, ownership of the airport passed from the city to the county. A sadder milestone came on March 20, 1984, when the takeoff of an A-10 Thunderbolt marked the delivery of Fairchild's last Hagerstown-built aircraft.[43]

Physical changes at the airport over the years have included the addition of acreage and the lengthening, in stages, of the two runways. Roughly 2,500 feet long when first paved in the late 1930s, they now measure 3,494 and 5,451 feet. The achievement of this length for the primary runway required that a section of U.S. Route 11 be moved eastward in 1958. A control tower has been added, now located north of the main runway. In September 1991, a new 15,000-square-foot terminal was dedicated. Henson's memory is honored in its name, and also in the current designation of the airport itself, adopted in October 1998. Hangars multiplied during the 1990s, and, by July 23, 2001, 200 aircraft were based at the facility. Operations during the preceding seventeen months totaled 55,834, including 845 by air carrier aircraft.[44]

Significance for Maryland air/space history: One of the state's oldest continuously operated airports, this facility has served as a testing and delivery point for important aircraft production, and also as a center for regional aviation.

Relevant years: 1928 - present

Lat/Long: 39-42-48N 77-43-77W

Map: ADC Md/Del 2000 *Num*: 4 *Grid*: D4 *Shows*: airport

Continued on page 52

From the Oral History Files...

Pioneering the Commuter Airline

An Interview with William "Bill" Rinn
by Dr. Barry A. Lanman

Bill Rinn worked for Dick Henson as manager of Henson Aviation from 1954 to 1966. In an oral history interview, Rinn describes how Dick Henson's new idea of a "commuter airline" was developed, grew, and provided air transportation for Marylanders.

"Hagerstown was served by Allegheny Airline. Originally, it was American Airways. They started in about 1948. And then they changed the name to Allegheny. Early on when they first started the service, which was called Local Service Airlines. [Allegheny] received [a] subsidy. All of them all over the United States received subsidies through an act of Congress that all communities with airports

Bill Rinn, age 20, perched on the wing of his war-surplus Vultee BT-13 trainer in 1952. Photo courtesy of William (Bill) W. Rinn.

should have air service. And they started out initially with four flights a day east and four flights a day west. They'd go west to Pittsburgh, east to Washington. By 1959, they'd cut the service to one flight each way, which really was very inadequate.

"Mr. Henson was on the Chamber of Commerce committee and they approached [Allegheny] a number of times and asked him to improve the service, put more flights on, and they refused to do it. There were some others [carriers] in the United States that started small commuter airlines—and Henson decided to start one in competition to Allegheny. Allegheny objected at first . . . If the aircraft doesn't weigh over twelve thousand five hundred pounds you can operate it as an air taxi, you can go at schedule, unscheduled, anything you want to do."

The first day of operation was April 23, 1962. "Well, prior to that day, we decided we would have, for publicity, an inaugural flight, and so. . .I invited the mayor of Hagerstown, Winslow Berhands, Tom Dwyer, who was with the Chesapeake Potomac Telephone Company. He was president of the Chamber of Commerce. And there was another gentleman. I can't remember who the third one was. And rather than just take them down to Washington National and back, [we flew them to Dulles Airport]. Dulles was brand new and there was no activity. There was no business at Dulles, and they welcomed anybody who wanted to come down. So, we flew them down to Dulles and parked right underneath the control tower, right at the terminal, and they walked right in and they looked over the new terminal building at Dulles. That was the inaugural flight. We had a photographer record it.

"So, initially we started three flights a day, five days a week from Hagerstown to Washington National Airport — same with wherever Allegheny did. And then eventually we increased it to four flights a day, and we used. . .a ten-place Beech-18 that had been an Air Force C-45 that we modified, installed executive interior in it. And, initially, that's all we flew, was just that exclusively, but we ended up flights with one passenger down, one back, and so forth, so that we decided we can't continue this. It's too expensive. So, then we started using a seven-place Aero Commander, twin-engine Aero Commander, five-place Beechcraft Travel Air, and four-place single-engine Beech Bonanza, and so forth. . . I never really saw anybody object . . . I saw people walk out of the gate in Washington and say, 'My goodness is that what I'm going in?' But I never saw anybody refuse." The trip between Hagerstown and Washington was about 70 miles and initially cost $9.50; the same price as a ticket on Allegheny Airlines.

"Henson was so concerned with passenger satisfaction and developing a record of reliability, he bought a station wagon. Thus, when weather grounded all airplanes, Henson had the pilots drive the passengers to Washington and back to Hagerstown. While it served as a good customer relations ploy, it was not popular with the pilots!"

Rinn was both manager and pilot; he also assumed a variety of tasks to keep the small airline operating efficiently. He often took tickets, handled baggage and assisted passengers with connecting flights. He explains the challenges of starting this endeavor. "Of course we had, counter people here in Hagerstown and line boys to do the baggage handling and so forth, but once you got to Washington National, we'd go into the general aviation gate. We didn't have an airline gate. We just went into the general aviation gate, and went in and paid cash to the FBO [fixed base operator: airport management] for our landing fees, and then utilized their counter. And they allowed us to put up a colored picture of the airplane and we printed up flight schedules in the size [of] a business card that you could put in your wallet. And this rack on the counter held these little flight schedules. They were very, very cooperative, but all this was new all over the country. [Henson] and the other ones were referred to as third level airlines. You had your major trunk airlines, local service airlines, and they started to call us third level airlines. Even, Washington National Airport, which was owned by the federal government, didn't know what to make of us...

"Initially, we would run a survey at the counter of the people who rode to and from Washington, and it turned out that eighty percent were not residents of the local area. Twenty percent were people who had business someplace and we're taking them to their connection in Washington, but eighty percent of the people who came in and went out were from someplace else, not local. So, if you walk into a travel agency or a ticket counter in St. Louis, Missouri, and ask how to get to Hagerstown, that ticket agent or travel agent is going to look in the *Official Airline Guide*, and it will list how to get to Hagerstown, Maryland, which said nothing but Allegheny Airlines. So, I tried and tried. I keep corresponding with an airline guy trying to get them to put us in there, and I finally succeeded after about two years. . .I got them to put our flights in." With this expanded visibility and advertising, business significantly increased.

Rinn describes a typical day of operation. *"You flew the first flight in the morning that left here at eight-thirty. . .We also did a lot of charter business, so we had five pilots, including myself, but we did a lot of charter for Fairchild and other local corporations. So, if there weren't that many flights, as manager, I would just stay home and do my paperwork and so forth, and the other pilots would handle the commuter and charter flights. But if we had enough charter flights to keep all the other pilots busy, then I did the commuter all day. I'd make three trips to Washington, three trips a day.*

"I think we had about twenty-five [employees]. We had about four or five linemen, had about five pilots, Marie, by herself, ran the office, and Ken Norick back in the shop. He had five or six mechanics under him. . .We were Cessna dealers. We always had at least one 172 or a 150 for rental, for flight training. He had the twin Beech, the D-18 for the commuter, an Aero Commander, and a Travel Air, and a Bonanza."

In 1966, Rinn left the company when Henson assumed operational control of the airline. *"In 1967, Allegheny called him and said, 'Hey, you've got the right idea. . .You're using the right size airplanes. . .How about we give you a contract to do Hagerstown. We'll call the Civil Aeronautics Board and we'll ask to be relieved, and tell them we'll give you a contract and we'll also tell the Civil Aeronautics Board you don't have to give us anymore subsidy. But we would like for you to take Salisbury,* Maryland, at the same time and we'll be relieved of subsidy down there and we'll give you a guarantee return on your contract. You can use our gates, our ticketing, our reservations, our ramp people, our baggage handlers and everything." And so he is the first commuter in the country to establish a contract with the air carrier, between [Henson Aviation] and Allegheny. [The] *Civil Aeronautics Board agreed to it and he became the first in the country. . .He's also credited with the term 'commuter' because he called the service The Hagerstown Commuter. In later years, all these operations are referred to—not as third level—but as commuter airlines. He's credited with that."*

In the decades that followed, Rinn took on other endeavors including the role of flight instructor. He has accrued over 7,000 hours of flight time. Rinn currently serves as the Aircraft Owners and Pilot's Association representative in the Hagerstown region as the Airport Support Network representative. In that capacity, he is involved in local discussions relating to airport and real estate development, security concerns relating to Camp David and all types of issues that impact flying in the area. For more than half a century, Bill Rinn has contributed to the development of commercial and private aviation in Western Maryland.

Bill Rinn, oral history interview, November 19, 2002,
MHT/OHC 002 (MD-AVC) 005, 29p.

After working as manager and chief pilot of Henson Aviation, Bill Rinn currently serves as the Aircraft Owner's and Pilot's Association representative in the Hagerstown region. Photo courtesy of William (Bill) W. Rinn.

KREIDER-REISNER AIRCRAFT COMPANY PLANT
FAIRCHILD PLANT NO.1
Hagerstown, Washington County
1929-1963

In 1929, the Kreider-Reisner Aircraft Company (KRA) constructed a large new plant at One Park Lane, just off Pennsylvania Avenue in Hagerstown. Four years earlier, the company had started production in a small shed in the same neighborhood, then expanded into a group of nearby buildings, and also built an airport north of town (see separate entries on pages 45 and 48). To continue to grow, however, KRA planned to construct a modern factory enclosing 32,000 square feet. It gained the resources to do this by becoming a subsidiary of the Fairchild

pleted plant. Even before this addition became operational, the onset of the Great Depression cut orders for new aircraft. A reduced staff at the plant engaged in such stopgap projects as manufacture of autogiro rotor blades. Soon, however, the facility began turning out new aircraft models, beginning with a light plane designated the Fairchild 22. A range of distinctive products followed during the 1930s, including cabin monoplanes, military cargo aircraft, and flying boats, as well as an unique Duromold 46 fabricated with an innovative Fairchild process. The Park Lane plant continued to grow, and an article published in January 1934 estimated its floor space as 90,000 square feet. The name Kreider-Reisner was discarded during that same year and the Hagerstown subsidiary became the Fairchild Aircraft Corporation, later the Fairchild Aircraft Division.[46]

A decisive upturn for the company came in the summer of 1939, when Armand J. Thieblot's design won a contract for a military trainer designated the PT-19. Production of this and other military aircraft during the wartime era required a major expansion of factory space. One part of the solution was massive new complex at the airport (see separate entry on page 80). The other was the "Hagerstown system." Under this plan, Fairchild took over a large number of the town's existing industrial facilities, many of which were inessential to the war effort. By December 1942, this multi-site estab-

Fairchild employees hold autogiro rotor blade in front of Plant No. 1, 1929, on Pennsylvania Avenue in Hagerstown. Photo courtesy of Kent A. Mitchell.

corporation, an arrangement formally announced on April 9, 1929. Nine days later, KRA concluded the purchase of seventeen acres just north of its existing multi-building complex. Construction work began almost immediately, and the company's move to the new facility is reported to have occurred that same summer.[45]

At the new plant, KRA continued to produce its successful line of Challenger biplanes, soon renamed the Fairchild models KRA 31, 34, and 21. In September 1929, the company decided to make an 8,000-square-foot addition to its recently com-

Fairchild Plant No. 1, built 1929 on Pennsylvania Avenue in Hagerstown. Photo courtesy of Kent A. Mitchell.

lishment included some thirty elements in and around Hagerstown. The Park Lane building was now Plant No. 1, functioning as the machine shop for the widely-dispersed production effort.[47]

In the postwar period, Fairchild received new orders that kept its Hagerstown establishment busy. An article in the company magazine *FAD* showed that some eight of the in-town plants were operating at least as late as July 1951. Plant No. 1 was still the machine shop, and was also described as housing the manufacturing department for sheet metal small parts. Directly behind it stood Plant No. 8. This Quonset-type structure, completed in 1948, served as a warehouse supporting activities at Plant No. 1. Fairchild's employment peaked in 1953, and the company eventually abandoned its in-town locations. Plant No. 1 remained in use until 1963, but Fairchild sold it to a division of the Roper Corporation two years later. In January 2003, the building is occupied by Air-Tech Products and other tenants of the owner, Vincent Grough.[48]

Despite its current designation as 881 Pennsylvania Avenue, the former Plant No. 1 fronts diagonally on Park Lane, the street to its north. The two-story brick façade is divided by four piers. Two of these piers closely flank the entrance, forming part of a central section that is slightly higher than the rest of the building. Originally, windows extended across the whole width of façade, interrupted only by the piers and by the entrance section. This fenestration has now been reduced to two sets of tall windows on the first floor, and smaller windows widely-spaced above. Behind the shallow front portion of the building, the main body of the plant extends toward the southwest. Its functional metal exterior appears to be basically unchanged since the Fairchild period.[49]

Significance for Maryland air/space history: A leading aircraft factory during the Depression era, this facility continued to support production during World War II and the postwar period.
Relevant years: 1929 – 1963 *Lat/Long*: 34-40N; 77-43W
Map: ADC Md/Del 2000 *Num*: 36 *Grid*: N/A *Shows*: area

HARBOR FIELD
Originally BALTIMORE MUNICIPAL AIRPORT
Baltimore City and County (BA-2094)
1929-1960

Harbor Field was located at the present Dundalk Marine Terminal, which is partly within the eastern edge of the city of Baltimore and partly in Baltimore County. The site is roughly bounded by Broening Highway on the northeast, Colgate Creek on the east, and the

Two Boeing 314 "clippers" in Colgate Creek at the Pan American Seaplane Terminal at Baltimore Municipal Airport. Behind the surrounding bulkheads, landfill is still being added for the landplane runways. Photo courtesy of the Dundalk-Patapsco Neck Historical Society.

Patapsco River on its other sides. Originally known as Baltimore Municipal Airport, the facility was planned as a successor to nearby Logan Field (see separate entry on page 41)[50]

In 1928, Baltimore's mayor announced selection of the 360-acre site at Dundalk. Most of the area would have to be created by a landfill along the river, but this seemed justified to obtain enough space for a major urban airport. The site also provided the waterfront needed for the seaplanes used in the era's trans-ocean travel. Construction of the necessary bulkheads began in 1929. Predictions that the airport would help to make Baltimore a great center of aircraft manufacturing seemed to be proving correct when the Curtiss-Caproni Corporation built a plant at the site in 1930 (see separate entry). In November of that year, the city's voters approved a $2.5 million loan for the airport. By July 1931, however, the project's viability was in question due to evidence that the fill was failing to harden properly. Despite attempted remedies, including long periods of drying and the introduction of sand-clay fill, this basic flaw was never wholly corrected. The project dragged on beyond the end of the decade, requiring another major loan and millions in federal grants.[51]

The landfill problem did not prevent Baltimore from dedicating a seaplane ramp at the airport in 1932, or from promoting the facility as a terminus for flying boats. In November 1936, Pan American Airways accepted an agreement under which it would begin regular transatlantic service within two years. In return, the city

*A DC-3 flies over the terminal on opening day
of Baltimore Municipal Airport, November 16, 1941.
Photo courtesy of the Dundalk-Patapsco Neck Historical Society*

undertook to lease ten acres to Pan Am on generous terms, and to build a base for the airline there. The resulting Pan American Seaplane Terminal was designed by W. Watters Pagon, who successfully overcame the unstable nature of the site. Four massive piers supported the structure, which measured 270 by 190 feet. In addition to hangar space, the building provided offices, a passenger concourse, lounge, and observation deck. Completed in 1938, the terminal served flights to and from Europe and Bermuda by the famous clippers produced by the Martin and Boeing companies[52]

For landplane travelers, Pagon designed a terminal in the Art Deco style. Constructed of brown brick, this Air Station had two-story wings flanking a three-story octagonal section that was topped by a control tower cab. Brick panels that rose above the roofline gave this central section's exterior a strong vertical effect. A single-story projection on the runway side supported an open-air observation deck. The terminal's interior included a concourse that was two stories high. Although the size of the Air Station had been reduced due to budget considerations, its aesthetic qualities received praise. Pagon also designed Hangar No. 1, which had an adjoining shop section and measured about 149 by 106 feet overall[53]

Another major building completed at Baltimore Municipal by the time of its opening was a base for the aviators of the Maryland National Guard. Funded by the Works Progress Administration, this facility was planned in two phases by the architect Laurence P. Sangston and

the engineer Rensselaer P. Saxe. The first phase was a steel-frame hangar, 130 by 250 feet, with a gable roof. To each side of this were added Georgian/Federal Revival sections for offices, quarters, shops, and storage rooms. The southeast façade was ornamented by a gabled portico with six square columns.[54]

After its opening on November 16, 1941, Baltimore Municipal Airport was served by three airlines. In May 1942, however, civilian traffic was suspended when the War Department took over the facility. World War II also prevented Maryland's Air Guard from moving into its spacious quarters at the airport until 1946. By the end of that first postwar year, some 136,000 airline passengers used the Air Station. Yet Baltimore had already adopted a plan for a new municipal airport. Located south of the city, the resulting Friendship International Airport was dedicated in June 1950. A state airport directory issued that same month showed a crucial difference between Friendship and what was now called Harbor Field. The new airport's runways ranged from 6,000 to 9,450 feet, while the older facility's longest was 4,520 feet. In addition, Harbor Field had near-by obstructions, and was still plagued by sinking surfaces that made it unsuitable for heavy aircraft.[55]

During the 1950s, Harbor Field lost its airline traffic but remained an Air Guard base and continued to serve private pilots and business aviation. In 1958, the city received $4.1 million for the airport, which was transferred to the Maryland Port Authority for conversion to a marine terminal. On the last day of 1960, a ceremony marked the closing of Harbor Field. In 1990, a historic sites survey reported on four major structures from the airport era that were still extant: the Pan American terminal; the Air Station; Hangar No. 1; and the Air Guard building. The Maryland Historical Trust subsequently found these buildings to be eligible for the National Register of Historic Places, based on their innovative design features and their associations with local transportation history. In January 2000, a historical context report prepared for the Maryland Port Administration further documented the four buildings, which have subsequently been demolished.[56]

***Significance for Maryland air/space history*:** Despite its defects, this major municipal airport was the site of developments and structures important to the history of Maryland air transportation.
Relevant years: 1929 - 1960 *Lat/Long*: 39-15-00N 76-31-45W
Map: ADC Md/Del 2000 *Num*: 15 *Grid*: F4 *Shows*: area

BERLINER-JOYCE (B/J) AIRCRAFT CORPORATION PLANT
(NORTH AMERICAN AVIATION PLANT)
Dundalk, Baltimore County
1929-c. 1945

The Berliner-Joyce Aircraft Corporation was formed by a group of executives who included Temple N. Joyce and Henry A. Berliner, president of the Berliner Aircraft Company of Alexandria, Virginia. On May 4, 1928, the new company began building a factory on a five-and-one-half-acre site at Dundalk, just east of Baltimore. A fly-over by thirty-five military aircraft celebrated the laying of the cornerstone. Berliner-Joyce was incorporated in Maryland on February 4, 1929, and took over the assets of the Berliner Aircraft Company at that time. The Alexandria plant was retained until June, when all personnel moved to Maryland.[57]

The Berliner-Joyce plant was near Logan Field, and also close to the site of the planned new municipal airport at the harbor. Enclosing some 54,000 square feet, the brick and steel factory had a rectangular main area under a nearly flat roof, as well as smaller projecting sections. A separate fifty-by-twenty-foot building was added during the facility's early years and housed the company's wind tunnel. The plant employed some 500 workers around 1934. An aerial view of Logan Field in 1935 includes a facility that matches other images of the Berliner-Joyce factory. The site was south of Logan and across a railway line from it, between Broening Highway and the Patapsco River.[58]

Berliner-Joyce had planned to introduce a new commercial aircraft, but conditions following the 1929 stock market crash did not favor this. Instead, the company worked on military contracts. In early 1930, a majority of its stock was acquired by the North American Aviation, a Delaware corporation. At the time of this transaction, Berliner-Joyce changed its name to the B/J Aircraft Corporation. In addition to a number of prototypes, B/J built a two-seat biplane fighter that the Army designated the P-16 (later PB-1). For the Navy, the company built light OJ-2 observation biplanes capable of shipboard operations.[59]

In 1933, North American Aviation added another Dundalk company to its holdings: the General Aviation Manufacturing Corporation, which had been operating at the nearby Curtiss-Caproni plant (see separate entry on page 61). North American then bought the remaining shares of B/J, and concentrated the manufacturing of both subsidiaries at the B/J plant.[60]

In mid-1934, General Aviation began building the GA-15, an observation monoplane in which seated two crewmembers in tandem under a long "greenhouse" canopy. Completed in July 1935, the prototype won an order from the Army and saw service as the O-47. Meanwhile, work proceeded on development of the first aircraft built under the North American name, the NA-16 trainer, which proved to be the first of a versatile and long-lasting group of planes. The Army placed its first order for aircraft derived from this design in September, giving it the designation B-19. The prototypes of both of these successful planes were built at Dundalk, but the

An experimental XFJ-1 Navy fighter stands in front of the door of the B/J factory in Dundalk. Photo courtesy of Stan Piet.

resulting production models were not built in Maryland. In November 1935, North American began moving its operations to a new factory in California.[61]

In March 1941, the Allied Aviation Corporation bought the former B/J factory, where it manufactured a range of products for the government. In addition to non-aeronautical items, these included aircraft components made of molded plastic that were substituted for similar parts made of duralumin. Allied Aviation filled a Navy order for a pair of prototype gliders, and these may also have been built at the Dundalk plant. These LRA-1 amphibious gliders had a crew of two and were able to carry ten passengers; however, the Navy decided to cancel the production order in 1943. In the postwar era, Allied Aviation turned to the manufacture of boats, and in 1947 the company was acquired by Moulded Products Inc.[62]

Significance for Maryland air/space history: This facility: produced military aircraft in 1930s; played a key part in the formative period of North American Aviation, a major manufacturer; and later supported aviation in World War II.

Relevant years: 1929 – c. 1945   *Lat/Long*: 39-14N 76-31W
Map: ADC Md/Del 2000   *Num*: 15 *Grid*: F4 *Shows*: area

GLENN L. MARTIN AIRCRAFT COMPANY PLANT NO. 1
**Currently MIDDLE RIVER AERO SYSTEMS/
LOCKHEED MARTIN MARINE SYSTEMS DIVISION
Middle River, Baltimore County (BA-2081, BA-3152)
1929-present**

The former Martin Plant No. 1 is located east of Baltimore in Middle River, south of Eastern Boulevard and west of Wilson Point Road. The facility was central in the development of Maryland's aircraft industry, and has since played an important role in the state's involvement in the production of rocket-based systems.[63]

During the late 1920s, aviation pioneer Glenn L.

The original 1929 Glenn L. Martin Aircraft plant at Middle River, including an administration building and factory divided into machine shop, receiving, and (with higher roofline) final assembly. Planes left either from the grass airfield or (if seaplanes) from adjoining Dark Head Cove. Photo courtesy of Glenn L. Martin Maryland Aviation Museum.

Martin decided to move his aircraft manufacturing business from Cleveland to a 1,260-acre tract that he purchased at Middle River. Philip Lindsay Small and Associates, a Cleveland architectural firm whose principal clients had been the Van Sweringen railroad interests, designed the new plant as well as a single-story Art Deco administration building placed just to its north. Both were constructed in 1929.[64]

What later came to be called A Building enclosed 298,000 square feet. It was probably the most advanced aircraft plant of its time. There, the Martin company began producing its remarkable series of Middle River aircraft, beginning with the BM-1 Navy biplane. An outstanding technical achievement of this period was the exceptionally fast B-10 bomber, an all-metal monoplane ordered by the Army in 1933. This era also saw the production of the M-130 Clippers that helped Pan American pioneer air service in the Pacific.[65]

In 1937, anticipating orders for large flying boats, Martin built the second stage of Small's original master plan. To design the new addition, he chose Albert Kahn, who has been called the American's most prominent architect to specialize in industrial building. The resulting B Building is considered to be one of the Kahn firm's finest achievements. Although smaller in area than A Building, this unit enclosed the world's largest unobstructed aircraft assembly floor. This was achieved by using flat span trusses of 300 feet, a size seen previously only in bridges. B Building also provided an unusually high interior clearance that facilitated the production of large aircraft such the Navy's Mariner flying boats. Beginning in 1938, Martin further enhanced its Middle River complex by replacing its simple landing field with a well-equipped airport (see entry on Martin State Airport on page 72).[66]

The World War II years brought urgent orders for military aircraft such as attack bombers, amphibious patrol bombers, and the huge Mars flying boat. During 1939-40, Martin added another unit in which 300-foot flat spans created an immense interior. This new C Building was built in just seventy-seven days in order to supply the beleaguered French with M-167 bombers (called "Glenns" or "Marylands"). This addition made Plant No. 1 the nation's largest single aircraft factory. Yet continuing wartime orders during 1940-41 led to a major expansion of B Building, and also to the creation of two more factory units, both built under the federal government's Emergency Plant Facilities program. One of these was D Building, on the south side of Plant No. 1, used for the production of Navy flying boats. The other was a separate facility to build the B-26 Marauder (see entry on Plant No. 2 on page 79). The war swelled the company's Middle River employment from 3,639 in January 1939 to 16,653 in 1940, then 30,326 in 1941, and finally to a peak of some 53,000 in 1942. This rapid growth triggered residential development nearby (see entry on Aero Acres on page 79).[67]

In the postwar era, Martin tried producing civil airliners, with limited success, and

A giant XPB2M flying boat takes shape inside skylit B Building in July 1941. Photo courtesy of Glenn L. Martin Maryland Aviation Museum.

Right: A PBM Mariner flying boat is dwarfed by the enormous doors of B Building, Albert Kahn's masterpiece of 1937 at Martin Aircraft. Photo courtesy of Glenn L. Martin Maryland Aviation Museum.

built further military aircraft that included British-designed Canberra jets. The company also became involved in the field of rocketry. Projects included such systems the Viking and Vanguard rockets, and the Matador missile, 1,000 of which had been produced at Middle River by 1957. In 1952, meanwhile, financial troubles prompted Glenn Martin's replacement as chief executive, and he died in December 1955. Earlier in that year, the company had launched its final design for a new flying boat, the P6M-1 SeaMaster. This innovative design was not accepted for full production, however, and Martin ceased to manufacture aircraft after turning out the last of its P5M-2 Marlins in December 1960.[68]

The following year saw a merger that produced Martin Marietta. Headquartered in Bethesda, this corporation was a diversified one, but the aerospace field remained the main focus at Middle River. The highlight of the 1960s for the plant was its role in the Project Gemini. This program paved the way for lunar exploration by orbiting pairs of astronauts, part of whose training was conducted in a simulation facility in B Building. The Titan launch vehicles for Gemini

When fully built up after 1943, Martin Plant No. 1 included A, B, and C Buildings in the main block, an Engineering Building in front and D Building to the rear (still in wartime camouflage in this photo). The two latter structures have since been demolished. Photo courtesy of Glenn L. Martin Maryland Aviation Museum.

From the Oral History Files...

Test Pilot for Glenn L. Martin

An interview with Jack King
by Dr. Barry A. Lanman

Jack King came to Baltimore in 1939 and acquired an entry-level position, with the Glenn L. Martin Company. To increase his education and to strive for career advancement, he took polytechnic courses in aeronautical engineering and was quickly promoted to the drafting department. He also worked at the old Curtiss Wright Airport on weekends. To earn his pilot's license at the age of eighteen, he bartered eleven hours of work at the airport for one-half hour of flight time. By World War II, he had received his instructor's rating. As with most young men, World War II interrupted their civilian careers and King was no exception. Assigned to Langley Field, he received B-25 training and was placed in the research division due to his experience at Glenn L. Martin.

After the war, King returned to the Martin plant and worked in the Power Plant Department and designed cowlings for new airline equipment such as the 2-O-2 and the 4-O-4. Because he was a licensed mechanic and had logged considerable flight time, King was offered a job as a co-pilot in the Flight Test Department.

The Test Pilot's Job

"We had every kind of conceivable thing you go through...except wrecking the airplane. What happens when one engine quits? You have to go up and do a lot of single engines, up and down, climbs and some of them a little boring. When you had to get up early in the morning to

Jack King presents veteran aircraft manufacturer Glenn L. Martin with the Associated Aviation Clubs of Maryland first annual award for outstanding achievements in aviation in January, 1951. Photo courtesy of Jack King.

get smooth air, and we'd fly down over the bay...we had some close calls. We had an engine reverse one time, on a 4-O-4 prototype that was fully loaded down with lead weights. We couldn't get back to the Martin Airport, and we had to land over at Great Oaks on the side strip...Somebody left a wire attached into a junction box that shouldn't have been there. The propeller wouldn't feather; it would go right back into reverse, so we had to go down. We also had the controls fail (on test flights) several times...That was about as close as anything.

"Oh we did a lot of unusual flight testing, and we had some close calls with icing programs. They'd let it snow on the airplane all day long and then go out and try to fly it and see if would fly, and that's where I got my gray hair, I think. I may have been too young or too enthused about flying to really have been scared...I think back on it and I get scared!"

Glenn L. Martin

King got to know his boss, Glenn L. Martin, a self-taught flyer who built and flew his first plane back in 1910. In 1933 he won the Collier Trophy for his firm's development of the first streamlined bomber from the National Aeronautic Association.

"He loved all of his airplanes he designed and he liked to talk about all his early flights... he loved the old days, to talk about it.

"He had his own ideas and he was a staunch Republican. He didn't want to give any money to the Democrats. He never married, but loved his mother. He stayed right here until she died. And he had his own ideas...Well, like one instance we had control problems with

Test pilots George Rodney (left) and Jack King in the cockpit of Martin 2-O-2A airliner developed for Trans World Airlines (TWA). Photo courtesy of Jack King.

the 2-O-2 Transport and we had to put a different tail on the airplane, so the engineers designed about three or four different types of tails on the back and he picked out the one that was least likely, least favorable to fly. . . And we called that the 'Presidential Tail' because Mr. Martin picked it!

"For his 65th birthday, The Associated Aviation Clubs of Maryland, for which I was an officer, gave him an award. I presented it to him in his office. . .He was so proud of that award that in his home on the Eastern Shore he had a special table and you'd come through the door and you almost fell over that thing. He was more proud of that than he was of the Collier Award for designing the B-10, because it represented an award from all the aviation clubs in Maryland."

Developing Patents

King is an inventor as well as a pilot. He received several patents. "Mine were all test flight equipment for testing airplanes. I was awarded the Purple Martin. That's a beautiful award and it hangs on my wall. . .it is signed by Mr. Martin. One of my inventions was a position transmitter. Everything that moves on an airplane, you had to make a record of it in flight and they put it on a photo panel. . .this even went into the space age testing years ago."

King is a member of the Quiet Birdmen, the OX-5 Aviation Pioneers, the Flying Shriners, and the Aircraft Owners and Pilots Association. In his role as an aviator, writer and corporate pilot, he helped launch the *Professional Pilot Magazine* in 1967. King has logged over 20,000 hours of flying time

Jack King, oral history interview, October 14, 2002, MHT/OHC 002 (MD-AVC) 007, 54 p..

As a member of the Martin Flight Test Group, Jack King (pointing) introduces TWA pilots to a new Martin 2-O-2, August 1950.
Photo courtesy of Jack King.

were assembled in what is now called the Vertical Assembly Building, a structure added east of C Building in 1963. In the 1970s, Middle River began manufacturing thrust reversers, an aircraft component that was to become one of its staple products; however, the decade was a generally poor one for the plant. The adjoining airport complex was sold to the state of Maryland in 1975 (see separate entry), and employment sank as low as 700.[69]

Early in the 1980s, Martin Marietta brought its Vertical Launching System (VLS) program to Middle River from its Orlando facility. The VLS, used to fire missiles from vessels at sea, proved to be an enduring product line. As of January 1984, other items manufactured at the plant included components for the Patriot missile and B-1B bomber. Employment then stood at 2,700. The E Building, an office structure north of B Building, was added in 1987. In that same year, increasing emphasis on naval products was reflected in a change of the division's name from Baltimore Aerospace to Aero & Naval Systems. Under the Lockheed Martin Corporation, formed by a merger in 1995, the unit's title is Naval Electronics and Surveillance Systems-Marine Systems. In early 2003, Lockheed Martin employed roughly 550 on naval projects, mostly in E Building.[70]

Meanwhile the thrust reverser business picked up to such an extent that employment rose to 1,500 in 1997. In October, 1997, Lockheed Martin sold most of the original Martin complex to General Electric. GE carried on the business as Middle River Aircraft Systems.[71]

A historic sites inventory report in 1997 found that Plant No.1 had been changed since the 1940s by factors that included the demolition of D Building and the addition of new structures. Aluminum siding, applied in the 1980s, had dramatically altered the exterior appearance of the complex. The report, however, found the site to be historically significant on several grounds. These were: its role in historical events such as aircraft development and World War II production; its associations with aviation leader Glenn L. Martin; and, its status as a major work of master architect Albert Kahn. It is also worth noting that the Middle River plant continued to be part of Maryland aerospace history after Martin's death. The Vertical Assembly Building, in particular, had a significant role in the space exploration program.[72]

Significance for Maryland air/space history: A facility of outstanding design that was an important center of aircraft innovation and manufacture, contributed to victory in World War II, and later played a role in production of rocket-based systems.

Relevant years: 1929 - present *Lat/Long*: 39-19N 76-24W
Map: ADC Md/Del 2000 *Num*: 16 *Grid*: A3 *Shows*: area

Maryland Air National Guardsmen, mascot goat, and O-16 biplanes at grassy Detrick Field, Frederick, 1930s. Braddock Heights looms in the background. Photo courtesy of Ann Arrundell County Historical Society.

DETRICK FIELD
INTERMEDIATE FIELD 5A,
WASHINGTON-CLEVELAND AIRWAY
Frederick, Frederick County (F-3-161)
1929-42

Detrick Field was located within the southern part of the present Fort Detrick, east of what is now Rosemont Avenue, north of Military Road, and west of West 7th Street. On July 29, 1929, Frederick municipal authorities purchased ninety-two acres at this site, then on the northwestern edge of their city. Three days later, they leased it to the federal government to become an intermediate landing field, one of several such facilities that the Department of Commerce was establishing along the Washington-Cleveland airway. Officially, these fields were for use in case of emergencies between airports, rather than for regular operations. Communities were eager to see them built, however, seeing the program as a chance to create an airport. Among the first landings at Intermediate Field 5A was made by a biplane dubbed the "Queen of Frederick County," and the facility continued to be used by local aviators. The airfield had two sod runways, configured as an "L." The northeast-southwest runway was 2,650 feet long, while the northwest-southeast strip measured 1,900 feet. The facility continued to be listed as an intermediate field as late as 1941, but by that time its main function had become military.[73]

In 1931, the Maryland National Guard's 104th Observation Squadron brought their DeHaviland O-38 biplanes to Frederick's airfield for the first of a series of annual summer camps. The facility then possessed three stone-block buildings that were used as a control tower,

a snack bar, and a rest room. In August, the squadron voted to name their summer base "Detrick Field" in honor of their respected medical officer, Capt. Frederick L. Detrick, who had died in June. As the danger of war increased in the late 1930s, a training program for pilots began at Detrick Field. New construction during this era included: prefabricated wooden barracks and administrative structures; a hangar; and paving of the main runway. After the United States entered the war, however, the 104th was reassigned elsewhere. Detrick Field was used to organize and equip the reestablished Second Bombardment Squadron during 1942, although that unit did not then have aircraft of its own.[74]

In 1943, the federal government acquired Detrick Field for $50,000, and the city began plans to establish an airport at a different location (see separate entry on page 98). Adding additional property, the Army converted the former airfield into a Chemical Warfare Service base that was designated Camp (later Fort) Detrick. In 1993, base historian Norman M. Covert wrote that current aviation at the Fort was restricted to a helipad used to shuttle visitors to and from the capital. Certain wooden buildings from the airfield era were then scheduled for demolition; however, two other structures continue to survive in 2003. One is the former hangar (Building 201), now used by the Directorate of Engineering and Housing for office and workshop space. The other, known as the Blockhouse Tower, consists of the control tower and two other stone buildings from Detrick Field's early days. Although designated Buildings 10, 11, and 12, these structures are today joined as a single unit that is used for offices. Traces of the grass landing strip may still be seen in the Blue and Gray Parade Ground. Part of the concrete runway now forms Hamilton Street, a short roadway that is northwest of Porter Street and parallel to it.[75]

Significance for Maryland air/space history: A facility that supported both civil aviation and air operations of the Maryland National Guard during the 1930s and early 1940s.
Relevant years: 1929 - 1942 *Lat/Long:* 39-26N 77-26W
Map: ADC Md/Del 2000 *Num:* 14 *Grid:* A1 *Shows:* area

RUTHERFORD FIELD

(BALTIMORE AIRPORT)
Woodlawn, Baltimore County
1929-c. 1965

Rutherford Field was located about eight miles west of Baltimore, at or near the present Rutherford Business Center. The facility was east of Rolling Road, south of Windsor Mill Road, and west of the present Interstate 695. It was established in 1929 by Oliver Rutherford, proprietor of a nearby gun and recreation club. Rutherford's company operated three aircraft and offered pilot training, rides, and aerial tours. In 1931, an Airway Bulletin described the 125-acre facility as an irregular sod field, 2,250 by 1,875 feet. A 1933 directory listed the operator as The Baltimore Airport, Inc; however, the hangar roof displayed a more modest designation, Rutherford Field.[76] The airport may have been closed for a period, since it was absent from aeronautical charts dated December 1936 through September 1938, and also from Airway Bulletins issued in January of 1937 and 1938. By November 1941, however, Rutherford Field had reappeared on the charts. A diagram of the airfield in July 1946 showed four landing strips, the longest being the 2,100-foot northeast-southwest runway. The airport had two hangars and a building containing an office and lounge. The facility operated in daylight only, providing fuel and minor repairs. The manager was Raymond V. McNemar.[77]

The state directory for June 1950 continued to list McNemar as manager, although the operator was now United Flying Service. The same directory showed a simplified airfield layout with only two turf runways. The longer runway, now 2,400 feet, extended the whole distance from Windsor Mill Road to Rolling Road. In 1955, a newspaper reported that McNemar and his wife had a staff of ten to help them with activities that included flight instruction, repairs, and aircraft sales. The airport was described as increasingly popular with business representatives flying in and out of Baltimore. The McNemars said that they would like to expand the facility, but noted that the adjacent farmland was now priced at residential levels. This rising land value was probably already a threat to the airport's future, but the tone of the article was highly optimistic. Rutherford Field continued to operate for another decade, and part of the main runway was surfaced with macadam. The facility appeared in a directory as late as 1965, but it was not included in the state airport listing for the following year, or in subsequent issues examined.[78]

Significance for Maryland air/space history: An airport that served general aviation for more than thirty years, beginning in 1929.
Relevant years: 1929 – c. 1965
Lat/Long: 39-20-15N 76-45-15W
Map: ADC Md/Del 2000 *Num*: 15 *Grid*: D3 *Shows*: area

CURTISS-CAPRONI CORPORATION PLANT

GENERAL AVIATION MANUFACTURING PLANT
Baltimore City (Dundalk)
1930-c. 1939

The Curtiss-Caproni Corporation was established in 1929 as a division of the Curtiss-Wright Corporation. The intent was to use the talents of famed Italian designer Gianni Caproni in building large, multi-engine aircraft. The site chosen for the new corporation's plant was a twenty-five-acre portion of the land that the city of Baltimore was developing for its planned water-side airport (see separate entry on Harbor Field on page 53). The factory's location in Dundalk was just east of Colgate Creek and within Baltimore's municipal limits. Completed in 1930, the plant was designed to accommodate up to 2,000 workers. It enclosed 200,000 square feet under saw-tooth roofs that were placed on either side of a double monitor.[79]

Because of the onset of the Great Depression, Curtiss-Caproni never operated the plant, and the company itself was absorbed by its parent corporation. In the autumn of 1931, the General Aviation Manufacturing

Army YO-27 observation planes in final assembly at General Aviation (formerly Curtiss-Caproni) plant at Dundalk. Photo courtesy of Stan Piet.

Corporation leased the facility. Among the products that General Aviation built at the plant were five flying boats for the Coast Guard. In 1932, one of these flying boats was launched as part of the dedication of the new airport's seaplane ramp. By this time, however, the airport project was already encountering trouble because of the instability of the fill being used at the site. The Curtiss-Caproni building itself had experienced settling as early as July of the previous year, even though it stood on natural land rather than fill.[80]

In 1933, North American Aviation acquired the General Aviation Manufacturing Corporation. Following this acquisition, North American concentrated General Aviation's work at the nearby plant of its other Dundalk subsidiary, the B/J Aircraft Corporation (see separate entry on the Berliner-Joyce factory on page 55). General Aviation gave up its lease on the former Curtiss-Caproni facility, and in 1935 North American began moving all its operations out of Maryland.[81]

Following General Aviation's departure from the Curtiss-Caproni building, Pan-American Airways used it for offices and maintenance before its own nearby facility opened in 1938. After the outbreak of World War II in Europe, the Glenn L. Martin Aircraft Company considered using the disused building for its booming production. In May 1941, however, Martin declared that reconditioning the facility would be too expensive. In July of that same year, the Western Electric Company occupied the plant, using it to produce cable. In 1955, the Bendix Aviation Corporation acquired the building, which was subsequently demolished.[82]

Significance for Maryland air/space history: A facility that was used for aircraft production in the 1930s, but not on the large scale for which it was designed.
Relevant years: 1930 – c. 1939   *Lat/Long*: 39-14N 76-31W
Map: ADC Md/Del 2000   *Num*: 15   *Grid*: F4   *Shows*: area

CURTISS-WRIGHT AIRPORT
Later PIMLICO AIRPORT
Baltimore (Pimlico), Baltimore City and County
1930-1947

Curtiss-Wright Airport occupied a site of roughly 250 acres that was about a mile north of Pimlico Race Course. It was on the south side of Smith Avenue, west of its intersection with Greenspring Avenue. Most of the property was in Baltimore County, although some may have been within the city limits. The facility was opened in 1930 by the Curtiss-Wright Corporation, whose widespread interests embraced nearly all aspects of aviation. Upon the new airport's completion, it replaced Logan Field as the primary base of the local Curtiss-Wright Flying Service. The "Million Dollar Airport" offered

instruction for pilots and mechanics, maintenance, flight services, and basing for private aircraft.[83]

As described in a 1931 bulletin, Curtiss-Wright provided pilots with 160 usable acres that included four landing strips, the longest measuring 3,000 feet. The airport was dominated by two imposing concrete-block hangars in the Art Deco style. On the airfield side, each hangar had rows of large windows, set in a single-story projection that was flanked by two-story sections. Awnings attached to the buildings helped to shade the crowds attending the spectacles for which the field became known. One memorable event in May 1931 was all-woman air show, billed as the nation's first of its kind. Stunts at the popular "aerial circuses" included maneuvers by planes tied together, bombing runs using sacks of flour, and delayed parachute jumps by Archie Seese, the "human bat." Among the participants at these events were members of the Thunderbird Flying Club, formed at the airport in 1933.[84]

Behind the excitement at Curtiss-Wright Airport was Col. William D. Tipton, who leased and ran the facility during its heyday. A World War I ace pilot, he commanded the Maryland National Guard air unit based at Logan Field, and was also a flying club president and a columnist on aviation topics. Curtiss-Wright Airport was an excellent stage for his promotion of air-mindedness; however, it lacked the space to become the air transportation hub that he may have envisioned, and seems not to have been particularly profitable as a business venture. Called to service in World War II, Tipton was still on active duty when he died in an Ohio air crash in December 1945.[85]

Curtiss-Wright Airport closed, at least for civilian operations, during the war. A commercial directory published in 1946 indicated that it was still owned by the Curtiss-Wright Corporation, and was operated by W. E. Mainville. During that same year, however, the facility was renamed Pimlico Airport, and presumably changed owners at that time. An article published in August 1946 reported that Cheston L. Eshelman had begun building his innovative "flying wing" aircraft at Pimlico Airport during June. A state directory issued in 1947 indicated that the airport was owned by Knipp Aviation Industries. In November 17 of the year, however, a revised listing showed that the facility was no longer in operation.[86]

Following the airport's closure, the Bendix Aviation Corporation used the facility for radar and electronic work. The buildings later served as storage space, but by the 1960s the property was disused and shabby. Photographs published by a local weekly in January 1963 showed that the hangars were still basically intact; however, the article reported that a retail complex was proposed for the property. The site is now occupied by the Greenspring Shopping Center and Pickwick apartments. No structures from the airport era remain.[87]

Significance for Maryland air/space history: A center of training for pilots and mechanics, as well as for aerial showmanship, during the golden age of aviation enthusiasm.
Relevant years: 1930 - 1947 *Lat/Long*: 39-22N 76-41W
Map: ADC Md/Del 2000 *Num*: 15 *Grid*: D2 *Shows*: area

TIPTON AIRPORT
Formerly FORT MEADE ARMY AIRFIELD, TIPTON ARMY AIRFIELD
Odenton, Anne Arundel County (AA-2240)
c. 1930-present

Tipton Airport occupies a 366-acre site at 81 General Aviation Drive, west of Odenton and south of Maryland Route 32. It is also just south of Fort George G. Meade, and was formerly that installation's airfield.[88]

Camp (later Fort) Meade was established by the Army in 1917 as part of the nation's military buildup during World War I. An emergency landing field was reported to exist there as early as 1920, and an auxiliary landing field was listed in a 1930 publication. A January 1936 bulletin stated that the airfield was three-fifths of a mile northeast of the barracks. The field was rectangular with three landing strips. The longest of three, which measured 1,800 feet, was paved and oriented northwest-southeast, a fact confirmed by several publications during the next four years.[89]

As described in a historical report by Clayton Davis, Fort Meade Army Airfield in 1957 was crossed by both MacArthur Boulevard and Mapes Road. Movable barriers were raised and lowered by the control tower to prevent surface traffic from interfering with air operations. Davis wrote that the single paved runway ran northeast-southwest, which differs from the orientation described in the 1936-40 period. Nevertheless, the generally similar location, and the fact that no other airfield is known to have existed at Fort Meade during these decades, make it virtually certain that this was the same facility. Davis noted that the airfield was used by civilian as well as military aircraft.[90]

The airfield's location within the built-up area of Fort Meade created safety and noise problems. In 1961, it was replaced by a new facility built on a landfill near the southern edge of the base. This was at first known by the same name as its predecessor, but in April 1962 it received the new designation of Tipton Army Airfield. The name honored Col. William D. Tipton, a Maryland native with a distinguished record as an aviator. During World War I, Tipton downed five enemy aircraft, and his decorations included Britain's Distinguished Flying Cross. He was an early commander of the Maryland National Guard's air unit, and a leader in the state's civil aviation affairs (see entry on Curtiss-Wright Airport on page 62). Tipton later served in World War II, and died in a military aircraft accident in December 1945.[91]

The Base Realignment and Closure Act of 1988 included provisions encouraging the conversion of military airfields to civil use. Tipton Army Airfield was one of the facilities designated under the program, and it closed in 1995. The conversion appealed to Anne Arundel County officials as a way to offset the loss of general aviation airports to residential development. One obstacle was the need to deal with environmental pollution at the site, a lengthy effort that was drawn out by the discovery of unexploded ordnance buried there. Meanwhile, the state legislature in 1997 established Tipton Airport Authority to operate the facility. The environmental cleanup was completed in June 1999, and the new civil facility opened on November 1 of that year.[92]

Continued on page 66

Tipton Airport, Odenton, when still under Army control, circa 1984. Photo courtesy of the Maryland Aviation Administration.

From the Oral History Files...

"America's Flying Family"
The Hutchinsons

An interview with Kathryn Hutchinson James and Janet Lee Hutchinson Simpson
by Dr. Barry A. Lanman

Today, most Marylanders are not familiar with the name Hutchinson or the ways in which the family promoted aviation and contributed to the development of flight in America. However, in the 1930s, the "Flying Hutchinsons" were a media phenomenon.

At the dawn of the "Roaring Twenties," George Hutchinson was a successful bank manager and appeared to be the typical Maryland family man. However, one day in 1922 would change his life forever. After visiting a Maryland race track, he came home with over $8,000 in cash! To put the amount of money in perspective, the average Marylander earned about $500 to $700 a year in the post World War I era. Thus, he was financially able to realize his dream of flying.

Hutchinson quickly learned how to fly, bought an airplane, and purchased a small airport in southern Pennsylvania. To earn revenue, he would take passengers for rides around the surrounding areas of Pennsylvania and northern Maryland. Because many of the potential customers were still concerned about the safety of airplanes, he had to demonstrate that the airplane flights were generally safe. So he took his two daughters on the excursions. Slowly, this created a small but steady stream of passengers. As a natural-born showman, he was not content with this endeavor so he hired show girls to participate in the rides: Business dramatically increased!

Flight to all 48 State Capitals in 1930

Motivated by his success in his first eight years as an aviator and aviation promoter, Hutchinson, his wife and two daughters were dubbed the "Flying Family" by the press. "Governor," the family's pet lion cub also participated in their adventures. The photogenic nature of the family expanded the media attention to a national level. To capture additional notoriety, to stimulate airport/aviation development and to promote Hutchinson's passion for the issue of aviation safety, he decided to fly to all of the state capitals in the United States. He acquired financial patrons and the President's blessing. Herbert Hoover officiated at the inauguration of the tour.

In an oral history interview, Janet Lee Hutchinson Simpson and Kathryn Hutchinson James, the daughters of George Hutchinson, Kathryn summarized the impact the promotional trip had on aviation expansion. *"The tour did have a favorable influence [on airport construction]...A lot of airports started out at this time.*

"We flew out of Logan...Maryland didn't have many airports... Governor Ritchie was very favorable toward aviation expansion...He was one of the important politicians that helped it expand...Maryland became a progressive state in aviation."

"The Flying Hutchinsons" Attempt Trans-Atlantic Flight in 1932 and a 1939 World Tour for Peace

In 1932, just five years after Charles A. Lindbergh made his historic first trans-Atlantic flight across the Atlantic, "The Flying Hutchinsons" decided to be the first family to accomplish this endeavor. Backed by wealthy financiers, Mr. Hutchinson obtained a Sikorsky S-38 seaplane, prepared for the trip and departed in September of 1932. While the first part of the trip went without incident, extreme weather forced the Hutchinsons to make a crash landing in Greenland, and they never completed the journey. However, as a result of this effort, better communications developed and the commercial airlines eventually accepted Hutchinson's route as the best one to cross the Atlantic.

Based on the tour of states and the success of that promotion, in 1939, Mr. Hutchinson sought to gain support for peace in a world that was highly unstable. He was once again successful in acquiring private funding for

The four members of the flying Hutchinson family flew their Fokker trimotor and its festoons of advertisements to every state capital in 1930. In a publicity photograph from the "classic era" of aviation, they pose with "Cheeta," the chimpanzee star of "Tarzan" movies. Photo courtesy of Kathryn Hutchinson James and Janet Lee Simpson.

a trip around the world in the name of peace. The plan was to visit sixty countries and have the heads of state sign a "Scroll of Nations" signifying their anti-war philosophy. Unfortunately, the trip was cut short due to the start of World War II.

As war expanded in Europe, Great Britain pleaded for assistance. While he was a man dedicated to peace, George Hutchinson had a change of heart. He helped organize a private venture to raise money for bombers and was one of the pilots who flew the planes to England before the United States officially entered World War II.

Janet Lee Hutchinson Followed in her Father's Footsteps

As World War II progressed, Hutchinson's daughter Janet Lee decided to follow in her father's footsteps and learned to fly. Thus, after high school graduation, she took flying lessons at Westminster Airport and applied to become a WASP (Women Airforce Service Pilot). She was accepted, and after seven months of training, at the age of nineteen, she served as a test pilot, as a ferry pilot and as an instructor. However, in December of 1945, the WASP's were disbanded. Janet Lee said, *"It broke our hearts!"*

After the war, Mrs. Janet Lee Hutchinson Simpson flew for the Reconstruction Finance Corporation and became a flight instructor at Rutherford Airport and at the Glen Burnie Airport in the 1950s and early 1960s.

The Impact of "America's Flying Family" on Aviation

Today, the Hutchinson sisters live in Florida and still refer to their father as their hero. They acknowledged that George Hutchinson was a man that had an eye for promoting aviation in a colorful manner and had a vision of making the airplane as common as the family automobile. Kathryn Hutchinson commented that *"it was all a big adventure"* – An adventure that expanded aviation in Maryland and throughout the United States.

Kathryn Hutchinson James and Janet Lee Simpson, oral history interview, August 8, 2003, interview not transcribed.

Clad in jodhpurs, boots, and hunting jackets, the "Flying Family" broadcast on CBS from the cabin of their airplane. Photo courtsy of Kathryn Hutchinson James and Janet Lee Simpson.

Above: The Flying Family: Blanche, George, Janet Lee, and Kathryn Hutchinson, September 1932. Photo courtesy of the Joseph Ruff family.

Left: The female Hutchinsons watch their Sikorsky flying boat slowly crushed by the ice off Angmagsalik, Kivdlak Island, Greenland, September 1932. Photo courtesy of the Joseph Ruff family.

The assets of Tipton Airport include a lighted 3,000-foot runway with a parallel taxiway, a broad apron, and four large hangars. Ninety-seven aircraft were based at the facility as of April 26, 2002. Operations for the preceding twelve months totaled 48,000, including 1,000 by air taxis.[93]

Significance for Maryland air/space history: A military airfield that was successfully converted to a civilian general aviation airport.
Relevant years: c. 1930 - present
Lat/Long: 39-05-06N 76-45-28W
Map: ADC Md/Del 2000 *Num*: 15 *Grid*: C5 *Shows*: airport

QUEEN'S CHAPEL AIRPORT
Hyattsville, Prince George's County
1930s-c. 1952

Queen's Chapel Airport opened in the mid-1930s, according to a paper by Karin Thiessen. The property was owned by the Barrett Brothers and managed by Bob Baber and William N. "Bill" Henderson. The airport was first included on the Washington section aeronautical chart in September 1940. The earliest directory found to list the airport was a Civil Aeronautics Administration bulletin issued in May 1941, which described it as a twenty-one-acre property at Hyattsville, four and one-half miles northeast of the U.S. Capitol. The facility offered fuel and major repairs. It possessed two hangars and two sod strips, 2,000 and 1,500 feet long. The 1941 bulletin warned of a nearby storage tank and radio towers, and sketches in later directories showed that these obstructions continued to flank the northwest end of the principal runway. Thiessen states that the facility closed during World War II, reopening shortly after its end.[94]

In the state directory for 1947, the owner was listed as Queen's Chapel Airport, Inc.; however, Henderson remained the manager until retiring in 1949. In that year, the operator became Maryland Flying Service and the manager was John E. Dorr, who received major assistance from his wife Debbie. The last directory found to list Queen's Chapel Airport, issued in June 1950, showed the modest layout generally unchanged from earlier descriptions. According to Thiessen, the airport closed between 1951 and 1953 (although aeronautical charts continued to include it as late as January 1955). Thiessen noted that the West Hyattsville Metro Station is now located at one end of the former airfield.[95]

Significance for Maryland air/space history: One of several small general aviation airports that formerly existed in the Maryland suburbs of Washington.
Relevant Years: 1930s – c. 1952 *Lat/Long*: 38-57-00 75-58-00
Map: ADC Md/Del 2000 *Num*: 20 *Grid*: A1 *Shows*: area

WEBB AIRPORT
Easton, Talbot County
1930s-1952

In 1930, Dorsey Webb established an airport on his farm about three miles east of Easton. Webb reportedly undertook the project as part of an understanding with Malcolm Hathaway, operator of Tred Avon Airport west of the city (see separate entry on page 47). Hathaway agreed to move his flying service to the new location, and to teach Webb to fly. According to local lore, Webb's objectives may have included the creation of a base for flying bootleg whiskey.[96]

The new airport was included in an Airway Bulletin as early as September 1931. Aeronautical publications listed the facility as Tred Avon Airport up until World War II, although it was known locally by the name of its owner. A directory issued for 1933 showed an aerial view of the 175-acre airport, which offered fuel, oil, limited repairs, and aircraft storage. The unpaved airfield was triangular in shape, its longest runway measuring 3,500 feet. Hathaway functioned as manager, and also continued his Tred Avon Flying Service, which soon became Chesapeake Air Ferries. His operations included scheduled flights to and from Baltimore, beginning in 1933 and lasting about a year.[97]

In 1942, Webb Airport closed for the duration of World War II. It was open again by at least 1946, although now overshadowed by the large new Easton Municipal Airport. A state directory issued in March 1947 showed that J. W. Dennis managed the facility for Webb. The runway layout was basically unchanged, although the longest was now listed as no more than 2,950 feet. Structures included one hangar measuring ninety-six feet square, three T-hangars, and an office. Webb Airport was also listed in a state directory issued in June 1950. In May 1952, however, a newspaper reported that it was being "plowed up for agricultural development," although the owner would retain a 600-foot landing strip for private use. How long this private strip may have remained operational is uncertain.[98]

The site of the former Webb Airport is on the east side of Black Dog Alley Road, north of its junction with Dover Road. Two surviving buildings are visible from the road. The smaller, a structure of the Quonset hut type, is believed to date from the airport's origin in 1930. The larger is a hangar that is currently incorporated into an industrial establishment. These buildings were the property of Norris Taylor, at least until recently. Cecil Gannon owns the farmland once occupied by the landing strips.[99]

Significance for Maryland air/space history: Talbot County's leading center of aeronautical activity before World War II, this airport reopened after the conflict to serve general aviation until the early 1950s.

Relevant years: 1930s-c. 1952
Lat/Long: 38-46-45n 76-01-30W
Map: ADC Md/Del 2000 *Num*: 21 *Grid*: F3 *Shows*: area

SERVICE FIELD
Pikesville, Baltimore County
1931-c. 1935

Service Field was a commercial airport that occupied a property of forty-six acres north of Baltimore, probably about a mile or less from the city limits. Airport directories published in 1931-34 stated that the irregularly-shaped field offered two landing strips: 2,205 by 536 feet, north-south; and 975 feet square, east-west. Lettering on the hangar roof displayed the airport's name. Servicing for aircraft was available only in daylight hours. Descriptions of the field's location were contradictory in some respects, but it was consistently described as one mile northwest of Curtiss-Wright Field (see separate entry on page 62). This would place it in the Pikesville area. Service Field was included in a Department of Commerce airport directory issued in September 1931. Since this seems to have been the earliest edition of that publication, it is possible that the airport was not new at the time. Service Field continued to be included in the commerce directories through September 1934 (no issue was found for 1935), and on aeronautical section charts dated through October 1934. The airport did not appear on the section chart dated August 1935, or in any subsequent charts or directories examined.[100]

Significance for Maryland air/space history: A general aviation airport that operated in the early 1930s.
Relevant years: 1931 – c. 1935   *Lat/Long*: 39-23N 76-40W
Map: ADC Md/Del 2000 *Num*: 15 *Grid*: E2 *Shows*: area

PRINCESS ANNE AIRPORT
Princess Anne, Somerset County
1932-c. 1933

Princess Anne Airport probably opened about 1932, since it was included in a Department of Commerce airport directory issued in September of that year, but not in the previous September's edition. The directory described it as a seventy-five-acre commercial facility located a mile and three quarters south-southwest of the town for which it was named. It was also south of the junction of Jones Creek and the Manokin River. The airport had three turf landing strips that were 2,800, 2,375, and 2,000 feet long. It serviced aircraft in the daytime only. A similar description appeared in a Commerce publication issued in June 1933. The facility was also featured in the Airport Directory Company's edition for that year, which favored it with an aerial photograph and listed

Charles C. Gelder as its manager. The airport was described as "on the Philadelphia-Norfolk airlane" and "just a short hop from all the large eastern cities." The publication noted that Princess Anne Airport was usable year round, since it was "practically free from ice, snow, and fog." Despite these reported advantages, the facility seems to have remained open only a short time. It did not appear in the commerce directory for September 1934, the aeronautical chart for October 1934, or in any later publication examined.[101]

Significance for Maryland air/space history: A short-lived airport of the early 1930s.
Relevant years: c. 1932 – c. 1933   *Lat/Long*: 38-11N 75-43W
Map: ADC Md/Del 2000 *Num*: 22 *Grid*: D4 *Shows*: area

CAPITOL AIRPORT
Bladensburg, Prince George's County
c. 1933-1941

According to a paper by Karin Thiessen, Capitol Airport's location in Bladensburg was near the Peace Cross, on River Road between Bladensburg Road and Kenilworth Avenue. Thiessen states that the facility was owned by Edward Stitt, who operated it, with his wife Evelyn, at least as early as 1933.[102] The earliest aeronautical section chart to include the airport was dated October 1934. A Department of Commerce bulletin issued in 1936 described Capitol Airport as a commercial airfield, five miles northeast of the national Capitol building for which it was named. The airport had two landing strips, 1,400 and 1,200 feet long, as well as at least one hangar and facilities for servicing in the daytime only. The Airport Directory Company's publications for 1939 and 1940 carried aerial photographs of Capitol Airport, and cautioned that it had a small house at the edge of one runway. In May 1941, a CAA bulletin described the facility's two sand-and-gravel strips as 2,400 and 1,800 feet long. The last aeronautical section chart to include the airport was dated in November 1941, and Thiessen reports that Mr. Stitt joined the military at the start of World War II. Capitol Airport did not reappear in available airport directories published during the postwar period.[103] Among the aviators using the field in its heyday was famed transatlantic pilot and barnstormer Clarence Chamberlain, who offered aerial rides to the public.[104]

Significance for Maryland air/space history: A general aviation airport that served the national capital area for about seven years prior to World War II.
Relevant Years: 1933, c. – 1941   *Lat/Long*: 38-56N 76-57W
Map: ADC Md/Del 2000 *Num*: 20 *Grid*: A1 *Shows*: area

SPRING HILL AIRPORT
Hebron, Wicomico County
c. 1934-present

Spring Hill Airport is located on Spring Hill Lane, roughly two miles northeast of Hebron. The airport occupies the site of an earlier facility of the same name. The original Spring Hill Airport appeared on aeronautical charts between October 1934 and November 1943. The first airport directory found that listed the facility was a Department of Commerce bulletin issued in January 1936. Spring Hill was described as a commercial airport that serviced aircraft in the daytime only. The airfield had three sod landing strips, the longest of which measured 1,780 feet. The last directory found that included the airport was issued in May 1941. That publication gave slightly more information, indicating that the airport covered twenty usable acres and had four individual hangars.[105] Spring Hill is reported to have been used by the military during the World War II era, according to the current owner, Mrs. Elizabeth A. Hastings. When she and her late husband purchased the property in 1983, Mrs. Hastings understood that the airport had been inactive for about forty years. The couple reopened the facility for private use. It has two turf runways, only one of which is currently in operation.[106]

Significance for Maryland air/space history: A small commercial airport of the 1930s and early 1940s, later reopened as a private-use facility.
Relevant years: c. 1934 – present
Lat/Long: 38-26-05N 75-39-04W
Map: ADC Md/Del 2000 *Num*: 27 *Grid*: D2 *Shows*: area

ENNIS AERODROME
Originally SALISBURY AIRPORT,
then DELMARVA AIRPORT
Salisbury, Wicomico County
1936-present

Ennis Aerodrome is located at 30365 Zion Road, two miles northeast of Salisbury and just north of the U.S. Route 13 bypass. Originally known as Salisbury Airport, the facility was established as a commercial enterprise in about 1936 by Fred E. Ennis, a veteran of World War I. In May 1936, Ennis and Col. William B. Tilghman, Jr., celebrated National Air Mail Week by taking an oath as temporary postal carriers and taking off from the field for a short mail flight. As described in a Department of Commerce bulletin issued earlier that year, the airport had two unpaved landing strips, the longest measuring 2,060 feet. A third runway had been added by 1937, and a fourth by 1938.[107]

When the large Salisbury Municipal Airport opened following World War II, Ennis changed the name of his facility to Delmarva Airport. A state airport directory issued in 1950 showed a layout with three turf runways. The airport continued as a commercial facility for general aviation until about 1958, when it shifted to private use. The Ennis family subsequently developed housing at the edges of the property, and reduced the number of runways to one. When the U.S. Route 13 bypass was constructed through the property in the early 1970s, the family sold the land south of the new highway and kept the northern portion containing the airfield. As late as the early 1980s, Fred Ennis continued to operate his 1929 Great Lakes biplane (still flown by his son, the airport's current owner). The open space now occupied by the airport is approximately fifty acres, and the single turf runway is 2,100 feet long. The name Ennis Aerodrome (Identifier 2MD4) was adopted in about 1992.[108]

Significance for Maryland air/space history: A private airport that served as a commercial facility and a local aviation center from about 1936 to about 1958.
Relevant years: 1936 - present
Lat/Long: 38-23-40N 75-33-26W
Map: ADC Md/Del 2000 *Num*: 27 *Grid*: F2 *Shows*: area

[Editor's note] In 1937, Japan invaded China, and Italy and Germany sent military aid to the rebel General Franco in the Spanish Civil War. The focus of Maryland's aviation activity switched back to military flying. At first, the emphasis was on training pilots. Smaller airports took the lead.

But in World War II Maryland was to be a center of large-scale aircraft production. Martin, Fairchild, ERCO, Bendix, and many smaller manufacturers turned out airplanes and parts. They attracted workers from all across the country. The establishment of big new military air bases, for the Army Air Forces at Camp Springs and the Navy along the Patuxent River, brought still more. Several new communities had to be built to house the new Marylanders. The big bases also spawned smaller satellite fields that were to serve as new municipal airports after the war. Finally, as existing laboratories in the District of Columbia were overwhelmed by wartime work, still more aviation research was moved into Maryland research facilities.

NAVAL AIR FACILITY ANNAPOLIS
(GREENBURY POINT)
Annapolis, Anne Arundel County
1937-1962

Naval Air Facility Annapolis was a seaplane base that occupied sixteen and one-half acres on the south shore of Greenbury Point. The site projects into the Severn River on the north side of the mouth of Carr Creek. It is downstream from the nearby David Taylor Research Center, and across the river from the United States Naval Academy.[1]

In 1937, construction of the base began in an effort to improve the flight training that squadron VN8-D5 provided to the Naval Academy (see separate entry on page 35). Builders created a concrete-paved rectangular area of 4,155 feet that included ramps, hangars, and space on which to taxi and park aircraft. The facility had fifteen buildings and about 280 assigned personnel. Emphasis on aviation instruction of midshipmen increased after World War II. Training utilized the combat information center aboard the carrier *Block Island*, towed to the facility in 1946 and later replaced by the USS APL-5. In 1947,

the base received the designation Naval Air Activity, and three years later it was recommissioned as a Naval Air Facility (NAF).[2]

During the 1950s, the ability of the NAF's seaplanes to provide realistic, modern training was questioned; however, attempts to acquire land for an airfield as a replacement were unsuccessful. Instead, a decision was made to transfer the functions of the installation to a naval facility at Andrews Air Force Base. The NAF at Greenbury Point officially closed on January 17, 1962. The property was transferred to the Naval Academy to use for storage and supply, and is now part of Naval Station Annapolis. A recent aerial photograph seems to indicate that the major buildings remained intact.[3]

Significance for Maryland air/space history: A naval air facility that fulfilled a training mission for about twenty-five years.
Relevant years: 1937 – 1962   *Lat/Long*: 38-59N 76-28W
Map: ADC Md/Del 2000 *Num*: 21 *Grid*: A1 *Shows*: area

GLEN BURNIE-WHIPP AIRPORT AND SEAPLANE BASE
Glen Burnie, Anne Arundel County
c. 1938-1950s

Glen Burnie-Whipp Airport was located about one mile east of Glen Burnie, between Furnace Branch Road and the northwest side of Marley Creek. Ed Whipp ran the facility and lived on its premises, beginning at least as early as 1938. The airport was closed or restricted during World War II, when Whipp flew Martin seaplanes as a test pilot. Robert E. Whipp was identified by his full name in the first airport directory found that included the facility, which was published for 1945.[4] The airport occupied 165 acres, with buildings that included a small administration building, a restaurant, and a hangar. A pictorial history of Glen Burnie, which shows the hangar as a large barrel-roofed structure of corrugated metal, includes scenes of convivial gatherings at the facility. In addition to the seaplane ramp, there were three turf landing strips, the longest of which was the northeast-southwest runway measuring 3,000 feet. The airport operated in daylight only, offering fuel, repairs, charter service, and aircraft sales. June 1950 saw the dedication of Friendship International, not more than five miles to the southwest. Thirty flying club airplanes took off from the small airport to mark the opening day of this huge new neighbor, "but Friendship essentially put Whipp out of business."[5] Another factor in the small airport's demise was increasing local development and the consequent rise in land values. The airport remained on aeronautical charts at least as late as February 1953, but closed later in the decade. The property became the Country Club Estates. In 1960, state authorities issued a commercial airport list that did not include Glen Burnie-Whipp; however, it showed that Whipp was now the manager of a facility for sea- and landplanes on the other side of the Chesapeake Bay (see Tilghman-Whipp Airport on page 120).

Significance for Maryland air/space history: An airport and seaplane base for general aviation that operated from the late 1930s into the 1950s.
Relevant years: c. 1938– 1950s   *Lat/Long:* 39-10-00N 76-36-15W
Map: ADC Md/Del 2000 *Num:* 15 *Grid:* E5 *Shows:* area

ENGINEERING AND RESEARCH CORPORATION (ERCO) PLANT
Riverdale, Prince George's County (PG: 68-22)
1938 – c. 1960s

The former plant of the Engineering and Research Corporation (ERCO) occupies a property of 11.55 acres

A gabled hangar at the still-rural Wipp Airport, Glen Burnie. Photo courtesy of the Ann Arrundell County Historical Society.

at 6501 Lafayette Avenue in Riverdale. The site is north of Tuckerman Road and east of the Baltimore and Ohio railway line.[6]

In 1932, Henry A. Berliner established ERCO in Washington, D.C. Early products included machine tools, such as a profiling device to assist in manufacturing airplane propellers. The company took a decisive turn when it was joined by Frederick E. Weik, a talented engineer with the National Advisory Committee for Aeronautics. Weik had already designed his W-1 and W-1A as possible prototypes of a personal airplane that could be flown safety by pilots with relatively little training. By further developing this concept for ERCO, he created the experimental Model 310, which first flew in 1937. This, in turn became the basis of the prototype of the first Ercoupe, the Model 415C, completed in late 1939. In the fall of 1938, meanwhile, the company moved to the new Riverdale site, which originally comprised more that 230 acres.[7]

The Riverdale plant was reportedly designed by ERCO's own staff engineers. The large main building, which faces south, has a two-story front section with a smooth concrete block exterior. Its Art Deco façade is ornamented by two wide, horizontal bands of glass block. Entrance is through a central projection, three bays wide. Behind the front section, which contains office space, is a spacious brick-and-steel factory area under a saw-tooth roof and clerestory windows. Single-story service buildings stand to the east of the main structure. Originally, the complex also included an airfield (see entry on ERCO Field on page 71).[8]

ERCO completed the prototype of the Model 415C in late 1939, and the highly innovative plane received its federal production certificate in January 1940. The Ercoupe's most notable feature was a two-control system using only ailerons and elevators (although rudders were optional on some models). The all-metal aircraft was supremely easy to fly, designed to protect against stalling, and equipped with a modern type of tricycle landing gear. The Ercoupe attracted strong consumer interest, but only 112 were manufactured before World War II intervened. One of these was purchased by the Army for use in developing the Jet-Assisted Takeoff (JATO) system. At a California airfield on August 23, 1941, it became the first aircraft ever to achieve a JATO takeoff.[9]

During the war years, ERCO manufactured gun turrets for Navy patrol bombers, components that were credited with reducing losses to enemy fighter attacks. Urgent demand for these and other company products, such propeller profilers, raised employment at the Riverdale factory to nearly 4,000. The influx of workers led to construction of the since-demolished Calvert Homes housing project across the railway. The boom also prompted expansion of the plant's floor space from about 42,000 to 92,000 square feet. This was accomplished by extension of the main building and construction of a new one, built by the government's Defense Plant Corporation and later acquired by ERCO.[10]

With the return of peace, ERCO resumed fast-paced production of several Ercoupe models. An aggressive sales campaign, including department store displays, produced a surge of orders. Contrary to expectations, however, the U.S. market for light planes became quickly saturated. ERCO diversified its line to include such items as school bus bodies, rocket launchers, and flight simulators. In 1948, it also switched to manufacturing Ercoupes and their parts for Sanders Aviation, rather than selling them directly. The last of the 5,140 Ercoupes built at Riverdale was completed in January 1952. Nevertheless, the demand for the easy-to-fly planes continued. Other companies later produced Ercoupes as late as 1970, although some of these were marketed as "Aircoupes."[11]

In the 1950s, meanwhile, ERCO was acquired by the American Car and Foundry Corporation, or ACF (later ACF Industries). During that decade, ERCO continued to produce such products as simulators and missile-related equipment, including material that supported the Korean war effort. ACF Industries eventually designated ERCO its Flight Simulation Division. It appears that this division left the Riverdale plant in 1965, when another company assumed its contract responsibilities. By 1985, several federal agencies were occupying the Lafayette Avenue plant, although ACF Industries was still the owner. The property now belongs to the University of Maryland.[12]

In 1986, the Keeper of the National Register of Historic Places determined that the ERCO plant and airfield were not then eligible for entry upon the register because they did not possess the exceptional historical significance required of sites less than fifty years old. In 2002, however, the Maryland Historical Trust recommended that the main building was now eligible for the

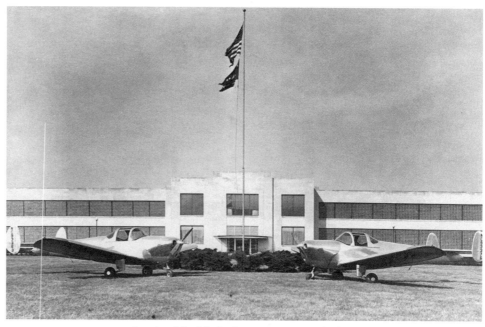

A pair of freshly built Ercoupes outside the ERCO Plant in Riverdale. Photo courtesy of the College Park Aviation Museum, ERCO Collection, Dunn.

register. Reasons cited included its association with production of the Ercoupe and of World War II material, as well as its status as a rare example of Art Deco industrial design in Prince George's County.[13]

Significance for Maryland air/space history: The site of the production of a unique light airplane, and of other aeronautical products, including material that supported the war effort in World War II and the Korean conflict.

Relevant years: 1938 – 1960s   *Lat/Long*: 38-58N 76-55W
Map: ADC Md/Del 2000   *Num*: 20   *Grid*: A1   *Shows*: area

ERCO FIELD
Riverdale, Prince George's County
1942/3-mid-1950s

ERCO Field was located in Riverdale on the grounds of the former Engineering and Research Corporation (ERCO) plant at 6501 Lafayette Avenue (see separate entry on page 70). ERCO was originally established in the District of Columbia, but moved to the Riverdale site in 1938. The company received a production certificate for its innovative light airplane, the Ercoupe, in January 1940 and began early flights at College Park Airport. Between 1942 and 1943, ERCO's own airfield began operations. ERCO used the airfield to test the planes and to send them off for delivery.[14]

Aeronautical section charts began including ERCO Field in November 1943, but no directories were found that described the airport before 1945. Publications for the 1945-47 period show that it had three sod runways, ranging in length from 3,600 to 2,650 feet, in a triangular configuration. The airfield lay just north and east of the plant area. In addition to serving its company, ERCO field offered fuel to transient pilots at least as early as 1947. By 1948, it was taking on the aspect of a full-service general aviation airport under the management of Sanders Aviation, which had also become the marketer of the Ercoupe line. The airport had nine T-hangars and two larger ones, as well as an office and sandwich shop. Although the longest landing strip was now replaced by a taxiway, the two remaining runways were paved for 1,500 feet from the point of their intersection. These runways were oriented roughly north-south and east-west, forming a wide "V" pointing toward the southeast.[15]

Flight instruction and aircraft rental were offered at ERCO Field in the postwar years, and an Ercoupe Flying Club was active during the era of Sanders management. Aircraft production at the Riverdale plant ended in January 1952, and ERCO was acquired by the ACF corporation at some point in the early 1950s. ERCO Field appeared on an aeronautical chart as late as July 1955, but appears to have closed about that time. The runways remained visible into the 1980s, but have since given way to building projects.[16]

Significance for Maryland air/space history: The airfield of the manufacturer of a distinctive series of light airplanes.

Relevant years: c. 1938 – c. mid-1950s
Lat/Long: 38-58-15N   76-55-45W
Map: ADC Md/Del 2000   *Num*: 20   *Grid*: A1   *Shows*: area

GLENN L. MARTIN STATE AIRPORT
Originally GLENN L. MARTIN AIRPORT
Middle River, Baltimore County (BA-2081)
1938-present

Martin State Airport occupies a tract that is roughly bounded on the north by Eastern Boulevard, on the east by Frog Mortar Creek, and on the west by Stansbury Creek and by Wilson Point Road. The facility originated as part of a manufacturing complex that Glenn L. Martin began to construct in 1929. (Most of the other surviving elements of the complex are now beyond the airport's borders: see separate entries on Glenn L. Martin Plants No. 1 and No. 2 on pages 56 and 79.) Built during 1938-41, the airport replaced a smaller airfield that was just south of the present intersection of Wilson Point Road and Eastern Boulevard. The facility was used for flight testing and for takeoff of new aircraft for delivery.

Above: Terminal and tower at Martin Airport, March 1945, with last production Martin B-26F medium bomber.

Right: Terminal and Hangars 4-6 (still in wartime camouflage) at Martin Airport, c. 1950. A Martin P4M Navy patrol plane warms up for takeoff.

Photos courtesy of the Glenn L. Martin Maryland Aviation Museum.

Like most of the rest of the original Martin complex, the airport was designed by the distinguished architect, Albert Kahn. Its features include a brick-and-concrete terminal, built in the "Streamlined Moderne" style, which is topped by a control tower. Because it is set on a hill, this structure has four stories at its rear elevation, but only three at its front, which faces the runway. The terminal is flanked by a pair of very large original buildings arranged to form a giant "V." Both of which are divided into three equal hangars, also built into the hillside, giving access on one side to basement offices and storerooms and on the other to the airport apron. Another Kahn-designed structure on the present airport property was the Seaplane Hangar at Strawberry Point, an important element of the Martin complex in view of the company's role in flying boat development. This hangar has been demolished, although the seaplane ramp survives. The site is the headquarters of the Maryland State Police Medevac service.[17] Parked on a nearby apron are the historic aircraft displays of the Glenn L. Martin Maryland Aviation Museum.

In response to an offer by the Martin company, the Maryland Air National Guard in 1956 began building a hangar and support facilities on a twenty-five-acre tract on the north side of the field. In the 1975, the company (by then Martin Marietta as the result of a merger) sold the part of its Middle River property containing the airport, comprising some 750 acres east of Wilson Point Road. The buyer was the state of Maryland, which intended the new Martin State Airport to relieve non-airline traffic from Friendship International. Four years later, the Air National Guard broke ground for a new 42-acre Multiple Facilities Complex at the airport. This installation was in 1982 designated Warfield Air National Guard base in honor of Maj. Gen. Ted Warfield. Today, the Martin State Airport continues to serve both general aviation and military aircraft with facilities that include a runway 6,996 feet long. Hangar No. 5 of the original complex houses the displays and archives of the Glenn L. Martin Maryland Aviation Museum.[18]

As historic sites surveys have noted, numerous structures have been added since the original complex was completed in 1941, and certain alterations have been made to the extant original buildings. In 1999, however, a review by the Maryland Historical Trust concluded that the airport, together with Martin Plant No. 1, should be

Annapolis Aero Service hangar, fuel pumps, and transient aircraft parking area at Lee Airport, 1988. Photo by Ashish Solanki, courtesy of the Maryland Aviation Administration.

eligible for the National Register of Historic Places.[19]

Significance for Maryland air/ space history: A civil/military airport with historical significance that includes design by a noted architect and association with an important aircraft manufacturing plant.
Relevant years: 1938 - present *Lat/Long*: 39-19-32N 76-24-50W
Map: ADC Md/Del 2000 *Num*: 16 *Grid*: B3 *Shows*: airport

LEE AIRPORT
Annapolis (Edgewater), Anne Arundel County
1939-present

Lee Airport is located at Edgewater, about five miles south of Annapolis. The facility is on the east bank of Beards Creek, south of the South River, and west of Solomons Island Road. The seventy-nine-acre property belongs to Mary Carroll Lee, daughter of the original owner, Charles Carroll Lee. The airport began operating in 1939 or 1940, with two turf runways. It closed during World War II, like most small airports in coastal areas, and then reopened in 1945.[20]

A state directory described Lee Airport in October 1946 as having one sixty-by-seventy-foot hangar with an office and shop, as well as a thirty-by-twenty-foot restaurant. The facility offered charters, student flying, fuel, and minor repairs. Its 2,700-foot primary landing strip ran northwest-southeast, with the northwest end near Beards Creek, an orientation similar to the single runway in operation today. There was also a short northeast-southwest runway, which by 1950 had been extended to 1,800 feet. By 1954, one of these runways had been abandoned for agricultural production.[21]

In June 1954, a newspaper reported that Lee Airport would close at the end of the month, despite the efforts of a citizens' committee to save it. The article explained that operation of the facility, under six different mangers since its opening, had been generally unprofitable. The State Aviation Commission was described as powerless to assist due to a cut in its budget. The airport may have won a brief reprieve, but by 1955 it had entered a period of closure.[22]

Lee Airport reopened within one or two years under the management of Mrs. Florence Parlett. During the late 1950s, the facility proved its worth for an Air Force C-47 pilot who landed safely there after losing an engine. The airport received a boost in the early 1960s when the Baltimore Aero Service maintenance facility moved there following the closure of Harbor Field. Improvements during that decade included lighting and paving for the single runway. In 1978, the airport figured in "The Seduction of Joe Tynan," a film starring Meryl Streep, who taxied an aircraft with the aid of Mrs. Parlett's off-camera coaching.[23]

In a work published in 1984, John F. R. Scott, Jr., noted that Lee Airport was surviving, without state or federal aid, in the face of rising prices and encroaching development. He praised Mrs. Parlett for her part in providing Annapolis with an airport for personal, business, and emergency uses. By 1987, the facility was being managed by the brothers Tom and Donald Parlett, who were involved in a dispute with nearby residents over how much of the land could be used for aviation. Although ruling against the Parletts, zoning officer Robert C. Wilcox called the case typical of controversies nationwide as "increased population demands meet head-on with shrinking, irreplaceable resources."[24]

Despite such trends, Lee Airport operates today as the only airport in the state capital's immediate vicinity. As of April 2002, one hundred and fifty-three aircraft were based at the facility. Operations during the preceding twelve months totaled 64,000, including 3,000 by military aircraft.[25]

Significance for Maryland air/space history: An airport that has served general aviation, with two interruptions, since before World War II.
Relevant years: 1939 - present *Lat/Long*: 38-56-34N 76-34-09W
Map: ADC Md/Del 2000 *Num*: 20 *Grid*: F1 *Shows*: airport

WASHINGTON EXECUTIVE/ HYDE FIELD
Clinton, Prince George's County
1940-present

Washington Executive/Hyde Field is located on Piscataway Road, about two miles southwest of Clinton and roughly six miles southeast of the District of Columbia. It was founded by Arthur C. Hyde, who had

interests in other airfields (see entry on Congressional Airport on page 40). Hyde Field opened in 1939 or 1940, and began appearing on aeronautical charts in September of the latter year. The Airport Directory Company's edition for 1940 indicated that it was a new facility, describing it as a sod field 3,950 feet by 2,600 feet.[26]

During World War II, the airfield reportedly became a base for the Civil Air Patrol, an organization in which Hyde held the rank of major. A State directory published in 1947 indicated that the airport now had an office building with a restaurant and lounge. Its assets also included twenty-eight hangars, mostly of the "T" design. The two paved runways, one of which was more than 3,000 feet in length, were set in an "L" configuration. The shorter runway closed in 1990.[27]

By 1996, Hyde was no longer the owner, and the airport had adopted its current name. As of September 28, 2001, flight operations for the preceding twelve months totaled 38,000. The terrorist attacks earlier that month resulted in security measures that affected Washington Executive/Hyde perhaps more than any other airport. After two periods of closure, authorities cleared the facility to reopen in September 2002, although still under special restrictions applying to the three small airports nearest Washington. The airport received a federal grant to help pay for security improvements that included a perimeter fence.[28]

Significance for Maryland air/space history: A general aviation airport that has provided services for more than sixty years.
Relevant years: 1940-present *Lat/Long*: 38-44-58N 76-55-58W
Map: ADC Md/Del 2000 *Num*: 20 *Grid*: A3 *Shows*: airport

TANEYTOWN AIRPORT
Taneytown, Carroll County
1941-1950

Taneytown Airport was located almost three miles west-northwest of the town for which it was named, on the north side of Route 32 (now Maryland Route 140). Landmarks included an automobile graveyard adjacent to the facility's southwest corner. On July 27, 1941, some 3,000 persons attended the airport's dedication, which was celebrated with parachute jumping and stunt flying that involved thirty airplanes.[29] No airport directories were found that listed the facility before the Haire Publishing Company's *Airport Directory* for 1945. That publication identified the owner as W. Z. Fair, and the operator as Robert W. Smith. *Decker's Airport Guide* for 1946 stated that there were two broad sod runways, 2,200 and 1,900 feet in length. Repairs were available, except on Sundays, and meals were served between 10 a.m. and 8 p.m. Aviators staying overnight could expect to pay fifty cents and up for tie-downs. A State directory issued in June 1950 showed that the airport's runways were arranged in an "X" configuration, with the southwest end of the longer strip close to the highway. The Taneytown School of Aeronautics was listed as operator, and Carroll J. Myers as manager. This 1950 directory also reported the demise of Taneytown Airport, since the pages describing the facility were stamped "closed."[30]

Significance for Maryland air/space history: A general aviation airport that operated about nine years, beginning in 1941.
Relevant years: 1941-1950 *Lat/Long*: 39-41-00N 77-13-3W
Map: ADC Md/Del 2000 *Num*: 5 *Grid*: D4 *Shows*: area

COLUMBIA AIR CENTER
Originally RIVERSIDE FIELD,
also known as CROOM AIRPORT
Croom, Prince George's County
1941-1956

The site of the former Columbia Air Center is on Croom Airport Road, about three miles east of Croom in Patuxent River Park. The airport was established by the Cloud Club, an organization of African American aviators formed in 1940. The group initially operated at an airport in Virginia, but racial discrimination there soon led them to plan an airfield of their own. The site chosen was 450 acres near Croom that had been used for potato farming. On behalf of the club, John W. Greene, Jr., and Dr. Coleridge M. Gill leased the property from Mrs. Rebecca Fisher.[31]

Known initially as Riverside Field, the new facility was the state's first airport to be operated by African Americans. Its manager, John Greene, was a pioneer black aviator who had learned to fly in 1922, before the era of federal pilot certification. He received his private pilot license in 1929, and later qualified as a transport pilot. Greene was also certificated as an engine and airplane mechanic in 1936, and became a teacher in that field. His association with the Cloud Club followed a move to Washington, D.C., where he organized a program in aviation mechanics at Phelps Vocational High School.[32]

Riverside Field opened in February 1941. In August, an air show there drew 800 spectators, about 150 of whom went aloft for rides. A parachute demonstration by Greene almost ended badly when a crosswind swept him into a wooded area, but he escaped injury. During this same general period, students from the Civilian Pilot Training Program at Howard University did their flight training at the field. This program may have continued there after the Pearl Harbor attack in December 1941, but wartime restrictions halted private

flying at Riverside. The Navy used the field for training purposes during the conflict.[33]

With the return of peace, the renamed Columbia Air Center continued to provide opportunities for African American fliers in a time of persisting segregation. In July 1946, the airfield consisted of 130 usable acres with seven marked landing strips (these were later increased to eight). The airport had one sixty-by-100-foot hangar, one forty-foot-square hangar, and a twenty-foot-square office building. The facility operated in daylight only, offering fuel, minor repairs, charter service, and a flying school attended by twenty-five students. The management's fleet included a Fairchild PT-19 trainer, Piper J3L, Aeronca Champion, and Aeronca L3. Postwar activities also included Civil Air Patrol operations. The CAP's first black unit in the national capital area, the Columbia Squadron, was formed at the airport.[34]

After John Greene's retirement, the airport was managed by Charles Wren and by Herbert Jones, who trained at the Tuskegee Institute after World War II. Closure of the field in 1956 followed the loss of its lease after the heirs of Mrs. Fisher decided to sell the land. In 1959, the property became part of the new Patuxent River Watershed Park. Today, a sign at the site provides historical information about Columbia Air Center, but little else remains besides a fuel pump and an empty field.[35]

Significance for Maryland air/space history: The state's first black-operated airport, this facility provided access to aviation for African Americans in an era of discrimination.
Relevant years: 1941 - 1956 *Lat/Long*: 38-45N 76-42W
Map: ADC Md/Del 2000 *Num*: 20 *Grid*: D3 *Shows*: area

BELTSVILLE AIRPORT
Beltsville, Prince George's County
1941-1981

Beltsville Airport was located about five miles east of the town for which it was named, and some three miles northwest of Bowie. The site is within the eastern portion of the Henry A. Wallace Beltsville Agricultural Research Center (BARC), northeast of Springfield Road and south of Powder Mill Road.[36]

The airport appears to have begun as one of the intermediate landing fields established by the Department of Commerce along the Atlanta-New York Airway. Airway Bulletins issued by commerce between January 1931 and January 1936 described this as a rectangular sod field, 3,000 by 500 feet, with a rotating beacon and green course light that flashed an identifying code. The field was designated number 57 in 1931, and then later as number 57B. A series of aeronautical section

Continued on page 78

From the Oral History Files...

The African American Aviation Experience in Maryland

An interview with Herbert Jones
by Dr. Barry A. Lanman

For many who have dreamed about becoming pilots, the considerations of money, time and the appropriate training have often been the limiting factors that kept them earth-bound. However, until the later part of the twenty-first century, African Americans faced one additional hurdle: segregation. Maryland, like the vast majority of states, generally excluded minorities from pilot training and from the use of airport facilities. It was the exception rather than the rule when an African American was granted the privilege of flight. Thus, John Greene and Herb Jones are aviation pioneers who helped Maryland aviation become more inclusive.

John Greene and the Columbia Air Center

Born in 1901, Greene lived in Georgia as a youth. To earn a degree in mechanical engineering, he moved to Virginia and attended the Hampton Institute. Greene then obtained a private pilot's license in 1929 and by 1933 had a commercial and

John Greene (far right) with fellow members of the Cloud Club, circa 1950s. Herb Jones is sitting in the cockpit of Vultee BT-13.
Photo courtesy of Herbert Jones.

transport license. While C. Alfred Anderson was the first, John Greene was the second African American to obtain this level of certification.

Herb Jones was interviewed about his association with John Greene and the ways in which he advanced aviation for minorities in Maryland. *"You have to realize at that time Black Americans were not in...aviation and they were systematically kept out because of what was going on in our country [segregation] at that time.*

"Los Angles, Chicago and Tuskegee and even Boston were areas...that supported Black aviation." When asked how Greene came to Maryland, Herbert Jones stated *"Well, some people [in] the Cloud Club [an African American group of Maryland, District of Columbia and Virginia flyers], especially John R. Pinkett...knew about Greene and they wrote a letter [October 15th, 1941] and asked him to come down here."* After Greene received his aviation mechanics certification, the opportunity of a job teaching airplane mechanics and an offer from the Cloud Club attracted him to the state he called home for the balance of his life. *"So, John Greene opened doors for people to get into aviation. For instance, the fellas who came back from World War II were pilots and wanted to fly. In most cases, they were not welcome at...airports, to the extent where they...wouldn't even rent them airplanes. So, by John Greene opening up his airport [Columbia Air Center] he made it possible for these guys to fly.*

"After World War Two, it [Old Riverside Airport] became Columbia Air Center when Dr. Gill [their financial backer] and Mr. Greene took over the operation of it." The airfield has also been called "Croom Airfield," from the road that led to the airport.

Columbia Air Center *"was used for commercial purposes. It was used as a flight school and also a full service airport like any other airport. They sold gasoline, they did maintenance...ground school...had flight instructors. And that's characteristic of most general aviation airports...I think the idea was that this was not only an airport, but a recreational place for people. They planned to have horseback riding, swimming, canoeing and all that sort of thing, but flying was the primary purpose of it...Of course, the runways were all sod runways... They had to spend money to keep the runways usable...The longest runway was 3,300 feet and the runways were about seventy-five feet wide... Eventually, they had eight [runways], I believe."*

During World War II, the Navy took over the use of the field. However, in 1946, Greene resumed control and initially had about twenty-five student pilots. Both African American and white students trained at Columbia Air Center. By the mid-1950s, according to Jones, there were no more than thirty-five African American pilots in Maryland.

"The first time I met John Greene was over at Phelps's Vocational Junior High School when he was running an airplane mechanics course at night...I noticed that he was a very quiet man and he was very large in stature. He was a very intense sort of per-

son. . .I came to the conclusion that he was a good instructor because he was able to impart information over to other people and I knew that he had a tremendous interest in aviation and he had an interest in aviation sciences. . . He [eventually] wrote a manual for the Auxiliary Coast Guard dealing with navigation, a new system of navigation."

Jones worked for Greene as an instructor and as an airport manager from 1949-1952. He is proud to say that from the early 1940s until it closed circa 1956, due to the loss of the lease on the land, the Columbia Air Center had a perfect record: no fatalities! Currently, the site is now the Patuxent River Park in Prince George's County.

Herbert Jones (center) remains active in aviation. Photo courtesy of Herbert Jones.

Herb Jones' Career in Aviation

Herb Jones obtained his aviation training in the Civilian Pilot Training Program at the Coffee School of Aeronautics during World War II. While there, he progressed to aerobatics and flew the Waco UPS-7. After the war, he returned to the Tuskegee Institute in Alabama on the GI Bill and took the instructor's course and a commercial pilot's course. He spent three years in the Army Air Corps and six years in the reserves. Jones then came back to Maryland and worked for Greene at the Columbia Air Center.

Following that opportunity, he stated *"I got a job as a corporate pilot flying a Cessna 195 between Ocean City, New Jersey and Savannah, Georgia. . .then I became involved in the operation of large transport type airplanes. . .My brother-in-law and my neighbor and myself formed a corporation called International Air Association. . . The idea was to acquire a transport type airplane. . .and we purchased a Douglas DC-7. . .Then we leased a Vickers Viscount [that formerly belonged] to singer Ray Charles."* Jones' company flew passengers to the Bahamas during the 1970s. However, because of rising fuel costs and competition from Eastern Airlines, the venture ended. In 1980, he formed Metropolitan Aviation based in Clinton, Maryland. To this day, the company serves as a flight training school and rents airplanes at Washington Executive Airport-Hyde Field, Prince George's County.

Jones Reflects on his Achievements and the Advancements of Minorities in Aviation

"We were the first people of color to operate a large transport type aircraft. . .About five years after us, there was another outfit called Air Atlanta, where they operated 727s. But, we were the first ones of color to operate large transport type airplanes."

In the late 1980s, "Maryland held a fair at BWI airport where they had Black History Month and they recognized. . . those in the aviation community who made contributions." Jones was recognized for a variety of accomplishments including his work on a program with Morgan State University and

the OBAP (Organization of Black Airline Pilots). In 1987, he was also instrumental in forming the Cloud Club II in honor of the original Cloud Club. He is still involved in the East Coast Chapter of the Tuskegee Airmen and he takes students to events held by the Coalition of Black Air Traffic Controllers. He has also received awards from the Black Pilots of America and the National Capital Wing of the Civil Air Patrol. It is his contention to promote, stimulate and provide opportunities for all young people interested in flight.

Jones is very proud of serving in the Civil Air Patrol and for flying search and rescues missions. *"We were flying Air Force airplanes, L-5s, L-14s, L16s and BT-13s. . .There was one mission where we were looking for a B-52 that crashed in Cumberland with a nuclear device on board. . .that stands out in my memory!"*

Jones retired from the Civil Air Patrol in 1972 as a Lieutenant Colonel.

Speaking about his current endeavor, Jones stated: *"we're about the only minority-owned flight school in this area, in Maryland. . . .We teach people primary flight training. We carry them through to their private license, and if they want, we take them through instrument training, to the commercial and to the CFI, which is Certified Flight Instructor."*

When Jones was asked about the future of minorities in aviation, he responded *emphatically, "I see that in the next few years there won't be a matter of black aviation or white aviation. . . it will be a matter of people who qualify for particular jobs. . .We've reached a stage now where people are not too concerned about the race. . .so I feel in the near future black aviation will not be an issue by itself. It will just be aviation."*

Herbert Jones, oral history interview, September 19, 2002, MHT/OHC 002 (MD-AVC) 004, 56p.

Right: An early-model B-26 taking off, July 1941, with the glass monitors of the nearly-completed Martin Plant No. 2 in background.

Below: In contrast to Martin Plant No. 1, the higher final-assembly bays at Plant No. 2 are on the south end of the building, with machine shops and preliminary assembly in lower sections to the north. The roof retains traces of wartime camouflage. Photos courtesy of the Glenn L. Martin Maryland Aviation Museum.

charts that began in May 1932 listed the field through December 1935. Operation was probably discontinued in 1936, since the facility did not appear on the chart dated in December of that year, or in the commerce directory for 1937. It seems, however, that the site or its close vicinity was later chosen for development as a defense facility.[37]

In March 1941, the Roosevelt Administration announced approval of an appropriation for the Works Progress Administration to construct an airfield at the Agricultural Research Center. The Civil Aeronautics Administration was also to contribute $125,000, bringing the total cost to $568,498. The facility's purpose was to train units of the District of Columbia National Guard and the Naval Reserve.[38] A tract of 186 acres was acquired from the Forest Service for the project at about this time. In 1942, the Civilian Conservation Corps provided labor to clear the land and prepare the site for its wartime role.[39]

The new Navy auxiliary field was appearing on aeronautical section charts by November 1944. The earliest airport directories found that included it were issued for 1946. These indicated that the facility, still operated by the Navy, had a 4,000-foot runway.[40] When military use ceased, the Civil Aeronautics Administration wished to take over the airport; however, the Department of Agriculture was granted control.[41] In May 1947, a newspaper article described the airport as having two runways. The article also reported that the Department of Agriculture had abandoned the facility due to the persistent bird hazard to aircraft operations there.[42] Any such closure, however, was not permanent. Reported uses of the Beltsville Airport included testing for pesticides and

crop dusting, local university flying club activities, and Reserve Officer Training Corps flight instruction.[43] One source even suggests that the Central Intelligence Agency was the facility's real operator.[44]

Directories published in the 1960s reported that the airport's runways were 4,400 and 3,960 feet in length.[45] By 1979, it appears that only one of these was in operation.[46] Beltsville Airport was closed permanently in about 1981. This was evidently done to avoid possible disruption of electronic testing at the nearby Goddard Space Flight Center.[47] By the late 1990s, the Plant Sciences Institute was using the former airport for a quarantine area.[48] Parts of the runway surface are reported to be extant.[49]

Significance for Maryland air/space history: A government airfield that served a variety of civil and military purposes over a period of more than fifty years.
Relevant years: 1941–1981 *Lat/Long*: 39-01-30N 76-49-15W
Map: ADC Md/Del 2000 *Num*: 15 *Grid*: A6 *Shows*: area

GLENN L. MARTIN
AIRCRAFT COMPANY PLANT NO. 2
Later MIDDLE RIVER DEPOT
Middle River, Baltimore County (BA-2824)
1941-present

The Glenn L. Martin Company Plant No. 2 was built in 1940-41 when demands for military aircraft surpassed the capacity of Plant No. 1 (see separate entry on page 56). This flood of orders resulted from the outbreak of World War II in Europe and the growing prospect of U.S. involvement. The federal government financed construction of the complex, which was located at the northeast corner of the Martin company's Middle River tract. The sole function of Plant No. 2 was production of Martin's B-26 Marauder Medium Bomber, of which 3,572 were manufactured here, and another 1,585 in Nebraska. The advanced aerodynamic design of the B-26 gave it great speed. The aircraft also possessed innovative features such as a plexiglass nose cone for the bombardier, an all-electric bomb release mechanism, and power-operated gun turrets. Although criticized as unsafe early in the war, the Marauder proved itself as a highly effective weapon for U.S. and Allied forces.[50]

In his design for Plant No. 2, noted architect Albert Kahn recycled elements used successfully in the original Middle River complex. The core of the former B-26 factory is a large structure formed by six connected buildings with concrete foundations and steel frames. This structure has concrete-block exterior walls, while an original administration building and storage facility have brick walls. There is extensive use of glass in wall surfaces and rooftop monitors.[51]

No longer needing Plant No. 2 after the war, the Martin company released it to the Army in 1946. In the following year, the federal government took possession of the almost-eighty-acre property for public use. During the 1950s aircraft production was resumed with Martin as tenant. Now known as the Middle River Depot, the complex at 2800 Eastern Boulevard is used by the Army as a storage and distribution point, and by the Navy as a warehouse site and Naval Reserve Industrial Facility. Although new buildings have been added since 1945, site surveys have found that the complex remains historically significant. The factors cited include: architectural excellence, a key role in wartime production, and association with the enterprises of aviation pioneer Glenn L. Martin. In 1999, an evaluation by the Maryland Historical

Trust concluded that the Plant No. 2 should be eligible for the National Register of Historic Places.[52]

Significance for Maryland air/space history: An industrial plant notable for its design and for its production of one of the important American-made bombers of World War II.
Relevant years: 1941-present   *Lat/Long*: 39-19N 76-24W
Map: ADC Md/Del 2000   *Num*: 16   *Grid*: B3   *Shows*: area

AERO ACRES and
RELATED HOUSING AREAS
Middle River, Baltimore County
1941-present

Aero Acres is a residential area between Martin Boulevard on the north and Orems Road on the south. It is probably the best known and most significant of several such neighborhoods originally developed for employees of the Glenn L. Martin Company. The outbreak of World War II in 1939 triggered urgent orders for military aircraft produced at Martin's Middle River establishment. The result was a rapid growth of the workforce that far outpaced available local housing, creating massive traffic jams as employees struggled to reach the plant from Baltimore. As a remedy, Martin first tried constructing conventional apartments near the plant, but these proved too expensive for most workers to rent. The

House in Stansbury Estates, identical to 999 others in Aero Acres and Victory Villa, built of two-and-three-quarter-inch-thick Cemesto panels fitted horizontally into a light wooden frame. Photo courtesy of the Glenn L. Martin Maryland Aviation Museum.

company then contracted for 600 identical, low-cost houses, built in 1941. Designed by Skidmore, Owings & Merrill, the structures measured only twenty-eight by twenty-four feet. Their plan was efficient, however, including two bedrooms, a bathroom, a dining alcove, and a living room with a pair of picture windows. The walls were constructed with panels of Cemesto, a new synthetic material made of pressed fibers coated with asbestos, which was able to provide both an interior and an exterior surface, and was designed for ease of construction. The houses were built in two new neighborhoods near the Martin establishment. One of these, Stansbury Estates, occupied the Wilson's Point peninsula across Cow Pens Creek from the main plant. Its layout featured "superblocks" in which the houses faced inward toward an open common. The other neighborhood, Aero Acres, adopted a plan now more typical of suburban areas, with curving drives and a central playground. Aero Acres streets carried such names as Fuselage Avenue, Left Wing Drive, and Right Aileron Street. Shops built to serve the area were grouped in an early example of the type of center in which storefronts, with a covered walkway, face a parking lot.[53]

The federal Farm Security Administration soon sponsored the construction of 400 more Cemesto houses on land adjoining Aero Acres, along with 600 more conventional plywood prefabricated houses on the opposite (northern) side of Martin Boulevard. Designed by the noted city planner Hale Walker, the Victory Villa neighborhood added a number of cul-de-sacs to the curving street pattern and aeronautical street names begun at Aero Acres. Victory Villa also included a automobile-oriented shopping center, a community building and nursery, and an elementary school. Subsequent Middle River housing developments Victory Villa Gardens, Edgewater, and Mars Estates carried on the street naming convention, adding the names of famous aviators (for example, Earhart and Glen Curtis Road) and air bases (McDill

From the Oral History Files. . .

Aeronautical Engineer at Fairchild

An Interview with Allen Clopper
by Dr. Barry A. Lanman

Fairchild Production During World War II

Allen Clopper joined Fairchild during 1943. "...by that time, you know, Pearl Harbor and the trainer build up had us up to a little over 8,000 [employees]. And I think, the all time peak at Hagerstown was a little over 10,000. When Franklin Delano Roosevelt said 'We need 50,000 airplanes next year'. . .the PT-19 was in production, and they were probably building about half a dozen a day, routinely. By 1943, I think they turned out, a hundred and seventy airplanes in one week. A hundred and seventy plus! And in the case of the flying boxcar, which was a pretty good piece of aircraft, they built thirty-four of those in one month, and Fairchild was very fortunate that, when World War II ended, the flying boxcar was just really getting into big production, and the Air Force was not about to give up the first real design from scratch, true cargo transport."

Working with the Legendary Test Pilot Dick Henson

"After three years in aerodynamics, which of course, is the heart of aeronautical engineering science, they decided to establish a flight test engineering group, and I was invited to help form that. So, I moved from the main engineering department, over to flight test. And from then on for twenty-seven years, I was in Dick Henson's department. My office was just upstairs from his, I was sometimes in and out of his office, I guess, a half a dozen times a day, because in a small organization, he was part of the flight test operation at times. He did some of the flying. Although we had other pilots who were, what we

called, 'experimental flight test pilots'. . .

"Dick Henson had a multiple role. He didn't often fly as a first, as the project pilot so to speak, on a test program, but if there was a critical test, and I guess I should say, if there was a test where an awful lot depended on it, he would do it. His style of flying was, went back, I guess, to his early days when he would give airplane rides, would sell the airplane rides and give demonstrations to stir up interest in the, in the young people particularly who just had to fly. And he developed a style, which he described as keeping the airplane close to the crowd, and that would mean that on take off, for example, and the crowd didn't need to know that he was carrying only a light load of fuel, but he had a knack of knowing just how far you could go with an airplane. I mean, he had an uncanny feel for the limits. And one illustration, which I've mentioned in Jack King's book, one of our senior electricians was riding as part of his crew at the Cleveland Air Races one time, when part of the program was for this flying boxcar to demonstrate for the crowd. And Dick was flying, and this electrician told me later, that when Dick pulled out of the top of his steep climb, keeping it close to the crowd, an instrument box on the table actually lifted off the table before he got the nose down. And so, I mean, that's going as far as you can go, but he could do that. And, of course, on maximum performance take offs, you were always at risk, because if an engine failed at the critical point, you had all you could do to handle it."

Testing a C-119

"We had an explosion on the leading edge of a C-119 wing. And I'm lucky to be here on that one. . .We were doing an engine cooling test, with a lot of instrumentation. And it called for stabilizing at normal rate of power, that's maximum acceptable take off power, in level flight at 2,000 feet, and in a test like that, you run until you know you got the least degree of stabilization. So, we were cruising down the valley at 2,000 feet, high power, and all at once, there's an explosion, right wing, leading edge. And we looked out, and there's the whole leading edge. . .lifted, but it hasn't curled under. If it had curled under,

Road, Hickham Road) as source. In all, there are more than seventy streets with aeronautical names in the vicinity of the Martin Plant.[54]

In 1999, an article by the historian John R. Breihan reported that the original houses of Aero Acres were still standing. The appearance of most, however, had been changed by adding vinyl or aluminum siding, as well as by other alterations. The common areas in the Stansbury Estates superblocks had been fenced in. These modifications were made by the individual homeowners who acquired the properties in the postwar era.[55]

Significance for Maryland air/space history: An innovative planned community built as part of the industrial mobilization in World War II.

Relevant years: 1941–present *Lat/Long*: 39-20-00N 76-27-30W
Map: ADC Md/Del 2000 *Num*: 16 *Grid*: A3 *Shows*: area

FAIRCHILD ENGINE AND AIRPLANE CORPORATION PLANT
Now TOP FLIGHT AIR PARK
Hagerstown, Washington County (WA-HAG-213)
1941-1984

Top Flight Air Park, formerly a major plant of the Fairchild corporation, is a large group of buildings that enclose more than one million square feet. It is located four miles north of Hagerstown, on the north side of Showalter Road. The property is roughly bounded on the east by Basore Drive and U.S. Route 11, and on the west and north by Hagerstown Regional Airport (see separate entry on the airport on page 48).[56]

Construction of this complex began in 1941, but the aircraft industry's association with the vicinity began much earlier. In 1928, the Kreider-Reisner Aircraft Company created here an airport that it used for final assembly and flight testing of airplanes built at its plant in

---

we'd've had a spoiled wing, and probably unable to control it laterally. But it stayed in place!

"The pilot decided he was going into the nearest airport, of course, which happened to be Martinsburg. He told us to get rid of the ballast. And normally, we would have twenty-five pounds of lead …made up in bags. So, you ballasted to the cg [center of gravity] and gross weight that you wanted…We had hundreds of pounds of lead shot tied down. They always laced it down to the rings in the floor. We, threw lead all over West Virginia, and never heard anything about it …we didn't hit a cow, we didn't hit a roof, we just dumped lead."

Good Times and Bad Times for Fairchild

"Well, in its golden years, I think Hagerstown was proud of Fairchild, in the fact that almost any hour of any day, you had Fairchild wings over the town… production test flights, if nothing else. Fairchild was big in the community as far as its support of organizations, and if you had, for example, the big Halloween parade, which is really a big event in this county, Fairchild would have a float, be well represented there. And the things like the Pegasus Club which were the supervisors of middle managers club sponsored by the company…The pension plan was pretty good, but late in coming. But I think Fairchild, was looked on with mixed feelings. In the early years, there was resentment, because wages went up and the old families of Hagerstown that had the pipe organ works and the sand blasting and there are some others that I could mention, shoe factories. This defense industry, the pay's better, and they wanted people badly enough after Pearl Harbor, that there were leaflets dropped over West Virginia for a radius of a hundred and fifty miles. I guess, not only West Virginia, but they actually dropped leaflets saying 'Opportunities at Fairchild, come to work'.

"Well the Fairchild name, I think has disappeared and that is one of the most interesting things about it to me. At a time when Fairchild had service representatives on at least three continents, when the employment level, even after the end of World War II, held 8-10,000 for years, now there's not a telephone number. So you have a prime exam-

ple of [the] defense industry. We could go back and Monday morning quarterback what happened as far as Fairchild's own part in that up and down, but basically it's [the] defense industry. If you miss on one big contract, you may just be hungry. If you miss on two, you're starved."

Allen Clopper, oral history interview, November 19, 2002,
MHT/OHC 002 (MD-AVC) 006, 29p.

Allen Clopper, (left) and pilot Jim Brown review test plan before take-off in Fairchild XNQ-1 prototype Navy trainer, 1946. Photo courtesy of Allen Clopper.

*The Fairchild plant alongside the Hagerstown Regional Airport in 1967.
The plant is busy with modifications to C-123 military transports and production
of F-27 airliners. Older airliners traded in for F-27s are parked on aprons.
Photo courtesy of Kent A. Mitchell.*

Hagerstown (see separate entry on page 45). During the following year, the company became a subsidiary of the Fairchild Aviation Corporation. Although the company sold most of the Hagerstown airport to the city government in 1934, it leased rights to operate at the facility and retained its hangar there.[57]

With the onset of World War II, Fairchild rapidly expanded its establishment both in and near Hagerstown. At the southeast corner of the airport, the federal government's Defense Plant Corporation built a large new plant for the company, which was given the option to buy it at war's end. This Plant 2A was completed on August 23, 1941. In March of the following year, a wing designated Plant 2B was added. A list of the company's plants in December 1942 showed that 2A was being used for engineering and for manufacture of PT series trainers and UC-61 light aircraft. In addition to offices, Plant 2B contained space for experimental work and for contract production of wings for Martin PBM seaplanes. In October 1943, a large hangar was completed just north of these buildings. Designed by noted architect Albert Kahn, this building has a barrel roof supported by 170-foot arches of laminated wood. April 1944 saw the completion of Plant 3, a concrete building topped by two rows of slanting roofs. Adjoining Plants 2A and 2B to their east, it provides more floor space than both of these

two earlier structures combined. This massive group of buildings helped Fairchild to make an impressive contribution to the war effort that included thousands of trainers and light aircraft. Before the end of the conflict, the Hagerstown complex also began turning out the C-82 Packet cargo planes.[58]

After the return of peace, the company received new orders for military aircraft that caused it to resume work on a large hangar left unfinished at war's end. Completed in April 1947, this flat-roofed structure was used as a flight test hangar also for such functions as machine tooling and packaging. It stands between the 1943 hangar and the larger buildings to the south. The last major addition to the complex came during the 1950s with a large extension on the eastern side of Plant 3. This structure has six arched supports that extend above the roof and help to bear its weight. It was intended to increase production of the C-119 Flying Boxcar, one of the best known designs of Fairchild's distinguished engineer, Armand Thieblot. Other examples of the wide range of products manufactured here in the postwar period include the F-27 Friendship turboprop airliner, C-123 Provider military transport, FH-1100 helicopter, SM-73 Goose decoy missile, and A-10 Thunderbolt II Attack Plane.[59]

The last aircraft produced at the airport plant, an A-10, made its delivery flight on March 20, 1984. Fairchild subsequently transferred the complex to the State of Maryland as an industrial development site. It was later acquired by the present owner, Barry Peterson, who operates it as Top Flight Air Park and leases space to multiple tenants. Among these is a unit of the Northrop Grumman Corporation that installs electronic systems aboard aircraft. Alterations have been made to the façade of the entrance section on Showalter Street; however, the exterior of the complex is otherwise little changed since its Fairchild period.[60]

Significance for Maryland air/space history: One of the state's most important centers of aircraft production from the World War II era until 1984.
Relevant years: 1941 - 1984   *Lat/Long*: 39-42-48N 77-43-77W
Map: ADC Md/Del 2000   *Num*: 4 *Grid*: D4 *Shows*: area

HAMILTON HOMES

Hagerstown, Washington County
1942-present

The development of Hamilton Homes was a response to the need for housing created by the great expansion of the Fairchild Aircraft Corporation in Hagerstown during World War II. Although the company recruited fewer workers from outside the community than did many war-boom employers in other localities, the city nevertheless expanded by more than 400 housing units during the conflict. This was accomplished by private developers without the assistance available from federal agencies for such wartime projects. Construction of Hamilton Homes, the largest project for Fairchild employees, was well advanced in September 1942.[61] It was located on the west side of Pennsylvania Avenue, the thoroughfare that ran between Fairchild's Plant No. 1 and its facility at the airport north of town. The 167 houses were built along a new Fairchild Avenue and on two intersecting streets, Beechwood Drive and Columbia Road. The basic material used was concrete block supplied by the local firm of H. E. Bester and Company. Priced at between $3,900 and $4,400, the structures have been described as an "assortment of cape-cods, bungalows, and salt boxes." The design that seems most typical was a single-story dwelling, two bays wide, with dormer windows. Today, many of the houses have been altered by the addition of siding, extensions, or other improvements. Examples of those that remain close to their original exterior appearance include 1008 Columbia Road and 1331 Fairchild Avenue.[62]

Significance for Maryland air/space history: A residential neighborhood that reflects the impact of the wartime aviation industry on a community's built environment.

Relevant years: 1942-present *Lat/Long:* 39-40N 77-43W
Map: ADC Md/Del 2000 *Num:* 4 *Grid:* D5
Shows: area

STEVENS AIRPORT

Lewistown, Frederick County (FR-3-86)
1942-1950

The site of Stevens Airport is located at 13102 Hansonville Road, about two miles southwest of Lewistown and some six miles north of Frederick. The property is on the west side of the road, which runs close to U.S. Route 15 and parallel to it. Howard L. Stevens built the facility in about 1942, the same year in which he acquired the farm on which it was located.

He operated the Stevens Flying Service, offering charter service, aircraft sales, fuel, repairs, and a lunch room. Photographs taken at the airport indicate that student flying and probably also Civil Air Patrol activities took place there. A diagram in a June 1950 state airport directory showed two intersecting turf runways that were 2,800 and 2,350 feet in length. The northeast end of the longer strip was not far from U.S. Route 15, and its southeast end was near a swimming pool. Overprinting on this 1950 directory page indicated that Stevens Airport had been recently closed[63]

In 1992, historic sites surveyor Janet L. Davis reported that the former airport's concrete-block hangar and adjoining control tower had been adapted for use as a cow barn. The converted structure stood about thirty yards west of a nineteenth century dwelling known as the Frederick A. Stull House. Davis wrote: "The hangar section has the distinctive arched roof with the original openings, now partially filled with concrete block, on the north and south elevations. The control tower is located at the southwest corner of the building and is a three-story square block with hipped composition roof. Two over two windows are located on each level. Adjoining the hangar on the east elevation is a gabled roof machine and repair shop with an open side on the east." At right angles to this opening was an office section that had probably been added in the 1960s. The report pointed out that Stevens Airport had been, for a time, the county's only airfield. This had occurred between the closure of Detrick Field in about 1943 and the opening of the fully-completed Frederick Municipal Airport in 1949 (see separate entries on pages 60 and 98).[64]

Significance for Maryland air/space history: An airport that provided access to general aviation during the World War II and postwar era.

Relevant years: 1942 – 1950 *Lat/Long:* 39-30-30N 77-24-45W
Map: ADC Md/Del 2000 *Num:* 5 *Grid:* B6 *Shows:* area

Hangar and control tower converted to agricultural use at the former Stevens Airport. Photo courtesy of the Maryland Historical Trust.

CARDEROCK DIVISION, NAVAL SURFACE WARFARE CENTER
Originally DAVID TAYLOR MODEL BASIN
West Bethesda (Carderock), Montgomery County
(MO: 29-54)
1942-present

The Naval Surface Warfare Center, Carderock Division, occupies 183.6 acres south of MacArthur Boulevard and north of Clara Barton Parkway. The facility originated as a successor to the Experimental Model Basin at the Washington Navy Yard, which was directed by Admiral David W. Taylor, a pioneer in hydrodynamics. The new facility was dedicated in November 1939, and received the name David Taylor Model Basin (DTMB). In February 1942, work began on an Aerodynamics Laboratory, including two subsonic wind tunnels, which were completed in April 1943. After the war, two German supersonic wind tunnels were transferred to the DTMB. A further advance occurred when a third supersonic tunnel, built in the United States, began operating in 1950. A decade later, the Aerodynamics Lab placed in operation a hypersonic wind tunnel for use in the development and design of missiles. Other work at the laboratory included such test subjects as airborne components, helicopters, and vertical- and short-takeoff aircraft. In 1967, DTMB became part of the Naval Ship Research and Development Center, whose other major component was an Annapolis facility now known as the David Taylor Research Center (see separate entry on page 37). Further reorganizations and name changes followed, and in 1992 the Carderock facility received its present designation.[65]

In 1985, meanwhile, four original (non-aeronautical) buildings of the David W. Taylor Model Basin were entered upon the National Register of Historic Places. Further site reports included a March 1996 National Register eligibility review concerning the facility's Building 11, which had originally contained the three supersonic wind tunnels mentioned above. This building was subsequently been renovated and is used for other purposes.[66] In 1999, a survey of the Subsonic Wind Tunnel Complex was performed prior to the scheduled demolition of three of its six buildings. The survey noted that the complex was not itself of exceptional significance, but contributed to the significance of the Carderock Division historic district as a whole. The facility currently operates only a single wind tunnel, a low speed system in Building 7.[67]

Significance for Maryland air/space history: A technical facility that has performed significant work related to aviation.

Relevant years: 1942 - present *Lat/Long:* 38-58N 77-12W
Map: ADC Md/Del 2002 *Num:* 19 *Grid:* D1 *Shows:* area

THE JOHNS HOPKINS UNIVERSITY APPLIED PHYSICS LABORATORY
(Original Site)
Silver Spring, Montgomery County
1942-c. 1955

The origin of the Applied Physics Laboratory (APL) lay in a wartime need for more effective artillery shells, particularly for use against aircraft. Under the National Defense Research Committee, work began at the Carnegie Institute to solve this problem by developing a more advanced type of fuse. Greater resources were needed, however, and Johns Hopkins University agreed to assist, formally establishing APL on March 10, 1942. The new organization was housed at the former Wolfe Motor Company building at 8621 Georgia Avenue in Silver Spring. A contemporary photograph shows this establishment as a two-story brick structure, with showroom windows on one side, and a taller section at least four stories high. By early summer, nearly 200 employees were working at his makeshift headquarters and laboratory, which APL adapted and expanded. A commercial postcard appears to show a substantial remodeling, including the addition of a floor to the two-story section.

The Silver Spring laboratory became the scene of important accomplishments. APL developed VT (Variable Time) fuses that could be used in rotating projectiles such as antiaircraft artillery shells. Radio-based devices detonated the shells when they detected a nearby target, greatly increasing their effectiveness. First used in combat in January 1943, proximity fuses proved to be among the major technical developments of World War II. Another important APL project begun during the conflict was the Bumblebee program to develop a guided missile for the Navy, an effort that eventually resulted in the Terrier and other missile systems. After the war, APL became involved in high-altitude research, at first using captured German V-2 rockets. The laboratory then helped to develop the Aerobee rocket as a practical vehicle for such experiments. As the APL staff grew to more than 1,000 in the early 1950s, the university acquired land upon which to build a more adequate facility. In September 1954, the first employees began moving to this new location in Howard County (see separate entry on page 107). The Silver Spring building appears to have been subsequently demolished, since no such structure is currently standing in the 8600 block of Georgia Avenue.[68]

Significance for Maryland air/space history: A technical facility that played an important role in the evolution of anti-aircraft weapons and rocketry.

Relevant years: 1942 – c. 1955 *Lat/Long:* 39-00N 77-02W
Map: ADC Md/Dl 2000 *Num:* 19 *Grid:* F1 *Shows:* area

BLOSSOM POINT PROVING GROUND
LaPlata, Charles County
1942-present

Blossom Point Proving Ground occupies a 1,600-acre peninsula between Nanjemoy Creek and the Potomac River, roughly six miles southwest of LaPlata. Established in 1942 by the National Bureau of Standards, the facility came under the control of the Army after 1953. Work at the site included testing of fuses and ordnance, aerial drops, and firing of rockets and projectiles. In 1956, the Navy received permission to use part of the property as a command and control base for satellites systems, and satellite tracking has continued there until the present. In 1976, testing operations ceased for a time at Blossom Point. The U.S. Army reactivated the facility in 1980 as an adjunct of the Harry Diamond Laboratories (later known as the Army Research Laboratory). Subsequent Army work at Blossom Point included testing of fuses, explosive devices, and electronic systems developed by the Laboratory. In July 1984, a historic properties report noted that the facility consisted of twenty buildings, all except one of which were simple and utilitarian in design. The exception was an historic farm house that predated the establishment of the proving ground.[69]

Significance for Maryland air/space history: A technical facility whose work has included aerospace-related research and satellite tracking.

Relevant years: 1942 - present

Lat/Long: 38-26N 77-06W

Map: ADC Md/Del 2000 *Num:* 24 *Grid:* E1 *Shows:* facility

Massive maintenance complex built in 1988 for Air Force One, Andrews Air Force Base. Photo courtesy of Andrews AFB.

ANDREWS AIR FORCE BASE
Originally CAMP SPRINGS ARMY AIRFIELD
Camp Springs, Prince George's County
1943-present

Andrews Air Force Base occupies an irregular, 4,300-acre tract at Camp Springs, about ten miles southeast of Washington, D.C. Principal roads that roughly border the base include: Maryland Route 5 on the west; Route 337 and Suitland Parkway on the northwest; and Maryland Route 4 (Pennsylvania Avenue) on the northeast.[70]

Discussed as a possible site for a civil airport as early as 1929, this area became a military airfield as the result of an order by President Franklin D. Roosevelt on August 25, 1942. The project spelled the end of the village of Meadows, and more than 100 families resident there and in the surrounding forests and farmland were displaced. Some 7,000 laborers hurried the work forward through the winter. By spring, a reporter described the nearly completed base as a "cross between a wilderness and a super highway," and explained that it was designed on the principal of dispersal. Parked aircraft were widely spaced, the single hangar used only for maintenance, and the administrative building was camouflaged as farm building. Extensive taxiways linked the four seemingly unrelated runways, each 5,500 feet long. To deal with this sprawling layout, the wooden control tower was raised to more than twice the usual height.[71]

Building 1535 at Andrews Air Force Base served as the first headquarters of the Strategic Air Command from 1946 to 1948. Photo courtesy of the Maryland Historical Trust.

Camp Springs Army Air Field became operational on May 2, 1943, and the first aircraft to land was a P-47 Thunderbolt. Besides aircrew training and defense of the capital, the base provided the headquarters for the Continental Air Forces. Additional wartime construction included two more hangars, more barracks, a hospital, and support buildings such as a theater and gymnasium. In March 1945, the facility was renamed Andrews Field in honor of Lt. Gen. Frank M. Andrews, commander of air forces in the European theater at the time that a plane crash in Iceland claimed his life. The name was modified to its present form in June 1948, following the separation of the Air Force from the Army during the previous year.[72]

After the war, the Strategic Air Command occupied a "baby pentagon" at Andrews for a time, and the base has since been home to other major commands. Units stationed here have engaged in missions ranging from training—including B-25 bomber crews during the Korean conflict—to airlift and helicopter operations. The naval air facilities at Anacostia and Annapolis moved to Andrews in 1963. The late 1950s and early 1960s saw a building program that transformed Andrews into the Air Force's chief facility serving the Washington area. The arrangement of runways placed at angles to one another was replaced by two 9,000-foot parallel runways, each flanked by taxiways, aprons, and hangars. A concrete control tower 150 feet high opened in 1967. The following decade saw further construction and improvement of housing and support buildings. An Advanced Airborne Command Post Facility, an aeromedical staging facility, and a data processing plant were all completed in 1976. Buildings added in the following year included a large personnel office building and a new facility for the operations of the District of Columbia's Air National Guard.[73]

The most remarkable structure at Andrews was completed in 1988: the Air Force One Maintenance Complex, a huge hexagon with a column-like cylindrical element at each corner. Inside, 151,000 square feet of hangar space housed two specially-equipped Boeing 747s. The structure reflected the base's longstanding role in presidential travel. This began on November 24, 1946, when Harry S. Truman boarded the "Sacred Cow" for a flight to Missouri. The Chief Executives' planes have been regularly based here since 1961. On November 22, 1963, Lyndon B. Johnson addressed the nation from Andrews after flying from Dallas with the body of his assassinated predecessor, John F. Kennedy. Another example of the many historic moments at the base was Richard M. Nixon's departure after his 1974 resignation. Andrews has received evacuees needing medical assistance, and has welcomed home freed hostages and prisoners. As the capital's primary gateway for state visitors, it has played a part in diplomatic missions by such figures as Menachem Begin of Israel, Anwar Sadat of Egypt,

and Mikhail Gorbachev of the Soviet Union.[74]

Further construction and improvements at Andrews have enhanced it as a military base, an official airport, and a community where some 24,000 people work and live. Examples from the late 1990s range from a new hydrant system for fueling aircraft to renovation of the passenger terminal—and even a controversial third golf course. In 1994, a historic site report indicated that only two flight line structures remained from the early days of the air-field, a pair of much-altered maintenance hangars dating from 1944. In physical terms, the installation has moved far from its origin as a hastily-built wartime fighter base. Yet its early air defense mission came to the fore again as F-16 pilots based here patrolled Washington's skies in the wake of the September 2001 terrorist attacks.[75]

Significance for Maryland air/space history: A major military air base for a half century and the scene of numerous events of historical importance.
Relevant years: 1943 - present *Lat/Long*: 38-48N 76-53W
Map: ADC Md/Del 2000 *Num*: 20 *Grid*: B3 *Shows*: base

NAVAL AIR STATION PATUXENT RIVER/TRAPNELL FIELD
Lexington Park, St. Mary's County (SM-357)
1943-present

Naval Air Station Patuxent River is northeast of Three Notch Road and occupies the whole of the Cedar Point peninsula, where the Patuxent joins the Chesapeake Bay. The station comprises 7,799 acres, including the non-contiguous Webster Field (see separate entry on page 87).[76]

The creation of the Patuxent River station stemmed from the need to consolidate naval aviation testing at a new base in the Washington area, one that would provide more space than the overcrowded facility in use at Anacostia, D.C. The site was approved by the Secretary of the Navy in January 1942, and a groundbreaking ceremony took place on April 4 of that year. Construction entailed disruption of local rural life and alteration of the landscape and shoreline; however, a number of archeological sites and landmarks of earlier times survive on the property today. Progress was slow at first, with problems including unstable terrain, lack of materials, and disorder among the 7,000 workers. On April 1, 1943, however, the station was officially commissioned. As completed, the facility had four seaplane ramps and three runways, one of which measured 10,000 feet, the greatest length then found at any of the Navy's continental bases. Notable among the structural features were six reinforced concrete hangars with barrel roofs 160 feet wide. Poor roads made overland access difficult, but the Navy built railway tracks that allowed it to operate train service between the new base and the town of Brandywine during the years 1944-54.[77]

Flight testing during World War II included such aircraft as America's first turbojet, the XP-59A Airacomet, as well as the FR-1 Fireball and FH-1 Phantom. Other activities included evaluation of captured enemy planes and development work in such fields as radar fire control, radar tracking, and instrument landing. Patuxent also

Navy AJ-1 bomber on the flight line at the Naval Air Station, Patuxent River, circa 1950. Terminal and control tower are in the background. Photo courtesy of Stan Piet.

Built in 1944, the Recreation Building at the Naval Air Station, Patuxent River, housed a USO and an enlisted men's club. It is now an aviation museum. Photo courtesy of the Maryland Historical Trust.

served as the east coast base of the Naval Air Transport Service during the war. The Naval Air Test Center (NATC) was established as a separate organization at the station in June 1945. During the following year, the Center conducted the nation's first test of adapting all-jet aircraft to carrier operations when a Phantom successfully flew to and from the U.S.S. *Franklin D. Roosevelt*.[78]

The Cold War era saw continued development work and the basing of early warning aircraft at the station. The Naval Pilot Test School, whose graduates were to include many astronauts, was established in 1958. Two years later, NATC launching of Bullpup missiles from a Marine HUS-1 helicopter provided an instance of the continuing and varied testing program. Other activities in the 1960s included a build-up of anti-submarine units that remained at the station into the next decade. In 1975, a "Hush House" for jet engine testing was constructed as part of work on noise reduction. Following the death in that same year of retired Vice Admiral Frederick M. Trapnell, a test pilot and NATC commander, the station's airfield was named Trapnell Field in his honor. A wave of upgrading and building in response to technological change began in the late 1970s and continued into the following decade. An example was the Electronic Warfare

Integrated Test Laboratory, established in 1980 in a converted hangar lined with copper screening to shield against interference.[79]

At the beginning of 1992, the Naval Air Warfare Center's Aircraft Division was established at Patuxent to provide a full range of research, development, testing, and evaluation in the aviation field. Subsequent construction and improvements followed as units were relocated to the station as a result of the legislatively-mandated closures of bases elsewhere. In 1997, the Naval Air Systems Command Headquarters moved to Patuxent. The station today has some 18,000 personnel and about 140 assigned aircraft. The longest of its runways measures 11,800 feet, and it has over 900 buildings. These installations include specialized hangars, laboratories, simulators, test ranges, and facilities for evaluating aircraft and their engines, components, instruments, ordnance, and electronic systems.[80]

Significance for Maryland air/space history: A major military airfield that has played an important role in the evolution of naval aviation.
Relevant Years: 1943 - Present *Lat/Long*: 38-17N 76-26W
Map: ADC Md/Del 2000 *Num*: 26 *Grid*: A3-B3 *Shows*: facility

NAVAL AIR WARFARE CENTER, AIRCRAFT DIVISION, SAINT INIGOES (WEBSTER FIELD)
Saint Inigoes, St. Mary's County (SM-8-94)
1943-present

Webster Field is two miles west of Saint Inigoes on the eastern shore of the Saint Mary's River. From its beginning, the base has been an auxiliary field for the larger Naval Air Station Patuxent River to its northeast (see separate entry on page 86). To create Webster Field, the Navy in 1942 acquired 773 acres of Saint Inigoes Manor, a Jesuit mission and plantation dating from the 17th Century.[81] In July 1943, the new base was named in honor of an officer long associated with naval aviation testing and development, Capt. Walter W. Webster, who had died in a Pennsylvania air crash earlier that year.[82]

"Flat-top" houses at Lexington Manor offered generous amounts of natural light. Photo courtesy of the Maryland Historical Trust.

Retrenchment following World War II reduced the facility's employment to just thirty-two in 1949, but it continued to survive periodic threats of closure. Technological development supported here included work on automatic landing systems for aircraft carriers in the 1950s and shipboard radio equipment in the 1970s.[83] A Coast Guard Station was established at Webster Field in 1976.[84] Recent developments have included the opening of the Navy's first permanent hangar for unmanned aerial vehicles (UAVs) in 2000. During the following year, the base hosted an international UAV exposition that included demonstration flights by the Predator and numerous other vehicles.[85] In October 2002, some 1,900 employees at Webster were engaged in projects such as the design of advanced communications systems for a number of government agencies. An example of their products was the Unified Command Suites system, created for National Guard units to use in the event of terrorist attacks or other disasters.[86] In addition to these activities, Webster Field remains an operating air station, with two of its three 5,000-foot runways in active status.[87]

Significance for Maryland air/space history: A naval airfield and technological center that has been active since 1943.

Relevant years: 1943-current *Lat/Long*: 38-08-45N 076-25-42W
Map: ADC Md/Del 2000 *Num*: 26 *Grid*: A5 *Shows*: facility

LEXINGTON MANOR
Originally LEXINGTON PARK
Lexington Park, St. Mary's County (SM-490)
1943-present

Lexington Park was a housing development built during World War II for civilian employees of the new Naval Air Station Patuxent. Located southwest of Three Notch Road and southeast of Great Mills Road, the complex included 350 single-story houses. The northern section, designed by the New York firm of Kahn and Jacobs, was completed in 1943, while the southern section, by architect Louis Justement, was finished in the following year. The streets of the complex were named for battles in which the carrier U.S.S. *Lexington* was engaged. The houses, fitted with flat, overhanging roofs of the modern movement in architecture, are still referred to locally as "flat tops." The complex also possessed a community building, dormitories, and a child care center, all now demolished, as well as a still-extant shopping area. In 1963, the federal government sold the property to a private owner, who gave it its present name. (The term "Lexington Park" now refers to a wider area of which Lexington Manor is a part.) In 1995, a historic sites survey found that Lexington Manor's fortunes had declined, and that many of the houses were boarded up. The survey report, however, found the property to be significant for three reasons: its design by prominent architects; its associations with World War II; and its place as the earliest planned community in St. Mary's County. [88]

Significance for Maryland air/space history: An example of the impact of aviation on community development and the built environment.

Relevant years: 1943 - current *Lat/Long*: 38-15N 76-28W
Map: ADC Md/Del 2000 *Num*: 26 *Grid*: A3 *Shows*: area

SALISBURY-OCEAN CITY: WICOMICO REGIONAL AIRPORT
Salisbury, Wicomico County (WI-541)
1943-present

Salisbury-Ocean City: Wicomico Regional Airport is located four miles southeast of Salisbury, on Airport Road south of Maryland Route 350. The facility was created in response to a 1940 defense plan in which the Civil Aeronautics Administration called for a large airport in the Salisbury area. The city and county together acquired some 695 acres for the project, and the Works Progress Administration provided the labor. Completed on a rush basis and dedicated in November 1943, Salisbury Municipal Airport had three concrete runways, each 5,000 feet long. In May 1944, the Navy leased the facility as an auxiliary air station, returning it to the civilian control in November 1945.[90]

Scheduled airline flights began in April 1946, with Chesapeake Airways as the first of several carriers. For many years, however, the service proved difficult to sustain at a profitable level. The situation improved after 1968, when Hagerstown entrepreneur Richard A. Henson began serving the airport with more frequent flights in smaller aircraft. Henson eventually switched to Salisbury as the base for his airline operation, which he later sold to Piedmont Airlines.[91]

Among structural improvements to the airport over the years have been: an administration building in 1949; an enlarged terminal and Henson Aviation offices and hangar in 1975; a new terminal in 1990; and, in 1999, a new tower operated by air traffic controllers under contract with the Federal Aviation Administration. The number of hangars has risen from one, in 1947, to the current total of well over seventy. The state airport directory for 1974 showed that the longest runway had been extended to its present length of 5,500 feet. All three runways remained active at that time, but the east-west strip had been closed by April 1981. The airport's name has also evolved over time, as authorities substituted "Wicomico County" for the original term "Municipal," then added the word "Regional," and finally adopted the present designation.[92]

Wicomico County's regional airport offers the only scheduled air service on the Delmarva peninsula, and ranks second in Maryland in terms of airline passenger traffic. In June 2002, the air carrier operations were at an annual level of more than 8,000, in addition to more than 38,000 general aviation operations.[93]

Significance for Maryland air/space history: A publicly-owned airport, with origins in World War II, that has become a major air transportation center for Maryland's Eastern Shore.

Relevant years: 1943 - present *Lat/Long*: 38-20-26N; 75-30-38W
Map: ADC Md/Del 2000 *Num*: 27 *Grid*: F2 *Shows*: airport

CARROLL COUNTY REGIONAL AIRPORT, JACK B. POAGE FIELD
Originally CIVIL AIR PATROL BASE 332, then WESTMINSTER AIRPORT
Westminster, Carroll County
1943-present

The facility now known as Carroll County Regional Airport had its origins in World War II. Beginning in August, 1942, members of the Baltimore Wing of the Civil Air Patrol began clearing a tract of some forty acres about two miles north of Westminster. The squadron members, many of whom were women, removed trees, stumps, and boulders to create their new base. They also made financial contributions to the project. The undertaking was sponsored by Base 332, Inc., a non-profit corporation whose president was the squadron's adjutant, Lt. E. Ridgely Simpson. Plans to name the field for Simpson may never have become official, since it appeared on aeronautical charts simply as Base 332. By the time of its dedication on June 6, 1943, the facility possessed three grass runways, a large hangar, an operations room, a flight office, and a room to be used for radio communications training.[94]

Cloud shadows dapple the 5,100-foot runway 16-34 at Carroll County Regional Airport, Westminster. Photo courtesy of Ashish Solanki, Maryland Aviation Administration.

Newspaper accounts of the establishment of Base 332 did not make clear to whom the property belonged; however, an airport directory published in 1945 identified the owner as the B. F. Schriver Company and the operator as the Civil Air Patrol. In the postwar period, the field became a commercial facility under the name Westminster Airport. Although it was still shown as Base 332 on an aeronautical chart dated as valid through October 22, 1946, the conversion had taken place at least several months earlier. A state directory of commercial airports described Westminster Airport, as of July 1, 1946, as offering student flying, charter services, fuel, and repairs. The three turf runways ranged in length from 1,600 to 2,000 feet. The longest, oriented east-west, was at right angles to the nearby highway.[95]

In 1976, Carroll County acquired the airport. During the following year, the county purchased additional land and built a paved runway 2,930 feet long. Improvements during 1978 included runway lighting and construction of a main hangar and administration building, as well as the first T-hangar. The name had been changed to Carroll County Airport by the 1980s, and the word "Regional" was added later in the decade after the completion of a new 5,000-foot runway. Beginning in 1979, the airport was operated by Westair, Inc., a firm formed by Jack and June Poage. In 1990, Jack Poage lost his life while performing an aerobatic demonstration, and the airfield designation honors his memory. June Poage continued as the airport operator until her own death in May 2002.[96]

Today, the runway and parallel taxiway at Carroll County Regional Airport are oriented northwest-southwest. Rows of hangars and an industrial park are placed to the west, while another business center is just across Littlestown Pike (Maryland Route 97). As of May 23, 2002, 121 aircraft were based at the airport, and operations for the preceding twelve months totaled 153,690.[97]

Significance for Maryland air/space history: Beginning as a wartime Civil Air Patrol base, this facility has evolved into a busy general aviation airport that is part of an industrial development area.

Relevant years: 1943 - present

Lat/Long: 39-36-30N 77-00-28W

Map: ADC Md/Del 2000 *Num*: 5 *Grid*: F5 *Shows*: airport

EASTON AIRPORT, NEWNAM FIELD
Easton, Talbot County
1943-present

Easton Airport/Newnam Field is located two miles north of the city that it serves, west of U.S. Route 50 and south of Airport Road. The facility originated as a defense measure in World War II. For its construction, the federal government appropriated $561,000. Some sources state that German prisoners of war provided the labor, but this has been questioned. By July 16, 1943, a newspaper was able to report that the project was within days of completion. Local authorities had contributed the 582-acre site, with the understanding that the airport would become theirs after the conflict. One writer noted, however, that the area of the city itself was smaller than that of the airport, which he called a "gigantic undertaking that outstrips Easton in many respects." [98]

With the return of peace, the community took possession of an Easton Municipal Airport with two paved runways, each 4,000 feet long. Aeronautical charts had already begun including the facility as an auxiliary field as early as May 1944, and by April 1946 it was shown as a commercial airport. Management was for a time entrusted to the Cities Service Oil Company. By October 1946, the company had completed an administration building, topped by a control tower, and was at work on a large barrel-roofed hangar. Only the latter structure remains extant.[99]

Scheduled airline flights began in 1946, but the modest number of passengers tended to make Easton an unprofitable stop, particularly after the opening of the Chesapeake Bay Bridge in 1952. Scheduled air carrier service ended in 1959. The airport's continued viability during the ensuing era has been credited to William S. D. (Bill) Newnam, Jr., the facility's manager from the 1960s into the 1980s. Newnam used the small aircraft of his Maryland Airlines to successfully link Easton with Washington National Airport, now known as Washington Reagan National Airport. He is posthumously honored in the current name of the airport, which became the sole property of Talbot County in January 1993.[100]

Features of an airport expansion plan begun in 1984 included a new terminal, designed by a local architect, Margaret Garey. Completed in 1987, this building has a large central section with a vaulted ceiling under a high peaked roof. Other improvements have included lengthening of the primary runway to 5,511 feet, accomplished during the 1990s, and the commissioning of an Instrument Landing System in July 2002. As of June 2001, 148 aircraft were based at the airport, including nineteen jets. Flight operations during the preceding twelve months totaled 90,000. Although none of these involved scheduled airlines, they included 10,000 air taxi operations.[101]

Significance for Maryland air/space history: Originating in World War II, this airport offered scheduled air carrier service and latter evolved into one of the state's larger general aviation facilities.

Relevant years: 1943–present *Lat/Long*: 38-48-19N 76-04-08W

Map: ADC Md/Del 2000 *Num*: 21 *Grid*: E3 *Shows*: airport

ESSEX SKYPARK
Originally DIFFENDAHL AIRPORT,
then EASTERN AIRPORT
Essex, Baltimore County
1943-present

Essex Skypark occupies 525 acres at 1401 Diffendahl Road, southeast of Essex on the west side of Back River Neck Road. The property includes Witchcoat Point, which projects into the eastern side of Back River.[102]

The airport is reported to have been established by

William Diffendahl in 1943, and was originally known as Diffendahl Airport. The earliest aeronautical chart found that included the facility was dated October 15, 1947. As depicted in a state directory issued in March of that same year, the airport had two intersecting turf landing strips: northeast-southwest, 2,200 feet long, and northwest-southeast, 1,800 feet long. Isabelle Diffendahl was listed as the owner and manager of the facility, which operated in daylight only, offering fuel, minor repairs, and student flying. Structures included an administration building, which is still extant, although altered on the interior. There were eight T-hangars, since destroyed by fire and rebuilt, as well as a forty-four-by-sixty foot hangar. This larger hangar was an open shelter consisting of a roof mounted on poles; it has subsequently been enclosed and extended.[103]

Runways and taxiways at Easton Airport/Newnam Field display a classic "V" alignment. Photo courtesy of the Maryland Aviation Administration.

Designed in 1987, the new terminal at Easton Airport/Newnam Field set the pattern for other regional airports across the state. Photo courtesy of the Maryland Aviation Administration.

In 1948 or 1949, J. S. Shapiro acquired the land, and the facility was renamed Eastern Airport. By 1963, it still had two turf runways. During mid-1960s, the airfield layout was converted to a single paved runway and the name changed again, to Essex Skypark. A newspaper article published in 1970 credited operators Earl and Lois Wilson with having revived the facility and making it profitable. The article also mentioned that, in addition to serving landplanes, the Skypark was currently the state's

only civilian base for seaplanes. (Essex Seaplane Base, which had been located further upstream, had closed in 1959; see separate entry on page 100.)[104]

Lois Wilson continued to manage the airport into the 1980s. After her death, Don Crouse and Jim Montgomery became the operators. The land remained in the Shapiro family until recent years, when it was acquired by Baltimore County under the Rural Legacy Program. The airport has continued to operate under an arrangement that includes restrictions on development and a cap on airport operations. The facility currently has a single lighted runway of 2,084 feet, as well as the seaplane beach. There are about thirty-eight T-hangars, in addition to the larger hangar mentioned above. As of October 5, 2001, thirty-six aircraft were based at the Skypark. Operations for the preceding twelve months totaled 3,050.[105]

Significance for Maryland air/space history: A general aviation airport that has operated since the era of World War II.

Relevant Years: 1943 - present   *Lat/Long*: 39-15-45N 76-26-00W

Map: ADC Md/Del 2000 Num: 16   Grid: A3   Shows: airport

Above: A 1934 model of the Fairchild 24 cabin monoplane stands outside the Fairchild hangar at Hagerstown airport. Later models of the Fairchild served the Army in World War II as UC-61 Forwarders. Photo courtesy of Kent A. Mitchell.

Right: As a publicity stunt, two Piper Cub airplanes were hoisted atop the wings of the giant XPB2M-1 Mars flying boat. The roof monitors of the B Building at Martin Plant No. 1, where the Mars was built, loom even larger in the background. Photo courtesy of the National Air and Space Museum, Smithsonian Institution.

Chapter Four:
Postwar and Cold War

World War II trained tens of thousands of pilots; thousands more learned to fly afterwards courtesy of the G.I. Bill of Rights. All across the country new general-aviation airports opened to cater to a new and larger flying clientele. Some, like Kentmorr, in Queen Anne's County, were "airparks," combining housing with an airfield. Meanwhile the Cold War and Space Race stimulated the continued growth of research laboratories and centers. Suddenly the airplane did not seem so benign; the suburbs of Baltimore and Washington sprouted nests of antiaircraft missiles designed to shoot down enemy bombers.

Nevertheless, towns and cities saw air access as key to economic growth. They put increasing federal and state subsidies to work building a new generation of municipal airports. The term "airpark" came more often to mean "industrial park." Daniel Henson experimented with regional commuter air service to smaller cities while Baltimore/Washington International Airport grew into a major hub. As the second century of aviation dawned, it was general aviation that seemed to be fading from the scene as economic and security concerns led the closing of many of the small fields begun so hopefully in the late 1940s.

GREATER CUMBERLAND REGIONAL AIRPORT
Wiley Ford, West Virginia, serves Cumberland, Allegany County
1945-present

Greater Cumberland Regional Airport occupies a 314-acre property that is about two miles south of Cumberland, across the North Branch of the Potomac River at Wiley Ford, West Virginia. During the 1930s, city authorities began seeking to establish an airport with greater potential than the existing one at Mexico Farms (see separate entry on page 43). A survey of available sites resulted in selection of level ground atop Knobley

Above: Runway 23-5 at the Greater Cumberland Airport in Wiley Ford, West Virginia, ends on a bluff along the Potomac River. Photo courtesy of Ashish Solanki, Maryland Aviation Administraton.

Left: New 1999 terminal and aprons at Greater Cumberland Regional Airport. Photo courtesy of Ashish Solanki, Maryland Aviation Administraton.

Mountain. Under an arrangement announced in February 1941, the federal government agreed to design the airfield and pay most of the projected $2.7 million cost of construction, while the city pledged $150,000. Labor shortages during World War II slowed the project, and the new airport did not open until after the return of peace in 1945.[1]

Owned and operated by the city, the new Cumberland Airport was rated Class 3, a ranking then shared or exceeded by only two other Maryland airports. A state directory that described the facility in October 1946 showed a triangular airfield with three paved runways. Structures included: one large hangar; fifteen single-plane hangars; and a building with office, lounge, and control tower. The airport offered charters, student flying, fuel, and repairs. Today, the airport has one less runway, but offers more in terms of air transportation.

Private houses line the grass runway at Kentmorr Airpark, Stevensville, 1987. Photo courtesy of Ashish Solanki, Maryland Aviation Administraton.

Changes during the 1990s have included adoption of the present name, which reflects the airport's regional service and its management by an interstate authority formed in 1976. Among the more recent improvements is a $3.5 million terminal, dedicated in July 1999. As of August 2001, fifty-seven aircraft were based at the airport. Commuter flights accounted for more than a third of the 22,757 operations during the preceding twelve months.[2]

Significance for Maryland air/space history: A municipal, and later regional, airport that has provided surrounding communities with access to aviation since 1945.
Relevant years: 1945-present *Lat/Long*: 39-36-54N 78-45-44W
Map: ADC Md/Del 2000 *Num*: 2 *Grid*: C5 *Shows*: airport

KENTMORR AIRPARK
Stevensville, Queen Anne's County
c. 1945-present

Kentmorr Airpark is located on twenty acres that are five miles southwest of Stevensville, between Romancoke Road and the Chesapeake Bay. There is a single unlighted turf runway, 2,400 feet long, with its western end near the bay shore. This simple layout is largely unchanged since Kentmorr's founding in about 1945.[3] The airport was established by Nathan "Bill" Morris, an inventor and avid pilot who operated an Aeronca from a field near his home in Silver Spring. After buying property on Kent Island for a residence, Morris decided to build a public-use airstrip. (The name is derived from the words "Kent Island" and "Morris.") Starting with two cottages, since demolished, Morris began what he believes was the nation's first residential airpark, a concept that combines houses with a landing field. Residents can literally taxi their planes to their front doors. In an interview with historian Barry Lanman, Morris recalled that sales were slow at first, in part because the size of the lots was too small. An early brochure billed the community as "A Private Pilot's Paradise," showed a plat of the lots, and also offered "hangar bungalows" for vacationers to rent. Later, Morris added a popular restaurant and a marina. Today, the development includes some 500 houses, about eleven of which border the runway itself. (During the 1960s, Morris also developed Bay Bridge Airport: see separate entry.) According to an article by Tom Vesey, the residential property owners formed an association and bought the airfield at Kentmorr in 1983. As of July 9, 2001, fifteen aircraft were based at the facility, and operations for the preceding twelve months totaled 4,500.[4]

Significance for Maryland air/space history: An early residential airpark, possibly the nation's first, that has operated since the period just after World War II.
Relevant years: c. 1945 - present
Lat/Long: 38-55-05N 76-21-30W
Map: ADC Md/Del 2000 *Num*: 21 *Grid*: B1 *Shows*: airport

HARFORD COUNTY AIRPORT
Originally ALDINO AIRPORT
Churchville, Harford County
c. 1945-present

Harford County Airport occupies fifty-nine acres on the north side of Aldino Road, three miles east of Churchville and six miles north-northwest of Aberdeen. Originally known as Aldino Airport, the facility was listed under that name in a commercial directory issued for the year 1945. The location was described as at the center of the town of Aldino, whose population was thirty-five persons. Owned by Christian Alder, the airport offered fuel and repairs. Structures included an administration building, six T-hangars, and an individual hangar. Two sod runways, both 2,000 feet long, formed an "L" configuration. A diagram in a 1950 directory showed that the airport then had three intersecting sod runways, the longest measuring

Hangars, fueling area, and terminal building at Harford County Airport, 1988. Photo courtesy of Ashish Solanki, Maryland Aviation Administraton.

Original 1947 office and terminal at Maryland Airport in Indian Head. Photo courtesy of Ashish Solanki, Maryland Aviation Administraton.

2,140 feet. In 1961, a trend in aerial sport reached Aldino when a thirty-member skydiving club set up its headquarters at the airport. Directory listings in the early 1970s indicated that the facility now belonged to the Harford County Investment Corporation. Under the new owner, the airport was renamed the Aldino-Churchville Industrial Airpark, a designation that lasted into the 1980s. By 1996, the proprietor was the Harford County Airport Owners Group, Inc., and the present name had been adopted. The layout had also been simplified to the current configuration of two runways, the longer of which is paved. As of March 29, 2002, operations for the preceding twelve months totaled 35,529. [5]

Significance for Maryland air/space history: An airport that has served general aviation since circa 1945.
Relevant years: c. 1945-present
Lat/Long: 39-34-02N 76-12-08W
Map: ADC Md/Del 2000 *Num:* 7 *Grid:* D6 *Shows:* airport

MARYLAND AIRPORT
Indian Head, Charles County (CH-597)
1945-present

Maryland Airport is located at 3900 Livingston Road, four miles east of Indian Head and less than a mile south of Pomonkey. The airport appeared on an aeronautical section chart dated December 26, 1945, although not on one issued less than a year earlier. A state airport directory described it, as of October 1946, as a 200-acre property owned by Charles Bauserman. The facility operated only in daylight, offering student flying, charter service, fuel, and minor repairs. It had two runways, 3,200 and 1,900 feet long. One of these runways is reported to have been graded by German prisoners of war at the end of World War II.[6] In October 1946, the airport also possessed office space, three existing hangars, and two more hangars under construction. The runway surfaces were described as sod in 1950, and as a sod and gravel combination in the early 1960s. By 1967, the longer of the two runways was paved. John K. Crawford, who was later a joint owner of the airport, became its manager at least as early as 1974. In March 2000, Maryland Airport was reported to be scheduled for a drastic overhaul as a designated reliever for Washington National Airport. The multi-year project was estimated to cost $10 million in federal, state, and private funds, and was planned to produce a completely new layout that included a 4,600-foot runway. In August 2000, a historic sites survey report indicated that, in addition to metal hangars, the airport's buildings consisted of two structures built in 1947 to provide a terminal and office. They were described as

From the Oral History Files...

Maryland's Oldest Aviator
Private Pilot for 65 Years

An interview with Nathan "Bill" Morris
by Dr. Barry A. Lanman

Nathan "Bill" Morris was born in East Baltimore on July 19, 1907. As he delights in telling the story, *"I was born just four years after the Wright Brothers flew at Kitty Hawk!"* His interest in flight was noted at a young age when he piloted his first soapbox airplane down the streets of Baltimore, and his desire to fly was fueled by the trans-Atlantic flight of Charles Lindbergh in 1927. As an engineer, designer and inventor, Morris saved his money and by 1938 began flight instruction at College Park Airport. He negotiated a deal with the instructor: a thirty-minute lesson each Sunday, in a J-3 Cub for $4. After sixteen lessons, he took a solo flight.

Maryland private pilots in the 1930s had few navigational aids or cockpit instrumentation in their planes. They usually flew at an altitude of 1,000-2,000 feet. From the lack of sophisticated equipment, Morris learned to fly in a safe manner and minimized the risks of flight associated with that era.

The first airplane he purchased was an Aeronca. The two-passenger airplane had a wooden propeller, a ten-gallon gas tank and cost a grand total of $950. His next adventure was to find a place close by to use as an airfield, since there were no commercial airports in the Silver Spring area where he lived. Eventually, he entered into a contract with a farmer to clear a 1,000-foot section of land for a runway. Once this was accomplished, he had his own airfield located a half-mile from his front door.

During the late 1930s and the early 1940s, Morris flew all over Maryland and neighboring states to attend air meets. After owning two Aeroncas, he purchased a 1937 Monocoupe, capable of acrobatics, which he performed on a regular basis.

Morris explained how he found and developed Kentmorr Airpark. *"I decided one day [in 1945] that I ought to have a private place down by the water somewhere so I can take the kids... So I took*

off and I flew as far as Nantucket, thinking I'd buy a piece of ground up there. But after I got there I found out it was an awful long way to Nantucket, so I gave up that idea and on my way home I happened to get a little bit off course and I went over Kent Island and I looked down. I said 'hey, there is the place for me, right close to Washington, close to Baltimore and easy to get to.' The next day I went down to here [Kent Island] with my family on a ferry boat and I bought a hundred and forty acres of land... That is it. That's how I got it. Wasn't planned, it just happened.

"Well, I got the idea of having a little airpark with a couple of

Bay Bridge Airport in the early 1960s when it was in its formative stages and Kent Island still rural. Kentmorr Park is in the distance at the far right near the horizon. Photo courtesy of Nathan "Bill" Morris.

weekend cottages, so I built two little cottages...and that was the beginning of the first residential airpark in the United States. There are over five hundred of them [residential airparks] now." Morris' sister named the facility by combining the name of the island with part of his last name. Thus, the airpark became known as Kentmorr Airpark.

"After I bought the land, I decided I'm going to clean this potato patch up and I spent seventy-five dollars and I had an airport when I got though... I had a farmer come in and level it out and it grew grass naturally." The airstrip is essentially the same today as it was when it was first cleared in 1945: 2,500 feet long, 250 feet wide and without navigational aids or lights.

Morris said that the Kentmorr Airpark started slowly but people got to know where Kentmorr was, especially the flying people. "So some weekends I'd throw a pancake party ... and a lot of planes would come in and none of the planes had starters ...I would spend my weekends cranking airplanes and selling three gallons of gas to this one and three gallons to that one."

The enterprising Morris eventually sold the lots along the airstrip, built a marina on the bay and opened the Kentmorr Restaurant so his wife did not have to feed the growing number of visitors. By the 1960s Morris saw a need for a commercial airport in the area. When a 180-acre farm came up for sale, he purchased it with a group of partners. The property became known as the Bay Bridge Airport due to its proximity to the bridge. As

Bill Morris in front of his Cessna 182-P Skylane "Spirit of Maryland" parked in a hangar attached to the Morris house at Kentmorr Park. Photo courtesy of Nathan "Bill" Morris.

compared to today's bureaucracy, Morris did not have to file for any major permits, participate in zoning hearings or be involved with environmental impact studies for either facility.

While airport development had been both an avocation and a financial endeavor, being in the air was Morris' true passion. Thus, after almost three decades of flying, he obtained his multi-engine rating and his instrument rating. In 1973, he purchased a new Cessna Skylane 182-P. There was only one name for his new Cessna: "The Spirit of Maryland." *"I wanted to emulate Lindbergh's trip to Le Bourget Field. . . and now people know* [the plane] *as 'The Spirit of Maryland.'*

"Since I got interested in what I call long distance flying and I don't know what airports I'm going into, the first thing I wanted was an airplane that could land very short. So, when I bought the airplane I had the Robertson-STOL [short take-off and landing] *system put on."* Other modifications over time have included an extra gas tank, fuel injection and a high performance engine.

Morris has made over fifty-five long distance flights over the last thirty years in "The Spirit of Maryland." Usually flying with co-pilots, he has made trips to every continent except the Antarctic. Alaska and Canada are places where he has traveled numerous times and he is proud of flying the routes traveled by Wiley Post and other early aviators.

One of Morris's dreams came true when he participated in the 1985 rally commemorating Charles A. Lindbergh's 1927 trans-Atlantic flight. Morris was 77 at the time and his co-pilot and good friend, George Allen, was 82. The "Spirit of Maryland" was one of sixty-eight planes that participated, and the team represented the most senior entry on the tour. While the planes and technology had vastly improved since Lindbergh made his trip, the trip was still a dangerous endeavor, as noted by one fatality during the tour.

At 94, Morris made a rare long distance solo trip. *"I circled the United States. I couldn't get anybody to go with me. I did it by myself. So I got in the plane, flew from here down to San Diego, all the way up the coast of California to British Columbia down through the Great Lakes and all the way back through Buffalo and back home."*

The subject of several books and articles, Morris has received a variety of aviation awards. However, one of the most significant honors came on June 18, 1997, when Maryland recognized him as a Maryland Aviation Pioneer. The Aircraft Owners and Pilots Association (AOPA) has also designated him as the oldest aviator to fly trans-Atlantic flights.

Currently, Morris is considered Maryland's oldest private pilot and one of the nation's most senior aviators. Born during the Teddy Roosevelt administration, with sixty-five years and 10,000 hours of flying experience, Morris has participated in two thirds of the powered flight era. His next trip is on the drawing board.

Nathan "Bill" Morris, oral history interview, November 22, 2002, MHT/OHC 002 (MD-AVC) 011, 34p

gabled, single-story concrete block buildings, connected by an addition.[7]

***Significance for Maryland air/space history*:** A general aviation airport dating from the post-World War II period.

Relevant Years: 1945-present   *Lat/Long*: 38-36-01N 77-04-25W
Map: ADC Md//Del, 2000 *Num*: 19 *Grid*: F5 *Shows*: airport

CECIL COUNTY AIRPARK
Originally LOVETT FIELD
Elkton, Cecil County
1945-1997

Cecil County Airpark, Identifier 2NO, was located about three miles northeast of Elkton, on the east side of Maryland Route 316, and north of the present Interstate 95. (Although sometimes listed as Cecil County Airport, it should not be confused with the later landing field of that name, Identifier 58M, which is southwest of the city.) Originally known as Lovett Field, the facility was listed under that name in an engineer's report in September 1945. The report described it as a Class 1 airport with a turf surface. More details were provided in a state directory that described the airport as of July 1, 1946. The facility had three hangars, an office, and seventy acres that were usable for landing, except for a soft area on the east side. It operated in daylight only, offering student flying, charter service, fuel, and minor repairs. Waldo R. Lovett, of nearby Newark, Delaware, was the owner and manager. Lovett continued to operate the airport as late as 1965. By 1966, however, the name had changed to Cecil County Airpark, and Mrs. Jane L. Stradley was the manager. Turf remained the runway surface as late as 1970, but by 1974 the airport possessed a paved runway 2,600 feet long. The state directory issued in October 1996 described a layout similar to that in 1974, and named Jane Stradley as both owner and manager.[8] Cecil County Airpark closed during the following year. According to Paul Freeman's website on airfield history, increasing land value prompted the owner to sell to the W. L. Gore Company. Paul Freeman reported that, in 2000, some of the former runway's pavement continued to exist at its north end, while an office complex was located at its south end.[9]

***Significance for Maryland air/space history*:** A general aviation airport that operated for roughly a half-century before closing in the increasingly urbanized 1990s.

Relevant Years: c. 1945 – 1997
Lat/Long: 39-38-57N 75-48-05W
Map: ADC Md/Del, 2000 *Num*: 8 *Grid*: C5 *Shows*: area

FREDERICK MUNICIPAL AIRPORT
Frederick, Frederick County
1946-present

Frederick Municipal Airport occupies a 588-acre tract on the eastern edge of the city, north of Interstate 70 and west of the Monocacy River. Planning for the airport began in 1943, when the city sold its first airfield to the federal government (see entry on Detrick Field on page 60). The site was selected during the following year. A planning committee member later remarked that "the key to the airport was getting the money from the federal government. At that time during World War II, money for any civilian project was hard to come by." With this assistance secured, the city purchased land in 1945 and construction began in March of the following year. The first stage of the project produced an airfield with sod runways used

Control tower at Frederick Municipal Airport.
Photo courtesy of Ashish Solanki, Maryland Aviation Administration.

only by recreational fliers. A second and more ambitious phase began in 1947, aided by both state funds and an award under the new Federal Airport Act. This stage included paved, lighted runways and an administration/terminal building topped by an air traffic control cab In September of the following year, the Baltimore *Sun* reported that the still-incomplete facility would be ranked as Category 3, making it one of the four top-rated airports in the state. Dedicated on April 27, 1949, Frederick's new airport was headlined as "One of the Most Modern in the East." The terminal building was named in honor of William T. Delaplaine III, a young Navy officer from Frederick who had been killed in a wartime plane crash. On the day after the dedication, a DC-3 landed to begin upgraded daily service by All American Airways.[10]

A diagram of Frederick Municipal in the 1950 state

directory showed the terminal and a large hangar to the west of a 3,000-foot north-south runway. This strip formed a "V" with the 3,800 feet primary runway, which was oriented northeast-southwest. Comparison with the diagram in the 1974 directory shows that the north-south runway had been lengthened to 4,000 feet. A northwest-southeast turf strip was active at that time, although this did not appear in the 1981 issue's sketch. In 1982, the Aircraft Owners and Pilots Association (AOPA) selected the airport as the new site for its national headquarters, which had been located in Bethesda, Maryland. In 1990, the Federal Aviation Administration awarded a grant of $40,000 as the first step in a program of expansion and upgrading for the airport. Subsequent improvements under the city's master plan have included a changed airfield design. This features a northeast-southwest runway lengthened to 5,220 feet, a northwest-southeast runway measuring 3,800 feet, and an extensive system of taxiways. In May 2002, aircraft based at Frederick Municipal numbered 216, including twelve jets. Operations for the preceding twelve months totaled 156,627, including 3,422 by air taxis and 724 by military flights.[11]

Significance for Maryland air/space history: One of the state's larger airports, this facility has provided its community with access to aviation since 1949.
Relevant years: 1946 – present
Lat/Long: 39-24-56N 77-22-34W
Map: ADC Md/Del 2000 *Num*: 14
Grid: B1 *Shows*: airport

DAVIS AIRPORT
Laytonsville, Montgomery County
1946-present

Davis Airport is located on a thirteen-and-one-half-acre property that is three miles north of Laytonsville at 7200 Hawkins Creamery Road, near that road's junction with Maryland Route 108. It began as one of many small postwar airports catering to veterans seeking pilot training with the aid of the G.I. Bill of Rights. Established by E. H. Davis in 1946, the facility was described in August of that year as possessing three hangars and two unpaved runways, 1,800 and 2,600 feet long. It operated in daylight only, offering fuel, repairs, and charter service, in addition to primary flight instruction.[12]

The fortunes of Davis Airport declined in the late 1940s, and by 1949 it was closed. During the following year, the airport reopened under the management of W. H. "Bill" Paille, a former military pilot. Paille bought Davis's three remaining Aeronca aircraft, and later purchased the land as well. He operated the airport with his wife, Mina Avery Paille, who became the owner after his death in 1977. Mrs. Paille was recognized as a Maryland Aviation Pioneer in 1997.[13]

In April 1956, a newspaper reported that the "tiny" airport was boarding about fifteen aircraft, and now had only a single runway. Due to a recent storm, its sole remaining building was an office-workshop. The article stated, however, that Paille expected his facility to benefit from the closure of its only competitor in the county at that time, Congressional Airport. In 1959, Davis Airport was reported to board about fifty aircraft, although it still lacked a hangar.[14]

By 1967, the runway surface was treated gravel, and by 1969 it was asphalt. The runway's reported length had slipped to 1,950 feet by 1996. By March 2000, however, the airport was slated for a state grant to assist in repaving and lengthening the runway to the 2000 feet usually required of public-use facilities. This work that had been accomplished by the following year. In mid-2002, twenty-nine aircraft were based at the airport, which still operated in daylight only.[15]

Original structures at the facility include the small office and adjoining maintenance hangar, both from 1946. Just northwest of these buildings are two "T" hangars from the 1950s. Among the airplanes that have been based at Davis Airport is a vintage 1973 Cessna 150L Commuter (N11213) that has been part of the National Air and Space Museum's collection since 1987.[16]

Significance for Maryland air/space history: A small general aviation airport that has continued to operate since the 1940s.
Relevant years: 1946-present   *Lat/Long*: 39-14-40N 77-08-56W
Map: ADC Md/Del 2000 *Num*: 14 *Grid*: E4 *Shows*: airport

SHEELER FIELD
Originally GILL AIRFIELD
Chestertown, Kent County
1946-c. 1992

Scheeler Field was just north of Chestertown, on the west side of U.S. Route 213 where that highway bends toward the northeast.[17] Originally known as Gill Airfield, the facility was built in 1946 by developer Henry Gill. It appeared on an aeronautical chart dated in October of that year. A November 6 newspaper article reported that students at Washington College were eager to use the new field to keep up flying skills learned during the war, and one Ercoupe owner planned to commute there from his residence near Baltimore. The article

described the airport as having an aluminum hangar large enough for four airplanes, and three long runways. As shown in a 1950 state airport directory, however, the field had only a single 3,300-foot turf runway paralleling the highway (north-northeast-south-southwest). A second intersecting runway (east-southeast-west-northwest) was then under construction, but diagrams in the 1974 and 1981 state directories showed only the single landing strip along the highway. The airport's name changed to Scheeler Field at some point between 1980 and 1984. The last directory examined that listed the airport, published for 1990, stated that there were now two lighted turf runways of 3,000 and 2,290 feet.[18] In 1992, the Wal-Mart company announced that it had purchased the property for $1.4 million; however, local opposition appears to have blocked construction of the retail store planned for the site.[19]

Significance for Maryland air/space history: A general aviation airport that operated for more than four decades.
Relevant years: 1946-c. 1992   *Lat/Long*: 39-14W 76-04 N
Map: ADC Md/Del 2000 *Num*: 16 *Grid*: F4 *Shows*: area

ABERDEEN AIRPARK
Aberdeen, Harford County
1946-1979

Aberdeen Airpark opened in about 1946.[20] Owned by Merrill R. Bowden, it then occupied a one-hundred-acre property less than a mile southwest of Aberdeen, between U.S. Route 40 on the south and a railway line on the north. The airport operated in the daytime only, offering student flying, charter services, fuel, and minor repairs. It had two runways, 1,800 and 2,100 feet long. By 1948, the operator was Thomas C. Hill.[21] Twenty years earlier, Hill had begun his career in aviation by winning a national model aircraft competition. After receiving an aeronautical engineering degree in 1933, Hill served with the Glenn L. Martin Company for thirteen years, and later worked in ballistics research at the Aberdeen Proving Ground. In early 1950s, Hill and his wife Betty received the fifth annual Pfeiffer Award for their contributions to Maryland aviation. In 1953, a local publication described Aberdeen Airpark as the center of aviation in the county, and the headquarters of the Albatross Flying Club. The 1950 state directory showed that the airport's two runways had been lengthened to 2,000 and 2,400 feet. By 1960, however, only the shorter one (oriented west-southwest/east-northeast) remained in operation. No state directories were found that listed the airport after July 1972, although the Aircraft Owners and Pilots Association publications continued to include it as late as 1979. The facility apparently closed around that year, and the property was developed as housing.[22] A document in the Maryland Aviation Administration files indicates that the site of the former airport is on Edmunds Street, south of the Hillsdale Elementary School.[23]

Significance for Maryland air/space history: An airport that served general aviation for more than thirty years.
Relevant Years: c. 1946 – c. 1979
Lat/Long: 39-30-15N   76-10-30W
Map: ADC Md/Del 2000 Num: 16 Grid: D1 Shows: area

ESSEX SEAPLANE BASE
Essex, Baltimore County
c. 1946-c. 1959

The earliest record found of Essex Seaplane Base is a description, as of August 27, 1946, in a state airport directory.[24] The facility was located one-half mile south of Essex and about three miles east of the Baltimore city boundary. It was on the north shore of Back River, roughly midway between the Eastern Avenue bridge and Cox Point. The unlighted base operated in the daytime only, offering student flying, charter services, fuel, and minor repairs. It had a dock and a ramp for light aircraft. In addition, a hangar and office building were reported under construction. The owner and manger was given as Harry R. Carl. Subsequent listings named Rena M. Carl as joint owner, and specify the facility's address as 536 Riverside Drive. The last directory found that listed Essex Seaplane Base was issued in June 1950. Hangar space was not yet available at that time. The facility continued appear on aeronautical section charts through January 22, 1959, but was not shown on the chart valid through July 27 of that year. It was not included in a state airport list issued in 1960.[25] (Essex Seaplane Base should not be confused with the later Essex Skypark, located farther downriver: see separate entry on page 90.)

Significance for Maryland air/space history: A general aviation seaplane base of the 1940s and 1950s.
Years: c. 1946 – c. 1959   *Lat/Long*: 39-18N   76-27W
Map: ADC Md/Del 2002 *Num*: 16 *Grid*: A3 *Shows*: area

ANNAPOLIS AIRPORT
Annapolis, Anne Arundel County
c. 1946-c. 1949

The first aeronautical section chart to include Annapolis Airport was dated October 22, 1946. A directory that described the facility as of the beginning of that same month stated that it was located on a 196-acre property, two miles south of Annapolis. It had two surfaced

runways, two hangars, and an administrative building. The unlighted airport operated in the daytime only, offering student flying, charter service, and repairs. Annapolis Airport, Inc., was listed as the owner in this directory, which was issued in 1947, and as the operator in the 1948 edition. A July 1949 state listing, however, gave the operator as Dixie Aero, Inc., a company that at the same time operated another Annapolis-area facility, Dixie Airport (see separate listing on page 102). This 1949 listing was the last that was found for Annapolis Airport.[26]

Significance for Maryland air/space history: A short-lived general aviation airport of the 1940s.
Years: c. 1946 – c. 1949   *Lat/Long*: 38-57N   76-30W
Map: ADC Md/Del 2002 *Num*: 21 *Grid*: F1 *Shows*: area

NAVAL ORDNANCE LABORATORY, WHITE OAK
(WHITE OAK LABORATORY)
White Oak, Montgomery County (MO: 33-25)
1946-1997

In 1939, the Navy acquired an 870-acre tract at White Oak that became the new location of the Naval Ordnance Laboratory (NOL), formerly at the Washington Navy Yard. Most of the site chosen was in Montgomery County, although its eastern extremity lay in Prince George's County. The cornerstone for the new facility was laid in August 1946, and command and administration of NOL officially moved there in June 1948. In 1969, the Navy transferred 137 acres of the site to the Army for establishment of its Adelphi Laboratory Center. In 1974, NOL became part of a combined organization, and as a result was renamed the Naval Surface Warfare Center, White Oak Detachment.

Over the years, research at White Oak addressed a broad spectrum of issues such as conventional and nuclear explosives, magnetic effects, materials testing, hydrodynamics, and aerodynamics. Work in the latter field was supported by a series of advanced wind tunnels. Capable of supersonic and hypersonic speeds, the tunnels were used to test aircraft and such missile systems as the Polaris and Minuteman. Hypervelocity Tunnel No. 9, for example, had the highest speed and largest object capacity of any wind tunnel in the nation when completed in the early 1970s. In 1995, the Navy transferred twenty-two acres of the White Oak property to the Army. Legislation enacted that same year resulted in the Navy's closure of the facility in 1997.[27] An historical survey report prepared in February 1997 noted that the site included 372 structures and landscape features.[28] The main entrance to the complex was at 10901 New Hampshire Avenue, the thoroughfare that formed its western boundary. The other three sides of the property were roughly bounded by a Perimeter Road that ran just inside its borders. The General Services Administration (GSA), which acquired this land from the Navy, leased the wind tunnel area to the Air Force. In 1998, GSA transferred an additional forty-nine acres to the Army for use in connection with activities at its Adelphi center. For the remainder of the property, roughly 660 acres, plans included environmental cleanup and redevelopment as the Federal Research Center at White Oak.[29]

Main building at the Naval Ordnance Laboratory, White Oak, was built in 1946. The laboratory conducted extensive wind-tunnel tests during the 1950s. Photo courtesy of the Maryland Historical Trust.

Significance for Maryland air/space history: A technical facility whose work has included research relevant to aviation and rocketry.

Relevant years: 1946 - 1997

Lat/Long: 39-02N 76-58W

Map: ADC Md/Del 2000 *Num:* 15 *Grid:* A6 *Shows:* facility

FREEWAY AIRPORT
Mitchellville (near Bowie),
Prince George's County
c. 1947-present

Freeway Airport is located about two miles northwest of Mitchellville at 3900 Church Road. The present owner reports that his father, Irvin Rodenhauser, built the airfield in the 1940s, and that aviation fuel was available there from 1947. The present name dates from the 1950s, when the U.S. Route 50 freeway was constructed. The highway was built across the northern portion of the facility, claiming its east-west runway. According to a Washington *Star* article, the airport was first licensed for commercial use in 1959. In November 1960, Maryland authorities issued a brief listing of commercial airports that included Freeway, which seems to have appeared in no such publication before that time. This 1960 listing described the facility as having two unpaved runways that were oriented north-south and northwest-southeast. A diagram in a 1974 state directory showed a single paved runway, 2,150 feet long, that was oriented north-south and at right angles to U.S. Route 50. Today's layout is similar, although the runway now measures 2,435 feet and has a parallel taxiway. As of September 2000, flight operations for the preceding twelve months totaled more than 61,000. Services at Freeway include aircraft rental, fuel, repairs, and flight instruction.[30]

Significance for Maryland air/space history: A general aviation airport that has provided services since 1947.

Relevant years: c. 1947 - present

Lat/Long: 38-56-25N 76-46-20W

Map: ADC Md/Del 2000 *Num:* 20 *Grid:* C1 *Shows:* airport

POTOMAC AIRFIELD
Formerly ROSE VALLEY AIPORT, then P.G. AIRPARK
Friendly, Prince George's County (PG6)
c. 1940s - present

Potomac Airfield is located at Friendly on a property of about fifty acres at 10300 Glen Way. It is less than a mile west of Washington Executive Hyde Field, and roughly six miles southeast of the District of Columbia. The airport has a single paved runway, 2,665 feet long, and offers services to general aviation that include fuel, repairs, and flight training. According to a paper by Karin Thiessen, the facility originated in the 1950s as a grass landing strip for private use. The current manager, however, has been told that operations began in the 1940s. In November 1960, a state listing of commercial airports included it under the name of Rose Valley Airport. The facility was described as having a lighted, hard-surface runway that was 3,000 feet in length. At some time between 1962 and the issuance of the state's 1966 airport directory, the name changed to P.G. Airpark. The current name had been adopted by 1996.[31]

As of August 2001, flight operations for the preceding twelve months totaled nearly 53,000. After the terrorist attacks of the following month, federal authorities closed Potomac Airfield until January 2002. It was then allowed to reopen, but under special security restrictions applying to the three small airports nearest Washington. Potomac Airfield received a federal grant to aid in defraying business losses and in making security improvements.[32]

Significance for Maryland air/space history: A general aviation airport that has provided commercial service at least 1960.
Relevant years: c. 1940s-present
Lat/Long: 38-44-51N 76-57-27W
Map: ADC Md/Del 2000 *Num*: 20 Grid: A3 *Shows*: airport

BERLIN AIRPARK
Berlin, Worcester County
c. 1947-c. 1953

A state airport directory described Midway Airpark, as of March 1947, as possessing two unpaved runways, two hangars, and an office. It offered training, charters, fuel, and minor repairs. Midway Airpark was five miles north-northeast of Berlin, on the east side of U.S. Route 113. The forty-acre facility was managed by C. D. Gumm, Jr., the son of the owner. Midway Airpark was included in the Haire Publishing Company's directory for 1947, but not in its editions for the previous or following years. No other directory listings were found for this airport; however, it continued to appear on aeronautical charts as late as February 1953.[33]

Significance for Maryland air/space history: A general aviation airport that appears to have offered commercial service for a short time in the postwar period.
Relevant years: c. 1947 – c. 1953. *Lat/Long*: 38-24N 75-13W
Map: ADC Md/Del 2000 Num: 28 Grid: D2 Shows: area

DIXIE AIRPORT
Annapolis, Anne Arundel County
1947-1951

Dixie Airport was located almost eleven miles west of Annapolis, south of U.S. Route 50 and east of the Patuxent River. It appears to have opened around 1947. The airport was listed in the Haire Publishing Company's directory for 1947, but not in the previous year's edition. Similarly, it appeared on the aeronautical section chart dated October 15, 1947, but not on one issued a year earlier. A state directory described it, as of March 1, 1947, as a forty-acre property owned by Dixie Aero Flying Service, Inc.[34] The airport had two unpaved runways, 2,490 and 1,900 feet long, as well as one hangar with office space. It offered student flying, charter service, fuel, and minor repairs. The facility operated during day-

light hours, although a June 1950 directory indicated that portable lights were available on request. In May 1952, a newspaper article named Dixie Airport as one of four Maryland airports that had closed since June 1950.[35]

Significance for Maryland air/space history: A short-lived general aviation airport of the late 1940s and early 1950s.
Relevant Years: 1947 – c.1951
Lat/Long: 38-59-15N 76-41-30W
Map: ADC Md/Del 2000 *Num*: 20 Grid: D1 *Shows*: area

FARMINGTON AIRPORT
Farmington, Cecil County
c. 1949-present

Farmington Airport is located just south of the town for which it is named, and about two miles southeast of the larger community of Rising Sun. The facility was established by Lloyd Gifford, whose interest in flying stemmed from his service as a mechanic aboard aircraft carriers in World War II. After completing pilot training in Oklahoma in 1949, Gifford returned home to Farmington, where he flew a rebuilt Taylorcraft from his father's farm. He bought a crossroads automobile repair shop, which became the nucleus of a hybrid business that combined farming equipment with aviation. Gifford used his flying skills for such tasks as locating lost livestock, carrying sportsmen to hunting grounds, and delivering newspapers and bread to snowbound farmsteads, according to an article published in 1960. In November of that same year, Farmington Airport was included in a state listing of commercial airports. The facility's two unpaved runways then measured 1,600 and 1,700 feet, slightly longer than the reported length today. Farmington disappeared from state listings of commercial airports in the early 1970s, but was still carried in AOPA directories into the 1990s. A current listing on the Air Nav.Com website states that hangars and servicing for airframes and engines are still available at the airport, which is owned by Mary V. Gifford Blevins.[36]

Significance for Maryland air/space history: A rural general aviation airport established about 1949.
Relevant years: c. 1949-present *Lat/Long*: 39-4N 76-02W
Map: ADC Md.Del 2000 *Num*: 7 Grid: F4 *Shows*: airport

GLENN L. MARTIN WIND TUNNEL
College Park, Prince George's County
1949-present

The Glenn L. Martin Wind Tunnel is located within the University of Maryland campus at College Park. The facility opened in 1949, and still occupies its original building. The location is on the east side of Stadium Drive, near its junction with Paint Branch Drive. The Glenn L. Martin Aircraft Company donated the low-speed wind tunnel to the university, with the intention that it be self-supporting. The company itself contracted to use the tunnel during the first five years of existence, but little work was actually accomplished for Martin before it left the field of aircraft manufacturing. The tunnel represented the state of the art at its inception, and it has received upgrades to keep pace with evolving technology. The staff has conducted

Above: Passengers arrived on one level and departed from another in the advanced design for the Friendship Airport Terminal, completed 1950. Photo courtesy of Glenn L. Martin Maryland Aviation Museum.

Left: Baltimore/Washington terminal retains the same traffic pattern and control tower location in 2003. Photo courtesy of BWI Airport.

more than 1,700 experiments and research projects in the fields of aerodynamics and hydrodynamics, covering a wide range of applications. Aviation-related work has involved studies of conventional airplanes, vertical take-off and landing (VTOL) aircraft, helicopters, airfoils, and turbofan thrust reversers.[37]

Significance for Maryland air/space history: A research facility that has assisted aviation design projects since 1949.

Relevant years: 1949 - present *Lat/Long*: 39-00N 76-57W
Map: ADC Md/Del 2000 *Num*: 20 *Grid*: A1 *Shows*: area

BALTIMORE/WASHINGTON INTERNATIONAL AIRPORT
Originally FRIENDSHIP INTERNATIONAL AIRPORT
Glen Burnie, Anne Arundel County
1950-present

Maryland's largest airport is almost nine miles south of Baltimore on a 3,170-acre tract that is just west of Glen Burnie. The facility's origin lay in a master plan that Baltimore authorities adopted in 1946 to remedy their

city's need for an airport more adequate than Harbor Field. The resulting Friendship International Airport was dedicated on June 24, 1950. (Its name honored Friendship Church, which had stood on the site.) Built at a cost of $15 million, the new airport was very impressive for its time. The terminal complex was dominated by a 110-foot control tower, and the main lobby covered an acre. It possessed three runways, of which the longest measured 9,450 feet.[38] Commercial service, which began a month after the dedication, grew slowly at first. Traffic experienced a spurt in the early jet era, dipped after the opening of rival Dulles International, and then resumed an upward trend.

The State of Maryland purchased the airport from the City of Baltimore in 1972. In the following year, the state gave the facility its present name and announced plans for a major upgrade. The most striking focus of the overhaul was the main terminal, which was more than double the previous size when work was completed in 1979. Instead of the central lobby of the old terminal, this structure offered ten entrances to a concourse curved around a parking area. Its roof of tubular steel construction was supported by twelve towers faced with red tile. Many subsequent improvements included such features

From the Oral History Files...

Air Traffic Controller

An interview with Paul Lebert
by John D. Willard, V

Whenever we get into an airplane, we see the flight attendants, and sometimes get to hear the pilot's voice over the intercom. Never do we see, and only rarely do we think about, the many men and women who ensure our safety when the plane takes off and lands, and flies to our destination. Considering the number of flights and passengers, the job of air traffic controllers is truly remarkable. Paul Lebert is one of these unrecognized people; he has spent most of his adult life in the field of air traffic control, with most of that time spent in the Baltimore Metropolitan area, serving at the now defunct Harbor Field, beginning in 1957, and then serving at Friendship Airport, which soon became Baltimore Washington International Airport. He retired in 1985.

As a child in Pittston, Pennsylvania, during the 1930s and 1940s, his interest in flight and flying started at an early age. He recalls that by the age of ten he was already eager about the idea of flying, *"Just being able to fly around the sky I thought was pretty super . . . I really wanted to fly, when I was ten years old."*

After being inducted into the United States Air Force in 1951, Lebert was able to enter into the field of air traffic control. *"[T]hey gave you options of what was available . . . [and] they gave me air traffic control. Being*

Paul Leibert controlling arrival aircraft in the Baltimore Approach air space at Friendship Airport, using radar screen and bay of paper strips, c. 1961. Photo courtesy of Paul Leibert.

that it was with aviation, I said, 'Sure, I'll take it.' " Air traffic control training was conducted at Keesler Air Force Base in Biloxi, Mississippi and Lebert was trained to be a control tower operator.

Lebert's first day on the job as an actual control tower operator proved to be uneventful, though the location was anything but typical, *"My first day was in Chinea, Korea. . . . you just look out and tell pilots to clear the landing strip for takeoff."* The station was a low-volume location with many periods of inactivity and long lulls without

out flights. *"You sat around for a lot of time just waiting. And that's all there was to it."* After serving an uneventful tour in Korea, Lebert was transferred to Andrews Air Force Base. He soon found out that the volume of air traffic was very different there. Instead of trying to keep occupied during long intervals of relative quiet, it was difficult to keep up with the sheer volume of flights. *"We used to have fifteen B-25's practicing landings almost daily, and in the beginning it scared the heck out of me. I figured, 'how am I going to handle that many airplanes?'"* But after a little experience, handling the large number of flights became easier.

In addition to developing the mental ability to keep track of so much information, there were more tools to help keep track of the flights and additional personnel. *"We had a flight data person. They had a little strip [of paper]. You'd write them down, and you knew who was who. They'd write the identification and type of airplane and keep it in a bay, in a sequence of the number one, two, three, to land. And also, the flight data person would help you keep an eye on the traffic and the traffic pattern."* This was a very simple paper system that helped keep information organized. As planes landed, the strips of paper were handed over to ground control personnel who ensured the planes taxied to the proper parking areas.

Above: Paul Leibert (standing, with sunglasses and mike) controlling taxiing aircraft to and from the runway at Friendship Airport, while Mike Harrington controls aircraft landing and taking off. A United Airlines DC-8 is parked in the background, circa 1963. Photo courtesy of Paul Leibert.

After completing his military service, Lebert entered the Civil Aeronautics Administration (CAA) in 1956. His first duty was as an Airway Operations Specialist in which he relayed air traffic control information and clearances, and reported weather observations. As part of the CAA he was transferred to Harbor Field, in Dundalk in late 1957. Like his post in Korea, Harbor Field control tower was completely visual, with relatively low flight volume. Flight traffic consisted mostly of smaller training planes, a few corporate planes, *"Nothing too big or too fast."* Lebert eventually got his private and commercial pilot's license and flew corporate Lear Jets while still working as an air traffic controller.

In 1959, Lebert started working at Friendship Airport (later rechristened BWI). At Friendship there was a lot more to learn and the overall operations were much more sophisticated. Friendship had two radar scopes and, like Andrews Air Force Base, had more personnel to handle a higher volume of traffic. It was during the period of the 1960s that air traffic began to increase sharply at Friendship and around the country. Over this period, the number of radar scopes increased from two to three, and then from three to four.

If any terms that can describe the environment in which Lebert worked they are expansion and increased air traffic. By the early 1970s there were eight radar scopes and a special room.

With the increase of traffic came more equipment and more complexity. Lebert cites an example of the changes, *"We had a little manual we called the ANC manual. It had sixty-three pages in it. Today that little manual is now called ATP 7110.65 . . . It's got over three hundred pages in it."*

Increased traffic and complexity began to elevate stress levels among people working at stations. The concern of making a mistake and possibly causing an accident was a real concern. *"[W]hen things weren't going right . . . Even with your best intentions . . . [The] fear of maybe almost killing somebody—that's not too nice a thought."* As a stress reduction method, controllers would rotate positions. *"The supervisor would assign you to the position to work [for] two hours and then they'd say, 'All right, go work another position,' or 'take a ten minute break,' or something to keep from getting too stressful."*

Not only did increased air traffic volume create greater air traffic control stresses, but also the greater speed and size of jet aircraft when they became more common in the 1960s and 1970s. The increase in air traffic volume and air speed led to new developments in electronics and air traffic management. The use of transponders that would help locate the positions of planes, as well as Traffic Collision Avoidance Systems (T-CAS), and improved radar systems helped ease the difficulties of controllers electronically. The new equipment proved to need more training and understanding, but helped increase air traffic volume. *"[T]here's a certain amount of complexity because you have to learn all these different pieces of equipment, but on one hand I guess you can say that that's difficult. But once you learn it, it allows you to do more, handle more traffic."* New rules helped also, including airspeed reductions and land-and-hold-short operations that increased the number of planes landing and taking off. Together, new electronics, and new practices helped allow a greater volume of air traffic.

In the late 1970 and early 1980s, Lebert continued to progress higher into the field of air traffic control by gaining higher and higher supervisory roles. Though he became management and no longer sat behind the scope he still appreciated the work, dedication and talent of the frontline controllers, *"[T]he challenge . . . being able to handle the volume of traffic, the complexity of it, and being so precise . . . knowing that not everybody can do that kind of stuff . . . the challenge was the fun of it. . . .[O]ne day when a guy gets up and says, 'I handled a hundred and twenty airplanes that hour.' That's a lot of airplanes in an hour."*

Asked about his impact to flight in Maryland, Lebert was humble in his response, *"I think we provided a service that allows a lot of people to fly and safely. I don't know of any other explanation it can be. I mean, that's what our purpose was."*

Paul Lebert, oral history interview, October 21, 2002, MHT/OHC 002 (MD-AVC) 021, 39 p.

as additional gates, runway extensions, a larger and better-equipped control tower, and new cargo facilities. A large new international terminal opened in December 1997.[39] Meanwhile, traffic grew rapidly in the era of airline deregulation. More than 19.6 million people used BWI in 2000, the year of its fiftieth anniversary. Passengers continued to increase even during the following year, when terrorist attacks had a devastating effect on the air travel system as a whole. During 2002, the U.S. Department of Transportation designated BWI as a test site for new security techniques, and it soon became the lead airport in the nationwide shift from the use of private to federal employees as security screeners.[40]

Significance for Maryland air/space history: The result of far-sighted planning, this major airport has provided the state with an efficient and profitable center of air transportation.
Relevant years: 1950 - present
Lat/Long: 39-10-31N 76-40-05W
Map: ADC Md/Del 2000 *Num*: 15 *Grid*: D4 *Shows*: airport

CRISFIELD MUNICIPAL AIRPORT
Crisfield, Somerset County
1950-present

Crisfield Municipal Airport is a 131-acre property located at 4784 Jacksonville Road, three miles north of the city for which it is named. The airport is east of James Island State Park, south of the Big Annemessex River, and northwest of Maryland Route 413. In September 1948, the Baltimore *Sun* reported that Crisfield had received a federal grant of $35,000. to build an airport. The newspaper indicated that the Civil Aeronautics Administration had approved the design, and that bids had been accepted for the project. Another article in May 1950 mentioned that the airport was "operable." The facility was not quite ready to open, however, to judge from a state directory issued on June 1 of the same year. That publication noted that information on the airport's operator, manager, and facilities would be available after July 1. The directory described the facility as possessing an asphalt runway 2,500 feet long, and an intersecting sod runway 2,800 feet long. The same general layout exists today, although the length of the unpaved runway is now 3,280 feet. Improvements at the airport include runway lighting and a Precision Approach Path Indicator (PAPI) system.[41]

Significance for Maryland air/space history: A small municipal airport that has operated more than half a century.
Relevant years: 1950 - present
Lat/Long: 38-01-00N 75-49-45W
Map: ADC Md/Del 2000 *Num*: 27 *Grid*: C6 *Shows*: airport

DEEP CREEK AIRPORT
Churchton, Anne Arundel County
1950-1988

Deep Creek Airport was about two miles northeast of Churchton at the end of Dent Road. The low-lying facility bordered on the creek for which it was named, and on the Chesapeake Bay.[42] The airport apparently opened about 1950, since a state directory issued in June of that year included its name with the notation "data pending." The next available state listing, for 1960, stated that the airport had two unpaved runways, 2,000 and 3,000 feet long. The manager was W. Neitzey, whom subsequent directories identified as Walter N. Neitzey, owner and operator as late as 1974. In January 1967, meanwhile, state authorities ordered the airport closed temporarily until utility lines at one end of it were placed underground. Descriptions from the 1970s reduced the length of the shorter runway to 1,800 feet, and also noted that the facility was "closed January to May, during periods of thaw and after rains." The last directory to include the facility was AOPA's 1987 issue, which named the operator as Deep Creek Airport and Marina, Inc. The runways were then listed as 2,100 feet (turf and gravel) and 1,500 feet (turf). Services available included instruction, aircraft rental, fuel and repairs. Beside conventional landplanes, operations included flying by seaplanes, gliders, and ultralights.[43] Deep Creek Airport closed in 1988. On his website, Paul Freeman noted a local pilot's report that a developer had purchased the property, but had been unable to obtain building permits as of 2002.[44]

Significance for Maryland air/space history: A general aviation airport that operated for about thrity-eight years.
Relevant Years: 1950 - 1988   *Lat/Long*: 38-48N 76-30W
Map: ADC Md/Del 2000 *Num*: 20 *Grid*: F3 *Shows*: town

RUSSELL AIRPORT
Chestertown, Kent County
1950-c. 1970s

Russell Airport was located near the Chesapeake Bay on a neck of land between Worton Creek on the north and Fairlee Creek on the south. The site was about three miles west of Melitota, and roughly seven or eight miles northwest of Chestertown. Russell Airport first appeared on the Washington section aeronautical chart in July 1950, having been absent from the previous one issued in January. A state listing of commercial airports issued in 1960 stated that its manager was F. C. Russell, and that it had one unpaved north-south runway 3,400 feet long. The last directory found that included Russell Airport, published by the state in 1974, still showed a sin-

gle turf runway. P. A. Sinclair was listed as the operator of the airport, which offered tiedowns and fuel, but no maintenance services. The name of the facility may have subsequently changed to Great Oak Airport, which had a similar location and description in listings by the Aircraft Owners and Pilots Association in 1979 and 1980.[45]

Significance for Maryland air/space history: A small general aviation airport that operated for at least twenty-four years.
Relevant years: 1950 – c. 1970s *Lat/Long*: 39-13N 76-11W
Map: ADC Md/Del 2000 *Num*: 16 *Grid*: D3 *Shows*: area

CAMBRIDGE-DORCHESTER COUNTY AIRPORT
Formerly CAMBRIDGE MUNICIPAL AIRPORT
Cambridge, Dorchester County
1954-present

Cambridge–Dorchester County Airport is located three miles southeast of Cambridge, south of U.S. Route 50 and east of Bucktown Road. According to an article by Clayton Davis, the facility originated in a 1952 understanding between the Airpax Corporation and local authorities. To secure relocation of Airpax to their community, the city agreed to establish an airport on farmland near an existing municipal dump site. The resulting facility opened in 1954.[46] A listing issued by the state's aviation commission in 1960 included Cambridge as a municipal airport with a hard-surface runway 3,000 feet long. A newspaper report in October 1969 stated that work was about to begin on an upgrade, described as part of a Federal Aviation Administration program to establish "new model airports" for small but growing cities. The municipal government allotted $5,500 toward the cost of these improvements, which would include lighting for the runway and its extension to 4,000 feet. The new length was reflected in an airport directory issued in 1972. Subsequent improvements included taxiway construction and new hangars. The airport was transferred from the city to the county in early 1979, and the received its present name at that time. In 1999, the runway was extended to its current length of 4,476 feet. As of December 2000, operations for the preceding twelve months totaled 22,000. Construction of a new terminal was in progress in early 2003. [47]

Significance for Maryland air/space history: A general aviation airport that has operated for more than fifty years.
Relevant years: 1954 - present *Lat/Long*: 38-32-21N 76-01-50W
Map: ADC Md/Del 2000 *Num*: 21 *Grid*: F6 *Shows*: airport

THE JOHNS HOPKINS UNIVERSITY APPLIED PHYSICS LABORATORY
Laurel, Howard County
1954-present

The Applied Physics Laboratory (APL) occupies 365-acre campus bounded by Sanner Road on the west and by Johns Hopkins Road on the south. The property lies just south of Simpsonville, although APL uses a mailing address in Laurel. Having outgrown its original facility in Silver Spring (see separate entry on page 84), APL broke ground at this new site in February 1953. The Laboratory accepted the first new building from the contractor in September 1954. Since then, the campus has grown into a multi-building complex that houses 130 facilities for research and testing. After the move to Howard County, APL continued its work in the missile field, including such vehicles as Terrier, Tartar, and Polaris. The Laboratory also became in involved in new space-related projects. The first APL-designed satellite to achieve orbit, Transit 1B, was launched on January 1, 1960. Recent examples of the Laboratory's involvement in rocketry and space include its support role for a successful flight test in 2001 of the Navy's Standard Missile-3. During the same year, an APL-built spacecraft that had been launched to provide data on asteroids capped its mission by a soft landing on the surface of 433 Eros.[48]

Significance for Maryland air/space history: A laboratory credited with notable accomplishments in aerospace development.
Relevant years: 1954 - Present
Lat/Long: 39-11N 76-54W
Map: ADC Md/Del 2000 *Num*: 15 *Grid*: B4 *Shows*: area

Baltimore-Washington Nike Missile Defenses

World War II had seen the establishment of air-raid wardens and the camouflaging of defense factories, but no serious threat of air attack on Maryland had developed. The Soviet Union's development of long-range bombers armed with nuclear bombs, however, was regarded as a very serious threat indeed. The U.S. Army was given the task of deploying anti-aircraft guided missiles to guard principal centers of population and production against enemy bombers.

The Nike system stemmed from development work that was begun during World War II, then later revived to counter the perceived Soviet threat. Deployment was in

Right: Nike Ajax anti-aircraft missiles on launcher. Photo courtesy of the Granite Historical Society

Below: Integrated Fire Control radar tower, Nike missile defense system. Photo courtesy of the Granite Historical Society.

two principal phases, beginning in 1954 with the Nike Ajax missile. More than thirty-two feet long, the Ajax was powered by a solid-fuel booster rocket and a liquid-fuel second stage. It traveled at supersonic speed, had a range of twenty-five miles, and carried warheads of conventional explosives. To operate the missiles, the Army converted battalions already manning 90mm and 120mm anti-aircraft gun batteries around major cities. The first operational Nike Ajax site in the U.S.A. was established at Fort George C. Meade on May 30, 1954. Fielding of the even faster Nike Hercules began in 1958. The Hercules version was more than thirty-nine feet long and powered entirely by solid fuel. It had a range of seventy-five miles, and was capable of carrying a nuclear warhead.[49]

Nike missile sites were established on existing federal property where possible, but they were often placed on land acquired for the purpose. Each site typically had three components: an administrative area, with offices and barracks; an Integrated Fire Control area, which included radar and other equipment for guiding the weapons; and the launch area, where the missiles themselves were kept. These components might be on three separate properties, but it was usual to combine the administrative and fire control functions at a single location. Typical buildings were constructed of cinder block with flat roofs. The earliest sites were entirely above ground, but underground magazines were soon introduced to store and maintain the missiles.[50]

The conversion of many sites to the longer-range Nike Hercules system that began in 1958 was accompanied by a change in the method of guiding the weapons, which had been done initially by the individual batteries. An electronic "Missile Master" system made possible a more coordinated type of control needed for the Nike Hercules. The first of these systems, which became operational on December 5, 1957, was located at the Fort Meade command post. Meanwhile, Army National Guard units began to assume operation of some Nike batteries in 1958. In Maryland, this first occurred at the Fork and Cronhardt sites in September 1959. In late 1962, the state became the first whose troops operated a Hercules facility when the Guard took over the site at Annapolis.[51]

The number of Nike sites in Maryland seems to have peaked at about nineteen in 1960. Those that were not converted from Ajax to Hercules were closed by 1964. The nationwide total of sites reached its height during 1963, but the program declined later in the decade. Factors working against the Nike system's continuance included the high manpower required to operate it, and a change in the main perceived threat from bombers to intercontinental ballistic missiles. The Baltimore-Washington defense area was combined with that of Hampton Roads in 1971, and all Nike facilities within the contiguous states were deactivated by 1974. In that year, there were about eight sites left in Maryland. Today, the Fort Meade Museum displays an Ajax missile at Building 4674 and a Hercules at Building 1978. (See also entries on individual sites.)[52]

NIKE MISSILE SITE W-13T ARMY AIR DEFENSE COMMAND POST (AADCP) FORT GEORGE G. MEADE
Odenton, Anne Arundel County
1954-1966

Fort George G. Meade occupies an irregularly-shaped tract that is east of Maryland Route 295 and west of Odenton. Originally known as Camp Meade, it was established by the Army in 1917 during World War I. In 1991, a large southern and western portion of the installation was transferred to the Department of the Interior, and this property is now part of the Patuxent Research Refuge. Fort Meade's associations with aviation have included operation of an airfield, now a civil facility known as Tipton Airport (see separate entry on page 63). During the Cold War era, the fort played a key role in the air defense of the region through a system of Nike sur-

face-to-air missile sites.[53]

On May 30, 1954, the nation's first operational Nike site, designated W-13T, was established at Fort Meade. It was a temporary installation within the fort's "western bulge," which is now part of the Patuxent Research Refuge. The Integrated Fire Control radar was evidently located on a high point described as Hill 85, while the launch area seems to have been one mile to the east. On April 14, 1955, one of this unit's missiles exploded in the air after an accidental launch. The mishap caused no serious injuries, but heightened public concerns about the safety of the Nike installations. The battery remained at Fort Meade until the summer of 1956, when its equipment and personnel were redeployed to Site 43, a new facility near Laytonsville.[54]

An Army Air Defense Command Post (AADCP) at Fort Meade controlled the defensive missile systems deployed around both Baltimore and Washington. On December 5, 1957, it was the first in the country to be equipped with the electronic "Missile Master" system needed to control the new Nike Hercules missiles. This in turn was replaced by a solid-state "Missile Mentor" system in 1966. The former AADCP, designated Building 1978, is on the north side of Maryland Route 175 about a mile and a half east of the Baltimore-Washington Parkway. The structure has been converted to office space, and is now occupied by the fort's Director of Information Services. The associated radar dome was dismantled in recent years.[55]

Significance for Maryland air/space history: The nation's first operational Nike missile site and the Nike system's command post for the Baltimore-Washington area, both components of a major air defense system of the Cold War era.
Relevant years: 1954 - 1974 *Lat/Long*: see note 54
Map: ADC Md/Del 2000 *Num*: 15 *Grid*: C5, D5 and 6
Shows: military reservation

NIKE MISSILE SITE BA-03, PHOENIX/SWEET AIR
Phoenix, Baltimore County
1955-74

Intended for the defense of Baltimore, BA-03 became operational in November 1955. Initially equipped with the Nike Ajax system, it was converted to the more advanced Nike Hercules during 1960-61. The site was deactivated in April 1974. BA-03 consisted of two locations, each of about seventeen acres in the vicinity of Phoenix. The former Integrated Fire Control area, which is on Sunnybrook Road, was used by the National Guard after the Nike deactivation in 1974 until 1981. The Army removed all improvements there in 1986, but retains ownership of the land. The site of BA-03's launch area at 3101 Paper Mill Road is listed as intact by *Rings of Supersonic Steel*, a Nike sites history and guide book by Mark A. Morgan and Mark L. Berhow. The property was transferred to Baltimore County in 1976, and is being used as a recreation center, senior center, and fire department training facility.[56]

Significance for Maryland air space history: A surface-to-air missile site that played a role in air defense during the Cold War era.
Relevant years: 1955 - 1974
Lat/Long: 39-30N 76-37W
Map: ADC Md/Del 2000 *Num:* 6
Grid: E6 *Shows:* area

Above: Four Nike Ajax missiles being lifted into position from underground silos. Photo courtesy of the Granite Historical Society, Zang Collection.

Twelve Nike Ajax missiles just emerging from silos. Photo courtesy of the Granite Historical Society.

NIKE MISSILE SITE BA-09, FORK

Fork, Baltimore County
1955-1962

BA-09 became operational in November 1955 in defense of Baltimore. On September 23, 1959, it became one of the first two Nike facilities in Maryland transferred from operation by the regular Army to the National Guard. The site was deactivated in December 1962. Morgan and Berhow's Nike site guide lists the Integrated Fire Control area as obliterated. The site is on private property at the end of Hutchensreuter Road, south of Maryland Route 147. The launch area, also on private property, is listed as intact. It is located on Stockdale Road, and is also south of Route 147.[57]

Significance for Maryland air/space history: A surface-to-air missile site that played a role in air defense during the Cold War era.
Relevant years: 1955 - 1962 *Lat/Long:* 39-26-51N 76-26-51W
Map: ADC Md/Del 2000 *Num:* 16 *Grid:* A1 *Shows:* area

NIKE MISSILE SITE BA-18, EDGEWOOD ARSENAL

Edgewood, Harford County (HA-1995)
1954-1974

Part of the northern defenses of Baltimore, BA-18 became operational in 1954 as a Nike Ajax site, and was equipped to accommodate the more advanced Nike Hercules system during 1958-59. The site was deactivated in April 1974. BA-18 was located within the Lauderick Creek Military Reservation at Edgewood Arsenal. (Since 1971, Edgewood Arsenal has been administratively a part of Aberdeen Proving Ground.) An associated headquarters facility at the Arsenal was known by the designation BA-14. In 1994, a Maryland Historical Trust review noted that BA-18 was larger than the average Nike site, with six magazines each containing twelve missiles. All the essential components of the facility remained intact: magazines, launch pads, radar equipment, control area, housing, and an administrative area. Because of this completeness and high degree of historical integrity, the Trust recommended that the site be eligible for the National Register of Historic Places. An article published on an Army website in December 2000 noted that, following inactivation of the Nike site, the silos were decontaminated and filled with concrete. Some of the other Nike-related structures had also been demolished. The remaining barracks building was serving as the field office of an environmental hazard removal project being carried on within the same Lauderick Creek area in which the missile site had been located. This area was defined as bounded by the Aberdeen Proving Ground property line on the north, Route 755 on the west, and the Bush River on the east.[58]

Significance for Maryland air/space history: A surface-to-air missile site that played a role in air defense during the Cold War era.
Relevant years: 1954 - 1974 *Lat/Long:* 39-35N 76-16W
Map: ADC Md/Del 2000 *Num:* 16 *Grid:* C2 *Shows:* area

NIKE MISSILE SITE BA-30/31, TOLCHESTER BEACH/ CHESTERTOWN
Tolchester Beach, Kent County
1954-1974

A double site in the ring around Baltimore, BA-30/31 became operational in 1954 as a Nike Ajax site, but was modified to accommodate the more advanced Nike Hercules system during 1958-59. The site was deactivated in April 1974. BA-30/31 included three locations near Tolchester Beach. The twelve-acre housing area is now privately owned as the Delta Heights Condominiums. The twenty-three-acre Integrated Fire Control Area on Route 21 is currently owned by Kent County and used as an agricultural center. The twenty-two-acre launch area of this double Nike site, which contains six magazines, is about one mile to the south of the control area on Route 445. The launch area is also county property, and is used by the highway department for storage. Morgan and Berhow's Nike site guide lists the control and launch areas as partially modified. In a 1996 letter, a Corps of Engineers official contrasted BA-30/31 with the less well preserved Nike site at Croom. The letter stated that the photographs of the Tolchester Beach site showed that it retained historic structures, fencing, signage, the original paint scheme, and other elements reflecting its function as a missile facility.[59]

Significance for Maryland air/space history: A surface-to-air missile site that played a role in air defense during the Cold War era.
Relevant years: 1954 - 1974 *Lat/Long*: 39-12N 76-14N
Map: ADC Md/Del 2000 *Num*: 16 *Grid*: D4 *Shows*: area

Twelve Nikes stand above their silos at the BA-79's launch area in rural Granite. Photo courtesy of the Granite Historical Society, Zang Collection.

NIKE MISSILE SITE BA-79, GRANITE
Granite, Baltimore County
1954-1974

BA-79 became operational in December 1954. As the prefix indicates it was part of the ring of sites around Baltimore. Initially equipped with the Nike Ajax system, it was modified to accommodate the more advanced Nike Hercules during 1958-59. The site was deactivated in April 1974. BA-79 consisted of two locations north of Granite. The Integrated Fire Control area was on Hernwood Road, a half mile north of Woodstock Road. Used for a time by the National Guard, the site is now an inactive property under the control of the Army Directorate of Public Works at Fort Meade. Reports posted on the World Wide Web describe the control area as in an unusually good state of preservation. The site of BA-79's launch area was 5.2 miles further north on Hernwood Road. It is described as partially modified and under the control of Maryland Police and Correctional Training Commission.[60]

Significance for Maryland air/space history: A surface-to-air missile site that played a role in air defense during the Cold War era.
Relevant years: 1954 - 1974 *Lat/Long*: 39-21N 76-51W
Map: ADC Md/Del 2000 *Num*: 15 *Grid*: B2 *Shows*: area

NIKE MISSILE SITE BA-92, CRONHARDT
Cronhardt, Baltimore County
1954-1959

BA-92 became operational in December 1954 in defense of the Baltimore area. On September 23, 1959, it became one of the first two Nike facilities in Maryland transferred from operation by the regular Army to the National Guard. The site was deactivated in September 1963. A history and guide book by Mark A. Morgan and Mark L. Berhow indicates that BA-92's Integrated Fire Control area is now the Jachman U.S. Army Reserve Center at 12100 Greenspring Road, north of Broadway Road. The guide lists the site as obliterated. The former launch area, also demolished, is the property of a private club at 2515 Baublitz Road. The sites are northwest of Cronhardt and about five miles northwest of the larger town of Brooklandville.[61]

Significance for Maryland air/space history: A surface-to-air missile site that played a role in air defense during the Cold War era.

Relevant years: 1954 - 1959 *Lat/Long*: 39-27N 76-43W
Map: ADC Md/Del 2000 *Num*: 15 *Grid*: D1 *Shows*: area

NIKE MISSILE SITE W-25, DAVIDSONVILLE
Davidsonville, Anne Arundel County (AA-993)
1955-1974

W-25 became operational in June 1955 as a Washington-ring Nike Ajax site, but was converted to the more advanced Nike Hercules system during 1958. In August 1963, the Davidsonville facility was named the "National Nike Site" to serve as a showcase for visits by national and foreign dignitaries. It remained active until April 1974. The site consisted of four locations southwest of Davidsonville: the eight-acre housing area on King Manor Drive, north of the intersection of Queen Anne Bridge Road and Wayson Road; the sixteen-acre integrated fire control area, south of the same intersection and west of Wayson Road; the ten-acre site of a collimation tower for testing the radar equipment, just south of the control area on the east side of Wayson Road; and the twenty-five-acre launch area, about a half mile east of the control area on the south side of Hagner Lane. The housing area, added in 1958, consisted of fifteen simple "Capehart" dwellings and three utility buildings. It was transferred to the U.S. Air Force following closure of the Nike site. In 1999, a proposed excess property disposal triggered a review by the Maryland Historical Trust, which concurred that the housing did not qualify for the National Register of Historic Places. The control area is currently used as a recreational center, and the launch area as a police academy. Both belong to Anne Arundel County, and are listed by the Morgan and Berhow's Nike site guide as intact. The collimation test area remained Army property as of 1985.[62]

Significance for Maryland air/space history: A surface-to-air missile site that played a role in air defense during nearly nineteen years of the Cold War era, and was the designated national showcase facility for the Nike program for more than ten years of that period.
Relevant years: 1955 - 1974 *Lat/Long*: 38-54N 76-39W
Map: ADC Md/Del 2000 Num: 20 Grid: E2 Shows: area

NIKE MISSILE SITE W-26, ANNAPOLIS/SKIDMORE/BAY BRIDGE
Annapolis, Anne Arundel County (AA-38)
1955-1968

Intended for the defense of Washington, Site W-26 became operational in 1955 as a Nike Ajax site, but was converted to the more advanced Nike Hercules system

Former integrated fire control radar towers at Granite Nike Site, Baltimore County. Photo courtesy of the Granite Historical Society, Zang Collection.

during 1960-61. In December 1962, this became the first Hercules-equipped site in the nation to be transferred from the regular Army to the Army National Guard. W-26 was deactivated in November 1968. The site consisted of two locations, both north of U.S. Route 50 on the Broadneck Peninsula across the Severn River from Annapolis. The seven-acre Integrated Fire Control area was located on property now used as the U.S. Army Reserve Center near the end of Broad Neck Road. The twenty-four-acre launch area is about one mile to the east, between Bayhead Road and Yorktown Road, on property belonging to the U.S. Navy. In 1997, a historic sites survey report evaluated four structures at the control area and nineteen at the launch area. The report concluded that W-26 did not possess the exceptional significance required for a site less than fifty years old to be eligible for the National Register of Historic Places. Only two structures, silos number 205 and 207, were found to retain sufficient integrity to convey their original function and appearance. The report noted that the site's subterranean silos were scheduled to be filled with concrete prior to the closure in 2000 of the Annapolis branch of the Naval Surface Warfare Center, to which the property belonged (see separate entry on David Taylor Research Center on page 37).[63]

Significance for Maryland air/space history: A surface-to-air missile site that played a role in air defense during the Cold War era.
Relevant years: 1955 - 1968 *Lat/Long*: 39-02N 76-27W
Map: ADC Md/Del 2000 *Num*: 16 *Grid*: A6 *Shows*: area

NIKE MISSILE SITE W-35, CROOM/MARLBORO

Croom, Prince George's County (PG: 86B-26)
1954-1963

The history and site guide by Mark A. Morgan and Mark L. Berhow indicates that W-35 was operational defending Washington from November 1954 to March 1963. According to a report to the Maryland Historical Trust, the site consisted of three locations: a twenty-one-acre launch area; a six-acre housing area; and a fifteen-acre control/administrative area. Bill Evan's website describes the control area as on Mount Calvert Road, about three-quarters of a mile from Croom Road. The housing is also on Mount Calvert Road, just east of Duvall Road, while the former launch area is nearby on Duvall Road. Both the launch and control areas are county property now used by Croom Vocational High School. The housing area was U.S. Air Force property in 1991. In a 1996 review, the Maryland Historical Trust noted that the historical integrity of W-35 was diminished, and concluded that it was not eligible for the National Register of Historic Places.[64]

Significance for Maryland air/space history: A surface-to-air missile site that played a role in air defense during the Cold War era.
Relevant years: 1954 - 1963 *Lat/Long*: 38-47N 76-45W
Map: ADC Md/Del 2000 *Num*: 20 *Grid*: D3 *Shows*: area

Nike Hercules missile of Battery B, 1st Missile Battalion (NH), 90th Artillery. Photo courtesy of the Granite Historical Society, Zang Collection.

NIKE MISSILE SITE W-36, BRANDYWINE/NAYLOR

Brandywine, Prince George's County
1957-1961

The Morgan and Berhow guide indicates that W-36 was operational from 1957 to December 1961. As the prefix indicates, it was part of the Washington defenses.

The abandoned launch area is on private property east of Brandywine on North Keys Road, one mile west of Route 382. W-36's Integrated Fire Control area was on the same road another mile to the west of Route 382. Its current ownership is unknown.[65]

Significance for Maryland air/space history: A surface-to-air missile site that played a role in air defense during the Cold War era.
Relevant years: 1957 - 1961 *Lat/Long*: 38-42-26N 76-45-39W
Map: ADC Md/Del 2000 *Num*: 20 *Grid*: C4 *Shows*: area

NIKE MISSILE SITE W-43, JACOBSVILLE

Jacobsville, Anne Arundel County (AA13)
1954-1962

The Morgan and Berhow guide indicates that BA-43 was operational from 1954 to December 1962, part of the ring of bases around Washington, D.C. The former Integrated Fire Control area is at 9034 Fort Smallwood Road, a half mile north of Woodstock Road. The site is controlled by the Anne Arundel County's Schools Maintenance and Operations division, and is listed as partially dismantled. The location of BA-43's launch area is on Old Nike Site Road, south of Fort Smallwood Road. The guide states that the road to the launch area is blocked, and the launchers are presumed to be abandoned.[66] According to a report by Tom Vaughn, however, the school system is using the launch area for maintenance work and storage, while the administrative area is providing office space. Vaughn's report also differs from Morgan and Berhow in giving the site's activation date as 1956.[67]

Significance for Maryland air/space history: A surface-to-air missile site that played a role in air defense during the Cold War era.
Relevant years: 1954 - 1962 *Lat/Long*: 39-07N 76-32W (town)
Map: ADC Md/Del 2000 *Num*: 15 *Grid*: F5 *Shows*: area

NIKE MISSILE SITE W-44, MATTAWOMAN/WALDORF/LA PLATA

Waldorf, Charles County (CH-677)
1955-1971

W-44 became operational in 1955 in defense of Washington. Initially equipped with the Nike Ajax system, it was converted to the more advanced Nike Hercules during 1958. The site was deactivated in June 1971. W-44 consisted of two locations, both on Country Lane in the Mattawoman area northeast of Waldorf. The former launch area of sixteenand one-half acres is transected by the line dividing Charles County from Prince George's County to the north. The former Integrated Fire Control area of eleven acres is about one mile west within Charles County. Following the deactivation of W-44, the majority of the land was transferred to Charles County, while portions were transferred to Prince George's County and to private parties. In October 1994, a Maryland Historical Trust review evaluated W-44 as ineligible for the National Register of Historic Places due to changes to the site since the Nike period. The launch area is now leased from Charles County by the Maryland Indian Heritage Society for use as a cultural center. The Melwood Horticultural Training Center leases part of the former control area as a training center for developmentally disabled persons.[68]

Significance for Maryland air/space history: A surface-to-air missile site that played a role in air defense during the Cold War era.
Relevant years: 1955-1971 *Lat/Long*: 38-39N 76-52W
Map: ADC Md/Del 2000 *Num*: 20 *Grid*: B5 *Shows*: area

NIKE MISSILE SITE W-45, ACCOKEEK
Accokeek, Prince George's County
1955-1961

The Morgan and Berhow guide indicates that W-45 was operational from 1955 from December 1961, guarding the national capital. The site is east of Accokeek and about four miles west of Waldorf, with the Integrated Fire Control area on the south side of Maryland Route 228 and the launch area on the north side. Both properties belong to the Naval Research Laboratory. The control area is listed as intact, while the launch area is listed as partially modified or dismantled.[69]

Significance for Maryland air/space history: A surface-to-air missile site that played a role in air defense during the Cold War era.
Relevant years: 1955 -1961 *Lat/Long*: 38-38N 77-04W
Map: ADC Md/Del 2000 *Num*: 19 *Grid*: F5 *Shows*: area

NIKE MISSILE SITE W-54, POMONKEY
Pomonkey, Charles County (CH-676)
1955-1961

The history and Nike site guide by Mark A. Morgan and Mark L. Berhow indicates that W-54, intended for the defense of Washington, was operational from 1955 to December 1961. The site consists of two locations several miles south of Pomonkey. The site of the launch area, located on Gwynn Road, is now used by the Pomonkey Naval Research Laboratory. The Integrated Fire Control area on Bumpy Oak Road is used by the Charles County Alternative School. Both areas are listed by Morgan and

Berhow as partially modified. In 1996, the Maryland Historical Trust found that W-54 did not possess sufficient historical integrity to be eligible for the National Register of Historic Places.[70]

Significance for Maryland air/space history: A surface-to-air missile site that played a role in air defense during the Cold War era.
Relevant years: 1955-1961 *Lat/Long*: 38-34N 77-04W
Map: ADC Md/Del 2000 *Num*: 19 *Grid*: F6 *Shows*: area

NIKE MISSILE SITE W-92, ROCKVILLE
Gaithersburg, Montgomery County (MO: 21-187)
1954-1974

According to the Morgan and Berhow guide, site W-92 was operational from 1954 to April 1974, which made it one of the longest-lasting of the sites located in Maryland. Part of the Washington ring, W-92 began as a Nike Ajax site, but was converted to the more advanced Nike Hercules system during 1958-59. The launch area was on property currently belonging to the National Institute for Standards and Technology (NIST), 770 Muddy Branch Road. The Integrated Fire Control area of W-92 is now used by the U.S. Consumer Products Safety Commission Engineering Laboratory, 10901 Darnestown Road.[71] Although W-92 was referred to as the Rockville site, the launch area is within present-day Gaithersburg.

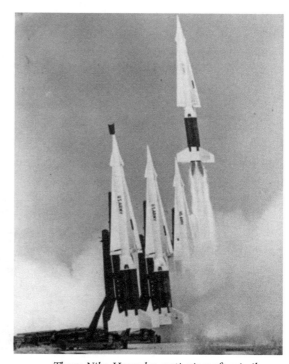

Three Nike Hercules anti-aircraft missiles on launchers as a fourth blasts off.
Photo courtesy of the Granite Historical Society.

Under a bill introduced into Congress in 2001, 13.71 acres at the former W-92 launch area would be transferred from NIST to Gaithersburg for use as a park.[72] The former integrated fire control area is beyond Gaithersburg's southeast edge. Comments posted on Ed Thelen's Nike website indicate that a number of original buildings there are intact.[73]

Significance for Maryland air/space history: A surface-to-air missile site that played a role in air defense during the Cold War era.

Relevant years: 1954 - 1974

Lat/Long: 39-07N 77-13W (launcher area)

Map: ADC Md/Del 2000 *Num*: 14 *Grid*: D5 *Shows*: area

NIKE MISSILE SITE W-93, LAYTONSVILLE/DERWOOD
Laytonsville, Montgomery County
1955-60

According to the Morgan and Berhow Nike history and site guide, Washington site W-93 was operational from September 1955 to August 1960. The site consisted of three locations east of Laytonsville. The former Integrated Fire Control area at 21515 Zion Road is now occupied by a facility for autistic children. Morgan and Berhow list this area as obliterated (Bill Evans' website notes that the guard shack is the sole remaining feature from the Nike era). W-93's administration area at 5115 Riggs Road is intact and in use by the Maryland Army National Guard. The launch area at 5321 Riggs Road is listed as partially modified by Morgan and Berhow. Their book states that this area is also occupied by the National Guard; however, information on the Evans and Thelen websites indicate that the Federal Emergency Management Agency is the user.[74]

Vacation gateway: terminal and fuelling station at Ocean City Municipal Airport, 1987. Photo courtesy of Ashish Solanki, Maryland Aviation Administration.

Significance for Maryland air/space history: A surface-to-air missile site that played a role in air defense during the Cold War era.

Relevant years: 1955 - 1960 *Lat/Long*: 39-12N 77-06W

Map: ADC Md/Del 2000 *Num*: 14 *Grid*: E4 *Shows*: area

NIKE MISSILE SITE W-94, GAITHERSBURG
Gaithersburg, Montgomery County
1955-1963

The Morgan and Berhow guide indicates that W-94 was operational as part of the Washington defenses from September 1955 to March 1963. The launch area was at the current location of the Hunton Memorial U. S. Army Reserve Center at 8791 Snouffer School Road. The launchers there have been abandoned. The Integrated Fire Control area was south of Snouffer School Road, at Strawberry Knoll Road and Cross County Place. It has been demolished, and the site is now a residential neighborhood.[75] A recent county map also shows Nike Missile Park on the south side of Snouffer School Road at Earhart Court.[76]

Significance for Maryland air/space history: A surface-to-air missile site that played a role in air defense during the Cold War era.

Relevant years: 1955 - 1963 *Lat/Long*: 39-10N 77-10W

Map: ADC Md/Del 2000 *Num*: 14 *Grid*: D5 *Shows*: area

OCEAN CITY MUNICIPAL AIRPORT
Ocean City, Worcester County
1958-present

Ocean City Municipal Airport is a 557-acre facility located about two miles southwest of the town, between Decatur Highway (Maryland Route 611) and Sinepuxent Bay. The airport was built as the result an agreement announced in October 1958. Under the plan, the city and state governments each pledged $50,000, and the federal government $150,000. State directories issued in the 1960s stated that the airport possessed a single paved runway 3,500 feet long, while others issued in the 1970s reduced that length by 100 feet. By 1981, the airport had two runways, 3,200 and 3,700 feet long. The length of the primary runway had been increased to 4,070 feet by 1996. Scheduled commuter service began at Ocean City Municipal at least as early as 1963. For a time, starting in April 1982, three daily round-trips were offered between the airport and Baltimore/Washington International. As of June 4, 2002, however, scheduled service was no longer available. Forty-six aircraft were based at the airport, and operations during the preceding twelve months totaled 37,000.[77]

Significance for Maryland air /space history: A municipal airport that has provided air transportation access to one of the state's major resort areas for more than four decades.

Relevant years: 1958 - present
Lat/Long: 38-18-64N 75-07-44W
Map: ADC Md/Del 2000 *Num*: 28
Grid: E3 *Shows*: airport

Open-sided hangars beneath the windsock at Fallston Airport, 1988.
Photo courtesy of Ashish Solanki, Maryland Aviation Administration.

FALLSTON AIRPORT
Fallston, Harford County
1958-present

Fallston Airport is a twenty-acre facility located about one mile south of the town for which is named, on the east side of Reckord Road north of its junction with Guyton Road. The airport opened in about 1958. A state listing of commercial airports issued in 1960 indicated that the facility had a single unpaved runway that was 2,000 feet long, which was 200 feet less than the reported length today. Structures at the airport include a pilot/crew shelter and T-hangars. It is normally open from dawn to dusk, offering fuel, repairs, and aircraft rental. As of February 22, 2002, flight operations for the preceding twelve months totaled 8,189. Fred R. Mills has been consistently identified as the airport's owner in those state directories providing ownership data, and he has usually been listed as its manager as well.[78]

Significance for Maryland air/space history: A general aviation airport that has operated since about 1958.
Relevant years: 1958 - present *Lat/Long*: 39-30-09N 76-24-66W
Map: ADC Md/Del 2000 *Num*: 16 *Grid*: B1 *Shows*: airport

NASA GODDARD
SPACE FLIGHT CENTER
Greenbelt, Prince George's County (PG: 64-9)
1959-present

The Goddard Space Flight Center (GSFC) at Greenbelt is one of the principal field facilities of the National Aeronautics and Space Administration (NASA). The facility consists of 1,121 acres owned by NASA, plus 149 outlying acres leased from the U.S. Department of Agriculture. The main site is bounded by Greenbelt Road to the south, Good Luck Road to the east, the Baltimore-Washington Parkway to the west, and the USDA Beltsville Agricultural Center to the north.

The origins of GSFC were contemporary with those of NASA itself, created in 1958 as part of the nation's determination to launch a space program that would out-match that of the Soviet Union. Originally known as the Beltsville Space Center, the nascent facility was renamed in May 1959 to honor rocket pioneer Robert H. Goddard (d. 1945). During the succeeding decades, GSFC supported many of NASA's successful undertakings, including aspects of manned space exploration. The facility's work made possible the use of satellites for weather observation, communications, astronomy, and environmental research. These achievements required the construction of a complex of advanced facilities for research, testing, tracking, and data processing. The first major structure, the Space Projects Building, was fully occupied by September 1960, and GSFC was formally dedicated on March 16 of the following year. Building 12, a tracking and telemetry laboratory, was completed in November 1963.[79] These original buildings were located west of Soil Conservation Service Road, while much of the recent development has concentrated on the newer East Campus on the opposite side of that road. Among the structures there are the Earth Observing System Data Information System and the Earth Systems Science Building, both of which reflect GSFC's lead role in the NASA program designated Mission to Planet Earth. The West and East campuses now include thirty-three major buildings devoted to various research, development, and support functions. Many of these structures house unique resources, examples of which include the Hubble Space Telescope

Continued on page 118

From the Oral History Files...

Maryland Recipients of the Distinguished Flying Cross

An Interview with Col. Paul Butler (Ret.) and Col. George "Hank" Henry (Ret.)
by Dr. Barry A. Lanman

The Distinguished Flying Cross

The Distinguished Flying Cross (DFC) is one of the highest honors bestowed in the United States for heroism and/or extraordinary achievement in aerial flight. Since the DFC was established in 1926, thousands of aviators have distinguished themselves under fire and in the line of duty. This file contains interviews with two Maryland residents who won the DFC during the Cold War.

Paul Butler: Aerial Combat in Korea

Col. Butler explains what it was like flying combat missions in a B-26 [Douglass Invader bomber] during the Korean War. "*Each squadron was assigned a given route, which is a segment of roads and railroads in Northern Korea that we patrolled. We attacked targets of opportunity most of the time, sometimes we went after specific targets. Our primary job was low-level night interdiction missions on supplies. You interdict [interfere] with ground transportation in any form: locomotives, trains, trucks, marching troops, whatever.*

"*We brought back pieces of our own bomb on a couple of days. It was winter and there was snow on the ground, and you get a clear night with the big moon out there. We had a route that was over fairly level terrain, we would interdict a railroad and fly right down until we saw the steam coming out of the locomotive. And we were flying at a hundred feet. We'd pop up to four hundred, drop a bomb...A five hundred pound bomb, with a parachute on it. The idea...you drop the bomb and it should open just before it hits. Lots of times it didn't, necessarily open quick enough, and it would explode and we brought back pieces in the tail a couple of times.*

"*On one mission, I think it was February, 1952, we flew several close air support missions for the ground troops...pretty close to the*

Paul Butler
in the cockpit
of a Douglas
B-26 Invader,
Korea, 1951.
Photo courtesy
of Col. Paul
A. Butler

front lines for two hours...did a lot of strafing and maneuvers like that. We had to keep track of where you were, because the Chinese were coming over the hill, and we were doing the best to protect our guys. The airplane got shot up pretty bad, but fortunately, no one got hurt and we were able to bring it home." For this mission, Col. Butler received the Bronze Star.

"*We were allocated specific routes, and they were numbered P, our number was P4. They were always numbered, purple four, purple seven and so forth. P4 was on the west part of Korea and a very, very level plain. North from Pyongyang to Sananga. Pyongyang is the capital of North Korea now. And that was a very good route for trains, it was a duel railroad track that comes right down from Sananga which crossed the Sananga River, down to Pyongyang, the Capital...And, at Pyongyang [there] was a big marshalling [train] yard. So, what we did that night, we were using the same technique, interdict the railroad, find the railroad and then fly right up or down it...until we found a train. Usually you found a train by the steam coming out of the engine. I was able to successfully drop a bomb in front of one and back of one. Wrecked the rails, they couldn't move. And they were stuck, two trains side by side. One of them was an ammunition train. Colonel Morgan did the strafing, and I did the bombing. That's how we received the Distinguished Flying Cross, we blew up two locomotives, fully loaded trains with ammunition.*"

On his forty-fifth and final mission, Col. Butler sustained personal injury and the nose of his B-26 was severely damaged. Thus, he was unable to complete fifty missions, which was customary for Korean era pilots. Col. Butler elaborates on what happened: "*I would line the targets up with a Norden [bombsight], and we would bomb from twenty-five hundred feet or less...very low level and high speed. Well, we needed to go high speed, and high speed then was 210 - 250. This was because the Chinese were very adapt at putting the anti-aircraft guns in tunnels or sidetracks, and have them well camouflaged. If you went over that area too close, they would throw up the camouflage and, and the anti-aircraft guns were usually on flatbeds. They would pepper the heck out of us. And that's what happened when I got shot up...we stayed there too long.*"

During his military career, Col. Butler earned two graduate degrees and was awarded the Distinguished Flying Cross, the Bronze Star, the Purple Heart and numerous Air Medals. After his retirement from the Air Force as a full Colonel, he worked for Martin Marietta as an engineer. He also worked on aerospace and telecommunications contracts associated with Fort Meade and the National Security Agency.

Col. Butler is currently president of the Nation's Capital Region of the Distinguished Flying Cross Society. The region, which includes Maryland, currently has twenty-seven members representing all wars and conflicts since World War II. The members are in good company. Charles A. Lindbergh, the Wright Brothers and Amelia Earhart were among the first to receive a DFC!

George "Hank" Henry: Aerial Combat in Vietnam

Col. Hank Henry flew into combat at the controls of a vintage airplane, the C-47 "Gooney Bird," the military version of the DC-3 airliner of the 1930s. The airplane was quite familiar to him because he had hopped rides on C-47's while in ROTC and learned to love the old plane in his early days. Now, he was flying one in combat. While the C-47 was used as a transport in

WWII and Korea, in Vietnam *"they had guns sticking out of the windows, they called it 'Puff the Magic Dragon'. They had antennas hanging all over it. Some flyers had actually flown the Gooney Bird in three different wars.*

"I ended up flying in the Gooney Bird working with security service. Our job was to fly a circular pattern around anybody with a teletype key and pinpoint where their transmissions were coming from. Those young men we had in the back were sharp. They could actually tell you whether the person on that teletype key was from the U.S. One time they were telling me, 'No, that's an Australian sending now.' But they could distinguish whether it was a VC [enemy Viet Cong] sending a message. I mean, just that sharp. We would do what they called 'dot points.' We'd fly a circle around the transmission and then pinpoint where it was, and then direct a strike in on it."

The first time in combat is a life-altering experience. Henry, in an oral history interview, explains the emotions of military engagement. **"*When you see it from a distance* [enemy fire], *the red balls coming up, you say, 'That's pretty. . . Let's get away from that.' When you look out your side window and see it coming right up at you, you know, it's 'Whoops, let's get the hell out of here'! Sometimes our intelligence wasn't too good and they would tell us where they thought gun points were, and, of course, we would direct fire suppression in on those points at times.***

"Well, your emotions change a bit. If we're being attacked, there's that 'where's the hole to get out of this?' There's a sudden fear that comes over you for a short moment, but you don't have time to be afraid. All you do is want to find a place to get out of it. If you're doing the attacking, then it's 'every one of these guys that we get—don't get to hurt our troops down south.' So you get a feeling of exhilaration . . . I will admit that on the trip back, after it's all over and you're headed back to your home station, you sometimes think, war never solved anything."

When asked about how he received his Distinguished Flying Cross, Henry responded in the following manner: *"Actually, my DFC came from the Electric Goon missions. . . After flying over 150 missions [in both C-47s and newer C-130s], I don't remember the specific event. . . I give full credit for my DFC to the young enlisted troops that we had in the back. They were just so experienced in locking onto an electrical signal that was being transmitted, and us just flying a circle around it, pinpointing where it was and then putting a strike in on it. We flew so many of them they just all run together. But we must've had something pretty important that happened during one of those missions."* After thinking for a moment, he added *"they were all important missions because every one of those radio points that we shut down, meant that there was no communications from one VC unit to another or to a North Vietnamese unit.*

"I think I got a better appreciation for the Distinguished Flying Cross by sitting on a panel making a determination on whether this person should get a Distinguished Flying Cross or whether they should be downgraded to an air medal. I got more of an appreciation for my Distinguished Flying Cross there than I did when I actually received it. Some of the stories, well, they leave a cold chill up your spine, and I realized some of the things that people went through. I knew just what an important part of history that meant to the individual, and the reason the country bestows something like the Distinguished Flying Cross on a person."

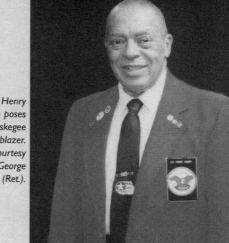

Col. George Henry (USAF Ret.) poses in his red Tuskegee Airmen blazer. Photo courtesy of Col. George Henry (Ret.).

Asked about his experience as an African American in the military, Henry replied, *"Sure, I ran into a lot of discrimination. I look back over my career and I find times when I was discriminated against, in assignments and things like that. But overall, I still must say that the military at that time offered more of an integrated society where I could compete. In fact, I give full credit to the Tuskegee Airmen for things like that. They were my first inspiration when I looked at flying. They told me something that I tell young people all the time. They called it 'rule number one' when they gave it to me. And rule number one was to believe in yourself. When you believe in yourself, you can do anything.*

"When I talk about Tuskegee Airmen, I'm not just talking about fewer than a thousand pilots, because it took everybody. . . the mechanics, the people in supply. Pilots get enough credit, you know, we're as cocky as can be. . . Oh sure, the pilot shot down the airplanes, but they couldn't have gotten off the ground without having that mechanic. So, when we talk about Tuskegee Airmen, we're talking about all of them."

Col. Henry retired from the Air Force in 1983 and has spent decades working with young people throughout the state of Maryland. He serves as a community activist so that that young people will have the same opportunities as he had. Over the years, Henry has spoken to hundreds of Maryland school children and delights in motivating students to consider careers in aviation. He is currently the head of the speakers' bureau of the East Coast Chapter of the Tuskegee Airmen.

Col. Paul Butler, USAF (Ret.), oral history interview, December 5, 2002, MHT/OHC 002 (MD-AVC) 013, 47p.

Col. George "Hank" Henry, USAF (Ret.), oral history interview, December 16, 2002, MHT/OHC 002 (MD-AVC) 003, 40p

The Spacecraft Systems Development/ Integration Facility in Building 29 (below) is the largest of NASA Goddard's "clean rooms" (left). Photos courtesy of Goddard Space Flight Center.

Control Center, the Space Environment Simulator, and the Spacecraft Fabrication Facility. GSFC is an evolving entity, and the interiors of many of its buildings have changed over the years in response to new requirements. In terms of its sustained contributions, however, the center as a whole is a site of great importance.[80] (Also see entry on Spacecraft Magnetic Test Facility on page 122.)

Significance for Maryland air/space history: A major field center in the history of the United States space program.

Relevant Years: 1959 - present   *Lat/Long*: 39-00N 76-51W
Map: ADC Md/Del 2000 *Num*: 20 *Grid*: B1 *Shows*: facility

An airport in the woods: single runway and taxiway at Suburban Airpark in Laurel. Photo courtesy of Maryland Aviation Administration.

SUBURBAN AIRPARK
Laurel, Anne Arundel County
1959-present

Suburban Airpark occupies fifty-two acres that are two miles southeast of Laurel, west of Brock Bridge Road, and also west of the Baltimore-Washington Parkway. The facility is in Anne Arundel County, but very close to Prince George's. Originally a hog farm owned by E. Burton Tidler, the property was used occasionally for light plane operations prior to the opening of the airport in 1959.[81] The runway was originally clay, and the first building was completed in 1960. By 1962, a state airport directory indicated that the single northeast-southwest runway had a hard surface. Operators managed the airport under lease agreements until 1995, when the Tidler family assumed direct control. (The current manager, Charles H. Crew, Sr., is E. Burton Tidler's son-in-law.) A major rehabilitation of the 2,324-foot runway, the taxiway, and ramp was completed in 1996, under a matching grant from the state. The 1999 state directory appears to have been the first such publication to use the word "Airpark" rather than "Airport" in the facility's name. As of April 19, 2002, sixty-five aircraft were based at Suburban Airpark. Operations in the preceding twelve months totaled 20,400.[82]

Significance for Maryland air/space history: A general aviation airport that has operated for more than four decades.

Relevant Years: 1959 - present
Lat/Long: 39-04-37N 76-49-40W
Map: ADC Md/Del 2000 *Num:* 15 *Grid:* C6 *Shows:* airport

MONTGOMERY COUNTY AIRPARK
Gaithersburg, Montgomery County
1960-present

Montgomery County Airpark is located three miles northeast of Gaithersburg, on Airpark Drive west of Woodfield Road. The facility's establishment followed the closure of Congressional Airport in 1958, an event that left

Montgomery County Airpark, Gaithersburg, in 1978 (top) and 2002. Photos courtesy of Maryland Aviation Administration.

the modest Davis Airport as the county's only commercial airfield. The key figure in the airport's creation was William E. Richardson, who won approval for a controversial plan. Richardson's development firm deeded the 115-acre site to the county, receiving in return a ninety-nine-year lease. The airport's operator became Freestate Aviation, Inc., made up of Richardson, his son, and a third partner. Constructed with the aid of a federal grant, the airport formally opened in October 1960. There were initially two runways, the shorter of which was eventually discontinued. The airport was well equipped, with assets that included a two-story administration building, and by 1969 it had some eighty T-hangars.[83] Montgomery County Airpark had been intended to attract light industry to an adjacent industrial park, but development of the surrounding area increasingly included housing. Many

residents opposed the airport's expansion, citing concerns over noise and safety. Nevertheless, the runway had reached a length of 4,200 feet by the early 1970s. The airport ranks among Maryland's busiest. As of May 2002, flight operations for the preceding twelve months totaled more than 140,500, including 11,200 air taxi operations.[84]

Significance for Maryland air/space history: A large county-owned general aviation airport that has operated for more than forty years.

Relevant years: 1960 - present
Lat/Long: 39-10-05N 77-09-59W
Map: ADC Md/Del 2000 *Num:* 14 *Grid:* E4
Shows: airport

BALTIMORE AIRPARK
Originally QUINN AIRPORT
Perry Hall, Baltimore County
c. 1960-2001

Baltimore Airpark occupied an irregular property of sixty acres on Forge Hill Road, just west of Interstate 95 and north of Joppa Road. The site is roughly two miles east of Perry Hall and a mile north of White Marsh. The facility was originally known as Quinn Airport. The earliest record examined in which that name was included was a brief state listing issued in 1960. A 1962 state directory reported that the airport was operated by Herbert Shanklin, and that it offered fuel and minor repairs. The publication described the 1,800-foot sod runway as

"Rough & Rolling." On the night of January 17, 1962, a fire at the airport destroyed three aircraft and badly damaged two others. The Baltimore *Evening Sun* named Fred D. Quinn as the airport's operator in its report on the fire. The state's brief 1966 directory listed the facility's name as "Quinn-White Marsh." The manager at that time was Dorothy M. Griffin.[85]

Robert E. "Ed" Whipp evidently established the facility after closing his somewhat larger one in Anne Arundel County (see Glen Burnie-Whipp Airport on page 69). Located on Tilghman Island, one mile south of the town of Tilghman, the new airport had an unlighted turf runway 1,800 feet long. There is no indication that a seaplane ramp was ever provided. The facility was attended on an irregular basis, offering services that included fuel and tie-downs, but no maintenance. Tilghman-Whipp Airport was listed in the state directory for 1970-71, but not in the issue for 1972.[87]

T-hangars at Baltimore Airpark, Perry Hall, 1988.
Photo courtesy of Ashish Solanki, Maryland Aviation Administration.

Significance for Maryland air/space history: A small airport and seaplane base for general aviation that operated for roughly decade, beginning about 1960.
Relevant years: c. 1960 - c. 1971
Lat/Long: 38-42N 76-20W
Map: ADC Md/Del 2000 *Num*: 21
Grid: B4 *Shows*: area

In 1967, the airport was acquired by C. Earle Mace and his wife Betsy Mace. They paved the runway before reopening the facility in 1968 as Baltimore Airpark. The new owners added hangars and an office building. Mrs. Mace later recalled that the airport prospered until about the time of Martin State Airport's opening in 1975. The new facility attracted pilots seeking a longer runway than the single 2,200-foot east-west strip available at Baltimore Airpark. The Maces eventually sold the land, and the airport closed in 2001. The property is planned for residential development. As of March 2003, however, construction has not yet begun.[86]

Significance for Maryland air/space history: A general aviation airport that closed in 2001 after operating for more than forty years.
Relevant Years: 1960, c. - 2001
Lat/Long: 39-24-16N 76-25-35W
Map: ADC Md/Del 2000 *Num*: 16 *Grid*:A2 *Shows*: airport

TILGHMAN-WHIPP AIRPORT AND SEAPLANE BASE
Tilghman, Talbot County
1960-1971

The earliest listing of commercial airports found that included Tilghman-Whipp Airport and Seaplane Base was issued by state authorities in November 1960.

GARRETT COUNTY AIRPORT
Oakland, Garrett County
1962-present

Garrett County Airport is located some thirteen miles northeast of Oakland on a 200-acre property east of U.S. Route 219. The facility stands on a hilltop to the north of the town of McHenry and of Deep Creek Lake. The county established the airport in order to increase access to its lake and skiing resort area. Construction was accomplished with the aid of a federal grant that was matched by state and local funds. The facility opened in 1962, and a state airport directory for that year shows that it then had a single paved runway 2,500 feet in length. This was lengthened to 3,000 feet in 1992. As of August 3, 2001, flight operations for the preceding twelve months totaled 17,800, including 300 air taxi operations and 500 military operations. Services available included fuel, flight instruction, T-hangars, tie-downs, and rental of aircraft.[88]

Significance for Maryland air/space history: A county-owned airport that has provided air transportation access since the early 1960s.
Relevant years: 1962 - present
Lat/Long: 39-34-48N 79-20-26W
Map: ADC Md/Del 2000 *Num*: 1 *Grid*: B6
Shows: airport

AQUALAND/CLIFTON SKYPARK

(AQUALAND SKYPARK)
Newburg, Charles County
c. 1962-1992

The earliest listing found for this airport was in the AOPA 1962 directory, which noted that Aqua-land Park was nearby. In the 1974 state directory, the facility's name was altered to include the name of Clifton, a community just to its north. The directory described Aqualand/Clifton Skypark as one mile southwest of Newburg at the Potomac River bridge. The facility offered a single paved runway 3,250 feet long, and its attractions included an adjoining "Aqua-Land Restaurant (crabs)." The airport shifted from public to private usage in 1990, and closed in 1992. Paul Freeman's website on abandoned airfields includes an aerial photo showing that the runway continued to exist in June 1999. A website on Charles County tourism in 2002 indicated that Aqualand still operated, but as a marina.[89]

Significance for Maryland air/ space history: An airport that existed for at least thirty years, providing aviation access to a recreational area.
Relevant Years: c.1962 - 1992
Lat/Long: 38-22-00N 76-58-24W
Map: ADC Md/Del map 2000
Num: 25 Grid: A2
Shows: Aqualand campground

BAR H SKY PARK
North East, Cecil County
c. 1962-c. 1965

The state directory of commercial airports for 1962 included Bar H Sky Park, located one half mile north of the town of North East. Managed by Edison C. Henderson, the airport offered fuel and repairs, both major and minor. It had a single sod runway 1,800 feet long. AOPA's directory for 1963 included the facility, based on a 1962 report, in its section on new entries. Slightly more detail was given in the 1965 edition, which showed the runway lengthened to 2,100 feet, and named Mr. Henderson as the operator. Bar H Sky Park did not appear in the next AOPA directory examined, the issue for 1967, or in subsequent issues.[90]

Significance for Maryland air/space history: A short-lived general aviation airport of the early 1960s.

Relevant Years: c.1962 –c.1965 *Lat/Long*: 39-36N 76-56W
Map: ADC Md/Del 2000 *Num*: 8 *Grid*: A5 *Shows*: Grid

CLEARVIEW AIRPORT/ CLEARVIEW AIRPARK
Westminster, Carroll County
1963-present

Clearview Airport occupies a forty-nine-acre site that is about seven miles south of Westminster, north of Bear Branch Road and west of Oak Tree Road. The airport is reported to have opened in about 1963. A brief airport directory issued by the state in 1966 indicated that the airport had two unpaved runways and that its

Office at Garrett County Airport, 1987, has the minimum requirements— windsock and soft-drink machine.
Photo courtesy of Ashish Solanki, Maryland Aviation Administration.

manager was Oliver Farinholt. The state directory for 1970-71 showed that the facility then had a single hard-surface runway, and listed Farinholt as both owner and operator. The airport today has a single 1,845-foot lighted runway and offers fuel, repairs, tiedowns, and hangars. As of April 12, 2002, operations for the preceding twelve months totaled 15,300. Forty-two aircraft, all single-engine airplanes, were based at the facility. [91]

Significance for Maryland air/space history: An airport that has served general aviation since the 1960s.
Relevant years: 1963 - present
Lat/Long: 39-28-01N 77-01-04W
Map: ADC Md/Del 2000 *Num*: 15 *Grid*: F1 *Shows*: airport

RIDGELY AIRPARK
Originally RIDGELY PELICAN AIRPORT
Ridgely, Carroll County
1966-present

Ridgely Airpark is located about two miles northeast of Ridgely on Racetrack Road. Established in 1966 by the Pelican Land Corporation, the facility was originally known as Ridgely-Pelican Airport. The state directory for 1970-71 reported that the airport had a 3,000-foot turf runway and that it offered fuel, maintenance services, tiedowns, and parachute jumping. In a work published in 1984, John F. R. Scott, Jr., noted that Ridgely-Pelican was almost entirely devoted to skydiving. During that same year, Tracy Coleman acquired the airport and gave it the current name. Skydiving at the airport was discontinued following fatalities and a resulting lawsuit. A paved and lighted runway was constructed in the autumn of 1992, but part of the original turf runway remains in use for glider and ultralight operations. A non-directional beacon was installed in 1992, and an automated weather observing system (AWOS) in October 1999.[92] In January 2001, county authorities published a notice of their interest in acquiring the airport as part of a business technology park. The county was still pursuing this multi-year project in February 2003, and had acquired some property near the airport as part of the planned business complex. Meanwhile, existing structures at Ridgely Airpark included two maintenance hangars, with an office between them, and ten storage hangars. As of July 25, 2001, operations during the preceding twelve months totaled 31,113. The twenty-nine aircraft based at the airport included fifteen single-engine airplanes, four ultralight vehicles, and nine gliders.[93]

The Spacecraft Magnetic Test Facility is located some distance away from the main campus of NASA Goddard.
Photo courtesy of Goddard Space Flight Center.

Significance for Maryland air/space history: An airport that has served general aviation since 1966.
Relevant years: 1966 – present
Lat/Long: 38-58-12N 75-52-00W
Map: ADC Md/Del 2000 *Num*: 22 *Grid*: B1 *Shows*: airport

SPACECRAFT MAGNETIC TEST FACILITY
Greenbelt, Prince George's County (PG: 64-6)
1966-present

The Spacecraft Magnetic Test Facility, also known as the Attitude Control Test Facility, was built in 1966. Its function is to test spacecraft and to allow calibration of their controls and instruments with minimal interference from the earth's magnetic fields. The facility stands in a magnetic-quiet area about two miles east of Goddard Space Flight Center (see page 115), north of Good Luck Road and south of Beaver Dam Road. It is a sixty-foot square building containing a coil system able to virtually cancel the earth's magnetic field over a six-foot-diameter spherical space, and to provide a stable artificial field. Tracks and dollies move the test item in and out of the coil system, and a powered turntable at the coil center permits positioning. The facility is unique within the U.S. and is essential to the successful deployment of large satellites used for weather observation, communications, and many other purposes. A survey by the National Park Service in May 1984 found the facility to be unaltered and in excellent condition. The site was subsequently nominated for inclusion on the National Register of Historic Places.[94]

Significance for Maryland air/space history: An important testing facility for the national space program.
Relevant Years: 1966 - present *Lat/Long*: 39-01N 76-50W
Map: ADC Md/Del 2000 *Num*: 15 *Grid*: B6 *Shows*: Area

CARROLL'S AIRPORT
Dominion, Queen Anne's County
1966-1969

Carroll's Airport was located on Kent Island, one-quarter-mile east of Dominion and three-and-one-half miles southeast of Stevensville. The section of the 1965 AOPA airport directory devoted to new entries described the airport as possessing one turf runway, 1,800 feet long, and named the operator as Carroll Behringer. The 1966 state directory of commercial airports listed Ms. Behringer as the manager rather than the operator, and noted that gas and oil were obtainable. The facility was also included in the AOPA's directory for 1967. In that publication, however, pilots were cautioned that Carroll's was a private facility, to be used at their own risk. This warning was absent from AOPA's 1969 issue, which simply noted that the hours that the facility was attended were not reported. The runway was now described as 2,000 feet long. Carroll's was included neither in the 1970 AOPA directory, nor the state directory for 1970-71, nor in any other directories examined.[95]

Significance for Maryland air/space history: A general aviation airport that was available for public use briefly in the 1960s.

Relevant Years: c. 1966 – c. 1969

Lat/Long: 38-57N 76-16W

Map: ADC Md/ Del 2000 *Num:* 21 *Grid:* C1 *Shows:* town

The Chesapeake Bay Bridge towers over the tie-down area at Bay Bridge Airport, Stevensville. Photo courtesy of Ashish Solanki, Maryland Aviation Administration.

BAY BRIDGE AIRPORT
Stevensville, Queen Anne's County
1967-present

Kent Island's Bay Bridge Airport is located on seventy-two acres just south of the eastern end of the structure for which it is named, and one mile southwest of Stevensville. The facility originated as part of a planned industrial center promoted by Nathan "Bill" Morris, principal partner of the Kent Island Limited Partnership. Morris was an aviator and land developer who had also established Kentmorr Airpark (see separate entry). He bought the land on which he built Bay Bridge Airport in 1966, and its dedication took place in September of the following year. The first structure was a small terminal with office space; later, he added a large marina nearby. The AOPA airport directory for 1969 described the airport as having a single paved runway 3,000 feet long, with lighting on request. The county acquired the property in 1988. A state airport directory issued in September 2001 showed a 2,910-foot lighted runway with parallel taxiways, and a Precision Approach Path Indicator (PAPI) system installed. Seventy-four aircraft were based at Bay Bridge Airport as of July 12, 2001, and operations for the preceding twelve months totaled 46,000.[96]

Significance for Maryland air/space history: A general aviation airport that has operated since the 1960s, originally as a private enterprise but later publicly owned.

Relevant Years: 1967 - present

Lat/Long: 38-58-36N 76-19-48W

Map: ADC Md/Del 2000 *Num:* 21 *Grid:* C1 *Shows:* airport

CAPTAIN WALTER FRANCIS DUKE REGIONAL AIRPORT AT ST. MARY'S,
formerly ST. MARY'S COUNTY AIRPORT
Leonardtown, St. Mary's County
1969-present

Captain Walter Francis Duke Regional Airport is four miles northeast of Leonardtown, on the west side of Three Notch Road south of Hollywood. Preliminary planning for a St. Mary's County Airport began in the late 1950s. The county acquired the site in 1968, and the facility began operations before the end of the following year. About thirty-eight percent of the cost of establishing the airport was funded by the Federal Aid Airport Program. By 1975, the county had completed a maintenance and storage hangar with adjacent office space and public areas. The state directory for 1970-71 indicated that the facility had a single lighted and paved runway 3,250 feet in length. Extension to the present length of 4,150 feet was accomplished in 1997, with ninety percent funding by the Federal Aviation Administration. federal grants assisted other improvements during the 1990s, including enlargement of the airport property to its current size of some 224 acres. In the spring of 2000, a new $3.5 million terminal was completed, with one-fifth of the costs supplied by the county and the rest by the Maryland Aviation Administration. The facility received its present name at that time. The designation honors a Leonardtown native who was the Tenth Air Force's leading "Ace" fighter pilot at the time of his death in combat over Burma in June 1944.[97]

Since the terrorist attacks of September 2001, the airport has been subject to periods of restriction due to its proximity to Washington and to the Calvert Cliffs

Continued on page 127

From the Oral History Files…

The Quintessential Aviator
An Interview with Mary Feik
by Dr. Barry A. Lanman

To know Mary Feik of Annapolis is to know the quintessential aviator. Throughout her sixty years in aerospace, Ms. Feik has advanced and promoted aviation as a pilot, test pilot, airplane mechanic, engineer, innovator, restorer, and educator. It is no wonder that she has received myriad prestigious awards and honors including the FAA's Charlie Taylor Master Mechanic Award, was named a Maryland Pioneer in Aviation and honored by NASA as one of forty-seven most significant women in aerospace. While she is considered a "legend" by the people who rely on her expertise and wisdom, Feik is a humble and a soft spoken individual who has the drive and motivation of teenager. The eternal optimist, she is the ideal educator/spokeswoman for her career, avocation and passion.

From Autos to Airplanes

Feik attributes her father with the development of her character, her personality and her mechanical ability. *"I got through high school in three years, instead of four and I wanted to go to engineering school… they wouldn't accept me purely on the basis that I was a girl, even though I had what would be equivalent to a 4.0 average. It was the Depression years and my father had a small automobile repair shop in the backyard in the garage… and we overhauled engines."* When he got thirteen engines to do all at one time, he needed his daughter's help and taught her how to re-build Model A Ford engines. Ultimately, she finished all of the engines herself. *"I learned about engines, I learned about brake systems, just about every aspect of how an automobile ran… So, that was about the time when the war really started and that's when I had a chance to leave and start on my aviation career.*

Above: Mary Feik and a P-51 "Captivair" simulator she designed, at Wright Field, near Dayton, Ohio.
 Right: Mary Feik and her crew with an early P-80 jet, at Wright Field, 1947. The P-80 "Captivair" was christened "Mary's Little Lamb." Photos courtesy of Mary Feik.

"I worked with my father all day and then at night I worked at Buffalo Evening News, and that's where I got the tele-type message from the U.S. Army Air Corps. It read, 'Desperately need aircraft maintenance instructors in… the Air Corp Training Command. Any who can fill this position, please apply'. I said, 'how different can an airplane be?'" She sent them a letter explaining her qualifications and was hired on the spot. So, in May, 1943, she reported to Seymour Johnson Field in Goldsboro, North Carolina.

Developing Simulators During World War II

Just two weeks after she arrived, she was instructing and learning at the same time. *"First of all it was airframe section, rigging, tubing, fabric work… The elevator of a B-17 was my first project. And then I went into my first engine course. I got through all of that because I could already weld. I knew metallurgy. I knew systems. I knew hydraulics… it's all the same principle* [as an automobile]." While her superiors did not want her to participate in the engine course, because they didn't think women could handle it, she quickly proved them wrong. In a very short time, she was working on B-17s, Douglas A-20s, AT-6s, BT-13s, and all of the training airplanes. *"We also went into the P-51's and those very, very early fighters, P-38s. Oh, my goodness, yes, loved those. But P-51s are my favorite… It was just a lot of airplanes that we could assemble, dissemble, run up, taxi and you had to be cockpit qualified so you could learn how to taxi."*

Because of the lack of training materials, she became frustrated in her role as a teacher. At nineteen years of age, she wrote the Air Technical Service Command at Wright Field. She expressed her concerns and also stated *"how are we going to teach these kids that are going into combat if we have nothing with which to teach?"* As a result of the letter, John C. Cunningham was so impressed with her potential that he took her under his authority. *"I almost fainted. John put me by a desk with a stack of projects, Fighter Pilot Transition Training and Maintenance Training."*

In this position, she helped develop the "Captivair," a stock model airplane mounted on a frame for ground-based "flying." *"They wanted a fire breathing aircraft, meaning everything functioning… The cadets, when they came from training, going into fighter pilot transition, [they] already knew how to fly, and they knew enough about the airplane, knowing the aerodynamics… It was basically emergency procedures training."* In just six weeks, Feik developed the first working simulator of its kind using a P-51. Though this process, training was dramatically improved for future combat pilots. Based on this successful model, Feik then wrote the specifications and engineering analyses for the "Captivairs" at other training bases. They not only adapted P-51s but P-47s, P-38s and related combat aircraft. Modern day simulators and trainers are based in part on this initial experiment.

To support her growing expertise, Mary's superiors suggested that she needed to learn to fly. Thus, she started out on a Stearman biplane and progressed to the hot P-51 fighter. She was a civilian flying military airplanes, and, while she actually logged over 400 hours in P-51s, the military record does not record this feat by a female civilian. Constantly learning, she was sent to Boeing and was checked out as a flight engineer for the B-29. She then used that training to direct flight simulations and tests. Even in the era of World War II, Feik has the distinction of being one of the few research and development engineers who never received a formal college education. Her entire knowledge base was acquired from personal study, experimentation and on-the-job training.

Perfecting her Craft: Jets

Feik continued learning and teaching as jets came to replace propeller-driven planes. When the Lockheed P-80 entered service, she was issued a brand-new model. *"Two airplanes had come to the base; one was for the instructor pilots and one for my "Captivair," and that had never been done before."* The P-80 was nicknamed "Mary's Little Lamb" in her honor.

Feik wrote several technical manuals and maintenance related documents during her civilian career with the Air Force. She characterizes the profession of aviation maintenance in the following manner: *"I find that with maintenance I keep impressing upon the young people that if you want to be a pilot, that's fine, but there is one person that can look at your airplane and determine whether you will fly it or not, and that's your maintenance man or woman...We are the most certified people in the aviation industry. When you sign a logbook, you're signing absolutely everything...including a person's life who is flying it."*

Close Calls While Testing Military Airplanes

Feik also worked at the dangerous job of flight-test engineer. *"I have the distinction of having been in a B-25 that cartwheeled...The B-25 [bomber] always had the problem after so many hard landings on rough fields that the left gear would usually come down and the nose gear, but the right gear, for some reason, would always hang up...and we wanted to see what that was like...So we flew over to Patterson Field to see if we could recreate this condition."* While simulating the problem on a calm day in 1943, they were hit with a sudden gust of wind on the landing and the up wing. *"We had no control at that time, everything was bled off—so we drifted off, the nose gear hit a rut next to the pavement, it dug in and we cart-wheeled...It was a total loss and they dragged me out through the wind screen...and as they pulled me out...I was still semi-conscious and I said, 'Wow, what a ride. Let's do that again!'"*

Some years later, Feik flew a P-59 jet fighter while tracer rounds were being shot two feet off the nose in a gunnery training exercise. *"I was the only person to ever fly open cockpit in a jet airplane...the airflow over this little windscreen was so great that I think I was off the seat no matter how tightly I was strapped down."* Other close calls occurred in a B-29 when she was nearly sucked out of the astrodome and when she almost had to bail out of a Fairchild C-82 due to an engine fire. Although dangerous, Feik knew that these activities were all part of being a test engineer and accepted the risks in order to reap the benefits of the knowledge gained and the safety it would provide for pilots in the future.

Aviation Restoration

Feik's wide range of experiences and flexible schedule now allowed her to focus on airplane restoration [at the Smithsonian Institution's famed Paul A. Garber Facility in Silver Hill]. *"Well, when*

One of Mary Feik's most rewarding restoration projects: a World War I Spad for the Smithsonian Institution. Photo courtesy of Mary Feik.

we came back here, I volunteered as a docent at the Garber facility and downtown 'cause I had such a big background...And so I started that way...I thought it was kind of fun to get into the docent aspect...At the Garber facility, they persuaded me to take a job there...So the first airplane that I did was the 1910 Wiseman-Cook...and working with Richard Horigan was a dream job. Then Charlie Parley asked for me for the Spad project, and we did it in just about three years." She also assisted the acquisition of the cloth used for Ken Hyde's reproduction of the Wright Flyer. In all, Feik helped to restore about twenty-four airplanes.

Civil Air Patrol and Aerospace Education

Feik is currently a member of the Composite Squadron of the Civil Air Patrol, located in Edgewater. *"They do bay patrol...we have airplanes in the Civil Air Patrol that are purchased by the Air Force for orientation flights... search and rescue of course is the big thing and of course the airplanes have to be maintained."* A veteran of the Civil Air Patrol, Feik has been involved with the organization for four decades. Her main foci have always been the cadet program, external aviation education and aerospace education. Promoting women in aerospace careers has also been a life-long avocation.

"I tell youngsters that you have to know the airplane, even if you're going to just fly as an observer. You ought to know what the airplane will do in case of an emergency...I am not a teacher. I am a mentor and a distinguishing feature of being a mentor is that you're teaching what you know personally...It's a different purview...than a classroom. Its hands on, a lot of bulletin board work, a lot of sketching and... analyzing."

Mary Feik's Legacy

To conclude the oral history interview, Feik was asked what she thought would be her legacy. Considering her vast achievements over six decades, this could have been a formidable task, but not for Mary. She quickly stated *"My legacy should lie with the people and the students I have instructed and mentored over the years in aviation maintenance and flight training, as well as with the many honors secured and given to me by my wonderful colleagues. The ultimate enduring honor comes from the Civil Air Patrol by creating a Cadet Achievement award in my name."*

Mary Feik, oral history interview,
Session I, June 26, 2002, Session II, November 25, 2002,
MHT/OHC 002 (MD-AVC) 002, 100 p.

From the Oral History Files...

To the North Pole
in a Stearman Open-Cockpit Biplane

An Interview with Gustavus "Gus" Aerous McLeod
by Dr. Barry A. Lanman

When people first read the headline about Gustavus Aerous McLeod's role in aviation history, they usually envision an aviation event that took place during the "Golden Age" or "Classic Era" of flight. However, they are startled to find out that the event took place in the twenty-first century!

When Gus McLeod purchased his two-seat Stearman biplane in 1993, it had already served as an Army flight trainer and as a crop duster. While he wanted to re-create the exploits of flyers such as Wiley Post and other early aviation pioneers, McLeod did not yet have a vision that would take him to the top of the earth.

Gus McLeod flew this sixty-year-old Stearman biplane to the North Pole, April 2000. Photo courtesy of Gustavus "Gus" Aerous McLeod.

"I started thinking about going to the North Pole in 1995 and spent the next three years planning it, and planning it, and planning it!"... Basically, your always in the planning mode and you never get from the planning stage to the actual doing stage."

While the actual flight was challenging and dangerous, the testing and modification of the equipment was equally hazardous and a major part of the experience. As an engineer, McLeod realized that he had to test the Stearman in cold weather conditions. From his research, he knew that the Canadians had used Stearmans for a brief period during World War II. However, they gave them back to the United States because they would not operate well in temperatures below twenty degrees Fahrenheit. In Canada during 1999, he experimented with the sixty-year-old airplane and its original Continental 220 engine. Two test trips were ultimately made.

On the first fact-finding excursion, McLeod solved the mystery that had existed for decades: "The fuel going from the updraft carburetor to the intake manifold and the pipes would super chill the fuel causing it to change from vapor back to a liquid. Therefore, the fuel would not burn efficiently... It was misting in the carburetor but not misting out at the cylinder end."

To reinforce this engineering limitation, McLeod had, as he described it, "a defining moment in the whole genre of the two trips when I left Churchville trying to beat a storm, The storm hit me and it was just vicious... eighty-mile-an-hour winds." Due to the ice and cold, the engine quit at 2,000 feet. Blown off course with his ELT (emergency locator transmitter) battery frozen, Gus knew he was in trouble. Luckily, the lower cylinders started firing at 600 feet and he was able to touch the front wheels on the ice with the tail in the air. After he confirmed that the engine was again operating at some efficiency, he powered the Stearman back to a village on the Renke Inlet.

That near disaster allowed McLeod to focus on the engine problem and how to personally survive minus-thirty to minus-forty degree temperatures. In addition to his engineering expertise, the local Inuet population "adopted" Gus and helped him solve the issues of surviving the cold. After insulating the carburetor, the manifold, the oil lines and oil tank choke with insulation, often four inches thick, and the judicious use of duct tape, the problem was brought under control. On the test flight, McLeod calculated that he made it to the magnetic North Pole, where it was located in 1950 (the magnetic north pole has been moving north according to McLeod's calculations).

From May of 1999 to April of 2000, intense preparation was conducted for the flight. Modifications to the Stearman were made along with personal preparations including the development and construction of specialized clothing.

On April 5, 2002, McLeod and his blue biplane, took off from the Montgomery Air Park for the historic trip. As luck would have it, a freak spring snow storm marked the opening leg of the journey and set a tone for the challenges ahead. During the eighteen days of the experience, McLeod averaged a speed of ninety knots and survived mechanical problems, severe winds and unusually frigid temperatures. He even overcame a nearly frostbitten hand.

While he had experienced many physical, mechanical and mental concerns on the two previous test flights, nothing could prepare him for the long hours without sleep, the monotony and the enduring cold, day in and day out. To overcome the elements and the psychological factors, McLeod played games in his mind. He often thought of how many songs he knew and how many songs he could sing with all the words. Even with these diversions, he experienced several periods where he hallucinated. However, he still continued to pilot his biplane north.

After all of the trials and the tribulations of weather and machine, on April 5, 2003, he approached the geographic North Pole. He stated "I had to rely on the chase plane's instrumentation... my GPS [Global Positioning System] was frozen solid... They [the chase plane] *saw their GPS register eighty-nine degrees, five minutes, and then it went haywire right at the geographic North Pole because it's where many longitudes converge."* McLeod's plane made three quarter-mile circles over the pole at an altitude of fifty feet. He wisely decided not to touch down. After accomplishing his goal, he flew thirty-six miles to a newly constructed base and landed for a brief ceremony. *"A lot of the reason I think I made it to the Pole, was nobody expected it first off. I didn't have a lot of money, so I couldn't over do it. I had to boil it down to the least common denominator."*

As he started his return trip, McLeod's Stearman biplane experienced major mechanical difficulties and forced him to land about fifty miles from the North Pole. He later returned with assistance to retrieve his Stearman. The historic airplane is now displayed at the College Park Aviation Museum.

The chase plane carried a crew from National Geographic EXPLORER television. Thus, part of McLeod's arctic adventure was captured on film and was the subject of a National Geographic EXPLORER television show.

McLeod believes *"the expedition will help people appreciate the challenges and risks early aviators faced."* Flying alone without the aide of air-traffic controllers, exposed to extreme weather, sitting for hours on a wooden seat, McLeod felt he succeeded. McLeod stated *"the most interesting part of the voyage of discovery were the people and places I visited along the way."*

Gustavus (Gus) McLeod, oral history interview, December 21, 2002, MHT/OHC 002 (MD-AVC) 009, 84p.

Gus McLeod's Stearman on the ice, April 2000.
Photo courtesy of Gustavus "Gus" Aerous McLeod

Nuclear Power Plant. One hundred aircraft were based at Captain Duke Regional Airport as of April 8, 2002. Operations for the preceding twelve months totaled 52,618, including 2,390 by air taxi aircraft. As of early 2003, goals for the future included a further runway extension, scheduled commuter service, and development of an industrial park using a portion of the property.[98]

Significance for Maryland air/space history: An airport that has provided access to aviation since 1969.
Relevant years: 1969 - present *Lat/Long*: 38-18-56N 76-33-06W
Map: ADC Md/Del 2000 *Num*: 25 *Grid*: F3 *Shows*: airport

BENNETT AIRPORT
Salisbury, Wicomico County
c. 1973-present

Bennett Airport is a fifty-five-acre property that is three and one-half miles northwest of Salisbury at 28890 Naylor Mill Road. The facility opened in about 1973, initially with a single north-south runway. The earliest directory examined that listed Bennett Airport was the AOPA publication for 1979. By the time of its publication, a second landing strip had been added to create the present "L" configuration, with two turf runways about 2,300 and 3,150 feet long. The longer runway is lighted. Structures include a pilot/crew shelter and T-hangars. Fuel is available, and operations include skydiving and crop dusting. The original owner continues to live on the airport and to manage it. Eleven aircraft were based at Bennett Airport as of May 14, 2002, and operations for the preceding twelve months totaled some 2,000.[99]

Significance for Maryland air/space history: A small general aviation airport that has operated since the early 1970s.
Relevant years: c. 1973 -present
Lat/Long: 38-24-45N 75-36-38W
Map: ADC Md/Del 2000 *Num*: 27 *Grid*: F2 *Shows*: airport

CECIL COUNTY AIRPORT,
formerly RAINTREE AIRPARK
Elkton, Cecil County
1979-present

Cecil County Airport, Identifier 58M, is located about three miles southwest of Elkton, on the west side of the Elk River. (It should not be confused with the defunct Cecil County Airpark, Identifier 2NO, which was northeast of the city; see entry on page 97.) Originally known as Raintree Airpark, the facility opened in 1979. It was described in the 1984 AOPA directory as possessing a turf runway 2,600 feet long, with transmitter-activated lighting. The operators were Aero Sport, Inc., and Raintree Associates, Ltd. In March 2000, an article indicated that the facility would receive $700,000 in state funds

Reminiscent of the earliest flying fields, 2,600-foot grass runway at Raintree Airpark (now Cecil County Airport, Elkton) had a gentle rolling surface. Since this photograph was taken in 1987, the runway has been paved. Photo courtesy of Ashish Solanki, Maryland Aviation Administraion.

runway that was 1,910 feet long, with lighting on request. Freddie R. Fair was named as the operator and manager. Fair's Airport was also listed in the AOPA directories for 1984 and 1987. Although evidently no longer a public-use airport, Fair's appeared in the Alexandria Drafting Company's 2000 map of Maryland and Delaware, located on the west side of Ocean Highway (U.S. Route 13).[101]

Significance for Maryland air/space history: A general aviation airport that functioned as a public-use facility in the 1980s.
Relevant Years: c. 1981 – c. 1987
Lat/Long: 38-02N 75-33W
Map: ADC Md/Del 2000 *Num*: 27 *Grid*: F6
Shows: airport

toward paving the runway and lengthening it to 3,000 feet. The grant would also assist in such other improvements as a new taxiway, runway lighting, and hangar. The state directory issued in Sept 2001 reflected this upgraded configuration, as well as the new name Cecil County Airport. In December of that year, the Raintree Airpark Seaplane Base reportedly opened near the airport, on property owned by the Elk Point Marina[100]

Significance for Maryland air/space history:
A general aviation airport that opened in 1979 and has been recently upgraded.
Relevant Years: 1979 - present
Lat/Long: 39-34-29N 79-52-09W
Map: ADC Md/Del, 2000 *Num*: 8 *Grid*: B6 *Shows*: area

FAIR'S AIRPORT
Pokomoke City, Worcester County
c. 1981-c. 1987

The only official state directory found that listed Fair's Airport was issued on April 28, 1981. One mile south of Pokomoke City, the facility possessed a single turf

Havre de Grace Seaplane Base in 1989. Ashish Solanki, MAA

HAVRE DE GRACE SEAPLANE BASE
Havre de Grace, Harford County
1986-present

Havre de Grace Seaplane Base is located in Havre de Grace, at the confluence of Susquehanna River and the Chesapeake Bay. The landing area is in the bay, and the base is next to the Amtrak railroad bridge on the river's south shore. The facility, which is reported to have opened in about 1986, offers water moorings and turf tiedowns, but not fuel. Six aircraft were based there as of March 14, 2002, and operations for the preceding twelve months totaled 1,280.[102]

Significance for Maryland air/space history:
A small seaplane base that has operated since the 1980s.
Relevant years: c. 1986 - present
Lat/Long: 39-32-49N 76-04-18W
Map: ADC Md/Del 2000 *Num*: 7 *Grid*: E6
Shows: town

Windsock hangs limp over hangars at rural Fair's Airport, Pokomoke City, in September 1987. Photo courtesy of Ashish Solanki, Maryland Aviation Administration.

The runway at Freeway Airport, a busy general-aviation field near Churchville, Prince George's County, ends at the edge of the U.S. Route 50 highway that gave the airport its name. Photo courtesy of the Maryland Aviation Administration.

An early-model PBM Mariner, built at the Glenn L. Martin Aircraft Company plant in Middle River, Baltimore County, flying over Pimlico Racecourse in Baltimore. The Navy patrol bomber bears a pre-war paint job. Photo courtesy of the National Air and Space Museum, Smithsonian Institution.

Montgomery County Airpark near Gaithersburg, photographed in 1994, surrounded by factories and businesses. Photo courtesy of Maryland Aviation Administration

County	Site Type	City	Name and Maryland Historical Trust number (if assigned)
Anne Arundel	APT	Annapolis	Annapolis Airport
Anne Arundel	APT	Annapolis	Dixie Airport
Anne Arundel	APT	Annapolis	Lee Airport
Anne Arundel	APT	Churchton	Deep Creek Airport
Anne Arundel	PT	Glen Burnie	Baltimore-Washington International Airport (Friendship)
Anne Arundel	APT	Glen Burnie	Glen Burnie-Whipp Airport and Seaplane Base
Anne Arundel	APT	Laurel	Suburban Airpark
Anne Arundel	APT	Odenton	Tipton Airport (Ft. Meade Army Airfield) AA-2240
Anne Arundel	AFLD	Annapolis	Naval Air Facility Annapolis
Anne Arundel	AFLD	Annapolis	Naval Aviation Camp
Anne Arundel	NIKE	Annapolis	Site W-26, Annapolis/Skidmore/Bay Bridge AA-38
Anne Arundel	NIKE	Davidsonville	Site W-25, Davidsonville AA-993
Anne Arundel	NIKE	Jacobsville	Site BA-43, Jacobsville
Anne Arundel	NIKE	Odenton	Ft. Meade Nike missile facilities (Site W-13T and command post)
Anne Arundel	SCI	Annapolis	David Taylor Research Ctr. (Navy Engineering Experiment Station) AA-2176
Anne Arundel	MISC	Annapolis	U. S. Naval Academy AA-359
Allegany	APT	Cumberland	Greater Cumberland Regional Airport
Allegany	APT	Cumberland	Mexico Farms Airport AL-111-A-153
Baltimore County	APT	Baltimore	Curtiss-Wright Airport (Pimlico Airport)
Baltimore County	APT	Baltimore	Harbor Field (Baltimore Municipal Airport) BA-2094
Baltimore County	APT	Baltimore	Service Field
Baltimore County	APT	Dundalk	Logan Field (Baltimore Municipal Airport)
Baltimore County	APT	Essex	Essex Seaplane Base
Baltimore County	APT	Essex	Essex Skypark
Baltimore County	APT	Halthorpe	Baltimore Aviation Field, Halethorpe
Baltimore County	APT	Middle River	Martin State Airport BA-2081
Baltimore County	APT	Perry Hall	Baltimore Airpark (Quinn Airport)
Baltimore County	APT	Woodlawn	Rutherford Field (Baltimore Airport)
Baltimore County	NIKE	Cronhardt	Site BA-92, Cronhardt
Baltimore County	NIKE	Fork	Site BA-09, Fork
Baltimore County	NIKE	Granite	Site BA-79, Granite
Baltimore County	NIKE	Phoenix	Site BA-03, Phoenix
Baltimore County	IND	Dundalk	Berliner-Joyce Aircraft Company plant
Baltimore County	IND	Middle River	Martin Plant No. 1 BA-2081, BA-3152
Baltimore County	IND	Middle River	Martin Plant No. 2 BA-2824
Baltimore County	MISC	Middle River	Aero Acres/Victory Villa/Stansbury Estates
Baltimore County	MISC	Edgemere	Bay Shore Park BA-2361
Baltimore City	IND	Baltimore	Curtiss-Caproni Corp. plant (General Aviation Mfr. Corp. plant)
Caroline	APT	Ridgely	Ridgely Airpark (Ridgely-Pelican Airport)

Carroll	APT	Taneytown	Taneytown Airport
Carroll	APT	Westminster	Carroll Co. Reg. Apt./Poage Field (Base 332, Westminster Apt.)
Carroll	APT	Westminster	Clearview Airpark
Cecil	APT	Elkton	Cecil County Airpark (Lovett Field)
Cecil	APT	Elkton	Cecil County Airport (Raintree Airpark)
Cecil	APT	Farmington	Farmington Airport
Cecil	APT	North East	Bar H Sky Park
Charles	APT	Indian Head	Maryland Airport CH-597
Charles	APT	Newburg	Aqualand/Clifton Skypark
Charles	APT	Shiloh	Site 11 intermediate field, Norfolk-Washington Airway
Charles	NIKE	Pomonkey W-54,	Pomonkey CH-676
Charles	NIKE	Waldorf	Site W-44, Mattawoman/Waldorf/La Plata CH-677
Charles	SCI	Indian Head	Indian Head Dv., Naval Surf. Warfare Ctr. (Ind. H. Prov. Gnd.) CH-492
Charles	SCI	La Plata	Blossom Point Proving Ground
Dorhester	APT	Cambridge	Cambridge-Dorchester Municipal Airport
Frederick	APT	Frederick	Detrick Field F-3-161
Frederick	APT	Frederick	Frederick Municipal Airport
Frederick	APT	Lewistown	Stevens Airport
Garrett	APT	Oakland	Garrett County Airport
Harford	APT	Aberdeen	Aberdeen Airpark
Harford	APT	Churchville	Harford County Airpark (Aldino Airport)
Harford	APT	Fallston	Fallston Airport
Harford	APT	Havre de Grace	Havre de Grace Seaplane Base
Harford	AFLD	Edgewood	Weide Army Heliport (Edgewood Arsenal Field)
Harford	NIKE	Edgewood	Site BA-18, Edgewood Arsenal, Aberdeen Proving Ground HA-1995
Harford	SCI	Aberdeen	Aberdeen Proving Ground and Phillips Army Airfield
Howard	SCI	Laurel	Johns Hopkins University Applied Physics Laboratory
Kent	APT	Chestertown	Russell Airport
Kent	APT	Chestertown	Scheeler Field (Gill Airport)
Kent	NIKE	Tolchester Beach	Site BA-30/31, Tolchester Beach/Chestertown
Montgomery	APT	Gaithersburg	Montgomery County Airpark
Montgomery	APT	Rockville	Congressional Airport M: 26-21-6
Montgomery	APT	Laytonsville	Davis Airport
Montgomery	NIKE	Gaithersburg	Site W-92, Rockville (now in/near Gaithersburg) M: 21-187
Montgomery	NIKE	Gaithersburg	Site W-94, Gaithersburg
Montgomery	NIKE	Laytonsville	Site W-93, Laytonsville/Derwood
Montgomery	SCI	Silver Spring	The Johns Hopkins University Applied Physics Lab (original)
Montgomery	SCI	West Bethesda	Carderock Dv., Naval Surf. Warf. Ctr. (D. Taylor Model Basin) M: 29-54
Montgomery	SCI	White Oak	White Oak Laboratory M: 33-25
Prince George's	APT	Beltsville	Beltsville Airport
Prince George's	APT	Bladensburg	Capitol Airport
Prince George's	APT	Clinton	Washington Executive/Hyde Field
Prince George's	APT	College Park	College Park Airport PG: 66-4
Prince George's	APT	Croom	Columbia Air Center (Riverside Field, Croom Airport)
Prince George's	APT	Friendly	Potomac Airfield (Rose Valley Airport, P. G. Airpark)

Prince George's	APT	Greenbelt	Schrom Airport
Prince George's	APT	Hyattesville	Queen's Chapel Airport
Prince George's	APT	Mitchellville	Freeway Airport
Prince George's	APT	Riverdale	ERCO Field
Prince George's	AFLD	Camp Springs	Andrews Air Force Base
Prince George's	NIKE	Accokeek	Site W-45, Accokeek
Prince George's	NIKE	Brandywine	Site W-36, Brandywine
Prince George's	NIKE	Croom	Site W-35, Croom PG: 86B-26
Prince George's	SCI	College Park	Glenn L. Martin Wind Tunnel
Prince George's	SCI	Greenbelt	NASA Goddard Space Flight Center PG: 64-5 and PG: 64-8
Prince George's	SCI	Greenbelt	Spacecraft Magnetic Test Facility, NASA Goddard PG: 64-6
Prince George's	IND	Riverdale	Engineering and Research Corp. (ERCO) plant PG: 68-22
Prince George's	MISC	Bladensburg	George Washington House (Indian Queen Tavern) PG: 69-2
Queen Anne's	APT	Dominion	Carroll's Airport
Queen Anne's	APT	Stevensville	Bay Bridge Airport
Queen Anne's	APT	Stevensville	Kentmorr Airpark
St. Mary's	APT	Leonardtown	Capt. Walter Francis Duke Regional Airport
St. Mary's	AFLD	Lexington Park	Naval Air Station Patuxent River/Trapnell Field SM-357
St. Mary's	AFLD	Saint Inigoes	Naval Air Warfare Ctr. Aircraft Div. Saint Inigoes (Webster Fld.) SM-894
St. Mary's	MISC	Lexington Park	Lexington Manor SM-490
Somerset	APT	Crisfield	Crisfield Municipal Airport
Somerset	APT	Princess Anne	Princess Anne Airport
Talbot	APT	Easton	Easton Airport/Newnam Field
Talbot	APT	Easton	Tred Avon Airport
Talbot	APT	Easton	Webb Airport
Talbot	APT	Tilghman	Tilghman-Whipp Airport and Seaplane Base
Washington	APT	Hagerstown	Doub's Meadow
Washington	APT	Hagerstown	Hagerstown Regional Airport/Richard A. Henson Field
Washington	IND	Hagerstown	Fairchild Engine and Airplane Corporation plant WA-HAG-213
Washington	IND	Hagerstown	Kreider-Reisner original plant and airfield
Washington	IND	Hagerstown	Kreider-Reisner plant, 1929 (Fairchild Plant No. 1)
Washington	IND	Hagerstown	Maryland Pressed Steel
Washington	MISC	Hagerstown	Hamilton Homes
Wicomico	APT	Hebron	Hebron Airport (Del-Mar-Va Airport)
Wicomico	APT	Hebron	Spring Hill Airport
Wicomico	APT	Salisbury	Bennett Airport
Wicomico	APT	Salisbury	Ennis Aerodrome (Salisbury Airport, Delmarva Airport)
Wicomico	APT	Salisbury	Salisbury-Ocean City Wicomico Regional Airport WI-541
Worcester	APT	Berlin	Midway Airpark
Worcester	APT	Pocomoke City	Fair's Airport
Worcester	APT	Ocean City	Ocean City Municipal Airport

ABBREVIATIONS
AOPA   Aircraft Owners' and Pilots Association
EPFL   Maryland Department, Enoch Pratt Free Libary, Baltimore
MAA   Maryland Aviation Administration
MHT   Maryland Historical Trust
MSAC   Maryland State Aviation Commission
ERRP   Environmental Restoration and Redevelopment Program

FROM BALLOONS TO ROCKETS:
MARYLAND AVIATION HISTORY IN CONTEXT
(1) Donald D. Jackson, *The Aeronauts* (Alexandria, Va.: Time-Life, 1980), pp. 14-21, 28; Tom D. Crouch, *The Eagle Aloft* (Washington: Smithsonian Institution, 1983), pp. 52-60.

(2) Crouch, *Eagle Aloft,* pp. 60-65; Raymond D. Hill, "The Search for Peter Carnes," *Richmond County History,* Vol. 10, No. 2 (1978), pp. 6-7.

(3) Crouch, *Eagle Aloft,* 65-66; Jackson, p. 28.

(4) Crouch, *Eagle Aloft,* pp. 66-69; Jackson, p. 28; Hill, pp. 7-8.

(5) Crouch, *Eagle Aloft,* pp. 69, 102, 106-108, 130.

(6) Ralph Robinson, "The Use of Rockets by the British in the War of 1812," *Maryland Historical Magazine,* Vol. 40, No. 1 (Mar. 1945), pp. 1-6; Frank W. Winter, *The First Golden Age of Rocketry* (Washington: Smithsonian Institution, 1990) pp. 24-28, 142-143.

(7) Tom D. Crouch, *Eagle Aloft,* pp. 143-169, quotation from p. 158; Carleton Jones, "Birdwoman of Baltimore," Baltimore *Sun,* Apr. 19, 1987. Jones credits Mrs. Warren with being the first woman to make a solo balloon flight in the Western Hemisphere; however, Crouch on pp.143-145 describes prior solo flights in the 1820s by Mme. Johnson in several states (of which Maryland was not one). Mme. Johnson's first name and nationality are unknown, although the "Mme." suggests that she was not American.

(8) Unsigned, "J. H. Pennington's Steam Balloon, 1842," petitions reprinted in the *Maryland Historical Magazine,* Vol. V (1910), pp. 134-139, quotations from pp. 136 and 138; Crouch, pp. 289-291.

(9) Frederick S. Haydon, *Aeronautics in the Union and Confederate Armies,* (Baltimore: Johns Hopkins, 1941), pp. 9-10, 345-350; Crouch, *Eagle Aloft,* pp. 341-364; Richard D. Layman, *To Ascend from a Floating Base,* (Cranberry, NJ: Associated University Presses, 1979), pp. 36-40; Eugene B. Block, *Above the Civil War. The Story of Thaddeus Lowe, Balloonist, Inventor, Railway Builder* (Berkeley, CA: Howell-North Books, 1966), pp. 64-65, 86-87.

(10) Haydon, pp. 350-359; Crouch, p. 371.

(11) Haydon, pp. 310, 359-367; Crouch, p. 370.

(12) Crouch, *Eagle Aloft,* pp. 336, 398-399, 410-412.

(13) George Gipe, "An Afternoon's Diversion in the Good Old Days," *The Sun Magazine,* Baltimore, Oct.14, 1973; Crouch, pp. 532-542; unsigned letter and illustration dated Baltimore, Aug. . 30, 1865, "A Natural Flying Machine," *Scientific American,* Vol. XIII (New Series), No. 13 (Sep.23, 1865), p. 195; Unsigned, "The Story of Aviation in Baltimore," *Baltimore,* Nov.1941, pp. 32-33. The last-named source also reports that another Baltimorean, W. F. Schroeder, built a flying machine in 1875; however, the invention was demolished by a storm before it could be tested.

(14) J. Gordon Vaeth, *Langley: Man of Science and Flight* (New York: Ronald Press, 1966), pp. 45-47, 79-87, and *passim;* Charles de F. Chandler and Frank P. Lahm, *How Our Army Grew Wings: Airmen and Aircraft before 1914* (New York: Ronald Press, 1943), pp. 96-97; Tom D. Crouch, *The Bishop's Boys: A Life of Wilbur and Orville Wright* (New York: Norton, 1989), pp. 138-142, 258, 261-263. *Charles County History* by Jack D. Brown, et al., states on p. 51 that Langley's first successful unmanned craft landed on the Maryland shore after overflying the Potomac in 1896; however, Vaeth (pp. 45-47) and Crouch (pp. 142-143) describe this test as ending with a landing in the water. Brown further reports that in 1903 Langley's launching boat was anchored off Liverpool Point in Charles County, Md., and was supplied by Charles Countians of Mallow's Bay. This Maryland connection is not mentioned in other sources examined.

(15) Chandler and Lahm, p. 162-166; Crouch, *Bishop's Boys,* p. 408-409; Catherine W. Allen, unpublished history of College Park Airport, undated, College Park Aviation Museum files, pp. 3-7, quotation from p. 6; William A. Aleshire and Robert F. Sellers, National Register of Historic Places Nomination Form, Aug. 30, 1976, MHT file PG 66-4, section 8, continuation pp. 6-8.

(16) Charles F. Elvers, "I Remember When I Built Maryland's First Plane," Baltimore *Sun,* June 25, 1954 (quoted); "Early Aviation in Baltimore," album compiled by the Enoch Pratt Free Library with pictures presented by Elvers in 1928; Unsigned, "The Story of Aviation in Baltimore," *Baltimore,* Nov.1941, p. 33; Rea Murdock, "Maryland Pacemaker as Aviation Pioneer," Baltimore *News American,* Apr. 3, 1966.

(17) Baltimore *Sun,* reprinted articles from Nov.7- 8, 1910, and album of clippings from Baltimore newspapers, June 1 – Nov.7, 1910, collection of Barry Lanman; Unsigned, "Practical Aviation:

Latham's Record Flight Over Baltimore," *The Book of the Royal Blue*, Vol. XIV, No. 3 (Dec.1910); Barry Lanman, "The Baltimore Air Show, 1910," script for a video presentation, 1980; Elvers, "I Remember . . ."

(18) Allen, pp. 8-10; Ralph C. Van Allen, "The History of the Aviation Field at College Park," 1928, pp. 10-13, Records of Phi Mu Fraternity, University of Maryland Libraries; Aleshire and Sellers nomination form, MHT file PG 66-4, section 8 continuation sheet, pp. 6, 18-19; Thomas Reilly, *Jannus, An American Flier* (Gainesville: University Press of Florida, 1997), pp. 11-15, 26.

(19) Reilly, pp. 24-25; unsigned, "The Story of Aviation in Baltimore," *Baltimore*, Nov.1941, p. 34.

(20) Chandler and Lahm, *How Our Army Grew Wings*, pp. 194-211, 214, 219-243; William F. Lynd, "The Army Flying School at College Park," *Maryland Historical Magazine*, Vol. 48 (1953), pp. 227-241; Catherine W. Allen, unpublished history of College Park Airport, pp. 11- 24; Aleshire and Sellers nomination form, MHT file PG 66-4, sections 7 and 8; Julyliet A. Hennessy, *The United States Army Air Arm, Apr. 1861 to Apr. 1917* (Washington: Office of Air Force History, 1958), pp. 33, 45-54, 60-62, 71-73; C. V. Glines, "Eighty Years at College Park," *Air Force Magazine*, Jan.1990.

(21) Deputy Chief of Naval Operations (Air) and Naval Air Systems Command, *United States Naval Aviation*, 1910-1970, NAVAIR 00-80P-1 (Washington, 1970), pp. 3-9; Thomas W. Ray, "First Year of Naval Aviation," *American Aviation Historical Society Journal*, Vol. 12, No. 3 (Fall, 1967), p. 209, "Annapolis: The Navy's First Aerodrome," *U.S. Naval Institute Proceedings*, Vol. 97, No. 19 (Oct. 1971), pp. 34-41; Jack Sweetman and Thomas J. Cutler, *The U.S. Naval Academy: An Illustrated History* (Annapolis: Naval Institute Press, 1995), pp. 165-166; ; George van Deurs, *Wings for the Fleet: A Narrative of Naval Aviation's Early Development, 1910-1916* (Annapolis: Naval Institute Press, 1966), pp. 49, 50, 63-66, 69-71, 82-87, 92-93, 103-104; H. B. Miller, "Shooting the Catapult," *U.S. Naval Institute Proceedings*, Vol. 59, No. 4 (Apr. 1933), pp. 549-551.

(22) Reilly, *Jannus*, p. 2; R. B. Clapp, "Gas and Electricity Used in Conquering the Air, *The Baltimore Gas and Electric News*, Nov.1914, p. 490.

(23) Reilly, 2, 165-167, 173-176, 190-191; Clapp, pp. 490-491.

(24) Unsigned, "The Story of Aviation in Baltimore," *Baltimore*, Nov.1941, p. 34; *Maryland Historical Magazine*, "In Memoriam," June 1919, pp. 109-110 and Sep.1919, pp. 293-294, 325-327; James H. O'Brien, "I Remember Baltimore's World War I Fliers," *Baltimore Sun*, Nov.11, 1956.

(25) "The Story of Aviation in Baltimore," *op. cit.*, pp. 34-35; William Joynes, "Maryland's Role in Aviation," *Baltimore American*, Nov.15, 1953; Kent A. Mitchell, "The Hagerstown Airport," undated manuscript in the MAA airport archives file; "Bellanca, Giuseppe Mario – 1993," National Aviation Hall of Fame site, nationalaviation.org, view Sep.20, 2002; "Belanca CF," National Air and Space Museum site, nasm.si.ed, viewed Sep.20, 2002.

(26) NAVAIR chronology, pp. 6, 10, 15; Keir Sterling, "Aberdeen Proving Ground: The Early Years," *Harford Historical Bulletin*,

No. 49 (Summer 1991), Aberdeen Room Archives and Museum; Leonard Weston, "Early Testing Takes to Skies," *APG News*, Aug. 15, 1990; Wernher von Braun and Frederick I. Ordway III, *History of Rocketry and Space Travel* (New York: Thomas Crowell, revised edition, 1969), p. 45.

(27) William M. Leary, *Aerial Pioneers: The U.S. Air Mail Service, 1918-1927* (Washington: Smithsonian Institution, 1985), pp. 37-38, 54, 100-101, 173, 216, 241-242; Allen, unpublished history of College Park Airport, pp. 25-27; Aleshire and Sellers nomination form, MHT file PG 66-4, section 8 continuation, pp. 19-20; Monroe, "The History of the Aviation Field at College Park Since 1918," pp. 5-7.

(28) Unsigned, "The Story of Aviation in Baltimore," *Baltimore*, Nov.1941, p. 36; Unsigned, "Saga of Logan Field, Once Called Finest Airport on the East Coast," Baltimore *Evening Sun*, Dec.28, 1948; John F. R. Scott, Jr., *Voyages into Airy Regions* (Annapolis: Ann Arundell County Historical Society and Fishgate Publishing, 1984), p. 17; Lampl Associates, Baltimore Municipal Airport Aviation Context Report, June 2000, MHT file BA-149; pp. 17-19; Clayton Davis, "Logan Field, Baltimore's First Municipal Airport," 1997, posted on geocities.com; Robert May, "Logan Field" in *Dundalk Then and Now, 1894-1980* (Dundalk: Dundalk-Patapsco Neck Historical Society, c. 1980), p. 27; Maryland Air National Guard, *The Maryland Air National Guard: A Commemorative History, 1921-2000* (Charlotte NC: Fine Books, 2000), pp. 25-31, 249.

(29) Howard A. Kelly, Jr., "I Remember a Flyer's Life in the Twenties," Baltimore *Sun*, Sep.7, 1952.

(30) Kelly; Ralph Barker, *The Schneider Trophy Races* (Shrewsbury, England: Airlife, 1971), pp. 103-122; Thomas G. Foxworth, *The Speed Seekers* (New York: Doubleday, 1974) pp. 49, 54-55; David A. Dorsey, National Register of Historic Places Inventory Nomination Form, Oct.30, 1979, MHT file AL-III-A-15; James H. and Martha R. Dolly, "Lily Pad on a Pond: The Golden Days of Aviation at Mexico Farms Airport," National Air and Space Museum library file; Wilbert F. Snyder and Charles L. Bragaw, *Achievement in Radio* (Boulder, CO: National Bureau of Standards, 1996), pp. 147-164; Monroe, "The History of the Aviation Field at College Park Since 1918," pp. 8-13; Catherine W. Allen, unpublished history of College Park Airport, pp. 30-31.

(31) Nick A. Komons, *Bonfires to Beacons: Federal Civil Aviation Policy under the Air Commerce Act, 1926-1938* (Washington: Federal Aviation Administration, 1978), 80-88, 168-172; Herbert M. Brune, Jr., "The Air Law of Maryland," Baltimore *Evening Sun*, Apr. 3, 1928; Maryland State Archives, "Department of Transportation, Historical Evolution," mdarchives.state.md.us; U.S. Civil Aeronautics Authority, Civil Aeronautics Bulletin No. 4, State Aeronautical Legislation Digest and Uniform State Laws (revised to Jan.1, 1939), Oct.1, 1939, pp. 38-40; Unsigned, "Baltimore's Singular Tribute to Lindbergh's Flight," *Maryland Gazette*, Vol. CCI, Sep.19, 1927, p. 107; William Joynes, "Maryland's Role in Aviation," *Baltimore American*, Nov.15, 1953.

(32) Joynes; Unsigned, "The Story of Aviation in Baltimore," *Baltimore*, Nov.1941, p. 36; Theodore Roosevelt McKeldin, "Making Baltimore a Center for the Airplane Industry," published transcript of a radio address, Nov.6, 1930 (or 1931), EPFL

vertical files; Christopher Pfrommer, "Harbor Field Ending Up as Marine Terminal," Baltimore *Evening Sun*, Dec.30, 1960.

(33) *Jane's All The World's Aircraft*, 1929 edition, p. 267c; "The Story of Aviation in Baltimore," *Baltimore*, Nov.1941, p. 39.

(34) *Jane's*, 1929, p. 242; "The Story . . .," *Baltimore*, Nov.1941, p. 39; Berliner-Joyce Aircraft Corporation, "New Quarter-Million Dollar Plant Now Building at Baltimore," pamphlet, c. 1929, EPFL (quoted); Robert May in *Dundalk Then and Now*, p. 28 (re fly-over); Anthony Robinson, *The Encyclopedia of American Aircraft* (New York: Galahad Books, 1979), p. 24.

(35) *Jane's*, 1931, p 266c; Baltimore Association of Commerce, "Aviation in Baltimore," pamphlet, early 1930s, EPFL; Unsigned, "The Story. . .," *Baltimore*, Nov.1941; John R. Breihan, Stan Piet, Roger S. Mason, *Martin Aircraft, 1909-1960* (Santa Ana, CA: (Santa Ana, Ca.: Narkiewicz//Thompson, 1995), pp. 5-7, 14-16, 35-40; William B. Harwood, *Raise Heaven and Earth* (New York: Simon and Schuster, 1993), pp. 113-120; Andrea Bakewell Lowry, Maryland Inventory of Historic Properties, Aug. .20, 1997, MHT: file BA-2081.

(36) Theron K. Rinehart, "Sherman M. Fairchild 'Discovered' Local Airplane Company and Bought It in 1929," *The Cracker Barrel*, Mar. 1979, pp. 16-19; Kent A. Mitchell, *Fairchild Aircraft, 1926-1987* (Santa Ana, Ca.: Narkiewicz//Thompson, 1997), pp. 6-7, 51-58.

(37) Unsigned, "General Aviation Manufacturing Corporation Locates All Its Activities in Baltimore," *Baltimore*, Oct.1931, and Unsigned, "The Story . . .," *Baltimore*, Nov.1941, p. 39; Norm Avery, *North American Aircraft, 1934-1998* (Santa Ana, Ca.: Narkiewicz//Thompson, 1998), Vol. I, pp. 8-18.

(38) Harwood, *Raise Heaven and Earth*, pp. 116, 120-123; Breihan, Piet, Mason, *Martin Aircraft*, pp. 42-52, 62-66.

(39) Unsigned, "The Fairchild Aviation Corporation," reprinted from *Aero Digest*, Jan.1934; Rinehart, "Fairchild 'Discovered. . .,'"pp. 19-21; Unsigned pamphlet, "Historical Summary, Fairchild Engine and Airplane Corporation, 1920-1951," Washington County Free Library, pp. 13-14, 21-22; Mitchell, *Fairchild Aircraft*, pp. 58-103.

(40) Kent A. Mitchell, "The Hagerstown Airport," unpublished and undated paper, MAA files, pp. 3-4, 7-8; Dickson J. Preston, *Talbot County: A History* (Centreville, Md.: Tidewater, 1983), pp. 300-301; Thomas F. Norton, transcript of untitled lecture at the Historical Society of Talbot County, Oct.2002; Norman M. Covert, *Cutting Edge: A History of Fort Detrick, Maryland, 1943 – 1993* (Headquarters, U.S. Army Garrison, Fort Detrick, 1993), pp. 3-8; Joshua Wilson Rowe, "Detrick Field in the Thirties," Baltimore *Sun*, July 8, 1978; *The Maryland National Guard*, pp. 36, 38, 40-41; Karin Thiessen, "Airports in Prince George's County: Past and Present," 1996, unpublished paper, MAA files; Catherine W. Allen, unpublished history of College Park Airport, pp. 32-33; Fred Rasmussen, "Flights of Fancy during the Depression," Baltimore *Sun*, Jan.18, 1998; H. Kelcey Gault, "The Air Circuses of the 1930s," Baltimore *Sunday Sun Magazine*, Feb.22, 1959; Gwinn Owens, "Early Aviation in Baltimore: A Personal Journey," Baltimore *Evening Sun*, June 2, 1983.

(41) Unsigned, "Saga of Logan Field . . . ," Baltimore *Evening Sun*, Dec.28, 1948; May, "Logan Field" in *Dundalk Then and Now, 1894-1980*, p. 27; McKeldin, "Making Baltimore a Center for the Airplane Industry," Nov.6, 1930 (or 1931); Pfrommer, "Harbor Field Ending Up as Marine Terminal," Baltimore *Evening Sun*, Dec.30, 1960; Scott, *Airy Regions*, p. 19; Lampl report, MHT file BA-149 pp. 17-19, 24-27, 36.

(42) Herbert M. Brune, Jr., "I Remember When We Almost Got a Zeppelin Base," Baltimore *Sun*, Oct.11, 1953; Unsigned, "Big Navy Dirigible Explodes at Holabird," Baltimore *Evening Sun*, July 1, 1919; Michele Benjamin, "Camp Holabird Witnesses Explosion of Navy Dirigible," DundalkEagle.com, viewed Aug. 21, 2002.

(43) Avery McBee, "Wings Over Maryland," *The Maryland Spectator*, May 1936, quotation from p. 29; Unsigned, "Pan-American Leases Airport Tract as Base for Ocean Plane Link," Baltimore *Sun*, Nov.5, 1936; Lampl report, MHT file BA-149, pp. 26-31.

(44) G. H. Pouder, "Regular Passenger Air Service Between Baltimore and Bermuda In Aug. Inaugurated," *Baltimore*, Dec.1937; Lampl report, MHT file BA-149, pp. 26-35.

(45) Lampl report, pp. 33-34, 36; *The Maryland Air National Guard*, p. 250.

(46) William B. Harwood, *Raise Heaven and Earth*, pp. 163-171; Breihan, Piet, and Mason, *Martin Aircraft*, pp. 55, 68-81.

(47) Harwood, pp. 171-181; Breihan, Piet, and Mason, pp. 82-89.

(48) Harwood, pp. 174-212; Breihan, Piet, and Mason, pp. 90-119.

(49) Mitchell, *Fairchild Aircraft 1926-1987*, pp. 104-129; Christopher Shank, "Wings over Hagerstown: Experiencing the Second World War in Western Maryland," *Maryland Historical Magazine*, Vol. 88, No. 4 (Winter 1993), pp. 444-461; Unsigned, "The Story of Aviation in Baltimore," *Baltimore*, Nov.1941, p. 39; Craig Swain, "Gliders for the Navy Department: 1940-45," microworks.net; General Motors Corporation, *A History of Eastern Aircraft Division, General Motors Corporation* (1944), pp. 21, 45, 54, 119-121.

(50) Chuck Hansen, "Engineering and Research Corporation," *Journal of American Aviation Historical Society*, Spring 1985, pp. 43-45; Stanley G. Thomas, *The Ercoupe* (Blue Ridge Summit, Pa.: Tabb, 1991), pp. 61-66; Milton Lehman, *This High Man: The Life of Robert A. Goddard* (New York: Farrar, Straus, 1963), pp. 341-399.

(51) Unsigned, "The Bendix Radio Story," *Baltimore*, Mar. 1963; Unsigned, "Short History of Bendix Radio," Baltimore Museum of Industry website, thebmi.org, viewed Aug. 1, 2002; Gene Strull, *Electronic Enterprise: Stories from the History of Westinghouse Electronic Systems* (Westinghouse Electronic Systems Division, 1996), pp. 5-9; Westinghouse Corporation, *Westinghouse in World War 2, Radio and X-Ray Divisions* (Westinghouse Corp., 1946), Vol. I, pp. 69-77.

(52) Strull, *Electronic Enterprise*, pp. 9-10 *Westinghouse in World War 2*, Vol. I, pp. 145-153; William K. Klingaman, *APL – Fifty Years of Service to the Nation*, pp. 6-20; George H. Callcott, *Maryland and America*, (Baltimore: Johns Hopkins, 1985), pp. 36-39.; Naval Historical Center, "Radio Proximity VT Fuzes," ;

Greg Gobel, "Microwave Radar at War,' , both viewed Sep. 29, 2003.

(53) Callcott, *Maryland and America,* pp. 33-34; *The Maryland Air National Guard,* pp. 39-46; Michael H. Rogers, *Answering Their Country's Call* (Baltimore: Johns Hopkins, 2002), pp. 1-12, 44-55, 72-87, 131-138, 195-207, 225-238, 254-262; Donald T. Fritz, "Bill Moore and the Last Enemy Plane," *Maryland Historical Magazine,* Vol. 90, No. 4 (Winter 1995), pp. 489-493.

(54) Covert, *The Cutting Edge,* pp. 7-8, 13-15; Harry I. Stegmaier, Jr., et al., *Allegany County: A History* (Parsons, W.Va.: Mcclain, 1976), pp. 360-361; Eric J. Mills: "50th Anniversary: Taking Flight at Easton Airport," Easton *Star Democrat (Sunday Star),* July 25, 1993; Scott, *Airy Regions,* p. 33; Norman P. Sullivan, "Baltimore Squadron of CAP Opens Westminster Airport," Baltimore *Sun,* June 7, 1943; Linda Drew, *The History of Naval Air Station, Patuxent River, Maryland* (Naval Air Systems Command, c. 1999), pp. 3-5; Paolo E. Coletta, ed., *United States Navy and Marine Corps Bases, Domestic* (Westport, Ct.: Greenwood, 1985), p. 426; Eugene L. Meyer, *Maryland Lost and Found . . . Again* (Baltimore: Woodholme, 2000) pp. 125-126.

(55) Meyer,, pp. 125-126; Drew, *Naval Air Station, Patuxent River,* pp. 3-5; Callcott, *Maryland and America,* p. 42; John R. Breihan, "Aero Acres," *Air & Space Smithsonian,* June/July 1999; Elizabeth Hughes, MHT Historic Sites Inventory Form, Mar. 1995, file SM-490.

(56) D. Cochrane and P. Ramirez, "Bernetta Miller," National Air and Space Museum, .si.edu, Dec.15, 1999, and information from Catherine Allen, College Park Aviation Museum; Patricia Strickland, *The Putt-Putt Air Force: The Story of the Civilian Pilot Training Program and the War Training Service, 1939-1945* (Federal Aviation Administration), especially p. 104; Betty Stagg Turner, *Out of the Blue and into History* (Arlington Hts., Il.: Aviatrix, 2000), excerpts supplied by Elaine Harmon; Katherine Scarborough, "Flying Hutchinsons Fold Wings," Baltimore *Sun,* Oct.29, 1939.

(57) John R. Breihan, "Between Munich and Pearl Harbor: The Glenn L. Martin Aircraft Company Gears Up for War, 1938-1941," and Christopher Shank, "Wings Over Hagerstown," *Maryland Historical Magazine,* Vol. 88, No. 4 (Winter 1993), pp. 408-409, 451-452; Harwood, *Raise Heaven and Earth,* pp. 213-216.

(58) Breihan, "Between Munich and Pearl Harbor"; Shank, pp. 452-453; Clayton Davis, "Columbia Air Center, Croom, Maryland," unpublished typescript, MAA files; Bianca P. Floyd, *Records & Recollections: Early Black History in Prince George's County, Maryland* (Maryland National Park and Planning Commission, 1980), pp. 95-99; list of Tuskegee Airmen from Maryland provided by William Holton; Charles E. Francis, *The Tuskegee Airmen* (Boston: Branden, 3rd ed., 1993), especially pp. 190 and 358.

(59) Geoffrey Arend, *Great Airports Worldwide* (New York: Air Cargo Books, 1998), pp. 89-91; Scott, *Airy Regions,* pp. 26-29; Paul E. Welsh, "Harbor Field Handles Nearly as Many Planes as Friendship," Baltimore *Sun,* Oct. 8, 1953; Murdock, "Maryland Pacemaker as Aviation Pioneer," Baltimore *News American,* Apr. 3, 1966.

(60) Arend, p. 91-92; Scott, p. 29; MAA "BWI Timeline," www

bwiairport.com, viewed Nov.25, 2002; Maryland State Archives, "Department of Transportation, Historical Evolution," www.mdarchives.state.md.us, viewed May 19, 2002; Carole Shifria, "BWI Airport at 30: Where It's Been and Where It's Going," *Washington Post,* June 23, 1980.

(61) Unsigned, "Discover Your Airport: Celebrating 50 Years, 1949-1999," Frederick *News Post* special section, June 3, 1999; Stephen A. Bennett, "State's Air Service Seen Substandard," Baltimore *Sun,* Mar.1, 1963 (quoted).

(62) Meyer, *Maryland Lost and Found . . . Again,* pp. 17-24; Eric J. Mills: "50th Anniversary. . .," Meredith Goad, "Bill Newnam's High-Flying Days Remembered," Easton *Star Democrat,* July 25, 1993 (the latter reprinted from Jan.12, 1988); Mary Coddry, "Aviation Pioneer Finds New Frontiers," *Maryland,* Spring, 1981; Robert A. Searles, "Richard "Dick" Henson, the Maryland Marvel," *Business and Commercial Aviation,* Aug. .2002.

(63) Unsigned, "Aviation Gains in Md. in 1946 Set record," Baltimore *Evening Sun,* Dec.28, 1946; "Kentmorr Airpark," brochure c. 1950s, EPFL vertical file.

(64) Unsigned, "34 Airports Now in State, Baltimore *Sun,* Sep.2, 1948; Unsigned, "2 More Shore Airports Close," Baltimore *Evening Sun,* May 28, 1952; William Welling, "State Legislative Moves on Flying Matters Few," Baltimore *Sun,* Jan.13, 1954, and "Business Flying Grows, Airports Shut Down," Baltimore *Evening Sun,* Mar. 1, 1954; Maryland State Aviation Administration, *Maryland Airport Directory,* Apr. 28, 1981; George H. Callcott, *Maryland and America,* p. 316; Edmund Preston, ed., *FAA Historical Chronology* (Washington: Department of Transportation, 1998), p. 192.

(65) Joseph L. Stanton, "There's a Plane in Your Future," *Baltimore,* Aug. 1946; Thomas, *The Ercoupe,* pp. 67-68, 77-83.

(66) Mitchell, *Fairchild Aircraft,* pp. 122, 140-151, 158-160, 168-175, and *passim*; Kurtis Meyer, list of Fairchild aircraft produced at Hagerstown, Sep.2002.

(67) Breihan, Piet, and Mason, *Martin Aircraft,* pp. 132-201; Harwood, *Raise Heaven and Earth,* pp. 231-271; Martin Marietta Aero and Naval Systems, "Sixty Years in Baltimore," *The Star,* Oct.1989, Baltimore Museum of Industry files.

(68) von Braun and Ordway, *History of Rocketry and Space Travel,* pp. 122-123; Klingaman, *APL,* pp. 43-46; Harwood, pp. 244, 248-257; Breihan, Piet, and Mason, pp. 198-201; Mitchell, *Fairchild Aircraft,* pp. 180-181, and conversation with Preston, Dec. 17, 2002.

(69) Joseph P. Smaldone, *History of the White Oak Laboratory, 1945-1975* (Silver Spring: Naval Surface Warfare Center, 1977), p. 2 and *passim*; Klingaman, pp. 90-91; Harwood, pp. 271-282; "Sixty Years in Baltimore," *The Star,* Oct.1989; Charles Cohen, "Westinghouse Legacy Stands Out in War, Peace," *Baltimore Business Journal,* Oct.29, 1999; Baltimore Museum of Industry "Maryland Milestones" exhibit information on Black and Decker, citing Otto Scott's *The Powered Hand*; William Hallstead, "On the Front of the Jet, Missile and Space Age," *Maryland,* Summer 1980, p. 26.

(70) Hallstead, pp. 25-28; "Sixty Years in Baltimore," *The Star,* Oct.1989.

(71) Merle T. Cole, "W-25: The Davidsonville Site and Maryland Air Defense, 1950-1974," *Maryland Historical Magazine*, Vol. 80, No. 3 (Fall 1985), and "The One That Got Away," *Anne Arundel County History News*, Vol. 32 (Jan.2001); Mark L. Morgan and Mark A. Berhow, *Rings of Supersonic Steel: Air Defenses of the United States Army, 1950-1979* (Bodega Bay, Ca.: Fort MacArthur Military Press, 2nd ed., 2002), *passim.*

(72) Paolo E. Coletta, ed., *Bases*, pp. 22-24, 428-430; Raymond D. Baker, *Historical Highlights of Andrews Air Force Base, 1942 – 1989* (Andrews AFB, Md.: Office of History, 1990), *passim.*; *The Maryland Air National Guard*, pp. 212, 250-251.

(73) Lockheed Martin, NE&SS-Marine Systems, "Heritage of Excellence," ness.external.lmco.com; Cohen, "Westinghouse Legacy," *Baltimore Business Journal*, Oct.29, 1999; Sun Staff, "Lockheed Lands Pact For Joint Strike Fighter," Baltimore *Sun*, Oct.27, 2001.

(74) Maryland Department of Business and Economic Development, "Maryland's Economic Base," Aerospace Industry section, viewed June 12, 2003; National Aeronautics and Space Administration, "The History of the Hubble Space Telescope," quest.arc.nasa.gov, viewed Aug. . 21, 2001.

(75) Kent A. Mitchell, *Fairchild Aircraft*, pp. 174-175; *The Maryland Air National Guard*, pp.166-209; Drew, *History of Naval Air Station, Patuxent River*, p. 26; Colleen Jenkins, "Longtime Navy Career Is Business Success Story," *Washington Post*, Oct.20, 2002; "Webster Field Annex" and "Severn River Naval Complex," globalsecurity.org; Clayton Davis, "Tipton Airport," July 1, 2000, MAA files.

(76) Edmund Preston, conversation with Betsy Mace re Baltimore Airpark, Mar. 27, 2003; Maryland Department of Natural Resources, "Population of Maryland's Jurisdictions, 1790 – 2000," dnrweb.dnr.state.md.us; Steven Ginsberg and Jessie Mangaliman, "Trying to Land Economic Growth; Outlying Areas Expand Airports," *Washington Post*, Sep. 12, 1999; Barry Lanman, oral history interview with Bruce Mundie, Dec.19, 2002.

(77) Chart on airport aid from 1978 through 2003, MAA June 27, 2003; Dec.1988 starting date of MAPA also provided by Bruce Mundie.

(78) Bradley Graham, "For Patrol Pilots, A Nightmare Scenario," *Washington Post*, Sep.29, 2001; Unsigned, "Washington Executive/Hyde Field Opens at Last," *EAA News*, eaa.org, Sep.27, 2002; Lanman interview with Mundie, Dec.19, 2002; Bureau of Transportation Statistics, bts.gov, Table 1-39, with data updated provided by Donald Bright, July 11, 2002; MAA bwiairport.com, "BWI Timeline," viewed July 11, 2003.

(79) Lanman interview with Mundie (quoted); Joe Nawrozki, "One Man's Plane Dream," Baltimore *Sun*, June. 10, 2003; Scott Moore, "Mr. Cool: Gus McLeod's North Pole Adventure, June 2, 2000, and "To the North Pole – and Back: Historic Plane Has Roundabout Trip to College Park Museum," *Washington Post*, Dec.29, 2000.

CHAPTER ONE:
PIONEERS

(1) Christopher Owens, MHT Worksheet, Nomination for the National Register of Historic Places, Mar. 2, 1973, MHT file PG 69-2. Although he dated the construction of the George Washington House as c. 1760, Owens noted that the dates 1732 and c. 1750 have also been ascribed. Owens' report differed from the usual accounts in concluding that the George Washington House had served as a store rather than as a tavern or inn during the 18th Century. This does not affect the structure's associations with the pioneer balloonist, however, since the report states that Carnes rented the whole commercial complex.

(2) Tom D. Crouch, *The Eagle Aloft: Two Centuries of the Balloon in America* (Washington: Smithsonian Institution Press, 1983), pp. 60-69, quotation from p. 63; Raymond D. Hill, "The Search for Peter Carnes," *Richmond County History*, Vol. 10, No. 2 (1978), pp. 5-10; Owens report. Owens states that Carnes' tenure at the Indian Queen establishment ended in 1783, while Crouch and Hill imply that he was still there in 1784.

(3) Owens report.

(4) Baltimore *Sun*, Nov.7-8, 1910, "Practical Aviation: Latham's Record Flight Over Baltimore," *The Book of the Royal Blue*, Baltimore and Ohio Railroad, Vol. XIV, No. 3, (Dec.1910), Album of clippings from Baltimore newspapers, June 1 – Nov.7, 1910, collection of Barry Lanman; Barry Lanman, "The Baltimore Air Show, 1910," script for a video presentation, 1980; Baltimore Aviation Company, Official Program of the Baltimore Aviation Meet, Nov. 2d to 8th, 1910 (Maryland Historical Society files). John F.R. Scott, Jr., *Voyages into Airy Regions* (Annapolis: Ann Arundell County Historical Society and Fishergate Publishing Co., 1984), pp. 82-85.

(5) Lanman album clippings. The closing date is from Richard D. Layman, *To Ascend from a Floating Base: Shipboard Aeronautics and Aviation, 1783-1914* (Cranberry, N.J.: Associated University Presses, 1979), p. 112.

(6) Lanman album clippings; Layman, *Floating Base*, pp. 111-112.

(7) Preston site visit with Lanman, whose previous research had included a trip to the location with Henry Rinn, an attendee at the 1910 event.

(8) MAA airport data sheet and directory, Sep.2001.

(9) Charles deForest Chandler and Frank P. Lahm, *How Our Army Grew Wings: Airmen and Aircraft Before 1914* (New York: Ronald Press, 1943), p. 162; Tom D. Crouch, *The Bishop's Boys: A Life of Wilbur and Orville Wright*, (New York: Norton, 1989), p. 408; Catherine W. Allen, unpublished history of College Park Airport, undated, College Park Aviation Museum files., pp. 3-5.

(10) Chandler and Lahm, pp. 163-166; Crouch, *Bishop's Boys*, pp. 408-409; Allen, pp. 6-7; William A. Aleshire and Robert F. Sellers, National Register of Historic Places Nomination Form, Aug.30, 1976, MHT file PG 66-4, section 8, continuation pp. 6-8.

(11) Allen, pp. 8-10; Ralph C. Van Allen, "The History of the Aviation Field at College Park" (1928), Records of Phi Mu Fraternity, University of Maryland Libraries, pp. 10-13; Thomas

Reilly, *Jannus, An American Flier* (Gainesville, Fla.: University Press of Florida, 1997). Aleshire and Sellers report, MHT file PG 66-4, section 8 continuation sheet, pp. 6, 18-19. According to Van Allen, flying at the airport ceased after U.S. entry into World War I (Apr. 1917) and did not resume until the establishment of the air mail station (Aug. 1918); however, Allen states that activities by some of the companies mentioned continued into early 1918, and that use by smaller organizations continued after their departure.

(12) Chandler and Lahm, Pp. 194, 202; William F. Lynd, "The Army Flying School at College Park," *Maryland Historical Magazine*, Vol. 48 (1953), pp. 227-41, pp. 227-229, 234; Allen, pp. 11-12, 17; Aleshire and Sellers report, MHT file PG 66-4, section 7. On p.6 of the section 8 continuation sheet, this report errs in stating that Smith was using the field before the Army's arrival in 1909; the cited source refers to 1911.

(13) Chandler and Lahm, pp. 194-211, 214, 219-243; Lynd, pp. 230-241; Julyiette A. Hennessy, *The United States Army Air Arm, April 1861 to April 1917* (Washington: Office of Air Force history, 1958), pp. 47-54; Allen, pp. 11-24; C.V. Glines, "Eighty Years at College Park," *Air Force Magazine*, Jan.1990, and commenting letter by Catherine W. Allen, May 1990; Aleshire and Sellers report, MHT file PG 66-4, section 8 continuation, pp. 8-18.

(14) Chandler and Lahm, pp. 221-222, 232-233; Allen, pp. 20-22. The two previous officer fatalities were: Lt. Thomas E. Selfridge at Ft. Meyer, Va., Sep.17, 1908; and Lt. George E. M. Kelly at Ft. Sam Houston, Texas, May 10, 1911 (Hennessey, pp. 33, 45).

(15) William M. Leary, *Aerial Pioneers: The U.S. Air Mail Service, 1918-1927* (Washington: Smithsonian Institution, 1985), pp. 54, 100-101, 173, 216, 241-242; Allen, pp. 25-27; Aleshire and Sellers report, MHT file PG 66-4, section 8 continuation, pp. 19-20; Benjamin Monroe, "The History of the Aviation Field at College Park since 1918," Jan.5, 1929, Records of Phi Mu Fraternity, University of Maryland Libraries, pp. 5-7. Monroe seems incorrect in stating that the route ended in 1920.

(16) Authors crediting Berliner with this "first" include Ken Beatty, *The Cradle of Aviation: The National Aviation Field, College Park, Maryland.* (Hagerstown Bookbinding and Printing, 1973; with errata sheet issued by College Park Aviation Museum), pp. 29, 43; Karin Thiessen, "Airports in Prince George's County: Past and Present," museum internship paper, 1996, MAA aviation history file, p. 4; and Allen (pp. 28-29); the Aleshire and Sellers report also lends some support (section 8 continuation, p. 20). For a variety of other views, see: Steve Wartenberg in Walter J. Boyne and Donald S. Lopez, eds., *Vertical Flight: The Age of the Helicopter* (Washington: Smithsonian Institution, 1984), pp. 9-10; Charles Gablehouse, *Helicopters and Autogiros: A History of Rotating-wing and V/STOL Aviation* (New York: Lippincott, rev. ed., 1969), p. 27; Richard G. Hubler, *Straight Up: The Story of Vertical Flight* (New York: Duell, Sloan and Pearce, 1961), pp. 29-30; Robert Jackson, *The Dragonflies: The Story of Helicopters and Autogiros* (London: Arthur Barker, 1971), pp. 21-22; Warren R. Young, *The Helicopters* (Alexandria, Va.: Time-Life Books, 1982)., p. 36; and R.D. Conner, ed., "Berliner No. 5" National Air and Space Museum document on website nasm.si.edu, viewed June 12, 2002.

(17) Wilbert F. Snyder and Charles L. Bragaw, *Achievement in Radio: Seventy Years of Radio Science, Technology, Standards, and Measurement at the National Bureau of Standards* (Boulder, Co.: National Bureau of Standards, Oct. 1996), pp. 147-164; Monroe, "History of the Aviation Field," pp. 8-13; Allen, pp. 30-31

(18) Allen, pp. 32-33. The airport remained on aeronautical charts throughout World War II, although it was shown as an auxiliary field. USCGS section charts, May 20, 1943, through Nov.30, 1944; MAA airport directories, Mar. 6, 1947 (with data as of July 1, 1946), June 1950, 1966, and 1970-71; AOPA directories, 1965, 1967, and 1969.

(19) Aleshire and Sellers, especially section 8 continuation, pp. 22-23; Allen, pp. 34-35; MAA airport directory Sep. 2001 and July 2002 data sheet; Katherine Shaver, "College Park Airport Almost Grounded," *Washington Post*, Sep.10, 2002.

(20) Lex Campbell and Martha Williams, R. Christopher Goodwin & Associates, MHT State Historic Sites Inventory Form, Oct.1996, MHT file AA-359, pp. 7.2 and 8.1.

(21) Layman, *Floating Base*, pp. 106-108.

(22) Thomas W. Ray, "First Year of Naval Aviation," *American Aviation Historical Society Journal*, Vol. 12, No. 3 (Fall, 1967), p. 209, "Annapolis: The Navy's First Aerodrome," *U.S. Naval Institute Proceedings*, Vol. 97, No. 19 (Oct. 1971), p. 36; Robert W. Murch, "N.A.S. Annapolis," *U.S. Naval Institute Proceedings*, Vol. 77, No. 10 (Oct. 1951), p. 1069; Jack Sweetman and Thomas J. Cutler, *The U.S. Naval Academy: An Illustrated History* (Annapolis: Naval Institute Press, 2nd ed., 1995), pp. 165-166; George van Deurs, *Wings for the Fleet: A Narrative of Naval Aviation's Early Development, 1910-1916* (Annapolis: U.S. Naval Institute, 1966). p. 49. Van Deurs casts doubt on the accuracy of Rodgers' flight log for this period; however, both Ray and Murch include the Washington flight in their accounts, and Murch quotes a contemporary news report describing it. Sweetman, who does not mention the Washington trip, includes a photograph of Rodgers preparing to takeoff on p. 167. Comparison with the contemporary ADC map suggests that the site is now occupied by newer buildings, although there is still a Farragut Field in this area.

(23) H. B. Miller, "Shooting the Catapult," *U.S. Naval Institute Proceedings*, Vol. 59, No. 4 (Apr. 1933), pp. 549-551; Van Deurs, *Wings for the Fleet*, pp. 69-71; NAVAIR chronology, pp.6-7; Sweetman and Cutler, *Naval Academy*, p. 166.

(24) Frank M. Hertel, "The Naval Academy and Naval Aviation," *U.S. Naval Institute Proceedings*, Vol. 74, No. 1 (Jan. 1948), pp. 37-38; Jack Stevenson, "Academy Aviation Training in Forty-Sixth Year," *The Log*, Mar.28, 1972, p. 34; Paolo E. Coletta, ed., *United States Navy and Marine Corps Bases, Domestic* (Westport, Conn.: Greenwood Press, 1985), pp. 21-22. Campbell and Williams seem mistaken in stating (p. 8.2) that aviation was introduced into the Academy's curriculum in 1911.

(25) NAVAIR chronology, pp. 3-4; Gerald E. Wheeler, "Naval Aviation's First Year," *U.S. Naval Institute Proceedings*, Vol. 87, No. 5 (May 1961), pp. 88-95.

(26) Ray, "First Aerodrome," pp. 34-36, including a photo of the hangar and an aerial view marked to show the camp's features; James C. Bradford, *Anne Arundel County, Maryland: A*

Bicentennial History, 1649-1977 (Annapolis: Anne Arundel County and Annapolis Bicentennial Committee, 1977), pp. 32-33, including building dimensions; van Deurs, *Wings for the Fleet,* pp. 50-1. Although van Deurs writes that the camp had no living quarters, this probably refers to a lack of accommodation for the officers, who lived at an inn near the Academy; both Ray and Bradford state that the camp had barracks space.

(27) Ray, "First Aerodrome," pp.34-41; NAVAIR chronology, p. 5; van Deurs, *Wings for the Fleet,* pp. 50-57.

(28) Van Deurs, pp. 50 and 63, including aerial photo of the 1912-14 camp; Bradford, p. 33; Archibald P. Turnbull, and Clifford L. Lord, *History of the United States Naval Aviation* (New Haven: Yale University Press, 1949), p. 17.

(29) Van Deurs, pp. 63-66, 82-87; NAVAIR chronology, pp. 6-8; "Centreville Visited by Its First Aeroplane," Centreville *Record,* June 29, 1912.

(30) Van Deurs, pp. 92-93, 103-104; NAVAIR chronology, p. 9. Bradford's statement on p. 33 that a hangar was built at the Severn River camp seems incorrect in the light of van Deur's more detailed study.

(31) Coletta, *Bases,* p. 21.

(32) Rodney P. Carlisle, *Where the Fleet Begins: A History of the David Taylor Research Center, 1898-1998* (Washington: Navy Historical Center, 1998), pp. 33-42, including photograph on p. 41; R. Christopher Goodwin & Associates, MHT State Historic Sites Inventory Form, Naval Engineering Experiment Station, U.S. Naval Academy, Annapolis Housing, Oct.30, 1996, MHT file AA-2176. (This report focuses on housing that was formerly part of the Engineering Experiment Station.), pp. 8.2-8.3.

(33) Van Deurs, *Wings for the Fleet,* pp. 50-51, 57, 63-64, including an aerial photo of the EES on p. 50; MHT file AA-2176, p. 8.3.

(34) Milton Lehman, *This High Man: The Life of Robert H. Goddard* (New York: Farrar, Straus and Company, 1963), pp. 341-399; Wernher von Braun and Frederick I. Ordway III, *History of Rocketry and Space Travel* (New York: Crowell, rev. ed., 1969), p. 101; Carlisle, *Where the Fleet Begins,* pp. 174-178.

(35) Carlisle, *Where the Fleet Begins,* pp. xvii, 178-179, 222-223, and *passim.;* MHT file AA-2176, pp. 8.4-8.5; "Severn River Naval Complex," www.globalsecurity.org; "Timeline, Carderock Division Milestones," both viewed Nov. 6, 2002.

(36) MHT file AA-2176, p. 7.1; websites globalsecurity.org and . "David Taylor Research Center," viewed on Nov.8, 2002.

(37) Larine Barr, et al., "Indian Head History, 1890-1997," and other information from www.ih.navy.mil, viewed Nov. 2002.; NAVAIR chronology, pp. 6, 10, 15, and 217; Lehman, *This High Man,* pp. 121-123.

(38) Rodney P. Carlisle, *Powder and Propellants: Energetic Materials at Indian Head, Maryland, 1890-1990* (Publication data not stated in volume, but presumably Washington: U.S. Navy, c. 1990), *passim;* Goodwin & Associates, MHT file CH-371.

(39) "Aberdeen Proving Ground," www.apg.army.mil, viewed Sep.11, 2002; Leonard Weston, "Early Testing Takes to Skies," *APG News,* Aug.15, 1990.

(40) Keir Sterling, "Aberdeen Proving Ground: The Early Years," *Harford Historical Bulletin,* No. 49 (Summer 1991), Aberdeen Room Archives and Museum, quotation, p. 63; Extracts from an unpublished historical report on Aberdeen Proving Ground, Mar.17, 1919, provided by Peter Kindsvatter; U.S. Army, Chief of Air Service, Airways Section, Aeronautical Bulletin No. 16, May 1, 1923.

(41) Weston, "Early Testing;" Extracts from *Sketches of the Ordnance Research and Development Center in World War II,* Aberdeen Proving Ground, 1945, provided by Kindsvatter, p.100.

(42) Weston, "Early Testing;" letter, Letter, Peter Kindsvatter, U.S. Army Ordnance Museum, to Edmund Preston, Sep.13, 2002, with attached documents.

(43) Von Braun and Ordway, *History of Rocketry,* pp. 46, 94-95; Ballistic Research Laboratories, Aberdeen Proving Ground, "The High-Speed Flexible-Throat Supersonic Wind Tunnel," undated, Maryland Room, University of Maryland.

(44) Websites "Phillips Army Airfield": atc.army.mil, viewed Mar.14, 2002; globalsecurity.org, viewed Sep.24, 2002.

(45) Edmund Preston: site visit, Dec. 17, 2002; notes on a meeting with Kent A. Mitchell, Dec. 17, 2002; notes on conversations with John Fry, Washington County Free Library, Jan. 10, 2003; History and photograph of the Moller Motor Car Company from www.fullorgan.com, viewed Jan. 10, 2002. The latter source, which gives the 1891 date, does not mention Maryland Pressed Steel. Mr. Fry reported, however, that the 1919 city directory confirms that Maryland Pressed Steel was at this location. The directory described it as on Pope Street between Howard Avenue and Maple Avenue (apparently the name of Wilson Boulevard before its renaming in honor of Woodrow Wilson).

(46) Kent A. Mitchell, "The Hagerstown Airport," undated manuscript in the MAA airport archives file; "Bellanca, Giuseppe Mario – 1993," National Aviation Hall of Fame site, viewed Sep.20, 2002. "Belanca CF," National Air and Space Museum site, viewed Sep.20, 2002; Undated advertisement illustrating Bellanca aircraft and the Maryland Pressed Steel plant, collection of Kent A. Mitchell.

(47) Moller company history; Preston, site visit and notes, Dec.17, 2002; conversations with Fry and Jeff Crampton, Jan.10, 2003.

(48) Edmund Preston, site visit, and notes on a meeting with Kent A. Mitchell, Dec. 17, 2002; Kent A. Mitchell, "The Hagerstown Airport," undated manuscript in the MAA airport archives file.

(49) Mitchell paper. The quotation is from U.S. Army, Office of the Chief of Air Service, Aeronautical Bulletin No. 19, State Summaries Series, May 1, 1925, Landing Facilities in Maryland, which summarized information reported in 1923.

(50) Preston site visit and notes, Dec.17, 2002; Photograph of a Bellanca aircraft at Doub's Meadow, c. 1917, collection of Kent A. Mitchell.

CHAPTER TWO:
THE CLASSIC ERA

(1) Baltimore Municipal Airport Aviation Context Report by Lampl Associates, June 2000, MHT file BA-149, p. 17; Scott, *Airy Regions*, aerial photo, p. 17; ADC Baltimore map 44.

(2) Unsigned, "The Story of Aviation in Baltimore," *Baltimore*, Nov.1941, p. 36; "Saga of Logan Field, Once Called Finest Airport on the East Coast," unsigned article, Baltimore *Evening Sun*, Dec.28, 1948; Scott, *Airy Regions*, p. 16; Lampl report, MHT file BA-149; Clayton Davis, "Logan Field, Baltimore's First Municipal Airport," 1997, posted on geocities.com.; Robert May, "Logan Field" in *Dundalk Then and Now, 1894-1980* (Dundalk-Patapsco Neck Historical Society, c. 1980), p. 27; Maryland Air National Guard, *The Maryland Air National Guard: A Commemorative History, 1921-2000* (Charlotte, N.C.: Fine Books, 2000), pp. 25, 249. These sources differ considerably on the details of Logan Field's early history. For example, the July 5, 1920, date of Lt. Logan's death is based on Davis and May, but the *Evening Sun* 1948 article gives Nov.15, 1920. Scott states that the airport was dedicated and renamed for Logan on July 10, 1920; however, Davis and the *Baltimore* 1941 article give Nov.15, 1920. That the city lease started in 1920 is supported by Davis, the *Baltimore* 1941 article, and MHT file BA-149; however, the *Evening Sun* 1948 article places this in 1922 or later. Davis and the *Baltimore* 1941 article state that the airport was dedicated on Nov.15, 1920, while *The Maryland Air National Guard* and the *Sun* 1941 article state that it formally opened in the spring of 1921.

(3) *The Maryland Air National Guar*d, pp. 25-28; Edward G. Meckel, "I Remember the Birth of the First Air Guard Unit," *Sunday Sun Magazine*, Dec.6, 1964; Army Aeronautical Bulletin No. 19, May 1, 1925; "Saga of Logan Field;" May, *Dundalk Then and Now*, p. 27.

(4) Scott, *Airy Regions*, p. 16. In regard to previous service by smaller airlines, see Paul Freeman, Abandoned & Little-Known Airfields website: .com/airfields_freeman/index.htm, revised Oct. 17, 2002, and Edward V. Twilley, "I Remember Baltimore's First Scheduled Service," *Sunday Sun Magazine*, Baltimore, July 11, 1965.

(5) Unsigned, "Aviation in Baltimore Progresses," *Power Pictorial*, May 1933, pp. 34-35; "Saga of Logan Field;" Civil Aeronautics Administration, Civil Aeronautics Bulletin No. 11, *Directory of Airports (Within the Continental United States)*, Washington: Government Printing Office, May 1, 1941.

(6) "Saga of Logan Field;" MHT file BA-149, p. 19; May, *Dundalk Then and Now*, p. 28. Logan was not listed in the Haire directory for 1945, or in subsequent directories examined. Various website references indicate that the name Logan Village still has some currency, and the cited Baltimore map shows Logan Village Shopping Center at the eastern edge of the former airport.

(7) ADC Maryland Delaware 2000 map; Jeffery K. Smart, "History of the U.S. Army Soldier and Biological Chemical Command," from the Command's website sbccom.army.mil, viewed Mar.13, 2003.

(8) Annual Report, Edgewood Arsenal, Fiscal Year 1922, extract (document provided by Jeffrey K. Smart, Command Historian, Soldier and Biological Chemical Command); Edmund Preston, conversations with Smart, Mar. 13 and 17, 2002.

(9) Army Aeronautical Bulletins No. 5, Sep.15, 1923, and No. 19, May 1, 1925; U.S. Department of Commerce, Aeronautics Branch, Airway Bulletin No. 2, *Airports and Landing Fields in the United States*, Sep.1, 1931; notes on Smart conversations, including a quotation from the FY 1926 Edgewood Arsenal annual report. The hangar is designated Building 4040 in the current inventory and is listed as enclosing 13,000 square feet. Another early structure at Weide Army Heliport, Building 4050, is a small brick storage facility. It was built in 1918 and hence appears to predate the airfield itself.

(10) Civil Aeronautics Administration, Bulletin No. 11, *Directory of Airports*, May 1, 1941; Photograph copy, "Airfield Construction, Oct. 30, 1941;" Preston conversations with Smart and with Lt. Col. Charles Schultz, Weide Army Heliport, Mar. 12, 2003.

(11) "ACC Air Field Named in Honor of Maj. Weide," article c. 1955 from *Armed Forces Chemical Journal*; Army Chemical Center, General Order No. 36, Designation of Weide Army Airfield, Sep.27, 1955 (documents provided by Smart).

(12) Smart and Schultz conversations; Aberdeen Proving Ground Guide, 1972.

(13) MAA airport data sheet, July 8, 2002; David A. Dorsey, Allegany Historic Sites, National Register of Historic Places Inventory Nomination Form, Oct.30, 1979, MHT file AL-III-A-15; James H. and Martha R. Dolly, "Lily Pad on a Pond: The Golden Days of Aviation at Mexico Farms Airport," article from the National Air and Space Museum library file on Mexico Farms Airport, pp.26-27.

(14) Army Aeronautical Bulletin No. 63, Sep. 15, 1923; Dorsey, MHT file AL-III-A-15.

(15) MHT file AL-III-A-15; Department of Commerce, Airway Bulletin No. 2, *Airports and Landing Fields*: Sep.1, 1931; Sep.1, 1932; June 1, 1933; Sep.1, 1934; and Jan.1 for 1936, '37, and '38; Harry I. Stegmaier, Jr., et. al., *Allegany County: A History* (Parsons, W.Va.: McClain, 1976), p. 360; Dollys, "Lily Pad," p. 32.

(16) Stegmaier, *Allegany County*, pp. 360-361; Haire Publishing Co., New York, *The Airport Directory*, 1945; MSAC Directory of Licensed Commercial Airports, Mar.6, 1947 (containing relevant data as of July 1, 1946).

(17) MHT file AL-III-A-15.

(18) MAA, Maryland Airport Directory, Sep.2001, and Airport data sheet, July 8, 2002.

(19) Ralph Barker, *The Schneider Trophy Races* (Shrewsbury, England: Airlife., 1971), pp. 103-122; Thomas G. Foxworth, *The Speed Seekers* (New York: Doubleday, 1974), pp. 49, 54-55; Roger E. Bilstein, *The American Aerospace Industry: From Workshop to Global Enterprise* (New York: Twayne, 1996), pp. 22-24; Maurice Maurer, *Aviation in the U.S. Army, 1919-1939* (Washington: Office of Air Force History, 1987), pp. 165, 172-173; North Point State Park history page, homestead.com/northpointstatepark, viewed Mar.23, 2002; Edmund Preston, conversation with ranger Steve Tacos, North Point State Park, Mar.23, 2003.

(20) The shed's move from Walnut St. is reported in Theron K. Rinehart, "How It All Began . . . 50 Years Ago," and unsigned features in *The Cracker Barrel*, Hagerstown, Mar. 1979, and Unsigned, "1928 Production at Hagerstown," and other features in *Fairchild World*, Sep.27, 1981. It is dated by Rinehart (p. 27) as occurring in 1925. However Herbert A. Poole, in an untitled memoir, Aug. 1977 (p. 5) stated that the Reisner brothers built Waco-like aircraft in a shed in this general vicinity, circa. 1918-21.

(21) Unsigned pamphlet, "Historical Summary, Fairchild Engine and Airplane Corporation, 1920-1951," Washington County Free Library, Western Maryland Room archives, gives KRA's incorporation date as Sep.5, 1925. Rinehart, "How It All Began," p. 2, states that Kreider joined Reisner in 1925, but incorporation followed in 1926.

(22) Kent A. Mitchell, "Hagerstown Airport," unpublished and undated paper in the MAA airport archives files, p. 2; Poole memoir, p. 5; *Cracker Barrel*, p. 14.

(23) Mitchell "Hagerstown Airport," pp. 3-4, and *Fairchild Aircraft, 1926-1987* (Santa Anna, Ca.: Narkiewicz // Thompson, 1997), pp. 51-55.

(24) *Fairchild World*, Sep. 27, 1981; Mitchell, "Hagerstown Airport," pp. 3-4.

(25) Rinehart, "How It All Began," pp. 17-19; Mitchell "Hagerstown Airport," pp. 4-5; Edmund Preston, Notes on a Meeting with Kent A. Mitchell, Dec. 17, 2002. The March 1979 *Cracker Barrel* includes an aerial view of the flying field and shed, c. 1926. Richard H. Avery III, *Wings Over Hagerstown* (Hagerstown, 1939), p. 22, shows a later aerial view of the plant built in 1929.

(26) Edmund Preston, site visit, Dec.17, 2002, and notes on a meeting with Mitchell. Publications that show photos of the shed during the 1920s include the cited *Cracker Barrel* and *Fairchild World* issues.

(27) Monroe, "History of the Aviation Field at College Park," p. 7. As Monroe explained, the early airmail service that had used College Park as its Washington-area terminus was discontinued in 1921. Bolling Field in the District of Columbia was the airfield used when Washington became part of an intercontinental route in the spring of 1927.

(28) Department of Commerce, Airway Bulletin No. 2, *Airports and Landing Fields*, Sep.1, 1931 and Sep.1, 1932; USCGS section chart, May 1932.

(29) "Official Program, Opening Del-Mar-Va Eastern Shore Airport, Hebron, Maryland, Sep. 3rd, 1928," EPFL vertical file.

(30) Airport Directory Company, *Airports and Established Landing Fields*, issues for 1931-33; Aeronautical Chamber of Commerce of America, 1922-45, *Aircraft Year Book*, 1930.

(31) Scott, *Airy Regions*, pp. 31-32.. Department of Commerce, Airway Bulletin No. 2, *Airports and Landing Fields*, 1936. Del-Mar-Va Airport should not be confused with the later Delmarva Airport northeast of Salisbury (see entry on Ennis Aerodrome).

(32) Mianna Jopp, "Profile: Malcolm Hatthaway [sic.]," Easton *Star Democrat*, Feb.23, 1972; Thomas F. Norton, untitled lecture at the Historical Society of Talbot County, Oct.2002, and con-versation with Edmund Preston, Jan.2, 2003.

(33) Department of Commerce, Aeronautics Branch, Airway Bulletins No. 1012, May 29, 1930, and No. 2, Sep.1, 1932. The Talbot County Historical Society owns a large collection of Hollyday's aerial photographs. Norton also provided the information on the site's present-day status and location, except that the name Ratcliffe Manor Road is from the mapquest.com website. Mills and Dickson state that Hathaway moved to Webb Field in 1930; however, Jopp quotes Hathaway directly as saying this took place in 1932. Eric J. Mills: "50th Anniversary: Taking Flight at Easton Airport," Easton *Star Democrat (Sunday Star)*, July 25, 1993; J. Preston Dickson, *Talbot County: A History* (Centreville, Md.: Tidewater Publishers, 1983), p. 300.

(34) Undated and unsigned information sheet, "Schrom Airport," College Park Aviation Museum files. Thiessen, "Airports in Prince George's County," MAA files, pp.17-19, gives the opening date as c. 1930, stating that other sources contradicted the 1928 date reported by Mary Lou Williamson, ed., *Greenbelt: History of a New Town, 1937-1987* (Virginia Beach; The Donning Co., 1987), on pp. 116, 120, 163. The quoted description of Schrom is from the same page. The airport did not appear on the USCGS section chart dated January 1939, but was included from Apr. 1940 through May 20, 1943. It was absent from the chart dated Nov.18, 1943, but reappeared for June 14, 1945, through Feb.17, 1953. Civil Aeronautics Administration, Bulletin No. 11, *Directory of Airports*, May 1, 1941; Section charts, Jan.1939 through Feb.17, 1953. MAA directories and listings: Mar.6, 1947 (with report as of July 1946); June 28, 1947; June 4, 1948; July 1949; and June 1, 1950.

(36) Anne Cissel, State Historic Sites Inventory Form, Oct. 1986, MHT file M:26-21-6: Department of Commerce, Airway Bulletin No. 2, *Airports and Landing Fields*, Sep.1, 1931. Cissel states that Arthur Hyde was president of Congressional Airport, Inc., when this 1929 transaction occurred. Hyde's obituary (Moorefield (WV) *Examiner*, Aug.11, 1999), however, shows that he would have been no more than about 20 years old at that time, and states that he owned Congressional Airport in the 1940s. According to the *Sunday Star* articles (Washington *Sunday Star*, Dec.25, 1955, and *Evening Star*, Mar. 3, 1958) cited by Cissel, Hyde began working at the airport in 1936, and became its owner ten years later. The state airport directory published in 1947 confirms that Hyde was the owner as of July 1, 1946. MAA airport directories dated Mar.6, 1947, and June 1, 1950. A different account of Congressional Airport's origins appears in a history of Montgomery County Airpark posted on that airport's website, www.montcoairpark.com, and viewed in Dec.2002. According to that version, the Wagner family had an airstrip on their farm in the late 1920s. W.C. and A. N. Miller purchased the facility, built a hangar there, and later sold the property to Arthur Hyde. See also Maria Longo-Swiek, "Soaring High Above It All," *Montgomery Miscellanea*, May/June 1997; Freeman, Abandoned & Little-Known Airfields website. Longo-Swiek and Freeman credit Horton as the founder.

(37) MAA airport data sheet and Sep.2001 directory.

(38) Kent A. Mitchell, "Hagerstown Airport," pp. 3-4; Department of Commerce, Aeronautics Branch, Airway Bulletin No. 588, Oct.6, 1930.

(39) Mitchell, "Hagerstown Airport," pp. 7-8.

(40) Mitchell, "Hagerstown Airport," pp. 8-9; Edmund Preston site visit and notes on conversations with Mitchell, Dec.17, 2002, and Jan.10, 2003; unsigned article from Baltimore *Sun*, June 20, 1938.

(41) Mitchell, "Hagerstown Airport," pp. 6-7, and *Fairchild Aircraft*, pp. 104-122, and *passim*; Jack L. King, *High Flight Beyond the Horizons: The Aviation Legend of Richard A. Henson* (Jack L. King Associates, Baltimore, and Richard A. Henson Foundation, Salisbury, 2002), pp. 22-23, 36-44, and *passim*; unsigned articles from Baltimore *Sun*, July 6 and 9, 1940, and July 1, 1941; Kurtis Meyer, list of aircraft produced at Hagerstown, Sep.2002.

(42) Mitchell conversation, Jan.10, 2002; King, *High Flight*, pp. 71-81; R. E. G. Davies, *Airlines of the United States Since 1914* (London: Putnam, 1972), pp. 485-486.

(43) Date of ownership transfer provided by airport manager Carolyn S. Motz, Memorandum to Ashish Solanki, May 31, 2000, MAA airport archives files; Mitchell, *Fairchild Aircraft*, p. 174.

(44) Department of Commerce, Aeronautics Branch, Airway Bulletin No. 588 (revised), Oct. 6, 1930; Airport Directory Company, Hackensack, N.J., *Airports and Established Landing Fields in the United States*,1939; MAA airport directories and lists, especially those dated Mar.6, 1947, June 1, 1950, 1974, Apr. 28, 1981, Oct.1996, and Sep.2001. MAA Airport data sheet, July 8, 2002; Motz memorandum; Mitchell conversation, Jan.10, 2002.

(45) Unsigned, "The Fairchild Aviation Corporation," reprinted from *Aero Digest*, Jan.1934; Theron K. Rinehart, "How It All Began," pp. 16-19; Mitchell, "Hagerstown Airport," pp. 4-5, and *Fairchild Aircraft*, pp. 57-58.

(46) *Aero Digest* 1934 article; Rinehart, "How It All Began," pp. 19-21; Unsigned pamphlet, "Historical Summary, Fairchild Engine and Airplane Corporation," pp. 13-14, 21-22; Mitchell, "Hagerstown Airport," pp. 4-8, and *Fairchild Aircraft*, pp. 58-103.

(47) Rinehart, "How It All Began," p. 21; Mitchell, *Fairchild Aircraft*, pp. 104-122; "Historical Summary," pp. 22-25; Christopher Shank, "Wings over Hagerstown: Experiencing the Second World War in Western Maryland," *Maryland Historical Magazine*, Vol. 88, No. 4 (Winter 1993), pp. 444-461; Unsigned, "Looking in on Fairchild in Hagerstown," *FAD*, clipping from the Mitchell files, undated, but with text that indicates it was published no earlier than July 1951.

(48) Shank, p. 458, states that Fairchild moved out of its leased locations in Hagerstown after the war, but the *FAD* article shows that this change was not immediate.

(49) Paula S. Reed, MHT historic site inventory report, June 10, 1992, MHT file WA-HAG-213; Edmund Preston, site visit, Dec. 17, 2002. Views of the building in the 1930s appear in Avery III, *Wings Over Hagerstown*, p. 22; Mitchell , *Fairchild Aircraft*, p. 52; and the *Aero Digest* article. Air-Tech Products provided the owner's name, Jan.6, 2003.

(50) Lampl Associates, Baltimore Municipal Airport Aviation Context Report by Lampl Associates, June 2000, MHT file BA-149, pp. 24-25; Map, 1930s, "New Baltimore Municipal Airport," EPFL; map included in Unsigned, "Pan-American Leases Airport Tract as Base for Ocean Plane Link," Baltimore *Sun*, Nov.5, 1936; maps in Richard D. Mayer, MHT Inventory Form, 1980,

MHT file B-3603/BA-2094.

(51) Theodore Roosevelt McKeldin, "Making Baltimore a Center for the Airplane Industry," script of radio address, Nov.6, 1930 (or 1931), EPFL; Baltimore Association of Commerce, "Aviation in Baltimore;" Christopher Pfrommer, "Harbor Field Ending Up as Marine Terminal," Baltimore *Evening Sun*, Dec.30, 1960; Scott, *Airy Regions*, p. 19; Lampl report, MHT file BA-149, pp. 24-27, 36.

(52) "Pan American Leases Airport Tract;" Lampl, MHT file BA-149, pp. 26-31.

(53) Lampl, MHT file BA-149, pp. 31-33, 34-35.

(54) Lampl, MHT file BA-149, pp. 33-34; *The Maryland Air National Guard*, p. 250.

(55) Lampl, MHT file BA-149, pp. 36-37, 52; *The Maryland Air National Guard*, p. 250; MSAC airport directory, June 1, 1950; Scott, *Airy Regions*, p. 19; Paul E. Welsh, "Harbor Field Handles Nearly as Many Flights as Friendship," Baltimore *Sun*, Oct.8, 1953.

(56) Pfrommer, "Harbor Field Ending Up as Marine Terminal;" Lample, MHT file BA-149, pp. 37-38, 52-53; Mayer, MHT file B-3603/BA-2094; Memorandum of Agreement, Maryland Port Authority and MHT, Dec.20, 1999. Although p. 24 of file BA-149 gives 1961 as Harbor Field's ending year, it cites a Jan.1, 1961, report for this. This fact and the Pfrommer article makes it seem that the closure came on Dec.31, 1960.

(57) Fred T. Jane, original ed., *Jane's All The World's Aircraft* (annual), 1929, p. 242; "The Story of Aviation in Baltimore," *Baltimore*, Nov.1941, p. 39; Berliner-Joyce Aircraft Corporation, "New Quarter-Million Dollar Plant Now Building at Baltimore," pamphlet, c. 1929 and no earlier than January of that year, EPFL; May, *Dundalk Then and Now*, p. 28, re fly-over.

(58) The space estimate is from the Berliner-Joyce pamphlet. The *Baltimore* article, which is the source of the employment figure, gives the space as about 60,000 square feet (p. 39). The aerial photo of Logan Field is on p. 249 of *The Maryland Air National Guard*. Other information and images of the plant are in the Berliner-Joyce pamphlet; Baltimore Association of Commerce, "Aviation in Baltimore," pamphlet, early 1930s, EPFL; and Norm Avery, *North American Aircraft, 1934-1998* (Santa Ana, Calif.: Narkiewicz // Thompson, 1998), Vol. I, p. 6.

(59) *Jane's*, 1930, p. 244, 1931, p. 247; Anthony Robinson, *The Encyclopedia of American Aircraft* (New York: Galahad, 1979), pp. 24-27;

(60) Avery, *North American Aircraft*, Vol. I, p. 6.

(61) Avery *North American Aircraft*, Vol. I, pp. 8-18.

(62) "The Story of Aviation in Baltimore," *Baltimore*, Nov.1941, p. 39; Craig Swain, "Gliders for the Navy Department: 1940-45," mircoworks.net; David Hanson, "Allied LRA-1," daveswarbirds.com; Hans Weichsel, "The Moulded Plywood Canoe, Part 2: On American Shores," *Wooden Canoe Journal*, Issue # 105, posted on wcha.org, all viewed Jan.30, 2003.

(63) John R. Breihan, National Register of Historic Places Multiple Property Documentation Report, Historical & Architectural Resources of Middle River, MD, Aug. 1996, MHT Field &

Research Reports (FRR) BaCo5; National Register of Historic Places Nomination Form, Glenn L. Martin Plant No. 1, Aug. 1996, MHT file BA-312; Andrea Bakewell Lowry, Maryland Inventory of Historic Properties form on Glenn Martin L. Airport and Plant, Aug.20, 1997, with eligibility recommendation Aug.8, 1999, MHT file BA-2081; Lampl Associates, Baltimore Municipal Airport Aviation Context Report, June 2000, MHT file BA-149, pp. 38-44. A diagram of the facility as it appears today is posted on the Lockheed Martin NE&SS Marine Systems website, ness.external.1mco.com.

(64) Breihan, "Martin Plant No. 1," MHT file BA-3152; Sec. 8 continuation sheet, pp. 1-3, "Middle River," pp. 6-10, MHT Field & Research Reports, FRR BaCo5.

(65) Lowry, MHT file BA-2081; John R. Breihan, Stan Piet, and Roger S. Mason, *Martin Aircraft, 1909-1960*, (Santa Ana, Ca.: Narkiewicz // Thompson, 1995). pp. 36-67 (On pp. 36-38, this book explains that the first Maryland-made Martin aircraft was the BM-1's prototype, the XT5M-1, built at a rented factory in Baltimore before the Middle River plant was completed.); Martin Marietta Aero & Naval Systems, "Sixty Years in Baltimore," *The Star*, Oct.1989, Baltimore Museum of Industry; William B. Harwood, *Raise Heaven and Earth: The Story of Martin Marietta People and Their Pioneering Achievements* (New York: Simon and Schuster, 1993), pp. 119-120.

(66) Breihan, "Martin Plant No. 1," MHT file BA-3152; Sec. 8 continuation sheet, pp. 3-4, "Middle River," pp. 15-18, MHT Field & Research Reports, FRR BaCo5; Lowry, MHT file BA-2081, Sec. 8 continuation sheet, pp. 3, 8-11, re Kahn's stature; Betsy Hunter Bradley, *The Works: The Industrial Architecture of the United States* (New York: Oxford University Press, 1999), p. 255, also supports this point; Martin Marietta, "Sixty Years in Baltimore;" Breihan, Piet, and Mason, pp. 68-71; Harwood, *Raise Heaven and Earth,* p. 171.

(67) Breihan, "Martin Plant No. 1," MHT file BA-3152; Sec. 8 continuation sheet, pp. 4-5, "Middle River," pp. 18-22, MHT Field & Research Reports, FRR BaCo5; Harwood, pp. 173-174, 176; Breihan, Piet, and Mason, *Martin Aircraft*, pp. 68-119, 124-131; Martin Marietta, "Sixty Years in Baltimore;" John R. Breihan, "Between Munich and Pearl Harbor: The Glenn L. Martin Aircraft Company Gears up for War, 1938-1941," *Maryland Historical Magazine*, Vol. 88, No. 4 (Winter 1993), pp. 389-419, especially pp. 392, 400-401 and 411. Employment statistics are from the Breihan article except for the 1942 figure, which is from Lampl, MHT file BA 2081, 1997 report, Sect. 8 continuation sheet, p. 4.

(68) Breihan, Piet, and Mason, *Martin Aircraft*, pp. 132-201; Martin Marietta, "Sixty Years in Baltimore;" Harwood, *Raise Heaven and Earth*, pp. 231-295.

(69) Martin Marietta, "Sixty Years in Baltimore;" James M. Grimwood and Barton C. Hacker, "Project Gemini Technology and Operations, A Chronology", NASA Special Pub. 4002, from nasa.gov, viewed Jan.2003; Unsigned, "Martin Marietta Ships 1,000th Reverser," *Flight International*, Sep.14, 1994; Harwood, *Raise Heaven and Earth*, pp. 355-358, 371-377.

(70) Martin Marietta, "Sixty Years in Baltimore;" Eugene Kozicharow, "Martin Baltimore Reverses Downtrend," *Aviation Week and Space Technology*, Jan.2, 1984; Harwood, *Raise Heaven and Earth,* pp. 558-559; Robert Little, "Middle River Plant Awarded

$142 Million Job," Baltimore *Sun,* June 26, 2002. Conversation with Deborah Isenhart, librarian, Lockheed Martin NE&SS-Marine Systems division, Feb.7, 2003, supplied the E D Building date and information on current products and employment.

(71) Greg Schneider, "Lockheed Sells Middle River Factory To GE," Baltimore *Sun,* Nov. 4, 1997; Greg Schneider, "Aviation Plant Tries Its Wings Identity: No Longer Martin or Lockheed, and Barely GE, Middle River Aircraft Systems Embraces Its Semi-Independence," Baltimore *Sun,* Aug. 16, 1998.

(72) Lowry, MHT file BA-2081, 1997 report and 1999 recommendation.

(73) Edmund Preston, conversation with Norman M. Covert, Jan.20, 2002., Covert, *Cutting Edge: A History of Fort Detrick, Maryland, 1943 – 1993* (Ft. Detrick, Md.: Headquarters, U.S. Army Garrison, 1993), pp. 3-8; L. Paul Norsworthy, "Frederick Municipal Airport Aviation Museum and Airport Facility," thesis submitted for the degree of Master of Architecture, University of Maryland, 1998, pp. 5-6; Nick A. Komons, *Bonfires to Beacons: Federal Civil Aviation Policy under the Air Commerce Act, 1926-1938* (Washington: Federal Aviation Administration, 1978), pp. 137-138; Unsigned, "Discover Your Airport: Celebrating 50 Years, 1949-1999," Frederick *News Post* special section, June 3, 1999; Department of Commerce, Airway Bulletin No. 2, *Airports and Landing Fields*: Sep.1, 1931; Sep.1, 1932; June 1, 1933; Sep.1, 1934; and Jan.1 for 1936, '37, and '38; Civil Aeronautics Administration, Bulletin No. 11, *Directory of Airports*, May 1, 1941. In Norsworthy's account, the city built the field as a municipal airport and did not lease it as an intermediate field until 1931 or later; however, the interpretation above follows Covert's book in describing the purpose of the initial Federal lease in Aug. 1929 as establishment of an intermediate field. Additional note: in the 1941 bulletin, the field's designation had changed from 5A to 5.

(74) Covert, *Cutting Edge*, pp. 3-7; Norsworthy, 'Frederick Municipal Airport," pp. 6-7; Joshua Wilson Rowe, "Detrick Field in the Thirties," Baltimore *Sun*, July 8, 1978; *The Maryland National Guard*, pp. 36, 38, 40-41.

(75) Covert conversation and *Cutting Edge*, pp. 7-8, 13-15; Norsworthy, 'Frederick Municipal Airport," p. 7.

(76) Lampl report, MHT file BA-149, p. 50. Baltimore *News Post*, Sep.23, 1955, clipping affixed to a query card at the Maryland Room, EPFL, states that the McNemars opened the airport in 1932, but this is contradicted by MHT file BA-149 and by the listing in Department of Commerce, Airway Bulletin No. 2, *Airports and Landing Fields*, 1931-34 and 1936-38; USCGS section charts, May 1932 through Dec.1935, and Nov. 1941; Airport Directory Company, *Airports and Established Landing Fields*, 1933.

(77) Department of Commerce, Airway Bulletin No. 2, *Airports and Landing Fields*, 1931. The data about the airport as of July 1946 is contained in the state directory issued on Mar.6, 1947.

(78) MAA directories and listings, Mar.6, 1947, June 28, 1947, July 1949, June 1, 1950, and 1962; *AOPA Directory*, 1962, 1963, and 1965; Freeman, Abandoned & Little-Known Airfields website suggests that the construction of Route 695 may have speeded the airport's demise.

(79) *Jane's*, 1931, p 266; Baltimore Association of Commerce, "Aviation in Baltimore;" "The Story of Aviation in Baltimore," *Baltimore*, Nov.1941, p. 39; Lampl report, MHT file BA-149, pp. 24-25, 36.

(80) Unsigned, "General Aviation Manufacturing Corporation Locates All Its Activities in Baltimore," *Baltimore*, Oct. 1931; "The Story of Aviation in Baltimore," *Baltimore*, Nov. 1941, p. 39; Unsigned, "Consolidation of Aircraft Groups Made," news clipping c. 1933, EPFL; Lampl, MHT file BA-149, pp. 25-26.

(81) "The Story of Aviation in Baltimore," pp. 39; Avery, *North American Aircraft*, pp. 6, 16-18.

(82) Unsigned, "Western Electric Company Leases Curtiss-Caproni Building at Airport," *Baltimore*, Aug.1941; "The Story of Aviation in Baltimore," p. 39; Unsigned, "Idle Despite Emergency," Baltimore *Sun*, May 7, 1941; Unsigned, "Martin Discusses Old Plane Plant," Baltimore *Sun*, May 8, 1941; Lampl, MHT file BA-149, pp. 28, 36, 38.

(83) Unsigned, "Curtiss Moves to Million Dollar Airport," *Baltimore*, June, 1930; Fred Rasmussen, "Flights of Fancy during the Depression," Baltimore *Sun*, Jan.18, 1998; Lampl Associates, Baltimore Municipal Airport Aviation Context Report, June 2000, MHT file BA-149, p. 50.

(84) Department of Commerce, Airway Bulletin No. 2, Sep.1, 1931 Unsigned, *Baltimore News-Post*, Apr. (day not given) 1938, EPFL; Avery McBee, "Wings over Maryland," *Maryland Spectator*, Vol. 2, May 1936, p. 54; Lampl, MHT file BA-149, pp. 50-51; Unsigned, "County Airport May Live Again as Shopping Center," *County News Week*, Jan.31, 1963; H. Kelcey Gault, "The Air Circuses of the 1930s," Baltimore *Sunday Sun Magazine*, Feb.22, 1959, and "I Remember the Fun of Flying with the Thunderbirds," *Sun*, Jan.12, 1964; Gwinn Owens, "Early Aviation in Baltimore: A Personal Journey," Baltimore *Evening Sun*, June 2, 1983; Rasmussen. "Flights of Fancy."

(85) "The Story of Aviation in Baltimore," *Baltimore*, Nov.1941,, p. 37; Gault, "Air Circuses;" Owens, "Early Aviation;" Rasmussen, "Flights of Fancy;" *Maryland Air National Guard*, p. 30.

(86) Clayton Davis, "Curtiss-Wright Airport, Baltimore, Maryland," undated article, MAA airport archives file; Haire *Airport Directory*, 1946; Rasmussen, "Flights of Fancy;" Joseph L. Stanton, "There's A Plane in Your Future," *Baltimore*, Aug.1946; MSAC airport directories, Mar. 6, 1947, and June 28, 1947, as revised Nov.17, 1947.

(87) Unsigned, "Bendix Leases Pimlico Airport," Baltimore *Evening Sun*, Feb.12, 1951, Pratt Library query card; "Airport May Live Again;" Rasmussen, "Flights of Fancy;" Freeman, Abandoned & Little-Known Airfields website.

(88) MAA Airport Directory, Sep.2001, and Airport data sheet, July 8, 2002; data from tiptonairport.org website, viewed Feb.14, 2003.

(89) Manufacturers Aircraft Association, *Aircraft Year Book*, 1920 (Boston: Small, Maynard & Co.), p. 316; Department of Commerce, Airway Bulletin No. 2, 1936-38; Airport Directory Company, *Airports and Established Landing Fields*, 1939-40.

(90) Clayton Davis, "Tipton Airport," report sent to Bruce Mundie, July 1, 2000, Maryland Airport Administration files;

Edmund Preston, conversation with Mark Henry and Robert Johnson of the Fort George G. Meade Museum, Feb.14, 2002.

(91) *The Maryland Air National Guard*, p. 30.

(92) TanNoah Morgan, "High Hopes Accompany Tipton Airport's Takeoff," Baltimore *Sun*, Nov.2, 1999; Jefferson Morley, "Arundel Launches Tipton Airport," *Washington Post*, Nov.2, 1999.; Davis, "Tipton Airport."

(93) MAA airport directory, Sep.2001, and airport data sheet, July 8, 2002; data from tiptonairport.org website, viewed Feb.14, 2003.

(94) Thiessen, "Airports in Prince George's County," MAA files, pp. 15-17; Civil Aeronautics Administration, Bulletin No. 11, *Directory of Airports*, May 1, 1941. As sources for her section on Queen's Chapel Airport, Thiessen cites her interviews with Walter M. Starling, Sr., and with Jane Straughan. The references above to Bob Baber and Debbie Dorr are based on Thiessen. Henderson was named as sole manager in all directory listings examined that gave such information between 1941 and 1948, except that the Haire *Airport Directory* for 1946 named Hugh Barrett as joint manager.

(95) The airport was not included in the USCGS section chart dated Apr. 1940, but appeared in charts for Sep. 1940 through Nov.18, 1943, and again on charts dated Nov.30, 1944 through Jan.12, 1955; MSAC airport directories and listings, Mar. 6, 1947, June 28, 1947, June 4, 1948, July 1949, and June 1, 1950.

(96) Thomas F. Norton, untitled lecture at the Historical Society of Talbot County, Oct.2002. The 1930 establishment date is also supported by Mills, "50th Anniversary."

(97) Department of Commerce, Airway Bulletin No. 2, *Airports and Landing Fields*, Sep.1, 1931; Airport Directory Company, *Airports and Established Landing Fields*, 1933. The Easton-Baltimore service is reported by Preston, *Talbot County*, p. 300, and by Unsigned, "Maryland Airlines Recalls Shore Flying," Sep.23, 1947, typescript from the Talbot County Free Library's Maryland Room

(98) Norton lecture; MSAC directories and listings, Mar.6, 1947 and June 1, 1950. The Haire *Airport Directory*, 1946, listed Mrs. D. G. Webb as the owner, but other directories examined did not support this change of ownership. Quotation from "2 More Shore Private Airfields Are Closed," Baltimore *Evening Sun*, May 28, 1952. In this context, "Private Airfields" meant a general aviation airports, and did not imply private use only.

(99) Edmund Preston, conversation with Thomas E. Norton, Jan.2, 2003.

(100) Department of Commerce, Airway Bulletin No. 2, *Airports and Landing Field in the United States*: Sep.1, 1931; Sep.1, 1932; June 1, 1933; Sep.1, 1934; and Jan.1, 1936; Airport Directory Company, *Airports and Established Landing Fields*, 1933; USCGS section charts, May 1932 through Aug. 1935; ADC Street Map of Baltimore, map 26. The cited directories also related the location of Service Field to an unnamed lake. The Commerce 1931 and ADC 1933 publications stated that it was 1/8 of a mile west of the lake; the Commerce issues for 1932-34 placed it the same distance to the east.

(101) Department of Commerce, Airway Bulletin No. 2, *Airports*

and *Landing Fields*, Sep.1, 1932, and June 1, 1933; Airport Directory Company, *Airports and Established Landing Fields*, 1933; USCGS section chart, May 1932 and Oct.1934.

(102) Thiessen, "Airports in Prince George's County," MAA files. In regard to Edward Stitt and Capitol Airport, Thiessen cites Marylee Schneider, "He's the Oldest Collegian in the U.S.," *Intelligencer Journal*, May 23, 1985: I, 6.

(103) Capitol Airport did not appear in the 1934 issue of Department of Commerce, Airway Bulletin No. 2, *Airports and Landing Fields* (no 1935 issue of Bulletin No. 2 was found). A "Capital Airport" appeared in the 1945-47 issues of the Haire *Airport Directory*; however, it was described as 9 miles east of Berwyn, which is inconsistent with Capitol Airport's location. See also Airport Directory Company, *Airports and Established Landing Fields*, 1939 and 1940; USCGS section charts, July 1934 and various dates through My 7, 1942; Civil Aeronautics Administration, Bulletin No. 11, *Directory of Airports*, May 1, 1941.

(104) Both Herbert Jones and Russ Seavers recalled their boyhood experiences of flying with Chamberlain from Capitol Airport. Edmund Preston, conversation with Russ Seavers, College Park Aviation Museum volunteer, Sep.17, 2002; Barry Lanman, draft transcript of an interview with Herbert Jones, Sep.19, 2002.

(105) The airport did not appear on the section chart dated July 1934, but was included in charts for Oct. 1934 through Nov.18, 1943. Beginning with the chart for May 25, 1944, it was no longer included. Department of Commerce, Airway Bulletin No. 2, *Airports and Landing Fields*, 1936-38; Civil Aeronautics Administration, Bulletin No. 11, *Directory of Airports*, May 1, 1941; USCGS section charts, July 1934 though May 25, 1944; Information from AirNav.com, viewed Dec. 1, 2002.

(106) Edmund Preston, conversation with Elizabeth A. Hastings, Dec. 2, 2002.

(107) Edmund Preston, conversation with Fred A. Ennis, Dec. 2, 2002; Scott, *Airy Regions*, p. 33; John E. Jacobs, Jr., *Salisbury and Wicomico County: A Pictorial History* (Virginia Beach, Va.: Donning Co. Publishers), p. 114; Department of Commerce, Airway Bulletin No. 2, *Airports and Landing Fields*, 1936, 1937, and 1938.

(108) MSAC airport directory, June 1, 1950; Preston conversation with Ennis. Some directories use the spelling "Delmarvia" for Fred Ennis' airport and flying service. See Airport Directory Company, *Airports and Established Landing Fields*, 1939-40; Haire *Airport Directory*, 1945-48; Information from Air Nav.com, Antique Aircraft Association's website, www.aaa-apm.org, viewed Dec. 1, 2002.

CHAPTER THREE:
THE IMPACT OF GLOBAL WAR

(1) Paolo E. Coletta, ed., *United States Navy and Marine Corps Bases, Domestic* (Westport, Ct.: Greenwood, 1985), p. 22; Paul Freeman, Abandoned & Little-Known Airfields website: www.members.tripod.com/airfields_freeman/index.htm, revised Oct. 17, 2002,; ADC Annapolis map.

(2) Coletta, *Bases,* pp. 22-23; Frank M. Hertel, "The Naval Academy and Naval Aviation," *U.S. Naval Institute Proceedings*, Vol.

74, No. 1 (Jan. 1948), pp. 37-38; Jack Stevenson, "Academy Aviation Training in Forty-Sixth Year," *The Log*, Mar.28, 1972, p. 34.

(3) Coletta, *Bases,* pp. 23-24; ADC Annapolis map; Freeman, Abandoned & Little-Known Airfields website photo.

(4) Haire *Airport Directory*, 1945. The first USCGS section chart found that showed the airport was dated as valid through June14 1945. See also MAA directories and lists, June 28, 1947, June 4, 1948, June 1, 1950, and Nov.9, 1960.

(5) John Himmelheber, *Glen Burnie: A Pictorial History, 1888-1988* (Northern Anne Arundel Chamber of Commerce, c. 1988), pp. 36-37, including quotations from a letter by G. Robert Donovan to Mark Schatz; Lampl Associates, Baltimore Municipal Airport Aviation Context Report, June 2000, MHT file BA-149, p. 49.

(6) Richard Meyer, John Milner Associates, Documentation for a Determination of Eligibility, 1985, MHT file PG-68-22, p. 1; Marina King, MHT Historic Sites Inventory Form, Apr. 1986, with attached summary sheet.

(7) Chuck Hansen, "Engineering and Research Corporation," *Journal, American Aviation Historical Society*, Spring 1985., pp. 42-43, 56; Stanley G. Thomas, *The Ercoupe* (Blue Ridge summit, Pa.: Tabb Books, 1991), pp. 11-53; Meyer report, MHT file PG-68-22, including MHT Determination of Eligibility Form, June 10, 2002, including Letter, William J. Pencek, Jr., Maryland Department of Housing and Community Development, to William P. Mallari, University of Maryland, June 26, 2002. The 1932 inception date for ERCO is from Hansen (p. 42); Meyer (p. 6) gives an incorporation date of 1936. Sources differ on the some of the events described in this paragraph. For example, the completion of the Model 415 prototype in 1939 is from Thomas (p. 53), while Hansen says it flew in 1938 (p.42). Both Hansen (p. 43) and Thomas (p. 53) place the move to Riverdale in 1938; however, Meyer (p. 6) states that the plant was built in 1939, although this may refer to its completion.

(8) Meyer report, MHT file PG-68-22, pp. 1-6; King inventory form, 1986; MHT eligibility form, 2002.

(9) Thomas, *The Ercoupe*, xv, 1, 39-43, 53-54, 64-66; Hansen, "Engineering and Research Corp.," pp. 42-43; National Air and Space Museum, Smithsonian Institution, "Erco 415-C Ercoupe," nasm.si.ed, viewed Jan.28, 2002; Meyer report, MHT file PG-68-22, pp. 6-8. For a negative assessment of the Ercoupe and the historical significance of the ERCO site, see C. Curtiss Johnson and Brian R. Bader, Historical Evaluation and Research Organization (HERO), The Historical Significance of the Engineering Research Corporation (ERCO) Main Plant and Airfield, Final Report, Mar.24, 1986.

(10) Hansen, "Engineering and Research Corp.," pp. 43-55; Thomas, *The Ercoupe,* p. 63.

(11) Meyer report, MHT file PG-68-22, pp. 8-11; Hansen, pp. 44-46; Thomas, pp. xvi, 67-83, 115. The Riverdale production end-date is from Thomas' detailed study, p. 83; however, Meyer states that production ended in 1951 (p. 9).

(12) Meyer report, MHT file PG-68-22, pp. 6, 9-10; Hansen, pp. 45-46; Bob Fuerst, "Riverdale's Industrial Evolution," *The Town Crier*, Jun-Jul y 1992, p. 7; MHT eligibility form, 2002; NASM web page. Meyer (pp. 6 and 10) and Fuerst state that ACF

bought ERCO in 1954, while Hansen (p 45) gives 1951.

(13) MHT NR-Eligibility Review Form, prepared by Marina King, Apr.17, 1986; final review by Jerry L. Rogers, Keeper of the National Register, National Park Service, May 28, 1986; Determination of Eligibility Notification, May 28, 1986, with accompanying sheet; Pencek to Mallari, June 26, 2002.

(14) Thiessen, "Airports in Prince George's County," MAA files, pp. 12-13. Both Hansen, "Engineering and Research Corp.," p. 43, and Thomas, *The Ercoupe,* p. 53 place the move to Riverdale in 1938; however, Meyer (report, MHT file PG-68-22, p. 6), states that the plant was built in 1939, although this may refer to its completion. The certification date is from Thomas, p. 53.

(15) The airport did not appear on the USCGS section chart dated May 20, 1943, but began appearing with the chart for Nov.18, 1943. Haire *Airport Directory,* 1945-48; MSAC directories, 1947, 1949, and 1950.

(16) Thiessen, "Airports in Prince George's County," MAA files, pp. 13, 22; Meyer report, MHT file PG-68-22, pp. 5-6; Freeman, Abandoned & Little-Known Airfields website. The Riverdale production end-date is from Thomas' detailed study, p. 83; however, Meyer (p. 9) states that production ended in 1951. Meyer (pp. 6 and 10) and Fuerst state that ACF bought ERCO in 1954, while Hansen (p 45) gives 1951. The airport appeared on the USCGS section chart dated July 25, 1955, but was absent from the chart for Jan.12, 1956.

(17) Breihan, Multiple Property Documentation Report, Historical & Architectural Resources of Middle River, Aug. 1996, pp. 20-21, MHT Field & Research Reports, FRR BaCo5; Lowry, Inventory of Historic Properties form on Glenn Martin L. Airport and Plant, Aug.20, 1997, MHT file BA-2081; Lampl Associates, Baltimore Municipal Airport Aviation Context Report, June 2000, MHT file BA-149, pp. 38-44.

(18) *The Maryland Air National Guard,* p 251; Joe Nawrozki, "One Man's Plane Dream," Baltimore *Sun,* June 10, 2003; MAA airport data sheet, July 8, 2002.

(19) Lowry, Inventory form, with eligibility recommendation Aug.8, 1999, MHT file BA-2081.

(20) MAA airport directory, Sep.2001, and airport data sheet, July 8, 2002; Gisele Mohler, draft "Chronology of Lee Airport," May 21, 1999, MAA files; Unsigned, "Lee Airfield to Close at Annapolis," Baltimore *Evening Sun,* June 28, 1954. Mohler gives 1939 as the opening date, while the *Sun* gives 1940. Lee Airport appeared in no bulletins or directories examined that were issued before the Haire *Airport Directory,* 1945. The first USCGS section chart found that listed it was dated Dec.26, 1945.

(21) MSAC airport directories, Mar.6, 1947 (with data as of Oct.1, 1946), and June 1, 1950. Although it seems likely that the northwest-southeast runway was the surviving one at the time of the June 28, 1954, report in the *Evening Sun,* the wording did not make that clear.

(22) "Lee Airfield to Close," *Evening Sun,* June 28, 1954. Mohler gives the closing date as 1955.

(23) Mohler, "Chronology of Lee Airport."

(24) Scott, *Airy Regions,* p. 39; Dennis O'Brien, "Airports in Md.

Face Hard Times," Baltimore *Sun,* Dec.28, 1987 (including Wilcox quotation); Unsigned, "Airport Reprieved in Zoning Squabble," *Washington Post,* Aug.27, 1987.

(25) MAA airport data sheet, July 8, 2002.

(26) Thiessen, "Airports in Prince George's County," MAA files,, pp. 8-9; Airport Directory Company, *Airports and Established Landing Fields,* 1940.

(27) References to Arthur C. Hyde's activities in the Civil Air Patrol appear in: the Westminster, Md., *Democratic Advocate,* June 11, 1943; and Nicholas E. Hollis, "Jennings Randolph: Aviation's Centurion for Peace," posted on website www., viewed Dec. 2002. Wartime USCGS section charts showed the field: as commercial through Nov.1942; as military on May 20, 1943; not shown, Nov.18, 1943; as an auxiliary field on May 25, 1944; and as commercial again, Nov.30, 1944. See also MSAC/MAA airport directories dated Mar. 6, 1947, June 1, 1950, Apr.28, 1981, Oct.1996, and Sep.2001.

(28) MAA Airport data sheet, July 8, 2002; David M. Pittman, "Nation's Last Shuttered Airport Cleared to Reopen," Sep.27, 2002; and "Some Maryland Airports Get Federal Funds to Enhance Security, Defray Closures." Capital News Service, published in *Maryland Newsline,* www.newsline.umd.edu.

(29) Baltimore *Evening Sun,* July 28, 1941.

(30) MSAC Airport Directory, June 1, 1950; Haire *Airport Directory,* 1945-48; Decker Air Service, Inc., Fairfield, Conn., *Decker's Airport Guide, Zone Five, South Atlantic,* 1946-47; USCGS section charts, Nov.1941, Jan.12, 1950, Jan.12, 1951. Taneytown Airport appeared on the section chart of Jan.12, 1950, but not on the issue for Jan.12, 1951.

(31) Freeman, Abandoned & Little-Known Airfields website; Maryland Department of Natural Resources, "African American Sites Along the Patuxent River, Columbia Air Center," from website, dnr.state.md.us, viewed Aug.28, 2002; Bianca P. Floyd, *Records & Recollections: Early Black History in Prince George's County, Maryland* (Maryland-National Capital Park and planning Commission, 1989), pp. 96-97; Clayton Davis with Sandra Martin, "Croom, Maryland, Where Dreams Soared," *New Bay Times,* Feb.22-28, 1996; Clayton Davis, "Columbia Air Center, Croom, Maryland," unpublished typescript, MAA files. pp. 1-2.

(32) Floyd, *Records & Recollections,* pp. 96-97; Von Hardesty and Dominick Pisano, *Black Wings: The American Black in Aviation* (Washington: Smithsonian Institution Press, 1983), p. 70; and Davis, "Croom," and "Columbia Air Center," pp. 4-5. These sources differ somewhat on the licenses that Greene earned.

(33) Davis, "Croom," and "Columbia Air Center," pp. 2-3, and 7; Unsigned, "Cloud Club Arranges Air Show for Sunday," *Afro-American,* Aug.16, 1941, Unsigned, "Cloud Club Show Draws 800 Spectators; 150 Go Up," clipping, c. Aug.1941, both from College Park Aviation Museum files; Sharahn D. Boykin, "Taking Flight," *The Gazette* (Prince George's Co., Md.), Apr. 18, 2002.

(34) MSAC airport directories and lists dated: Mar.6, 1947; June 28, 1947; June 4, 1948; July 1949; and June 1, 1950; Floyd, *Records & Recollections,* p. 97-98; Boykin, "Taking Flight."

(35) Davis, "Croom," and "Columbia Air Center," pp. 3 and 7 Barry Lanman, draft transcript of an interview with Herbert

Jones, Sep.19, 2002; Freeman, Abandoned & Little-Known Airfields website; Department of Natural Resources, "African American Sites." The last named states that the airport closed in 1958, but all other sources examined give the date as 1956.

(36) Department of Agriculture, Beltsville Agricultural Research Center: Potential Areas of Concern Subject to Screening, June 1998, with map dated May 1997, forwarded by Claudette Joyner.

(37) USCGS section charts, May 1932 - Dec.1936, Nov. 25, 1944; Department of Commerce, Airway Bulletin No. 2, *Airports and Landing Fields*, 1931-34, 1936-38 (No bulletin for 1935 was located.). The bulletins described the field as 3 miles northwest of Bowie (or 2 ½ miles, in the 1932 issue), which corresponds to the location of the later Beltsville Airport. Bernard Johnson Young, Inc., definitely identifies the airport with Department of Commerce field 57B, although the report seems wrong in giving a construction date of 1933. Karin Thiessen also notes that Beltsville Airport was originally under the control of Commerce and dated from the 1930s. Comparison between the Dec.1936 chart showing the Commerce site and the Nov.25, 1944 section chart showing the Navy field is difficult due to a change in format; however, the Navy installation may have been slightly to the northwest of the original site. Bernard Johnson Young, Inc., Historic Sites Survey, Beltsville Agricultural Research Center, Vol. II, June 1998, excerpts forwarded by Claudette Joyner of BARC, Dec.16, 2002; Thiessen, "Airports in Prince George's County," MAA files, p. 13.

(38) "Fund For Beltsville Apt. Approved," Baltimore *Evening Sun*, Mar. 22, 1941. In addition, Bureau of Agricultural Research, Timeline, on website, www.ba.ars.usda.gov, viewed Feb.16, 2003, states that an airport was constructed in the1940-49 period.

(39) Bernard Johnson Young, Inc., Historic Sites Survey, 1998.

(40) USCGS section Chart dated Nov.25, 1944 and various dates through Jan.19, 1951. The runway length is from Decker Air Service, *Decker's Airport Guide, Zone Five, South Atlantic*, 1946. The coordinates provided by the Haire *Airport Directory* match the site on current maps. Both directories identified the Navy as the operator. The Navy affiliation continued on the USCGS charts until July 18, 1950, but this may have been an error.

(41) Thiessen, "Airports in Prince George's County," MAA files, pp. 13-14; "Birds Win Long Feud," Baltimore *Sun*, May 25, 1947.

(42) Baltimore *Sun*, May 25, 1947. The Haire *Airport Directory*, 1948, reported the airfield as inactive, although it still described the facility as a military one.

(43) Thiessen, p.14; Bernard Johnson Young, Inc., Historic Sites Survey, 1998.

(44) Freeman, Abandoned & Little-Known Airfields website

(45) MAA directories, 1960 and 1962; AOPA, *Airport Directory*, 1962-63.

(46) AOPA, *Airports USA*, 1979-80.These were the last directories found to list Beltsville Airport.

(47) Thiessen, p. 14.

(48) Bernard Johnson Young, Inc., Historic Sites Survey, 1998..

(49) Freeman, Abandoned & Little-Known Airfields website; Beltsville Agricultural Research Center, Potential Areas of Concern document and map.

(50) John R. Breihan, Stan Piet, Roger S. Mason, *Martin Aircraft, 1909-1960* (Santa Ana, CA: (Santa Ana, Ca.: Narkiewicz/Thompson, 1995),, pp. 101-119; William B. Harwood, *Raise Heaven and Earth* (New York: Simon and Schuster, 1993), pp. 193-212.

(51) Breihan, Piet, and Mason, p. 176; Virginia Busby, et al., Berger and Associates, MHT Inventory form, Martin Plant No. 2/GSA Depot, June 1993, MHT file BA-2824; Breihan, Multiple Property Documentation Report, Historical & Architectural Resources of Middle River, Aug. 1996, pp. 20-21, MHT file FRR BaCo5; Lowry, Inventory of Martin Airport and Plant, Aug. 20, 1997, and National Register evaluation, Aug.3, 1999, MHT file BA-2082, Sec. 8, pp. 3-4.

(53) Breihan, "Between Munich and Pearl Harbor," pp. 393, 404-405; Harwood, *Raise Heaven and Earth,* pp. 178-179. Neal A. Brooks and Eric G. Rockel, *A History of Baltimore County* (Towson, Md.: Friends of the Towson Library, Inc., 1979) are incorrect in asserting (p. 367) the Federal Public Housing Authority built Aero Acres.

(54) ADC Street Maps, Baltimore City and County, p. 37; John R. Breihan, "A History of Wartime Middle River (Essex-Middle River Civic Council, 1996); Breihan, "Necessary Visions: Community Planning in Wartime," *Maryland Humanities*, Nov. 1998, pp. 11-15.

(55) Breihan, "Aero Acres, The Town that Glenn Martin Built," *Air & Space Smithsonian*, Vol. 14, No. 2, June/July 1999.

(56) Edmund Preston, site visit, and notes on a meeting with Kent A. Mitchell, Dec. 17, 2002; notes on a conversation with Mitchell, Jan.10, 2003. On Jan.10, 2003, Top Flight Air Park provided the area figure as 1.3 million square feet; Paul Smith, "Last A-10," Hagerstown *Herald Mail*, Mar.3, 1984, gives this as 1.1 million.

(57) Mitchell, "Hagerstown Airport," MAA files, pp. 3-4 and 7-8.

(58) Shank, "Wings over Hagerstown," pp. 447-448; "Historical Summary," Washington County Free Library, pp. 23-25; [Fairchild], List of plants and their uses, Dec.12, 1942, collection of Kent A. Mitchell; "Looking in on Hagerstown," *FAD* clipping; Unsigned, "Hagerstown Hangar," *The Pegasus*, Oct.1943; Richard H. Depew, Jr., "Yesterday's 'Touch of Tomorrow' – VI, " *The Pegasus*, May 1944, p. 14; Mitchell, *Fairchild Aircraft*, pp. 71-75, 104-122, and *passim*; and Meyer, list of Fairchild aircraft produced at Hagerstown.

(59) "Historical Summary," pp. 25-28; "Looking in on Hagerstown;" Preston site visit and notes on Mitchell conversations, Dec.17, 2002, and Jan.10, 2003; Mitchell, *Fairchild Aircraft*, p.122-182; Meyer, aircraft list. In addition to its complex at the southeast corner of the airport, Fairchild operated a bonding shop built in 1957 for manufacture of the F-27. In the 1980s, the company sold this facility to Rohhr Industries, which used it to manufacture aircraft components. Now a warehouse, it is located north of Showalter Road and west of the airport terminal.

(60) Preston notes on Mitchell conversations, Dec.17, 2002, and

Jan.10, 2003; Mitchell, *Fairchild Aircraft*, pp. 174 and 182; Smith, "Last A-10."

(61) The Baltimore *Sun* (*Sunday Sun Magazine*), for Sep. 27, 1942, showed a photo of a row the houses in largely completed condition. The newspaper described the project as "in Hamilton Park," possibly another name for Hamilton Homes. Alternatively, the Hamilton Homes structures may have been part of a larger area designated Hamilton Park, as is the case are today.

(62) Shank, "Wings over Hagerstown," p. 456; Edmund Preston, site visit, and notes on a meeting with Kent A. Mitchell, Dec. 17, 2002.

(63) Davis, MHT file F-3-86; J. E. Greiner Co., "Maryland Airports," report to Red Star Motor Coaches, Inc., Sep.21, 1945; MSAC Maryland Airport Directory, June 1, 1950. The airport had been shown in the USCGS section chart valid through Jan.12, 1950.

(64) Undated photographs of Stevens Airport, Md., posted on Library of Congress website, loc.gov. Some limited recreational flying had also taken place at Frederick Municipal Airport in 1946 during an early stage of its development, according to a special sectionentitled "Discover Your Airport," Frederick *News Post*, June 3, 1999.

(65) "The David Taylor Model Basin: A Brief History," Naval Historical Foundation Publication, Series II, No. 15, 1971; "Time Line, Carderock Division Milestones," www.dt.navy.mil, viewed Nov.6, 2002; Carlisle, *Where the Fleet Begins;* Unsigned article, "The David Taylor Model Basin," *Proceedings, U.S. Naval Institute*, Vol. 89, No. 3 (Mar. 1963).

(66) David K. Allison, Historian of National Laboratories, MHT inventory form, Aug.26, 1985; file M-29-47; Lex Campbell, R. Christopher Goodwin & Associates, MHT eligibility review form, Mar. 27, 1996; inventory form, Aug.1, 1998, and associated eligibility review form, Aug.18, 1998; file M-29-52.

(67) W. Patrick Giglio, Goodwin & Associates, MHT inventory form, Oct. 7, 1999, file M-29-54; Edmund Preston, conversation with Denis Clark of the Carderock Division, Nov.19, 2002.

(68) William K. Klingaman, *APL—Fifty Years of Service to the Nationn* (Laurel, Md.: The Johns Hopkins University Applied Physics Laboratory, 1993), pp. 1-90, photograph on p. 9; Postcard, Silver Spring Historical Society; Rexmond C. Cochrane, *Measures for Progress* (U.S. Department of Commerce, 1966), p. 390.

(69) Building Technologies, Inc., Historic Properties Report on Harry Diamond Laboratories and Satellite Installations, prepared for the Historic American Building Survey/Historic American Engineering Record, National Park Service, July 1984 (associated with MHT file CH-371); "Blossom Point." www.globalsecurity.org, viewed Nov.8, 2002.

(70) Maryland Department of the Environment, Environmental fact sheet on Andrews AFB, mde.state.md.us, viewed Nov.26, 2002. This is the source for the acreage, which excludes remote sites associated with the base. See also "Capsule History of Andrews Air Force Base," USAF Fact Sheet, c. 1980; "Andrews," an installation guide," Marcoa Publishing, San Diego, Ca., 1992; Andrews AFB history, dcmilitary.com, viewed July 23, 2002, pp.

5-13; "Andrews AFB, Maryland," globalsecuiry.org, viewed Nov.8, 2002

(71) Raymond D. Baker, *Historical Highlights of Andrews Air Force Base, 1942– 1989* (Andrews AFB, Md.: Office of History, 1776th Air Base Wing, 1990), pp. 2-6; Meyer, *Maryland Lost and Found*, pp. 125-126; Robert R. Hare, "Upper Marlboro Airport Near Completion," Baltimore *Evening Sun*, Apr.6, 1943 (quoted); Unsigned, "Camp Spring Fighters Like Hornet Nest," Baltimore *Sun*, May 31, 1943.

(72) Baker, *Historical Highlights of Andrews,* iv-v, 5-53; Robert Mueller, *Air Forces Bases*, Vol. 1, (Washington: Office of Air Force History, USAF, 1989), pp. 5-7; "Camp Springs, Md., to be Named . . .," War Department press release, Mar.20, 1945, EPFL.

(73) Baker, *Historical Highlights of Andrews,* pp. v-vii, 55-320, and *passim.*; Mueller, *Air Forces Bases*, Vol. 1, pp. 5-7.

(74) Unsigned, "Insulated Panels Shelter Air Force One," *Building Design & Construction*, Vol. 31, No. 6, June 1990; Robert F. Dorr, *Air Force One*, (St. Paul, Minn.: MBI Publishing Co., 2000), pp. 9-14; Baker, *Historical Highlights of Andrews*, pp. v-ix, 55-57, 232-241, 301, 373-374, and *passim.*

(75) Figure on residence and employment from andrews.af.mil website, Jan.17, 2002.; Angie Cannon, "New Golf Course at Andrews Generates Controversy," Knight Ridder News Service, Sep.21, 1995; B. R. Sargent, "Andrews Building Better Lives, One Brick at a Time," Jan. 23, 1998; Larry A. Carson, "Andrews Keeps Busy Construction Pace in '98," July 17, 1998; Serge E. Ladd, "Renovations on 89th APS Terminal Near Completion," Dec.17, 1999, all from *Capital Flyer*, Andrews AFB'. B. R. Sargent, "Andrews Building Better Lives, One Brick at a Time," Jan.23, 1998; Larry A. Carson, "Andrews Keeps Busy Construction Pace in '98," July 17, 1998; Serge E. Ladd, "Renovations on 89th APS Terminal Near Completion," Dec.17, 1999, all from *Capital Flyer*, Andrews AFB; Bradley Graham, "For Patrol Pilots, A Nightmare Scenario,", p. A17, Sep.29, 2001; Steve Vogel, "Flights of Vigilance over the Capital, p. B1, Apr.8, 2002, both from *Washington Post*.

(76) Naval Air Warfare Center Aircraft Division, "Patuxent River Facilities," pamphlet, 1994; "Pax Info" and "Base History" sections of Naval Air Station Patuxent River website, nas.nawcad.mil, viewed Nov.10, 2002.

(77) U.S. Navy, Bureau of Yards and Docks, *Building the Navy's Bases in World War II: History of the Bureau of Yards and Docks and the Civil Engineer Corps, 1940-46*, Vol. 1 (Washington: GPO, 1947), pp. 236, 239, 248-249; Coletta, *Bases*, p. 245; Linda Drew, *The History of Naval Air Station, Patuxent River, Maryland* (U.S. Navy, Naval Air System Command, c. 1999), pp. 5-7; Naval Air Station Patuxent River and Jefferson Patterson Park and Museum, "Life at Cedar Point: A Cultural and Natural History Tour of Naval Air Station Patuxent River, Maryland," undated pamphlet, pp.1-2, 5-7; Unsigned, "'Pax River': The Naval Air Test Center," *U.S. Naval Institute Proceedings*, Vol. 95 (Dec.1969), pp. 93-106.

(78) Coletta, *Bases*, pp. 427-428; Drew, *History*, pp. 8-10; "Base History," nas.nawcad.navy.mil.

(79) Coletta, *Bases*, pp. 428-430; Drew, *History,* pp. 11-25; "Base History," nas.nawcad.navy.mil.

(80) Drew, *History*, pp. 26-32; Joel McCord, "Patuxent Welcomes New Naval Research Center," Baltimore *Sun*, Mar.5, 1992.; "Base History" and "Pax Info," nas.nawcad.navy.mil.

(81) "St. Mary's County Historic Background," somd.com, viewed Feb.1, 2003.

(82) "Navy and Marine Corps Air Stations and Fields Names," history.navy.mil, appendix 11, viewed Feb.1, 2003.

(83) Colleen Jenkins, "Longtime Navy Career Is Business Success Story," *Washington Post*, Oct.20, 2002.

(84) "Webster Field Annex," globalsecurity.org, viewed Nov.11, 2002.

(85) Naval Aviation Systems Team, U.S. Navy, "Inaugural UAV Flight Demonstration a Great Success," news release, Aug.1, 2001.

(86) Jenkins, "Longtime Navy Career."

(87) Page on Webster Field, airnav.com, viewed Feb.9, 2003.

(88) Elizabeth Hughes, MHT inventory form, Mar. 1995, file SM-490.

(89) Steven Gray, "St. Mary's Officials Move to Find Housing Answers," *Washington Post*, May 27, 2001. Vernon Gray, campaign position paper for the Nov.5, 2002 election on www.vernongray.com.

(90) MSAC/MAA airport directories and lists dated May 6, 1947, June 1, 1950, 1962, 1966, 1972, 1974, Apr. 28, 1981, and Sep.2001, airport data sheet July. 2002; Charles J. Truitt, *Historic Salisbury Updated, 1662-1982* (Salisbury: Historical Books, Inc., 1982), p. 143; Scott, *Airy Regions*, pp. 32-33.

(91) Truitt, *Historic Salisbury*, 144-145; Scott, *Airy Regions,* pp. 33-37; Mary Coddry, "Aviation Pioneer Finds New Frontiers," *Maryland*, Vol. 13, No. 3, (Spring,1981); Jacques Kelly, "Richard Henson, 92, Airline Founder," Baltimore *Sun*, June 14, 2002.

(92) Truitt, *Historic Salisbury*, p. 144; Unsigned photo caption, "Dedication of Terminal," Salisbury *Daily Times*, Nov.12, 1975; Salisbury Area Chamber of Commerce, www.salisburyarea.com viewed Nov. 2002; MAA airport directories, particularly for 1974 and 1981.

(93) Chamber of Commerce, www.salisburyarea.com; MAA airport data sheet July, 2002

(94) Baltimore *Sun* and *Evening Sun* articles, May 13 through June 7, 1943, EPFL clippings files, especially Carroll E. Willliams, "Air Volunteers Clear Ground And Build Field For Own Use," Baltimore *Sun,* May 13, 1943; Norman P. Sullivan, "Baltimore Squadron of CAP Opens Westminster Airport," Baltimore *Sun*, June 7, 1943.

(95) Haire *Airport Directory,* 1945. The description as of July 1, 1946, was provided in a MSAC directory dated Mar.6, 1947. That directory listed Pan-American Transport, Inc., as the owner; in fact, however, that company was probably the operator rather than the property owner. The B. F. Shriver Company was again listed as owner in the MAA directory for 1970-71. On the USCGS section chart, the airport was: not shown, Nov.5, 1942; appeared as CAP Base 332 from May 20, 1943, through Oct.22, 1946; and first appeared as Westminster airport, Oct.15, 1947.

(96) Town Council of New Windsor, North Windsor Community Planning Area Comprehensive Plan, May 7, 1997, posted on ccgov.carr.org; "Brief History of the Airport," Carroll County Regional Airport, carrollcountyairport.com, viewed Oct.12, 2002; Mary Gail Hare, "Airport Operators Face Battle for Control," Baltimore *Sun*, Sep.29, 2002.

(97) MAA directory, Sep.2001 and data sheet, July 9, 2002; Carroll County Commissioners, Carroll County Road Map, updated 1996.

(98) MAA airport data sheet, July 8, 2002; Mills: "50th Anniversary: Taking Flight at Easton Airport," Easton *Star Democrat*, July 25, 1993; unsigned articles, probably from the Easton *Star Democrat*, Feb. 5, 1943, May 7, and July. 16, 1943, clippings from Talbot County Free Library, Maryland Room; quotation from Easton *Star-Democrat*, Aug.13, 1943, EPFL. Dickson, *Talbot County . . .*, p. 301, states that the airport was built with the labor of German prisoners. According to Norton, however, the prisoners built only paths and gardens at the facility (lecture, Oct. 2002).

(99) Mills, "50th Anniversary;" USCGS section charts, Nov.18, 1943, May 25, 1944, Dec.26, 1945, and Apr.16, 1946; MSAC airport directory, Mar. 6, 1947, with information as of Oct.1, 1946.

(100) Mills, "50th Anniversary;" Dickson, *Talbot County*, pp. 336-337; Eugene L.Meyer, *Maryland Lost and Found . . . Again* (Baltimore: Woodholme House Publishers, 2000), pp. 17-24.

(101) Mills, "50th Anniversary;" AOPA airport directory, 1990; MAA airport data sheet, and directories Oct.1996 and Sep.2001; Edmund Preston, conversation with airport manager Joseph B. March, Dec.30, 2002.

(102) MAA airport directory, Sep. 2001, and airport data sheet, July 8, 2002; ADC Baltimore map p. 45.

(103) Edmund Preston, notes on conversations with Jim Montgomery and Don Crouse, Mar. 7, 2003. Montgomery and Crouse confirmed the 1943 opening date, which is given as an estimate on MAA's July 2002 data sheet. Crouse provided the name of the original owner, and also the data on the current status of the structures. An earlier building, which included a bar, was located at the river shore but was destroyed by fire. The airport was shown under the name Diffendahl on USCGS section charts dated Oct.15, 1947 and Oct.18, 1948.

(104) MSAC airport directories, July 1949, June 1950. AOPA directories, 1963, 1965, 1967; Unsigned article, *Extra*, Sep.30, 1970, EPFL vertical files.

(105) Montgomery and Crouse conversation, 2003; Joe Nawrozki, "County Saving a Pristine Forest," June 8, 2000, and "Airfield to Fade into Past," Baltimore *Sun,* Jan. 7, 2001; MAA airport directory, Apr.28, 1981, data sheet, July 8, 2002; O'Brien, "Airports In Md. Face Hard Times."

CHAPTER FOUR:
POSTWAR AND COLD WAR

(1) MAA airport data sheet, July. 8, 2002; Haire *Airport Directory*, 1945; Unsigned, "Cumberland Set to Build Airport, Baltimore *Evening Sun*, Feb.19, 1941, and other clippings from the *Sun* and *Evening Sun*, May 19, 1939 through July 24, 1940, EPFL ver-

tical file; Stegmaier, et al., *Allegany County,* pp. 360-361.

(2) MSAC airport directory, Mar. 6, 1947, containing data as of Oct.1, 1946; Virginia McCord, "$10 Million Cumberland Airport Bill Gets Preliminary OK," Capital News Service, Sep.25, 1998, from journalism,umd.edu; Maryland Department of Transportation, news release on terminal dedication, July 15, 1999; MAA airport data sheet, July 8, 2002, and directory, Sep.2001.

(3) Bill Morris, oral-history interview with Barry A. Lanman, Nov. 22, 2002, draft transcription by Sue Lanman. Morris stated that he bought the land in 1945 and established the airfield "right away." According Tom Vesey, "Community Spirit Soaring at Kentmorr," *Washington Post,* Apr. 9, 1988, however, it was begun in 1947. The airport did not appear on the USCGS section chart dated Oct.22, 1946, but was shown on the chart for Oct.15, 1947.

(4) "Kentmorr Airpark," brochure c. 1950s, EPFL vertical file; MSAC commercial airports listing, Nov. 9, 1960; MAA airport directory, Sep.2001, airport data sheet, July. 9, 2002.

(5) Haire *Airport Directory,* 1945-48; MSAC/MAA airport directories and lists dated June 1, 1950, 1962, 1966, 1970-71, 1972,1974, Apr. 28, 1981, 1996, Sep.2001, airport data sheet, July 2, 2002; Baltimore *News Post,* June 1, 1961. The Professional Marketing Association map, 1988, Aberdeen Room Archives and Museum, shows a variant name, Harford County Air Park

(6) USCGS section charts, Nov.30, 1944, and Dec.26, 1945; Haire *Airport Directory,* 1945-46; MSAC airport directory, June 1, 1950; AOPA airport directories, 1962, 1963, 1965, and 1967; Joanna Carter Jones, Coastal Carolina Research, Inc., MHT inventory form, Feb. 14, 2000, MHT file CH-597.

(7) Jones, inventory form, Anne Bruder, eligibility review, Aug. 18, 200, MHT file CH-597; "Maryland Private Reliever Airports to Get Public Funds," Mar.17, 2000, *GA News,* California Aviation Association on-line archives; MAA airport directory, Sep. 2001, airport data sheet, Cecil County Airport, July 8, 2002.

(8) Lovett Field appeared on the USCGS section chart dated Oct.15, 1947, but not on the chart for Oct.22, 1946. See also J. E. Greiner Co., Baltimore, Md., "Maryland Airports," report submitted to Red Star Coaches, Inc., Sep.21, 1945, EPFL; USCGS section chart, Oct. 15, 1947; MSAC/MAA airport directories, Mar. 6, 1947, June 1950, 1966, 1974, 1996, and 1999; AOPA airport directories, 1965 and 1967.

(9) Closed Airports by Name, listing, Oct.30, 2001, MAA files; Freeman, Abandoned & Little-Known Airfields website.

(10) MAA airport data sheet, July. 8, 2002; L. Paul Norsworthy, "Frederick Municipal Airport Aviation Museum and Airport Facility," thesis submitted for the degree of Master of Architecture, University of Maryland, 1998; headline quotation from Unsigned, "Discover Your Airport: Celebrating 50 Years, 1949-1999," Frederick *News Post* special section, June 3, 1999, pp. 8, 12; Unsigned, "34 Airports Now in State," Baltimore *Sun,* Sep.2, 1948. The dedication date given here follows the *News Post* 1999 article rather than Norsworthy.

(11) MSAC/MAA airport directories and lists, June 1, 1950, 1974, Apr. 28, 1981, and Sep.2001, data sheet, July. 8, 2002; *Washington Post,* Sep.10, 1990, p. WB3; "Discover Your Airport;"

Norsworthy, "Frederick Municipal Airport," pp. 12-14.

(12) MAA airport directories, Mar. 6, 1947 (with description of the airport as of Aug. 27, 1946), 2001, airport data sheet, July. 8, 2002; "Tiny Etchison Airport Slated For New Life," *Montgomery County Sentinel,* Apr. 26, 1956.

(13) *Sentinel,* Apr. 26, 1956; Clayton Davis, "Mina Avery, Class of 1933," a 1997 article posted on website geocities. com/Athens/Forum; MSAC airport directories, Mar. 6, 1947; June 28, 1947; June 4, 1948; July 1949; June 1, 1950. The *Sentinel* article stated that the property, which then belonged to Col. E. Brooke Lee, had changed hands several times before Lee purchased it. W. H. Paille had acquired the property by at least July 1972, when he was listed as owner by a state directory.

(14) *Sentinel,* Apr. 26, 1956, and July 30, 1959.

(15) AOPA airport directories,1967, 1969; Unsigned, "Maryland Private Reliever Airports to Get Public Funds," Mar.17, 2000, *GA News,* California Aviation Association on-line archives.

(16) "Cessna 150L Commuter," pages from National Air and Space Museum's nasm.si.edu website, viewed Oct.19, 2002; Edmund Preston, conversation with airport manager Frank Schmidt, Dec.26, 2002.

(17) USCGS section chart, Oct.22, 1946; MSAC/MAA airport directories, June 1, 1950, 1974 and Apr. 1981; AOPA airport directories, 1980, 1984, 1990; Kent County Commissioners and Chamber of Commerce, "Driving Tour of Kent County, Maryland," undated but in distribution during 2003..

(18) Unsigned, "Airport at Chestertown Built with Private Funds," Baltimore *Evening Sun,* Nov.6, 1946. The approximate date of the name change is based on a comparison of the 1980 and 1984 AOPA directories.

(19) Brian Shane, "Court of Special Appeals OKs Chestertown Wal-Mart Plan," Capital News Service, Sep.15, 1999. As of 2003, however, the Wal-Mart remains unbuilt.

(20) *The Harford County Directory* (1953, Aberdeen Room Archives and Museum) gives an opening date of 1947; however, the MSAC airport directory published on Mar.6, 1947, stated that its data on Aberdeen Airpark was as of Nov. 20, 1946. The airport appeared in the Haire *Airport Directory* for 1947 but not the previous year. The earliest USCGS section chart found that showed the facility was valid through Apr.26, 1948.

(21) MSAC/MAA airport directories and lists dated Mar.6, 1947, June 1, 1950, Nov.9, 1960, 1962, 1966, 1970-71, and 1972. Hill was later cited as the owner, as well as the operator, by both the 1953 county directory and the MAA airport directory, 1970-71.

(22) O'Brien, "Airports in Md. Face Hard Times," indicates that the land was used for housing. The article identifies the closure time only as between 1979 and 1987; however, 1979 seems the likely ending date since the airport was not included in the AOPA airport directory for 1980. A similar *Washington Post* article places the airport among those closed 1978-87, and also mentions its conversion to housing. Unsigned, "Small Airports Face Development Pressure," *Washington Post,* Dec.31, 1987.

(23) Undated note on Aberdeen Airpark's location, MAA archives.

(24) The description as of Aug.27, 1946, appeared in the Mar. 5, 1947 MSAC airport directory. The base was not included on the USCGS section chart dated as valid through Oct. 22, 1946, but did appear on the chart dated Oct. 15, 1947.

(25) USCGS section charts Jan. 22, 1959, July 27, 1959; MSAC airport directories, Nov. 17, 1947, June 4, 1948, July 1949, June 1, 1950.

(26) Greiner Co., "Maryland Airports," report to Red Star Motor Coaches, Inc., Sep.21, 1945; Haire *Airport Directory*, 1945-48; MSAC airport directories and listings, Mar. 6, 1947, June 28, 1947, July 1949, and June 1, 1950; USCGS section charts, Apr. 19, 1946, and Oct. 22, 1946.

(27) Joseph P. Smaldone, *History of the White Oak Laboratory*, 1945-1975 (Naval Surface Weapons Center, White Oak, Silver Spring, Md., 1977); William B. Anspacher, et al., *The Legacy of White Oak Laboratory* (Naval Surface Warfare Center, Dahlgen, Va., 2000); U.S. Navy, White Oak Fact Sheet, May 18, 2000; "White Oak, Maryland," from www.globalsecurity.org, viewed Nov.19, 2002.

(28) Christopher Martin and David Bert. G & O Inc., MHT inventory form, Feb. 1997, file M-33-25.

(29) Maryland Department of the Environment, Environmental Restoration and Redevelopment Program, ERRP Fact Sheet, from www.mde.state.md.us, viewed Nov.26, 2002; Environmental Protection Agency, "Federal Research Center," from www.epa.gov, viewed Nov. 19, 2002.

(30) MSAC/MAA airport directories and lists, Nov. 9, 1960, 1974, Sep. 2001, airport data sheet, July 8, 2002; Thiessen, "Airports in Prince George's County," MAA files, pp. 6-7; Edmund Preston, conversation with Stanley Rodenhauser, Dec. 3, 2002. The Washington *Star*, ("Bowie City Council Backs Airport, Endorses Plan For Improvements") Aug.2 6, 1964, described Bowie City Council support for Freeway Airport, but gave 1940 as the year that the it was built.

(31) MAA airport directories and lists dated Nov. 9, 1960, 1962, 1966, 1996, and Sep. 2002; Thiessen, "Airports in Prince George's County," MAA files, p. 9; Edmund Preston, conversation with airport manager David Wartofsky, Mar. 31, 2003.

(32) MAA Airport data sheet, July 8, 2002; Pittman, "Nation's Last Shuttered Airport Cleared to Reopen," "Some Maryland Airports Get Federal Funds," www.newsline.umd.edu

(33) Haire *Airport Directory*, 1947; MSAC airport directories, Mar. 6, 1947, June 28, 1947, revised Nov. 11, 1947. On USCGS section charts, the airport: was not included, Oct. 22, 1946; appeared Oct. 15, 1947, through Feb. 17, 1953; and was no longer included, July 17, 1953.

(34) Haire *Airport Directory*, 1946 and 1947. MSAC airport directories, Mar.6, 1947, June 1, 1950; USCGS section charts, Oct. 22, 1946, and Oct. 15, 1947.

(35) About 1949, Dixie Aero acquired another facility in the same county, Annapolis Airport (see that entry); both fields closed within a few years. "2 More Shore Private Airfields Are Closed," Baltimore *Evening Sun*, May 28, 1952.

(36) Isaac B. Rehert, "Cecil County Crossroads," Baltimore *Sun*,

Oct. 23, 1960; MSAC/MAA airport directories and lists, Nov. 9, 1960, 1962, 1966, 1970-71, and 1972; Air Nav.Com, viewed Nov.28, 2002; AOPA airport directory, 1990.

(37) Information on website windvane.umd.edu, viewed Nov.22, 2002; Edmund Preston, conversation with Dr. Jewel Barlow, facility director, Nov. 26, 2002.

(38) Unsigned, "Baltimore Dedicates $15,000,000 Friendship Airport," *Construction*, Vol. 17, No. 7, (July 1950); Scott, *Airy Regions*, pp. 25-29.

(39) Geoffrey Arend, *Great Airports Worldwide* (New York: Air Cargo Books, 1988), pp. 88-92; Carole Shifria, "BWI Airport at 30," *Washington Post*, June 22, 1980. Susanne S. Pickens, Greiner, Inc., MHT inventory form, Hangar No. 1, Friendship International Airport, Dec.17, 1993, file AA-30.

(40) MAA airport directory, Sep. 2002, airport data sheet, July 8, 2002; "BWI Timeline," from , viewed Nov. 25, 2002.

(41) "34 Airports Now In State," Baltimore *Sun*, Sep. 2, 1948. "National Airport Plan Fails To Show Change in Md.," Baltimore *Evening Sun*, May 11, 1950; MSAC/MAA airport directory. June 1, 1950, Sep. 2001, airport data sheet, July 8, 2002.

(42) The location description is based on Paul Freeman, Abandoned & Little-Known Airfields website: www.members.tripod.com/airfields_freeman/index.htm, revised Oct. 17, 2002, and the MAA airport directory, 1981. Comparison with a Mapquest.com map, viewed Oct. 26, 2002, confirmed the creek's identity.

(43) MSAC/MAA airport directories and lists, dated June 1, 1950, 1962, 1966, 1970-71, 1972, 1974, and Apr. 28, 1981; AOPA airport directory, 1987; David Runkel, "Increasing Number of Pilots Using Fewer Airfields," Baltimore *Evening Sun*, July 18, 1967.

(44) The closing date is from the MAA list, Closed Airports by Name, Oct. 30, 2002. See also Freeman, "Abandoned & Little-Known Airfields" website.

(45) USCGS section charts, Jan.12 and July 12, 1950; MSAC/MAA airport directories, Nov. 9, 1960, 1974; AOPA airport directories, 1979, 1980; Kent County Commissioners and Chamber of Commerce, "Driving Tour of Kent County, Maryland," undated but in distribution during 2003.

(46) Clayton Davis, "Cambridge Dorchester Airport," undated and unpublished article, with a history of 1974-1993 improvements by Airport Commissioner Elvin Thomas, MAA files; Edmund Preston, notes on a conversation with airport manager Don Satterfield, Jan.15, 2003. The Baltimore *Sun*, Oct. 1, 1969, stated that the city bought the airport from private owners in 1960, but Davis and Satterfield contradict this. Satterfield is the source for the 1954 opening date and for recent developments.

(47) Preston/Satterfield interview; MSAC/MAA airport directories and lists dated 1960, 1962, 1966, 1970-71, 1974, 1981, 1996, 1999, Sep. 2001.

(48) Klingaman, *APL—Fifty Years of Servicee*, pp. 87-252; Information from www.jhuapl.edu, viewed Nov. 2002.

(49) Mark L. Morgan and Mark A. Berhow, *Rings of Supersonic Steel: Air Defenses of the United States Army, 1950-1979, An Introductory History and Site Guide* (Bodega Bay, Calif.: Fort

MacArthur Military Press, 2nd edition, 2002), pp. 3-17; Von Braun and Ordway, *History of Rocketry,* pp. 144-145.

(50) Morgan and Berhow, *Rings of Supersonic Steel,* pp. 9-14, 45, 173, 175; Merle T. Cole, "W-25: The Davidsonville Site and Maryland Air Defense, 1950-1974," *Maryland Historical Magazine,* Vol. 80, No. 3, (Fall 1985); pp. 1-2.

(51) Morgan and Berhow, *Rings of Supersonic Steel,* pp. 14-15; News release, Dec. 5, 1957, ftmeade.army.mil, viewed Oct. 3, 2002; Cole, "Davidsonville Site," p. 245-246.

(52) Cole, "Davidsonville Site," p. 243; museum web page on ftmeade.army.mil; Morgan and Berhow, *Rings of Supersonic Steel,* pp. 34, 173. Estimates of the number of sites in Maryland are based on the "Units(years)" column of this book's site guide, pp. 45-48, and 173-178. BA-30 and BA-31 at Tolchester Beach are counted separately

(53) "Fort Meade History" website, www.ftmeade.army.mil, viewed Oct. 2, 2002; Cole, "Davidsonville Site," "The One That Got Away," *Anne Arundel County History News,* Vol. 32 (Jan.2001) (pages from the latter cited as posted on community-2.webtv.net, viewed Nov.21, 2002), "Army Air Defense Installations in Anne Arundel County, 1950-1973," www.ftmeade.army.mil, viewed Oct.3, 2002.

(54) Morgan and Berhow, *Rings of Supersonic Steel,* p. 8. In "The One That Got Away," p. 1, Cole states that the battery was located at Hill 85 and gives the coordinates as 39-05-178N/ 076-48-234W. In a report posted on Ed Thelen, "Ed Thelen's Nike Missile Website," ed-thelen.org, viewed Mar. 18, 2003, Morgan described his Nov. 2002 visit to this area, guided by Rick Potvin of the Fish and Wildlife Service. Potvin did not recognize the term "Hill 85," but pointed out a high point believed to be the site of the Integrated Fire Control radars (coordinates 390466/0764729). No structural remains were seen at the hill; however, Potvin also showed Morgan the site of a buried bunker (390454/0764729) and also the probable site of the launchers (390466/0764714), which was one mile to the east of the presumed radar position.

(55) Morgan and Berhow, *Rings of Supersonic Steel,* pp. 15, 45; Bill Evans, "U.S. Army Air Defense Command (ARADCOM), Baltimore-Washington Defense," hosted on website www.nike-missile.net, viewed Mar. 2003; Missile Master News Release, Dec.5, 1957, "Fort Meade History" website; Preston, conversation with Barbara Taylor, Fort Meade Museum, Mar. 14, 2003.

(56) Morgan and Berhow, *Rings of Supersonic Steel,* especially p. 47; Evans, "Baltimore-Washington Defense" website; Maryland Department of Environment, ERRP Fact Sheet, mde.state.md.us, viewed Nov. 26, 2002.

(57) Morgan and Berhow, *Rings of Supersonic Steel,* especially p. 47; Evans "Baltimore-Washington Defense" website; Cole, "Davidsonville Site," p. 245 (re Guard takeover). The coordinates above are, for the launch area, were posted by S. Murdock on Thelen, "Ed Thelen's Nike...Site;" the coordinates that Murdock gave for the control area were 39-26-55N, 76-27-41W.

(58) Morgan and Berhow, *Rings of Supersonic Steel,* especially p. 47 (including the activation and deactivation dates); Evans, "Baltimore-Washington Defense" website; Laura Bowlin, MHT eligibility review form, May 20, 1994, MHT file HA-1995; Doug

Garmen, "Early Chemical Weapons Sought at Aberdeen Proving Ground," Engineer Update, hq.usace.army.mil/cepa/dec00/ story8.htm., viewed Dec. 2000.

(59) Morgan and Berhow, *Rings of Supersonic Steel,* especially p. 48; Evans, "Baltimore-Washington Defense" website; Fred G. Usilton, *History of Kent County, Maryland* (Chestertown: Perry, c 1980), p. 277; Maryland Department of Environment, ERRP Fact Sheet; .James F. Johnson, Baltimore District, U.S. Army Corps of Engineers, letter to Lauren Bowlin, MHT, Apr. 29, 1996, file PG 86B-26.

(60) Morgan and Berhow, *Rings of Supersonic Steel,* especially p. 48; Evans, "Baltimore-Washington Defense" website; Maryland Department of Environment, ERRP Fact Sheet. In 1999, Tom Vaughn described the control area as an extremely well preserved; Tom Vaughn, "Recent Pictures of Nike Missile Sites," web page linked to Thelen, "Ed Thelen's Nike . . . Site;" Freeman, "Abandoned & Little-Known Airfields" website includes aerial and surface photos of the location.

(61) Morgan and Berhow, *Rings of Supersonic Steel,* especially p. 48; Evans, "Baltimore-Washington Defense" website; Cole, "Davidsonville Site," p. 245 (re Guard takeover).

(62) Morgan and Berhow, *Rings of Supersonic Steel,* especially p. 176; Cole, "Davidsonville Site," especially pp. 250, 253, and 256; Mark L. Baker, U.S. Army Corps of Engineers, MHT inventory form, May 14, 1998, eligibility review form, July 1, 1999, file AA-993; Evans, "Baltimore-Washington Defense" website.

(63) Morgan and Berhow, *Rings of Supersonic Steel,* especially p. 176; Evans, "Baltimore-Washington Defense" website; Cole, "Davidsonville Site," p. 246 (re Guard takeover); Cole, "Installations in Anne Arundel County, 1950-1973," ftmeade. army.mil, viewed Oct. 3, 2002; Lori O. Thursby, R. Christopher Goodwin & Associates, MHT inventory form, Feb. 21, 1997, file AA-38.

(64) Morgan and Berhow, *Rings of Supersonic Steel,* especially p. 176; Evans, "Baltimore-Washington Defense" website; James F. Johnson, Baltimore District, U.S. Army Corps of Engineers, letter to Lauren Bowlin, MHT, Apr. 29, 1996, with Corps of Engineers site report documents, 1991, MHT file PG 86B-26.

(65) Morgan and Berhow, *Rings of Supersonic Steel,* especially p. 176. The coordinates given above are for the launch area are from Thelen, "Ed Thelen's Nike...Site," which gives 38-42-37N, 76-46-16W for the fire control area.

(66) Morgan and Berhow, *Rings of Supersonic Steel,* especially p. 48.

(67) Tom Vaughn, "Recent Pictures of Nike Missile Sites," web page linked to Thelen, "Ed Thelen's Nike . . . Site," viewed Mar. 20, 2003.

(68) Morgan and Berhow, *Rings of Supersonic Steel,* especially p. 176; Evans, "Baltimore-Washington Defense" website; Lauren Boulin, MHT eligibility review forms, Oct. 4 and 10, 1994, file CH-677; Maryland Department of Environment, ERRP Fact Sheet. The ERRP Fact Sheet's states that the control area is east of the launch site, but this seems to be an error given the context and the other sources, including a map in MHT file CH-677.

(69) Morgan and Berhow, *Rings of Supersonic Steel,* especially p. 177; Evans, "Baltimore-Washington Defense" website provides

driving directions which appear to place both locations south of Maryland Route 228.

(70) Morgan and Berhow, *Rings of Supersonic Steel*, especially p. 177; Evans, "Baltimore-Washington Defenses" website; Thelen, "Ed Thelen's Nike...Site;" Lauren Baumgardt, MHT eligibility review form, May 20, 1996, file CH-676.

(71) Morgan and Berhow, *Rings of Supersonic Steel*, especially p. 178; Unsigned, "Community Quietly Accepts Missilemen," *Montgomery County Sentinel*, May 7, 1957.

(72) U.S. House of Representatives, Resolution 3355, Nov. 27, 2001, introduced by Rep. Morella.

(73) Thelen, "Ed Thelen's Nike. . .Site."

(74) Morgan and Berhow, *Rings of Supersonic Steel*, especially p. 177; Evans, "Baltimore-Washington Defenses" website; Thelen, "Ed Thelen's Nike. . .Site;" "Community Quietly Accepts Missilemen," *Montgomery County Sentinel*. Despite its apparently customary inclusion in W-93's designation, Derwood is further from the site than Brookeville, Olney, or Redland.

(75) Morgan and Berhow, *Rings of Supersonic Steel*, especially p. 178; "Community Quietly Accepts Missilemen," *Montgomery County Sentinel*.

(76) ADC Montgomery County Map, 2002, map 19, grid J4,

(77) MSAC/MAA June 1, 1960, 1962, 1966, 1970-71, 1972, 1974, Apr. 28, 1981, Oct. 1996, and Sep. 2001, airport data sheet, July 8, 2002; Baltimore *Evening Sun*, Oct. 2, 1958, and July 11, 1963; from EPFL query cards; Mary Corddry (sic), "Henson Sets Daily Flights From Baltimore To Ocean City," Baltimore *Sun*, Apr. 20, 1982.

(78) MSAC/MAA airport directories and lists Nov. 9, 1960, 1962, 1966, 1970-71, 1972, 1974, Apr. 28, 1981, Sep. 2001, airport data sheet, July 8, 2002; Professional Marketing Association map, 1988, from the Aberdeen Room Archives and Museum.

(79) Alfred Rosenthal, *Venture into Space: Early Years of Goddard Space Flight Center* (Washington: NASA, 1968), especially pp. 52-59.

(80) Lane E. Wallace, *Dreams, Hopes, Realities: NASA Goddard Space Flight Center: The First Forty Years* (Washington: NASA History Office, 1999); GSFC website, www.gsfc.nasa.gov, viewed Oct-Nov.2 002, especially sections: "GSFC History;" "Unique Goddard Resources;" and "About Goddard, Facilities;" Edmund Preston, conversation with Kim Tousectis, Facilities Master Plan officer, GSFC, Nov. 4, 2002. N.B. See separate entry on the GSFC's Spacecraft Magnetic Test Facility.

(81) The opening date given was provided by Charles H. Crew, Sr. The Thiessen Paper, "Airports in Prince George's County," MAA files, states that the airport was established in the mid-1950s; the MAA airport data sheet, July 8, 2002, indicates circa 1958.

(82) Mr. Crew stated that he had been told that the runway was first paved in the 1970s era. He noted that the surface was very thin prior to the rehabilitation completed in 1996. Edmund Preston, conversation with Charles H. Crew, Sr., Mar. 28, 2003; MSAC/MAA airport directories and lists 1960, 1962, 1966, 1970-71, 1974, 1981, 1996, 1999, and Sep. 2001.

(83) The fortunes of the airpark may be traced in a series of headlines from the Washington *Evening Star*: Charles Yarborough, "Montgomery To Open New Airport In Bid To Attract More Business," June 26, 1960, "Optimism On The Wing In County As New Airport Formally Opens," Oct. 23, 1960, "County Airpark Is Soaring," Oct. 14, 1969; Marvin Coble, "Montgomery Residents Fight Against Airpark Expansion," Dec. 5, 1969; Thomas Love, "Montgomery Airpark: Roars Above, Below," June 2, 1971; and Willliam Taafe, "Montgomery To Sue Airpark For Removal Of New Runway," June 9, 1971; see also City of Gaithersburg, *Gaithersburg – The Heart of Montgomery County*, 1978, pp. 314-315.

(84) MSAC/MAA airport directories Nov. 9, 1960, July 1972, and Sep.2001, airport data sheet, July 8, 2002; Maria Longo-Swiek, "Soaring High Above It All," *Montgomery Miscellanea*, May/June 1997; "Airpark History" and other information from www.montcoairpark.com, viewed Dec.2002.

(85) MSAC airport directories, 1960, 1962, 1966. (Quinn Airport did not appear in the state directories for 1950 or 1970-71, or in the AOPA directory for 1967.) *Evening Sun*, Jan. 18, 1962 (EPFL query card file).

(86) Edmund Preston, conversation with Betsy Mace, Mar. 27, 2003; MAA airport directory, 1999; Jay Apperson, "Small Airfield Awaits Developer's Landing," Baltimore *Sun*, Apr. 7, 1999; Charlie Muth, "Green Light for Forge Landing," *The Northeast Booster*, June 28, 2000.

(87) MSAC/MAA airport directories and lists dated Nov.9, 1960, 1962, 1966, 1970-1, and 1972.

(88) MSAC/MAA airport directories. 1962, 1966, 1970-71, July 1972, 1974, Apr. 28, 1981, Oct. 1996, airport data sheet, July 8, 2002; AOPA airport directories, 2001-2002; Edmund Preston, conversation with Gary Mulloch, Garrett County General Services office, Mar. 31, 2003.

(89) AOPA airport directory, 1962; MAA airport directory, 1974: letters, Theodore Mathieson to Carl R. Baldus, Jan.15, 1990; Bruce Mundie to Baldus, Aug. 17, 1992, MAA Closed Airports file; Charles County website, charlescounty.org, visited Oct. 14, 2002; Freeman, "Abandoned & Little-Known Airfields," website. N.B., Clifton on the Potomac does not appear on the ADC state map for 2000, but is shown on the Chamber of Commerce, Map of Charles County, 1995-96.

(90) MSAC airport directory, 1962; AOPA airport directories, 1962, 1963, and 1965.

(91) MSAC/MAA airport directories, 1966, 1970-71, Sep. 2001, airport data sheet, July 8, 2002. The approximate opening date is from the MAA Airport data sheet. Airport manager Thomas Chapman did not have the exact date.

(92) AOPA airport directories, 1969, 1990, 2001-02; MSAC/MAA airport directories and lists, 1970-71, 1972, 1974, Apr. 28, 1981, Oct.1996, 1999, Sep.2002; Scott, *Airy Regions*, p. 37.

(93) Commissioners of Caroline County, Airport Project Public Notice, Jan. 17, 2001 (ridgelymd.org), and minutes, Feb. 13, 2001 (carolinemd.org); Edmund Preston, conversation with airport manager Thomas R. Davis, Feb.. 3, 2003; MAA airport data sheet, July 8, 2002.

(94) Harry A. Butowsky, National Park Service, MHT inventory form, May 15, 1984, file PG 64-6; "Unique Goddard Resources," gsfc.nasa.govsection, viewed Oct.31, 2002. (See also separate entry on the Goddard Space Flight Center main site.)

(95) MCAC airport directory, 1966; AOPA directories, 1965, 1967, 1969.

(96) AOPA airport directories, 1969, MAA airport directories, 1970-71, 1972, 1974, 1996, Apr. 28, 1981, Sep. 2001, airport data sheet, July 8, 2002; Unsigned, "Developer Offers County Land at Bay Bridge for Airport," and "Dedication Held at Bay Bridge Airport," *Queen Anne's Record Observer*, Mar. 17, 1966 and Sep. 28, 1967; Clayton Davis, "Bay Bridge Airport," unpublished and undated article, MAA files; Barry A. Lanman, oral history interview with Bill Morris, Nov.22, 2002, draft transcription by Sue Lanman; Edmund Preston, Conversation with airport manager John Kirby, Mar. 11, 2003.

(97) MAA airport directories, 1970-1971, Sep. 2001; Airport history and Capt. Duke biography, co.saint-marys.md.us, viewed Feb. 11, 2003; two articles in the Washington *Post*: Steven Ginsberg and Jessie Mangalman, "Trying To Land Economic Growth; Outlying Areas Expand Airports," Sep.12, 1999, and Steven Gray, "St. Mary's Will Extend Airport Runway To Attract Commuter Planes," Nov.30, 2000.

(98) MAA airport data sheet, July 8, 2002; Michael Amon and Steven Gray, "Returning To Business, But Not As Usual," Sep.20, 2001, and Monte Reel, "Owner Of Charles County Facility Hopes Flights Will Resume Soon," Nov. 15, 2001—both from Washington *Post*.

(99) MAA airport directories, Apr. 28, 1981, Sep. 2001, airport data sheet, July 8, 2002; AOPA airport directory, 1979; Edmund Preston, conversation with Mrs. Howard Bennett, Mar. 31, 2003.

(100) MAA airport directories, 1981, Sep. 2001, airport data sheet, July 8, 2002; AOPA airport directory, 1980, 1984; "Maryland Private Reliever Airports to Get Public Funds," Mar.17, 2000, *GA News*, California Aviation Association on-line archives; AirNav.com web page on seaplane base, viewed Oct.19, 2002; Edmund Preston, conversations with Mrs. Cathy Powell, Apr. 1, 2003. Mrs. Powell confirmed the MAA data sheet specifying 1979 as the opening date.

(101) MAA airport directories, 1974, Apr. 28, 1981, 1996; AOPA airport directories, 1984 and 1987.

(102) MAA airport directory, Sep. 2001, airport data sheet, July 8, 2002.

Bibliography

CONTENTS

AIRCRAFT MANUFACTURING, GENERAL

Bilstein, Roger E., *The American Aerospace Industry: From Workshop to Global Enterprise* (New York: Twayne Publishers, 1996).

Bradley, Betsy Hunter, *The Works: The Industrial Architecture of the United States* (New York: Oxford University Press, 1999).

Bright, Charles D., *The Jet Makers: The Aerospace Industry from 1945 to 1972* (Lawrence: The Regents Press of Kansas, 1978).

Cunningham, William Glenn, *The Aircraft Industry: A Study in Industrial Location* (Los Angeles; L. L. Morrison, 1951).

Hallstead, William, "On the Front of the Jet, Missile and Space Age," *Maryland*, Vol. 12, No. 4, Summer 1980, pp. 25-28.

Holley, Irving Brinton, Jr., *Buying Aircraft: Materiel Procurement for the Army Air Forces* (Washington: Office of the Chief of Military History, Department of the Army, 1964).

Loftkin, Laurence K., Jr., *Quest for Performance: The Evolution of Modern Aircraft* (Washington: NASA, 1985).

Miller, Ronald E and David Sawers, *The Technical Development of Modern Aviation* (London: Routledge & Kegan Paul, 1968).

Rae, John B., *Climb to Greatness: The American Aircraft Industry, 1920-1960* (Cambridge, Mass.: The MIT Press, 1968).

Robinson, Anthony, *The Encyclopedia of American Aircraft* (New York: Galahad Books, 1979).

Stanton, Joseph L., "There's a Plane in Your Future," *Baltimore*, August 1946.

Swanborough, F Gordon, and Peter M. Bowers, *United States Navy Aircraft Since 1911* (Annapolis: Naval Institute Press, 1968).

Vander Meulen, Jacob A., *The Politics of Aircraft: Building an American Military Industry* (Lawrence: University of Kansas Press, 1991).

AIRCRAFT MANUFACTURING, FAIRCHILD

Depew, Richard H., Jr., "Yesterday's 'Touch of Tomorrow' – VI, " *The Pegasus*, May 1944

[Fairchild], List of plants and their uses," Dec. 12, 1942," collection of Kent A. Mitchell.

Meyer, Kurtis, list of Fairchild aircraft produced at Hagerstown, Sept 2002.

Mitchell, Kent A., *Fairchild Aircraft, 1926-1987* (Santa Anna, Ca.: Narkiewicz // Thompson, 1997).

Poole, Herbert A., untitled memoir, Aug 1977.

Rinehart, Theron K., "Sherman M. Fairchild 'Discovered' Local Airplane Company and Bought It in 1929", *The Cracker Barrel* (Hagerstown), Vol. 8, March, 1979, p.15 ff.

Rinehart, Theron K., *Yesterday, Today, Tomorrow: Fifty Years of Fairchild Aviation* (Steven C. Patton, publisher, 1970).

Shank, Christopher, "Wings over Hagerstown: Experiencing the Second World War in Western Maryland," *Maryland Historical Magazine*, Vol. 88, Winter 1993, pp. 444-461.

Smith, Paul, "Last A-10," Hagerstown *Herald Mail*, Mar 3, 1984

Unsigned, "The Fairchild Aviation Corporation," reprinted from *Aero Digest*, Jan.1934.

Unsigned, "Hagerstown Hangar," *The Pegasus*, Oct 1943

Unsigned, "Looking in on Fairchild in Hagerstown," *FAD*, clipping, undated, but with text that indicates it was published no earlier than July 1951, Kent A. Mitchell collection.

Unsigned pamphlet, "Historical Summary, Fairchild Engine and Airplane Corporation, 1920-1951," Washington County Free Library, Western Maryland Room.

Unsigned, "1928 Production at Hagerstown," and other features in *Fairchild World*, Sep.27, 1981.

AIRCRAFT MANUFACTURING, MARTIN

Breihan, John R., "Aero Acres: The Town Glenn Martin Built," *Air & Space Smithsonian* magazine, June/July 1999, Vol. 14, No. 2, pp. 36-43

Breihan, John, R., "Between Munich and Pearl Harbor: The Glenn L. Martin Aircraft Company Gears up for War, 1938-1941," *Maryland Historical Magazine*, Vol. 88, (Winter 1993), pp. 389-419.

Breihan, John R., Stan Piet, and Roger S. Mason, *Martin Aircraft, 1909-1960* (Santa Ana, Ca.: Narkiewicz // Thompson, 1995).

Breihan, John R., "When Did Glenn Martin First Fly?" *Journal of the American Aviation Historical Society*, Vol. 44, No. 2 (Summer 1999), pp. 148-54.

Glenn L. Martin Company, "Box Kites to Bombers: The Story of the Glenn L. Martin Company," originally published c. 1946, reprint courtesy of the Glenn L. Martin Aviation Museum.

Harwood, William B., *Raise Heaven and Earth: The Story of Martin Marietta People and Their Pioneering Achievements* (New York: Simon and Schuster, 1993).

Little, Robert, "Middle River Plant Awarded $142 Million Job," *Baltimore Sun,* Jun. 26, 2002

Lockheed Martin, NE&SS-Marine Systems, "About Us" and "Heritage of Excellence," ness.external.lmco.com, viewed Nov.27, 2002.

Martin Marietta Aero and Naval Systems, "Sixty Years in Baltimore," *The Star*, Oct.1989, Baltimore Museum of Industry files.

Nawrozki, Joe, "One Man's Plane Dream," Baltimore *Sun*, Jun. 10, 2003

Piet, Stan, and Al Raithel, *Martin P6M Seamaster* (Bel Air, Md.: Martineer Press, 2001).

Greg Schneider, Greg, "Lockheed Sells Middle River Factory To GE," Baltimore Sun, Nov. 4, 1997

Greg Schneider, Greg, "Aviation Plant Tries Its Wings Identity: No Longer Martin or Lockheed, and Barely GE, Middle River Aircraft Systems Embraces Its Semi-Independence," Baltimore *Sun*, Aug. 16, 1998.

Still, Henry, *To Ride the Wind: A Biography of Glenn L. Martin* (New York: Julian Messner, Inc., 1964).

Sun Staff, "Lockheed Lands Pact For Joint Strike Fighter," Baltimore *Sun*, Oct.27, 2001.

AIRCRAFT MANUFACTURING, OTHER COMPANIES

Avery, Norm, *North American Aircraft, 1934-1998* (Santa Ana, Calif.: Narkiewicz // Thompson, 1998).

Baltimore Museum of Industry "Maryland Milestones" exhibit information on Black and Decker, Incorporated.

Berliner-Joyce Aircraft Corporation, "New Quarter-Million Dollar Plant Now Building at Baltimore," pamphlet, c. 1929, Enoch Pratt Free Library.

General Motors Corporation, *A History of Eastern Aircraft Division, General Motors Corporation* (Printed by E. Rudge's Sons, place not indicated, 1944).

Hansen, Chuck, "Engineering and Research Corporation," *Journal of American Aviation Historical Society*, Spring 1985, pp. 42-56.

Saletri, Frank R., *The Ercoupe: A Touch of Class!* (Agony House, 1981).

Swain, Craig, "Gliders for the Navy Department: 1940-45," microworks.net, viewed Jan.30, 2003.

Thomas, Stanley G., *The Ercoupe* (Blue Ridge Summit, Pa.: Tabb Books, 1991).

Unsigned, "General Aviation Manufacturing Corporation Locates All Its Activities in Baltimore," *Baltimore*, Oct.1931.

AIR MAIL AND AIRLINES

Air Transportation Survey Commission, State of Maryland, *Report on Air Transportation Service Needs in Maryland, February 1, 1963.*

Bennett, Stephen A., "State's Air Service Seen Substandard," Baltimore *Sun*, Mar.1, 1963.

Coddry, Mary, "Aviation Pioneer Finds New Frontiers," *Maryland*, Vol. 13, No. 3, Spring,1981.

Davies, R. E. G., *Airlines of the United States Since 1914* (London: Putnam, 1972).

Jackson, Donald Dale, *Flying the Mail* (Alexandra, Va.: Time-Life Books).

Josephson, Mathew, *Empire of the Air: Juan Trippe and the Struggle for World Airways* (New York: Harcourt, Brace and Company, 1944).

Kelly, Jacques, "Richard Henson, 92, Airline Founder," Baltimore *Sun*, Jun. 14, 2002.

King, Jack L., *High Flight Beyond the Horizons: The Aviation Legend of Richard A. Henson* (Jack L. King Associates, Baltimore, and Richard A. Henson Foundation, Salisbury, 2002).

Leary, William M., *Aerial Pioneers: The U.S. Air Mail Service, 1918-1927* (Washington: Smithsonian Institution Press, 1985).

Maryland Airlines, "Maryland Airlines Recalls Shore Flying," Sept 23, 1947, typescript summary of remarks by Thomas B. Bourne, Talbot County Free Library.

Pan American Airways, Inc., "Baltimore and Its Opportunity in the Air Age," 1945, pamphlet, Enoch Pratt Free Library.

Pouder, G. H., "Regular Passenger Air Service between Baltimore and Bermuda Inaugurated," *Baltimore*, Dec.1937.

Searles, Robert A., "Richard "Dick" Henson, the Maryland Marvel," *Business and Commercial Aviation*, Aug.2002.

Smith, Henry Ladd, *Airways: The History of Commercial Aviation in the United States* (New York: Alfred A. Knopf, 1942).

Twilley, Richard V., "I Remember Baltimore's First Scheduled Air Service," Baltimore *Sunday Sun*, Jul. 11, 1965.

Unsigned, "Pan-American Leases Airport Tract as Base for Ocean Plane Link," Baltimore *Sun*, Nov.5, 1936.

AIR NAVIGATION AND ELECTRONICS

Breniman, William A., ed., *The Airway Radio Story: The First Fifty Years, 1920-1970*, special issue of *The Airway Pioneer*, published by the Society of Airway Pioneers, c. 1970.

Buderi, Robert, *The Invention That Changed the World* (New York: Simon & Schuster, 1996).

Cochrane, Rexmond C., *Measures for Progress: A History of the National Bureau for Standards* (U.S. Department of Commerce, 1966).

Cohen, Charles, "Westinghouse Legacy Stands Out in War, Peace," *Baltimore Business Journal*, Oct.29, 1999.

Klingaman, William K., *APL—Fifty Years of Service to the Nation: A History of The Johns Hopkins University Applied Physics Laboratoryy* (Laurel, Md.: The Johns Hopkins University Applied Physics Laboratory, 1993).

Snyder, Wilbert F., and Charles L. Bragaw, *Achievement in Radio: Seventy Years of Radio Science, Technology, Standards, and Measurement at the National Bureau of Standards* (Boulder, Colo.: National Bureau of Standards, October 1996).

Strull, Gene, *Electronic Enterprise: Stories from the History of Westinghouse Electronic Systems*, Westinghouse Electronic Systems Division, February 29, 1996, Historical Electronics Museum library.

Unsigned, "The Bendix Radio Story," *Baltimore*, March 1963.

Unsigned, "Short History of Bendix Radio," Baltimore Museum of Industry website thebmi.org, viewed Aug.1, 2002.

Westinghouse Corporation, *Westinghouse in World War 2, Radio and X-Ray Divisions* (3 vol.s), October 1946, Historical Electronics Museum library.

Winkler, David F., *Searching the Skies: The Legacy of the United States Cold War Defense Radar Program* (USAF Air Combat Command, 1997).

Young, D. C., "Airways Lighting," a paper presented to the Convention of the Illuminating Engineering Society, Pittsburg, Pa., October, 1931, Federal Aviation Administration history files.

AIRPLANE PIONEERS BEFORE 1914

Baltimore Aviation Company, Official Program of the Baltimore Aviation Meet, November 2d to 8th, 1910, Maryland Historical Society files

Crouch, Tom D., *The Bishop's Boys: A Life of Wilbur and Orville Wright*, (New York: W. W. Norton & Co., 1989).

Elvers, Charles F., "I Remember When I Built Maryland's First Plane," Baltimore *Sun*, Jun. 25, 1954.

Elvers, Charles F., "Early Aviation in Maryland," an album compiled by the Enoch Pratt Free Library, with pictures presented by Elvers in 1936.

Lanman, Barry, "The Baltimore Air Show, 1910," script for a video presentation, 1980.

Reilly, Thomas, *Jannus, An American Flier* (Gainesville, Fla.: University Press of Florida, 1997).

Vaeth, J. Gordon, *Langley: Man of Science and Flight* (New York: The Ronald Press Company, 1966).

Unsigned, album of clippings from Baltimore newspapers, June 1 – Nov.7, 1910, concerning the Baltimore Aviation Meet at Halethorpe, collection of Barry Lanman.

Unsigned letter and illustration dated Baltimore, Aug.30, 1865, "A Natural Flying Machine," *Scientific American*, Vol. XIII (new series), No. 13, Sept 23, 1865, p. 195.

Unsigned, "Practical Aviation: Latham's Record Flight Over Baltimore," *The Book of the Royal Blue*, Baltimore and Ohio Railroad, Vol. XIV, No. 3, Dec.1910.

AIRPORT DIRECTORIES AND LISTINGS
Non-governmental Directories:

Aircraft Owners and Pilots Association, Frederick, Md. (originally Washington, D.C.), *AOPA Airport Directory* (title variants include *AOPA's Airports USA*, etc.), annual beginning in 1962.

Airport Directory Company, Hackensack, N.J., *Airports and Established Landing Fields in the United States*, issued c. 1933 to c.1940.

Decker Air Service, Inc., Fairfield, Conn., *Decker's Airport Guide, Zone Five, South Atlantic*, annual, 1946 and 1947 issues.

Haire Publishing Co., New York, N.Y., *The Airport Directory*, annual, 1945-1948.

J. E. Greiner Co., Baltimore, Md., "Maryland Airports," report submitted to Red Star Coaches, Inc., Salisbury, Md., September 21, 1945, Enoch Pratt Free Library.

Manufacturers Aircraft Association (1919-1921), Aeronautical Chamber of Commerce of America (1922-45), *Aircraft Year Book*, annual.

Federal and State Directories:

Civil Aeronautics Administration, *Directory of Airports (Within the Continental United States)*, Civil Aeronautics Bulletin No. 11, Washington: Government Printing Office, May 1, 1941.

Department of Commerce, Aeronautics Branch, Airway Bulletin No. 588 (revised), Hagerstown Airport, Oct. 6, 1930, Enoch Pratt Library vertical file.

Department of Commerce, Aeronautics Branch, Airway Bulletin No. 2, *Descriptions of Airports and Landing Field in the United States*, 1931-1934, 1936-1938.

Freeman, Paul, Abandoned and Little-Known Airfields website: .com/airfields_freeman/index.htm, revised October 17, 2002.

Maryland State Aviation Commission, *Directory of Licensed Commercial Airports*, (title varies); March 6, 1947; Jun. 28, 1947, revised Nov.17, 1947; Jun. 4, 1948; Jul. 1949; Jun. 1, 1950; Nov.9, 1960; 1962; and 1966.

Maryland State Aviation Administration, *Maryland Airport Directory* (title varies slightly); 1970-71, with a transmittal note to Pratt Library dated Jan.5, 1971;1972 (revision date); 1974; April 28, 1981; Oct.1996; 1999; Sept 2001.

Maryland State Aviation Administration, *Maryland Airport Directory*, n.d., c. 1985.

U.S. Army, Office of the Chief of Air Service, Aeronautical Bulletins:

Apr.15, 1923, No. 7 (no series given), Md., Baltimore, Logan Field

May 1, 1923, No. 16, State Series, Md., Aberdeen, Aberdeen Proving Ground

Sep.15, 1923, No. 63, State Series, Md., Cumberland, Government Field

Sep.15, 1923, No. 5, Route Information Series, Washington, DC, to Philadelphia, PA

Dec.1, 1923, No. 95, State Series, Md., Hagerstown, Emergency [sic.]

Jan.2, 1924, No. 122, State Series, Md., Hagerstown, Emergency Field No. 4

Jan.15, 1924, State Series, No. 131, Md., Chesapeake City Emergency Field

Jan.15, 1924, State Series, No. 132, Md., Elk Mills, Emergency Field

Feb.15, 1924, No. 160, State Series, Landing Facilities in Maryland

May 1, 1925, No. 19, State Summaries Series, Landing Facilities in Maryland

Dec.28, 1925, No. 383, State Series, Md., Md. Shore of Potomac. . ., Emergency Field

Apr.10, 1926, No. 450, State Series.

AIRPORTS, GENERAL

Arend, Geoffrey, *Great Airports Worldwide* (New York: Air Cargo Books, 1988).

Ginsberg, Steven, and Jessie Mangaliman, "Trying to Land Economic Growth; Outlying Areas Expand Airports," *Washington Post*, September 12, 1999.

Jacobson, Joan, "Unregulated Airports Posing Problems," Baltimore *Evening Sun*, December 30, 1974.

Lanman, Barry, oral history interview with Bruce Mundie, Dec.19, 2002.

O'Brien, Dennis, "Airports in Md. Face Hard Times," Baltimore *Sun*, Dec.28, 1987.

Runkel, David, "Increasing Number of Pilots Using Fewer Airfields," Baltimore *Evening Sun*, Jul. 18, 1967.

Thiessen, Karin, "Airports in Prince George's County: Past and Present," unpublished paper, 1996, Maryland Aviation Administration files.

Unsigned, "34 Airports Now in State, Baltimore *Sun*, Sep.2, 1948.

Unsigned, "2 More Shore Airports Close," Baltimore *Evening Sun*, May 28, 1952.

Unsigned, "Washington Executive/Hyde Field Opens at Last," *EAA News*, eaa.org, Sept 27, 2002.

Welling, William, "State Legislative Moves on Flying Matters Few," Baltimore *Sun*, Jan.13, 1954.

Welling, William, "Business Flying Grows, Airports Shut Down," Baltimore *Evening Sun*, March 1, 1954.

Wilbur Smith Associates, at. al., Maryland Airport Economic Impact Study, prepared for Maryland Aviation Administration, April 1997.

AIRPORTS, SPECIFIC

Baltimore:

Davis, Clayton, "Logan Field, Baltimore's First Municipal Airport," 1997, posted on geocities.com.

Galbraith, Kathleen L., "Trends at BWI Since Deregulation," State Aviation Administration, Office of Marketing, Jun. 1984.

Gault, H. Lelcey, "The Air Circuses of the 1930s," Baltimore *Sunday Sun Magazine*, Feb.22, 1959.

Maryland Aviation Administration, "BWI Timeline," bwiairport.com, viewed Jul. 11, 2003.

May, Robert, "Logan Field," in *Dundalk Then and Now, 1894-1980* (Dundalk: Dundalk-Patapsco Neck Historical Society, c. 1980).

Pfrommer, Christopher, "Habor Field Ending Up as Marine Terminal," Baltimore *Evening Sun*, Dec.30, 1960.

Rasmussen, Fred, "Flights of Fancy during the Depression," (re Curtiss-Wright Airport), Baltimore *Sun*, Jan.18, 1998.

Shifria, Carole, "BWI Airport at 30: Where It's Been and Where It's Going," *Washington Post*, Jun. 23, 1980.

Unsigned, "Baltimore Dedicates $15,000,000 Friendship Airport," *Construction*, Vol. 17, No. 7, Jul. 1950.

Unsigned, "Saga of Logan Field, Once Called Finest Airport on the East Coast," Baltimore *Evening Sun*, Dec.28, 1948.

Welsh, Paul E., "Harbor Field Handles Nearly as Many Planes as Friendship," Baltimore *Sun*, October 8, 1953.

College Park:

Allen, Catherine W., unpublished history of College Park Airport, undated, College Park Aviation Museum files.

Beatty, Ken, *The Cradle of Aviation: The National Aviation Field, College Park, Maryland.* (Hagerstown Bookbinding and Printing, 1973).

Glines, C.V., "Eighty Years at College Park," *Air Force Magazine*, Jan.1990.

Lynd, William F., "The Army Flying School at College Park," *Maryland Historical Magazine*, Vol. 48 (1953), pp. 227-41.

Monroe, Benjamin, "The History of the Aviation Field at College Park since 1918," Jan.5, 1929, Records of Phi Mu Fraternity, University of Maryland Libraries.

Van Allen, Ralph C., "The History of the Aviation Field at College Park," 1928, Records of Phi Mu Fraternity, University of Maryland Libraries.

Shaver, Katherine, "College Park Airport Almost Grounded," *Washington Post*, Sep 10, 2002

Easton:

Mills, Eric J., "50th Anniversary: Taking Flight at Easton Airport," Easton *Star Democrat (Sunday Star)*, Jul. 25, 1993.

Goad, Meredith, "Bill Newnam's High-Flying Days Remembered," Easton *Star Democrat (Sunday Star)*, Jul. 25, 1993 (reprinted from Jan.12, 1988).

Fort Meade:

Davis, Clayton, "Tipton Airport," report sent to Bruce Mundie, Jul. 1, 2000, Maryland Airport Administration files.

Frederick:

Norsworthy, L. Paul, "Frederick Municipal Airport Aviation Museum and Airport Facility," thesis submitted for the degree of Master of Architecture, University of Maryland, 1998 (Hornbake Library, Maryland Room).

Rowe, Joshua Wilson, "Detrick Field in the Thirties," Baltimore *Sun*, Jul. 8, 1978.

Unsigned, "Discover Your Airport: Celebrating 50 Years, 1949-1999," Frederick *News Post* special section, Jun. 3, 1999.

"Kentmorr Airpark," brochure c. 1950s, Enoch Pratt Library vertical file.

Hagerstown:

Mitchell, Kent A., "The Hagerstown Airport," unpublished paper, Maryland Aviation Administration files.

Mitchell, Kent A., "The Hagerstown Airport," *American Aviation Historical Society Journal*, Vol. 48, No. 3 (Fall 2003), pp. 215-29.

Mexico Farms:

Dolly, James H. and Martha R., "Lily Pad on a Pond: The Golden Days of Aviation at Mexico Farms Airport," National Air and Space Museum library file.

Prince George's County:

"Schrom Airport," undated and unsigned information sheet, College Park Aviation Museum files.

Westminster:

Mary Gail Hare, "Airport Operators Face Battle for Control," Baltimore *Sun*, Sept 29, 2002.

Sullivan, Norman P., "Baltimore Squadron of CAP Opens Westminster Airport," Baltimore *Sun*, Jun. 7, 1943.

BALLOONS AND AIRSHIPS

Alphonso, A. M., "Celebration Planned in City to Mark Forgotten Flight," Baltimore *Sun*, Jul. 29, 1934.

Benjamin, Michele, "Camp Holabird Witnesses Explosion of Navy Dirigible," DundalkEagle.com, viewed Aug.21, 2002.

Block, Eugene B., *Above the Civil War: The Story of Thaddeus Lowe, Balloonist, Inventor, Railway Builder* (Berkeley, Calif.: Howell – North Books, 1966).

Brune, Herbert M., Jr., "I Remember When We Almost Got a Zeppelin Base," Baltimore *Sun*, Oct.11, 1953.

Crouch, Tom D., *The Eagle Aloft: Two Centuries of the Balloon in America* (Washington: Smithsonian Institution Press, 1983).

Gipe, George, "An Afternoon's Diversion in the Good Old Days," *The Sun Magazine*, Baltimore, Oct.14, 1973.

Hill, Raymond D., "The Search for Peter Carnes," *Richmond County History*, 1978, Vol. 10, No. 2, pp. 5-10.

Haydon, Frederick Stansbury, *Aeronautics in the Union and Confederate Armies, With a Survey of Aeronautics Prior to 1861* (Baltimore: The Johns Hopkins University Press, 1941). This book was published as Vol. 1, but no second volume followed.

Jackson, Donald Dale, *The Aeronauts* (Alexandria, Va.: Time-Life Books, 1980).

Jones, Carleton, "Birdwoman of Baltimore, " Baltimore *Sun*, April 19, 1987 (copied)

Layman, Richard D., *Before the Aircraft Carrier: Development of Aircraft Vessels, 1849-1922* (1989).

Layman, Richard D., *To Ascend from a Floating Base: Shipboard Aeronautics and Aviation, 1783-1914* (Cranberry, N.J.: Associated University Presses, 1979).

Mitton, John H., "The History and Construction of the George Washington House," April 28, 1930, records of Phi Mu Fraternity, University of Maryland at College Park Libraries.

Soderberg, Susan Cooke, *A Guide to Civil War Sites in Maryland* (Shippensburg, Pa.: White Mane Books, 1998).

Unsigned, "Big Navy Dirigible Explodes at Holabird," Baltimore *Evening Sun*, Jul. 1, 1919

Unsigned, "J. H. Pennington's Steam Balloon, 1842," petitions to Congress by John H. Pennington, reprinted for the collection of the Maryland Historical Society, *Maryland Historical Magazine*, Vol. V, 1910, pp. 134-139.

GENERAL WORKS ON AVIATION HISTORY

Bilstein, Roger E., *Flight in America: From the Wrights to the Astronauts* (Baltimore: Johns Hopkins Univ. Press, revised edition, 1994).

Corn, Joseph J, *The Winged Gospel: America's Romance with Aviation, 1900-1950* (New York: Oxford Press, 1983).

Josephy, Alvin M., ed., *The American Heritage History of Flight* (American Heritage Publishing Co., 1962).

Komons, Nick A., *Bonfires to Beacons: Federal Civil Aviation*

Policy under the Air Commerce Act, 1926-1938 (Washington: Federal Aviation Administration, 1978).

Preston, Edmund, ed., *FAA Historical Chronology: Civil Aviation and the Federal Government, 1926 –1996* (Washington: Department of Transportation, 1998).

HELICOPTERS AND ROTORCRAFT

Boyne, Walter J., and Donald S. Lopez, ed.s, *Vertical Flight: The Age of the Helicopter* (Washington: Smithsonian Institution Press, 1984).

Conner, R.D., ed., "Berliner No. 5," National Air and Space Museum document at .si..edu, revised 11/19/01.

Gablehouse, Charles, *Helicopters and Autogiros: A History of Rotating-wing and V/STOL Aviation* (New York: J. B. Lippincott Company, revised edition, 1969).

Hubler, Richard G., *Straight Up: The Story of Vertical Flight* (New York: Duell, Sloan and Pearce, 1961).

Jackson, Robert, *The Dragonflies: The Story of Helicopters and Autogiros* (London: Arthur Barker, Ltd., 1971).

Young, Warren R., *The Helicopters* (Alexandria, Va.: Time-Life Books, 1982).

MARYLAND HISTORY, GENERAL

Brugger, Robert J., *Maryland: A Middle Temperament, 1634-1980* (Baltimore: Johns Hopkins University Press, 1988).

Brune, Herbert M., Jr., "The Air Law of Maryland," Baltimore *Evening Sun*, April 3, 1928.

Callcott, George H., *Maryland and America, 1940 to 1980* (Baltimore: Johns Hopkins University Press, 1985).

Graham, Stirling, *You Will Find It in Maryland* (Baltimore: Records & Goldsborough, Inc., 1945).

Joynes, J. William, "Maryland's Role in Aviation," *Baltimore American*, Nov.15, 1953.

Kelly, Howard A., Jr., "I Remember a Flyer's Life in the Twenties," Baltimore *Sun*, Sept 7, 1952.

Maryland Department of Natural Resources, "Population of Maryland's Jurisdictions, 1790 – 2000," dnrweb.dnr.state.md.us, viewed Jul. 8, 2003

McBee, Avery, "Wings over Maryland," *The Maryland Spectator*, Vol. 2, May 1936, pp. 23-30, 54, 69-72.

Meyer, Eugene L., *Maryland Lost and Found . . . Again* (Baltimore: Woodholme House Publishers, 2000).

Murdock, Rea, "Maryland Pacemaker as Aviation Pioneer," Baltimore *News American*, April 3, 1966.

Scott, John F. R., Jr., *Voyages into Airy Regions* (Annapolis: Ann Arundell County Historical Society and Fishergate Publishing Co., 1984).

Unsigned, "Aviation Gains in Md. in 1946 Set record," Baltimore *Evening Sun*, Dec.28, 1946

MARYLAND HISTORY, COUNTY AND LOCAL

Allegany County:

Poling, Bob, and Bill Armstrong, *Wings over Cumberland: An Aviation History* (Cumberland: Commercial Press, 2002).

Stegmaier, Harry I, Jr., et al., *Allegany County: A History* (Parsons, W.Va.: Mcclain Printing Co., 1976).

Anne Arundel County:

Bradford, James C., *Anne Arundel County, Maryland: A Bicentennial History, 1649-1977* (Annapolis: Anne Arundel County and Annapolis Bicentennial Committee, 1977).

Himmelheber, John, *Glen Burnie: A Pictorial History, 1888-1988* (Northern Anne Arundel Chamber of Commerce, c. 1988).

Kelly, Jacques, *Anne Arundel County: A Pictorial History* (Norfolk, Va.: The Donning Compnay, Publshers, 1989).

Baltimore City and County:

Baltimore Association of Commerce, "Aviation in Baltimore," pamphlet, early 1930s, Pratt Library

Brooks, Neal A. and Eric G. Rockel, *A History of Baltimore County* (Towson, Md.: Friends of the Towson Library, Inc., 1979).

Cover, Patricia Root, "Baltimore's Air Transportation Problem: A Case Study in Intergovernmental Administrative Relations in the Field of Aviation," Master of Arts thesis, Johns Hopkins University, 1970.

Clapp, R.B., "Gas and Electricity Used in Conquering the Air, *The Baltimore Gas and Electric News*, Nov.1914

Gault, H. Kelcey, "I Remember the Fun of Flying with the Thunderbirds," Baltimore *Sun*, Jan.12, 1964.

McKeldin, Theodore Roosevelt, "Making Baltimore a Center for the Airplane Industry," published transcript of a radio address, Nov.6, (1931?), Enoch Pratt Library vertical files.

O'Brien, James H., "I Remember Baltimore's World War I Fliers," Baltimore *Sun*, Nov.11, 1956.

Olson, Sherry H., *Baltimore: The Building of an American City* (Baltimore: The Johns Hopkins university Press, 1980.

Owens, Gwinn, "Early Aviation in Baltimore: A Personal Journey," Baltimore *Evening Sun*, Jun. 2, 1983.

Unsigned, "Baltimore's Singular Tribute to Lindbergh's Flight," *Maryland Gazette*, Vol. CCI, Sep.19, 1927, p. 107.

Unsigned, "The Story of Aviation in Baltimore," *Baltimore*, Nov.1941, pp. 31-39.

Kent County:

Usilton, Fred G., *History of Kent County, Maryland* (Chestertown: Perry, c 1980),

Montgomery County:

Gaithersburg, City of, no author cited, *Gaithersburg – The Heart of Montgomery County*, 1978.

Offutt, William M., *Bethesda: A Social History of the Area through World War II* (Bethesda: McNaughton and Gwinn, 1995).

Offutt, William M., "Miracle in Bethesda," *Montgomery County Story*, Vol. 38, No. 2, May 1995.

Prince George's County:

Williamson, Mary Lou, ed., *Greenbelt: History of a New Town, 1937-1987* (Virginia Beach; The Donning Co., 1987).

Talbot County:

Jopp, Mianna, "Profile: Malcolm Hatthaway [sic.]," Easton *Star Democrat*, Feb.23, 1972.

Maryland Airlines, "Maryland Airlines Recalls Shore Flying," Sept 23, 1947, typescript summary of remarks by Thomas B. Bourne, Talbot County Free Library.

Norton, Thomas F., transcript of untitled lecture at the Historical Society of Talbot County, Oct.2002.

Preston, Dickson J., *Talbot County: A History* (Centreville, Md.: Tidewater Publishers, 1983).

Wicomico County:

Jacobs, John E., Jr., *Salisbury and Wicomico County: A Pictorial History* (Virginia Beach, Va.: Donning Co. Publishers).

Truitt, Charles J., *Historic Salisbury Updated, 1662-1982* (Salisbury: Historical Books, Inc., 1982).

Washington County:

Avery, Richard H., III, *Wings Over Hagerstown* (Hagerstown, 1939)

Worcester County:

Hurley, George M., and Susan B., *Ocean City: A Pictorial History* (Virginia Beach, Va.: Donning Co. Publishers, 1979)

MARYLAND HISTORICAL TRUST SITE FILES

Allegany County:

AL-III-A-153: Mexico Farms Airport.

Anne Arundel County:

AA-30: Baltimore/Washington Airport Hangar No. 1

AA-38: Annapolis-Bay Bridge Nike Missile Site W-26

AA-359: U.S. Naval Academy (primarily non-aviation in focus)

AA-993: Davidsonville Nike Missile Battery W-25 Housing Area

AA-2127, AA-2188 through 2193: Naval Radio Transmitter Facility, Annapolis (adjacent to Greenbury Point aviation sites.)

AA-2176: U.S. Naval Engineering Experiment Station, Annapolis, housing

AA-2179: U.S. Naval Engineering Experiment Station, Annapolis

Baltimore City and County:

Field & Research Reports FRR BaCo5: Historical & Architectural Resources of Middle River

Field & Research Reports FRRBaCo5: NR Nomination Forms: Aero Acres Shopping Center, Glenn L. Martin Plant No. 1, Mars Estates, Pierce-Cemesto Houses, Victory Villa Community Building

BA-149: Baltimore Municipal Airport (Harbor Field) Aviation Context Report, Jun. 2000: includes discussion of the history of other airports in the area.

BA-2094/ B-3603: Baltimore Municipal Airport (Harbor Field): combined report

BA-2081: Glenn L. Martin Airport and Plant

BA-2824: Glenn L. Martin Co. Plant No. 2

BA-3152 Glenn L. Martin Co. Plant No. 1

Charles County:

CH-371: Indian Head Naval Surface Warfare Center

CH-597: Maryland Airport

CH-676: Nike Missile Site W-54, Pomonkey

CH-677: Nike Missile Site W-44, Mattawoman/Waldorf/La Plata

Frederick County:

F-3-86: Stevens Airport

F-3-161: Fort Detrick

Harford County:

HA-1959: Aberdeen Proving Ground, Trench Warfare Range

HA-1995: Nike Missile Site BA-18/BA-14, Edgewood Arsenal, Aberdeen Proving Ground

Montgomery County:

M: 26-21-6: Congressional Airport

M: 29-47, David Taylor Model Basin

M: 29-52, Naval Surface Warfare Center, Carderock (specific buildings)

M: 29-54, Subsonic Wind Tunnel Complex, Naval Surface Warfare Center, Carderock

M: 33-25, Naval Ordnance Laboratory, White Oak

Prince George's County:

HSR Ch 9: Harry Diamond Laboratories, Adelphi, Md., including Blossom Point Field Test Facility in Charles County

PG-66-4: College Park Airport

PG-64-6: Goddard Space Flight Magnetic Test Facility

PG-68-22: Engineering Research Corporation (ERCO)

PG-69-2, George Washington House (Indian Maid Tavern)

PG-77-19, 40, 41, and others: Andrews Air Force Base.

PG-85B-13, Brandywine Receiver Station, Andrews Air Force Base

PG-86B-26: Nike Missile Site W-36, Croom

St. Marys County:

SM-357: Naval Air Station Patuxent River (specific buildings)

SM-490: Lexington Park Survey District

SM-894: Naval Air Station St. Inigoes, Webster Field

Washington County:

WA-HAG-179: Moller Organ Works (used for wartime aviation manufacture)

WA-HAG-213: Fairchild Engine and Airplane Corporation

Wicomico County:

WI-541: Salisbury-Ocean City Wicomico Regional Airport Survey District

MILITARY AVIATION, GENERAL

Baker, Raymond D., *Historical Highlights of Andrews Air Force Base, 1942 – 1989* (Andrews AFB, Md.: Office of History, 1776th Air Base Wing, 1990).

Balkoski, Jospeh M., *The Maryland National Guard: A History of Maryland's Military Forces, 1634-1991* (Baltimore: Maryland National Guard, State of Maryland Military Department, 1991).

C. F. Boone Nationwide Publications, Inc., "Washington Salutes Andrews AFB," undated pamphlet, University of Maryland, Maryland Room vertical file.

Chandler, Charles deForest, and Frank P. Lahm, *How Our Army Grew Wings: Airmen and Aircraft Before 1914* (New York: The Ronald Press Co., 1943)

Cole, Merle T., "W-25: The Davidsonville Site and Maryland Air Defense, 1950-1974," *Maryland Historical Magazine*, Vol. 80, No. 3, Fall 1985.

Cole, Merle T., "The One That Got Away," *Anne Arundel County History News*, Vol. 32, Jan.2001.

Covert, Norman M., *Cutting Edge: A History of Fort Detrick, Maryland, 1943-1993* (Headquarters, U.S. Army Garrison, Fort Detrick, Md.,1993).

Cooke, James J., *The U.S. Air Service in the Great War, 1917-1919* (Westport, Conn.:Praeger, 1996).

Dorr, Robert F., *Air Force One*, (St. Paul, Minn.: MBI Publishing Co., 2000).

Graham, Bradley, "For Patrol Pilots, A Nightmare Scenario," Sept 29, 2001, *Washington Post*.

Hennessy, Juliette A, *The United States Army Air Arm, April 1861 to April 1917* (Washington: Office of Air Force history, new imprint, 1985, originally published 1958).

Hueley, Alfred F., and William C. Heimdahl, "The Roots of U.S. Military Aviation," in Bernard C. Nalty, ed., *Winged Shield, Winged Sword: A History of the United States Air Force*, Vol. 1, (Washington: USAF, 1997).

Maryland Air National Guard, *The Maryland Air National Guard: A Commemorative History, 1921-2000* (Charlotte, N.C.: Fine Books Publishing Co., 2000).

Maurer, Maurice, *Aviation in the U.S. Army, 1919-1939* (Washington: Office of Air Force history, 1987).

Meckel, Edward G., "I Remember the Birth of the First Air Guard Unit," *Sunday Sun Magazine*, Dec.6, 1964.

Rogers, Michael H., ed., *Answering Their Country's Call: Marylanders in World War II* (Baltimore: Johns Hopkins University Press, 2002).

Smart, Jeffrey K. "History of the U.S. Army Soldier and Biological Chemical Command," printed from the Command's website sbccom.army.mil, Mar 13, 2003.

Sterling, Keir, "Aberdeen Proving Ground: The Early Years," *Harford Historical Bulletin*, No. 49 (Summer 1991), pp. 55-75.

Mueller, Robert, *Air Forces Bases*, Vol. 1, Active Air Force Bases . . . 1982 (Washington: Office of Air Force History, USAF, 1989).

Tilman, Stephen F., *Man Unafraid* (Washington: Army Times Publishing Co., 1958).

Weston, Leonard, "Early Testing Takes to Skies," *APG News*, Aug.15, 1990.

MILITARY AVIATION, NAVAL

Carlisle, Rodney P., *Where the Fleet Begins: A History of the David Taylor Research Center, 1898-1998* (Washington: Navy Historical Center, 1998).

Coletta, Paolo E., ed., *United States Navy and Marine Corps Bases, Domestic* (Westport, Conn.: Greenwood Press, 1985).

Deputy Chief of Naval Operations (Air) and Naval Air Systems Command, *United States Naval Aviation*, 1910-1970, NAVAIR 00-80P-1 (Washington, 1970).

Drew, Linda, *The History of Naval Air Station, Patuxent River, Maryland* (U.S. Navy, Naval Air System Command, c. 1999).

Fritz, Donald T., "Bill Moore and the Last Enemy Plane," *Maryland Historical Magazine*, Vol. 90, No. 4 (Winter 1995), pp. 489-493.

Jenkins, Colleen, "Longtime Navy Career Is Business Success Story," *Washington Post*, Oct.20, 2002.

Hertel, Frank M., "The Naval Academy and Naval Aviation," *U.S. Naval Institute Proceedings*, Vol. 74, No. 1 (Jan.1948).

Howe, David P., "Investigation of U.S. Navy PBM-3 Bureau of Aeronautics Number 6672, Choptank River, Maryland," *Maryland Archeology*, Vol. 26, No. 2, pp. 20-30, Sept. 2000.

Knott, Richard C., *A Heritage of Wings: An Illustrated History of Navy Aviation* (Annapolis, Naval Institute Press, 1997).

Miller, H. B., "Shooting the Catapult," *U.S. Naval Institute Proceedings*, Vol. 59, No. 4 (April 1933).

Murch, Robert W., "N.A.S. Annapolis," *U.S. Naval Institute Proceedings*, Vol. 77, No. 10 (Oct.1951).

Naval Air Station Patuxent River and Jefferson Patterson Park and Museum, "Life at Cedar Point: A Cultural and Natural History Tour of Naval Air Station Patuxent River, Maryland," undated pamphlet.

Naval Air Warfare Center Aircraft Division, "Patuxent River Facilities," pamphlet c. 1994.

Ray, Thomas W., "The First Year of United States Naval Aviation," Master of Arts thesis, American University, Washington, D.C., 1959.

Ray, Thomas W., "Annapolis: The Navy's First Aerodrome," *U.S. Naval Institute Proceedings*, Vol. 97, No. 19 (Oct.1971).

Ray, Thomas W., "First Year of Naval Aviation," *American Aviation Historical Society Journal*, Vol. 12, No. 3 (Fall, 1967), pp. 198-214.

Stevenson, Jack, "Academy Aviation Training in Forty-Sixth Year," *The Log*, Mar 28, 1972, p. 34

Sweetman, Jack, and Thomas J. Cutler, *The U.S. Naval Academy: An Illustrated History* (Annapolis: Naval Institute Press, second edition, 1995).

Turnbull, Archibald P., and Clifford L. Lord, *History of the United States Naval Aviation* (New Haven: Yale University Press, 1949)

Unsigned, "The David Taylor Model Basin," *U.S. Naval Institute Proceedings*, Vol. 89, No. 3 (March 1963), pp. 88-103

Unsigned, "'Pax River': The Naval Air Test Center," *U.S. Naval Institute Proceedings*, Vol. 95 (Dec.1969), pp. 93-106.

Unsigned, "Severn River Naval Complex," globalsecurity.org, viewed Nov. 6, 2002.

Unsigned, "Webster Field Annex," globalsecurity.org, viewed Nov.11, 2002.

U.S. Navy, Bureau of Yards and Docks, *Building the Navy's Bases in World War II: History of the Bureau of Yards and Docks and the Civil Engineer Corps, 1940-46*, Vol. 1 (Washington: GPO, 1947).

Van Deurs, George, *Wings for the Fleet: A Narrative of Naval Aviation's Early Development, 1910-1916* (Annapolis: U.S. Naval Institute, 1966).

Wheeler, Gerald E., "Naval Aviation's First Year," *U.S. Naval Institute Proceedings*, Vol. 87, No. 5 (May 1961), pp. 88-95.

RACING

Barker, Ralph, *The Schneider Trophy Races* (Shrewsbury, England: Airlife Publishers, Ltd., 1971).

Foxworth, Thomas G., *The Speed Seekers* (New York: Doubleday & Company, 1974).

North Point State Park history page, homestead.com/north-pointstatepark, viewed Mar.23, 2002.

Vogeler, Edward Jerome, "Thirty Minutes Over Baltimore with Doolittle," *Maryland Living*, May 10, 1970.

ROCKETRY AND SPACE FLIGHT

Anspacher, William B., et al., *The Legacy of White Oak Laboratory* (Naval Surface Warfare Center, Dahlgren, Va., 2000).

Ballistics Research Laboratories, Aberdeen Proving Ground, Md., "The High-Speed Flexible-Throat Supersonic Wind Tunnel," pamphlet, undated, c. 1948, University of Maryland, Maryland Room vertical file.

Barr, Larine, et al., "Indian Head History, 1890-1997," and other information from www.ih.navy.mil, viewed November 2002.

Burrows, William E., *This New Ocean: The Story of the First Space Age* (New York: Random House, 1998).

Carlisle, Rodney, *Powder and Propellants: Energetic Materials at Indian Head, Maryland, 1890-1990* (Publication data not stated in volume, but presumably Washington: U.S. Navy, c. 1990).

Lehman, Milton, *This High Man: The Life of Robert H. Goddard* (New York: Farrar, Straus and Company, 1963).

McCurdy, Hugh E., *Inside NASA: High Technology and Organizational Change in the U.S. Space Program* (Baltimore: The Johns Hopkins University Press, 1993).

Morgan, Mark L., and Mark A. Berhow, *Rings of Supersonic Steel: Air Defenses of the United States Army, 1950-1979, An Introductory History and Site Guide* (Bodega Bay, Calif.: Fort MacArthur Military Press, 2nd edition, 2002).

National Aeronautics and Space Administration, "The History of the Hubble Space Telescope," quest.arc.nasa.gov, viewed Aug.21, 2001.

Newell, Homer G., *Beyond the Atmosphere: Early Years of Space Science* (Washington: National Aeronautics and Space Administration, 1980).

Robinson, Ralph, "The Use of Rockets by the British in the War of 1812," *Maryland Historical Magazine*, Vol. XL, No. 1 (March 1945), pp. 1-6.

Rosenthal, Alfred, *Venture into Space: Early Years of Goddard Space Flight Center* (Washington: NASA, 1968) NASA SP-4301.

Smaldone, Joseph P., *History of the White Oak Laboratory, 1945-1975* (Naval Surface Weapons Center, White Oak, Silver Spring, Md., 1977).

Von Braun, Wernher, and Frederick I. Ordway III, *History of Rocketry and Space Travel* (New York: Thomas Y. Crowell Company, revised edition, 1969).

Wallace, Lane E., *Dreams, Hopes, Realities: NASA Goddard Space Flight Center: The First Forty Years* (Washington: NASA History Office, 1999).

Winter, Frank W., *The First Golden Age of Rocketry* (Washington: Smithsonian Institution, 1990).

WOMEN AND MINORITIES IN AVIATION

Boykin, Sharahn D., "Taking Flight," *Gazette* (Prince George's Co., Md.), April 18, 2002.

Breihan, John R., "Wings of Democracy? African Americans in Baltimore's World War II Aviation Industry," *From Mobtown to Charm City: New Perspectives on Baltimore's Past*, ed. Jessica Elfenbein, John R. Breihan, Thomas L. Hollowak (Baltimore: Maryland Historical Society: 2002), pp. 172-97.

Cochrane, D., and P. Ramirez, "Bernetta Miller," National Air and Space Museum, nasm. si.edu, Dec.15, 1999.

Davis, Clayton, with Sandra Martin, "Croom, Maryland, Where Dreams Soared," *New Bay Times*, Feb.22-28, 1996.

Davis, Clayton, "Columbia Air Center, Croom, Maryland," unpublished typescript, Maryland Aviation Administration files.

Floyd, Bianca P., *Records & Recollections: Early Black History in Prince George's County, Maryland* (Maryland-National Capital Park and planning Commission, 1989).

Francis, Charles E., *The Tuskegee Airmen* (Boston: Branden Publishing Company, 3rd edition, 1993).

Hardesty, Von, and Dominick Pisano, *Black Wings: The American Black in Aviation* (Washington: Smithsonian Institution Press, 1983).

Holton, William, list of Tuskegee Airmen from Maryland, undated.

Lanman, Barry, oral history interview with Herbert Jones, Sept 19, 2002, draft transcription.

Scarborough, Katherine, "Flying Hutchinsons Fold Wings," Baltimore *Sun*, Oct.29, 1939.

Turner, Betty Stagg, *Out of the Blue and into History* (Arlington Heights, Ill.: Aviatrix Publishing, Inc., 2000).

MISCELLANEOUS PUBLICATIONS

Aeronautical Chamber of Commerce of America, *Aircraft Year Book*, 1920-22, and 1930.

Civil Aeronautics Authority, Civil Aeronautics Bulletin No. 4, State Aeronautical Legislation Digest and Uniform State Laws (revised to Jan.1, 1939), Oct.1, 1939.

Department of Commerce, Aeronautics Branch, *Domestic Air News*, No. 8, pp. 4-6.

Jane, Fred T., original ed., *Jane's All The World's Aircraft*, annual.

Maryland Department of Business and Economic Development, "Maryland's Economic Base," viewed June 12, 2003.

Maryland State Archives, "Department of Transportation, Historical Evolution," mdarchives.state.md.us, viewed May 19, 2002.

Moore, Scott, "Mr. Cool: Gus McLeod's North Pole Adventure, June 2, 2000, and "To the North Pole – and Back: Historic Plane Has Roundabout Trip to College Park Museum," Dec.29, 2000, *Washington Post*.

Presidential proclamation, July 13, 1919, announcing an end to the wartime licensing program, begun by an earlier proclamation of Feb.18, 1918, and attached list of those licensed under the program, Federal Aviation Administration history files.

St. James Press, *International Directory of Company Histories*, London, annual since 1988.

Strickland, Patricia, *The Putt-Putt Air Force: The Story of the Civilian Pilot Training Program and the War Training Service, 1939-1944* (Department of Transportation, Federal Aviation Administration).

Maryland Aviation History Resources

Note to readers: This survey describes an evolving body of resources, and much of the information given here is subject to change. The material is arranged into six categories: Civilian Federal Organizations, Military Organizations, State Organizations and Public Libraries, Other Libraries, Museums, County Historical Societies, and Miscellaneous.

CIVILIAN FEDERAL ORGANIZATIONS

Library of Congress, 101 Independence Ave., SE, Washington, DC 20540; 202-707-5000. The website, www.loc.gov, includes catalogues, links, and on-line documents. As the world's largest library, this institution naturally has much material relevant to Maryland aviation history. Due to its size, however, LOC can be a difficult research venue and is best used to find items unavailable elsewhere. Manuscript collections of individuals associated with Maryland aviation include papers of Henry H. "Hap" Arnold, Washington I. Chambers, Sherman M. Fairchild, Benjamin D. Foulois, the Wright Brothers, and Glenn L. Martin (whose LOC papers are described on the Martin Aviation Museum's website). The Library's ongoing Veterans History Project is a possible source for wartime narratives of Maryland aviators. The on-line catalogue of prints and photos includes about half of LOC's huge collection of images, many of which are digitized on-line. A preliminary search yielded examples of relevant material that included images relating to early aviator Hubert Latham and to the Fairchild and Martin companies. The Photographic Services Department offers reproduction for a fee. The large collection of the Motion Picture and Television section (Madison Bldg: 202-707-8572) has not been fully cataloged, but is searchable, mainly by title, in the on-line catalogues and other finding aids at the section's reading room.

National Aeronautics and Space Administration:

NASA History Office, 300 E St., NW, Mail Stop IQ, Washington, DC 20546; 202-358-0384; histinfo@hq.nasa.gov. The history office's website (http://history.nasa.gov) provides a range of on-line publications and information about the agency. Researchers may visit the office by appointment. Relevant records available there include about 2-3 feet of files on the Goddard center, containing such items as newsletters, press releases, photos, and manuscripts. The office also has files on the Maryland Alliance for Space Colonization and the Maryland Business Space Roundtable.

NASA Headquarters Library, 300 E St., NW, Room 1J20, Washington, DC 20546. Tel. 202-358-0168; references service provided. The collection includes publications by and about NASA, as well as about aerospace-related disciplines. The library's catalogue is accessible to the public only through terminals in the facility itself; however, its website, www.hq.nasa.gov/office/hqlibrary, offers links to NASA documents and to a variety of information sources. The website also links to the "NIX" search engine covering the agency's very large collection of digital images and photographs. A preliminary search confirmed that the collection includes Maryland-related items, such as photos of equipment at the Goddard facility. Video cassettes available at the library, listed by title, may possibly contain pertinent footage.

Goddard Space Flight Center (GSFC), Greenbelt, Md. 20771; 301-286-8955. The website, www.gsfc.nasa.gov provides an internal search engine, a biography of Robert H. Goddard, and data on the center's history. The GSFC library has a web-accessible catalogue; however, its historical holdings are limited to published material. The contact is the librarian and additional-duty historian (301-286-9161). Like all Federal facilities, GSFC transfers its historical records to a Federal Record Center, and some are eventually accessioned by the National Archives (Record Group 255). There is, however, no archive at the GSFC itself. The GSFC Editorial Office has a collection of relevant photographs (301-286-7976).

National Archives and Records Administration. Permanent government records generally reach the National Archives after a period in which they remain under the initiating agency's control in a Federal Records Center. The original Archives building is at 700 Pennsylvania Avenue, DC 2008, but more of the records relating to Maryland aviation are held by Archives II at 8601 Adelphi Rd., College Park, Md. 20740-6001 (customer service: 866-272-6272). Sections relating to both of these research centers are included on the website, www.nara.gov, which also provides links to Presidential libraries and other NARA facilities.

The website contains much information for researchers, including an Archival Record Catalogue (ARC) that covers about 13 percent of the records. The collection's vast size and complexity, however, makes it advisable to seek the help of archivists in locating records. Below are examples of Record Groups (RGs) containing relevant documents:

RG18 (Yokelson), Army Air Force, 1917-64; examples of material include Series II, Army Air Forces Central Decimal Files, 1917-18; Subseries 1 on airfields, with an alphabetical index that includes the Aberdeen Proving Ground; and Subseries 7, National Guard, which includes records on the Maryland ANG.

RG40 (Lewis), Commerce Department, includes general correspondence files with a large, indexed section on aviation (no. 8327); Defense Plant Corporation (World War II) records, with company-specific files; and War Production Board records.

RG71 (Smith), Bureau of Yards and Docks; includes Naval Property Case files, c. 1940-65, whose finding aid lists multiple Maryland facilities.

RG72 (Livingston for pre-1941, Smith for later era), Navy Bureau of Aeronautics, includes items on a board range of topics going back as far as early Naval aviation at Greenbury Point. (RG24 has also been cited for this subject.)

RG111, War Department, Office of the Chief Signal Officer, 1860-1982, source for such topics as the 1911 Army flight school at College Park.

RG167 (Ciarlante), Bureau of Standards; a possible source regarding the Bureau's technical development work at College Park.

RG168, National Guard Bureau, records include correspondence and a state file, 1941-49, containing items concerning Maryland.

RG181 (Smith), Records of Naval Districts and Shore Establishments, including: Naval Air Facilities, Annapolis, 1944-47; Naval Engineering Experimental Station, Annapolis, 1951-53; Naval Ordnance Station, Indian Head, 1907-25; and the Severn River Naval Command, 1944-50.

RG197 (Pfeiffer), Civil Aeronautics Board, a source regarding such issues as airline route decisions (1938-88) and accident investigation (1938-67); also includes records of FAA's earlier predecessors (1926-38), and of the Federal Aviation Commission (1934-35).

RG237 (Pfeiffer), Federal Aviation Administration (from 1958) and its more immediate predecessors (1938-58); examples of records include plans of airports built with WPA funds; airport designs, 1941-47; airport site files by state, 1941-43; airport specifications and charts, 1941-43; U.S. airway maps, 1926-38 (twelve items); plans and profiles of airways, showing fields and beacons, 1926-37; airport construction, 1935-37; and FAA records relating to airports.

RG 255 (Ciarlante), National Aeronautics and Space Administration, a possible source regarding the Goddard Space Flight Center and NASA contractors in Maryland.

For photographs, a prime source is the Still Picture Branch at Archives II (301-713-6625. Many thousands of images, about a third of which are in ARC on-line catalogue (an example: fabrication of aircraft at the Martin plant in 1943). Card files at the Branch index various agency collections. Among these, the U.S. Information Agency collections, 1948-81, include non-governmental subjects such as civil airports. Among the paper finding aids are: 18-WP, Aircraft 1903-59, listed by maker and type; a binder on the Air Force, pre-1959; a binder on the Army Signal Corps; and a finding aid for the Wright Brothers collection.

The Cartographic and Architectural Branch (301-713-6885) includes an aerial photo division has material not in the Still Pictures Branch. The aerials date c.1938-55, in addition to later satellite photos. The map division (301-837-1780) has relevant aeronautical charts.

Archives II also has a very large collection of moving images, about sixty-four percent of which are in the ARC catalogue (an example is "Wings for the Army," which includes footage on the Wright Brothers, the Martin B-10, etc.) The card index provides a description of each film. Call 301-837-1970 for examples of cards by topic, provided free of charge.

The NARA website facilities section links to the web pages of the **National Personnel Records Center**, 9700 Page Ave., St. Louis, MO 63132-5100 (314-538-4243). The web pages explain how to obtain the personnel records of deceased military personnel and Federal employees.

National Institute of Standards and Technology (NIST), 100 Bureau Drive, Gaithersburg, MD 20899-2500. **NIST Library's** section of the website, www.nist.gov, provides an on-line catalogue. The collection, mainly published materials, includes items on the history of technology and of NIST and its predecessors. The library itself is closed to the public, but permits interlibrary loan. The **NIST Museum** is also at Mail Stop 2500. The museum's section of the website describes the exhibits and offers on-line information. In addition to artifacts, the museum has an archive that includes subject files, biographical files, photographs, and employees' personal papers. This material contains items relevant to Maryland air/space history, due to NIST's work in these fields since its move to Gaithersburg, which began in 1955. Other pertinent topics include the National Bureau of Standards work at College Park. Researchers may contact Ms. Greenhouse concerning access.

National Park Service:

Fort McHenry National Monument, East Fort Ave., Baltimore MD 21230-5393. website: www.nps.gov/fomc. Tel: 410-922-4290, ext. 244. The site's collections include original artifacts, papers, and publications relating to the Congreve rockets used against the Fort in 1814.

National Register of Historic Places, National Park Service, 1201 Eye St., NW, 8th Floor, MS 2280, Washington, DC 20005; 202-354-2213/2210. The website, www.cr.nps.gov/nr, includes a data base that researchers may use to search for National Register properties by state, name, and location. As of mid-November 2002, however, the website states that the office in process of moving, and refers inquiries to the State Historic Preservation Officer.

Department of Transportation Library, Headquarters: Room 2200, 400 7th St,, SW, Washington, DC, 20590, Tel. 202-366-0745; Aviation Branch, Bldg. FOB10A (Federal Aviation Administration), Room 925, 800 Independence Ave., SW 20591, Tel. 202-267-3174. The website, http://dotlibrary.dot.gov, includes an on-line catalogue (however, some older material is not yet included.) It also offers digital collections of historical documents that include aircraft accident reports for most air carrier crashes, 1934-65. Most pertinent materials are concentrated at the Aviation Branch, which maintains books, periodicals, and government publications, both current and historical.

MILITARY ORGANIZATIONS

Aberdeen Proving Ground, Aberdeen, Md. 21005. Tel.: 410-306-1403. The website (www.apg.army.mil) includes two separate histories of APG, which has absorbed the formerly separate Edgewood Arsenal. Print-outs of these histories are in the project's place files. The library (410-278-3417) deals only with technical subjects and has no historical information on the site. There is no base historian.

The U.S. Army Ordnance Museum is located at APG, Bldg. 2601, Aberdeen Blvd. (410-278-3602). Its mission, however, is to interpret the history of Army ordnance in general, rather than of APG itself. The museum has only a small collection of records on the facility. The museum contributed copies of items that relate to the airfield and to the testing of aerial weapons. The original records on APG are part of NARA's Record Group 165 concerning the Ordnance Corps. For further research, the Ordnance Museum seems a possible source of information only on particular weapon systems identified as produced or deployed in Maryland.

Air Force Historical Research Agency (AFHRA), 600 Chennault Circle, Bldg. 1440, Maxwell AFB, AL 36112-6424 (334-953-2395). AFHRA's collection includes such items as unit histories, oral histories, and record cards on individual aircraft. Its scope is not limited to Air Force records, but embraces Army flying before the creation of the USAF as a separate service. The website, www.maxwell.af.mil/au/afhra, lists the holdings of personal papers and of numbered studies, and also offers a photo album that includes pictures of Wright aircraft up to 1913. An electronic mail form is provided for public inquiries concerning specific topics. Personnel at AFHRA respond to the messages by forwarding abstracts of documents that appear to relate to the inquiry. The researcher may then view the documents at the library, or purchase microfilm reels that contain them. A related resource at Maxwell is the Air University Library, whose website, www.au.af.mil/au/aul, offers an on-line catalogue and a link to the MERLN search engine for other military libraries.

Air Force History Support Office Library, 200 McChord St., Box 94, Bolling AFB, DC 20332-111. The website (www.airforcehistory.hq.af.mil) includes lists of publications, some of which are on line, and advice about researching Air Force history. The Office's collection is similar to, but smaller than, that of the Air Force Historical Research Agency (see above). The Office is open to the public by appointment, according to the website; however, the librarian reports that visits and inquiries by non-government researchers are not encouraged.

Andrews Air Force Base, Maryland 20331. There is an historian for the 89th Military Airlift Wing and for the base as a whole. The historian maintains approximately ten cabinets of records, consisting primarily of annual unit histories. The collection also includes about fifteen file drawers of photos and a few videotapes. Researchers may view this material by appointment. The website (www.andrews.af.mil) includes a base history.

Fort George G. Meade, Md. 20755. No historian is listed for the base, but the website, www.ftmeade.army.mil, includes a brief history. The site also links to that of the **Fort George G. Meade Museum** at 4674 Griffin Avenue on the base. Its web pages include information, photos, and articles relating to the Fort's role in air defense through artillery and missiles. A Nike Ajax and a Nike Hercules missile that were deployed at the base are among the outdoor exhibits. Although the museum's files contain no original records, there is a small collection of secondary material and photographs that may be viewed by appointment.

Maryland Air National Guard: The website, www.mang.ang.af.mil, includes no history or historical office. Public Affairs: 410-576-6179. A useful contact for this topic is the chief of **Air National Guard History**, NGB-PAH, Jefferson Plaza 1, Suite 11200, 1411 Jefferson Davis Hwy., Arlington. Va. 22202-3231; tel. 703-607-2668; fax 607-3686.

Naval Air Station Patuxent River, Md. 20670. Public Affairs: 301-757-1487. The base website, http://nas.nawcad.naut.mil provides a history of the facility; however, there is currently no historian for the base as a whole.

Closely related is the **Patuxent River Naval Air Museum**, POB 407, Patuxent River, Md 20670, www.paxmuseum.com, 301-863-7418. The museum is located temporarily near Gate No. 1 of the base whose history it interprets. Its website gives a brief description of the collections, which include more than 1,600 artifacts. Displayed outdoors are thirteen aircraft that were tested at Patuxent, and four others that represent types tested there. Indoor exhibits tell the story of the facility and its research, development, and testing activities. The archival holdings of more than 15,000 items include publications, documents, and personal papers, as well as a large number of slides, photos, and films.

Naval Historical Center, Washington Navy Yard, 805 Kidder Breese SE, Washington, DC 20324-5060. The website, www.history.navy.mil, provides a large selection of historical information and research aids that include a listing of sources on naval history in Maryland, D.C., and nationwide. Among the elements of the Center are the:

The **Navy Department Library** (202-433-4132), which has an on-line catalogue, possesses an extremely large collection of published material on naval history, as well as such resources as vertical files and a collection of manuscripts listed on-line.

The **Aviation History Branch** (202-433-4355), whose holdings include aviation command history reports since 1941, as well as information on aircraft types, individual aircraft, and accident summaries. The Branch's section of the website includes further information and publications, as well as a listing of records related to naval aviation at other repositories.

The **Operational Archives** (202-433-3224), which houses operational records of commands, including their shore facilities, and well as such other material as personal papers and oral histories. The Operational Archives will be closed for reorganization through the end of February 2003.

The **Photographic Section** (202-433-2765) which maintains images that are reproducible by patrons directly, or by order in accordance with instructions posted on the website. Although the Section has its own search engine, it frankly recommends the major commercial search engines as a more efficient key to its collections.

Researchers wishing to visit the Naval Historical Center should call the Library 24 hours in advance to arrange entry through security, and a separate appointment is also required for the other offices named above.

Naval Surface Warfare Center, Carderock Division, 9500 MacArthur Blvd., West Bethesda, Md. 20817-57000. The website, www.dt.navt.mil, includes a timeline of this facility, originally known as the David Taylor Model Basin, which has performed much aviation-related research. The Technical Information Center library is primarily a technical resource and is closed to the public; however, its holdings include bound volumes of correspondence of the Model Basin's early leaders, as well as a small collection of documents assembled to assist in preparing a published history of the facility. Researchers may contact the center at 301-227-1433 concerning access to this material.

U.S. Army Military History Institute, 22 Ashburn Drive, Carlisle, Pa. 17013-5008. The website, http://carlisle-www.army.mil/usamhi/index.html, provides email links for reference inquiries, which are not accepted by telephone. It also offers descriptions and finding aids for the collection, which includes published material, personal papers, and oral histories. The National Archives and Records Administration, however, maintains official records material such as unit histories. The Institute provides some documents on-line, and these are listed both alphabetically and chronologically. Another feature of the website is a series of reference bibliographies, which include listings

for several Maryland installations that have air/space associations. The map collection is searchable only at the Institute. The large photo collection is also basically usable only at the Institute, although a small sample is digitized on the website.

U.S. Naval Academy, Annapolis, Md. 21402-5029; switchboard, 410-293-1000. The principle resource at the Academy is the **Nimitz Library**, whose general collection is catalogued on the website, www.nadm.navy.mil. This catalogue also includes some of the newer items from the Special Collections and Archives Division (410-293-6922); however, the primary finding aid for this material is a card catalogue. The Special Collections contain items on various topics relevant to naval aviation, including vertical files and reference files. In particular, the Division maintains the National Archives' Record Group 405, Records of the USNA. Of special interest in RG 405 are the five-boxes of the Naval Air Facilities series from the Records of the Superintendent, General Correspondence, Support Facilities. The Division possesses over 10,000 photographs, most of which are reproduced as numbered digital images on disks, and some 8,000 additional images are available at other USNA departments. Finding aids for the photos include an alphabetical paper listing and a searchable database. The library will reproduce the photos for a fee. The library does not have known films or videotapes relevant to Maryland aviation. (Note: identifying Marylander USNA graduates through the library is impractical, since the state from which candidates are appointed does not necessarily reflect their actual residence.)

The Academy website links to that of **Naval Station Annapolis**, which provides an on-line unit history. No historian is listed for the station, but the public affairs number is 410-293-2291. Also accessible through the Academy website is the site of the **U.S. Naval Academy Museum**, (410-293-5220), while also offers its own institutional history on-line. The museum possesses artifacts of naval aviation, but the only items that relate specifically to Maryland are a group of photos of a 1911 flight by Lt. John Rodgers.

STATE ORGANIZATIONS AND PUBLIC LIBRARIES

Enoch Pratt Free Library, 400 Cathedral St., Baltimore, Md. 21201; 410-396-5430. The website, www.pratt.lib.md.us, includes a general catalogue, and a page describing the resources of the Maryland Department. In that department itself, a large "query" card subject file contains brief information and cross references to the extensive vertical files and to other sources. Many of the vertical files contain useful clippings and pamphlets about aviation. This also a large system of biographical card files. The Maryland Department possesses a broad range of publications on the state's past, including county and local histories, and several cabinets of historical maps. The photo collection contains about 24,000 items dating through the 1950s, including some relating to aviation. The photos are arranged in cabinets, primarily by the names of companies, persons, and streets, and may be searched directly by patrons. Films and videos, in the Social Science Division, are covered in the on-line catalogue.

In its capacity as the State Library Resource Center, the Pratt Library manages **Sailor, Maryland's Public Information**

Network. The Sailor website, www.sailor.lib.md.us, includes an internal site search engine, as well as links to public libraries statewide and to many historical sources and organizations.

Maryland Aviation Administration (MAA), POB 8766, Terminal Bldg. 3rd Floor, BWI Airport, Md. 21240-8766; 410-859-7061. The website, www.marylandaviation.com, provides historical information on the two largest state-run airports, as well as current data on airports statewide, MAA programs, etc. Useful records are maintained at MAA's **Office of Regional Aviation Assistance**, 991 Corporate Blvd., Linthicum, Md. 21090 (410-859-7064). These include files pertaining to airports and to the state's program of regulation and assistance for general aviation. Among topics covered are: forms describing airports; correspondence files on closed and current airports; archival files on certain airports; aviation system plans; aviation conferences; economic impact studies; state aeronautical charts; airport directories; and grant programs. Although there is a file on aviation history, the records generally do not predate 1971. An extensive collection of aerial photos of airports is maintained.

Maryland Department of the Environment. This Department's website, www.mde.md.state.us, includes ERRP Fact Sheets prepared by the Environmental Restoration and Redevelopment Program. Some of these documents, which are listed by county, contain historical information on aviation-related sites.

Maryland Historical Society, 201 W Monument St., Baltimore, Md. 21201-4674; 410-685-3750. The website, www.mdhs.org, includes a catalogue for the Society's library, and an internal search engine for on-line information. The site also provides a search engine for the extensive photograph collection. Among the photo holdings are: the collection of Van Lear Black, a Marylander noted for his international air travels, c. 1925-30; the Clarence Beckett-Maryland National Guard aerial photo collection, 1935-40; the Howard Cruett Wilcox-Halethorpe Air Meet collection, 1910; and the Robert F. Kniesche collection, 1920s-'70s, including aerials shots and images of such aircraft as the *China Clipper*. There are also other personal collections that contain some aviation photos. The museum provides photo reproduction services for a fee. Manuscripts include Charles F. Elvers' three albums on early aviation, and the papers Hammond James Dugan, a Navy officer and aeronautical engineer who died in the *Akron* crash. Vertical file topics include such topics as airports, aviation, and balloons.

Maryland Historical Trust Archives and Library, 100 Community Place, Crownsville, Md. 21032. The website, www.marylandhistoricaltrust.net, describes the collection, which includes publications on Maryland history and on the disciplines of archeology, historic preservation, oral history, and community documentation. (An on-line catalogue is under construction.) The website also provides lists of historic maps at the library, and of National Register and National Landmark sites statewide. The library maintains data and files on these sites, as well as others covered by the Maryland Inventory of Historic Properties. At the library, computerized finding aids are available for the inventory forms, archeological reports, and compliance reports. Much of this material is directly or indi-

rectly related to the state's aerospace history. A list of relevant files is included in the context report bibliography.

Notable aviation related resources include:

The Maryland Centennial of Flight Celebration Oral History Project (2002-2003) conducted by the Martha Ross Center for Oral History University of Maryland, Baltimore County (UMBC). The project focused on the acquisition of oral history interviews and supporting photographic documentation of the most significant individuals who contributed to the development of Maryland aviation, had knowledge of Maryland aviation and/or had a Maryland aviation connection.

As a result of the research conducted, twenty-five "official" interviews were completed. Two additional interviews were accomplished because of their unique content and the need to capture the accounts in a timely fashion. From the twenty-five "official" interviews, the following items were produced: fifty-five audio recordings, four video tapes, sixty hours of oral history content, 1,000 pages of transcripts and over 150 supporting photographs and documents.

An oral history portfolio was created for each interview. The portfolios include the original and edited transcripts of the interview, the tape recordings, current and historical photographs and supporting documents. An interview abstract was written by the interviewee and in some cases, a three to five page historical vignette was produced. The portfolio also included legal agreements, legal permission to reproduce photographs and UMBC, Institutional Review Board documents for research involving human subjects. The original research portfolios are archived with the Maryland Historical Trust and copies of the portfolios reside at the Martha Ross Center for Oral History. Use by scholars, researchers and the general public is encouraged.

In assessing the value of the information collected, over ninety years of Maryland aviation history was documented. While the important facts, figures and aviation data were recorded, the unique nature of the content was in the narratives that captured the interviewees' personal accomplishments, eyewitness experiences, subjective reflections and insights into Maryland aviation that could not be accomplished in any other manner. Thus, the "Maryland Centennial of Flight Celebration Oral History Project," with its richness of human experience, compliments the research on Maryland aviation sites, aircraft and events. Together, the research establishes an initial set of documentation chronicling Maryland's aviation history and provides a cornerstone on which additional research may be accomplished.

Interviewees included: Betsey Weick (Fred Weick and the Ercoupe), Mary Feik (aviation mechanics / The "Captivair," the Civil Air Patrol, airplane restoration, Col. George Henry (Ret.) (aerial combat in Vietnam), Herbert H. Jones (John Greene, African Americans in Maryland aviation), Bill Rinn (Fairchild and Henson Aviation), Allen Clopper (Fairchild and aeronautical engineering), Jack King (Glenn L Martin, Dick Henson / Henson Aviation), Aubrey Patterson (aerial photography, early parachuting), Mr. Gustavus (Gus) McLeod (Flight to the North Pole in a Stearman biplane), Bruce Mundie (Maryland Aviation Administration, general Maryland aviation history), Bill Morris (Kentmoor Airpark, Bay Bridge Airport, Maryland's most senior pilot), Joe Frichera (aviation mechanics, aviation restoration),

Col. Paul Butler (Ret.) (aerial combat in Korea, Distinguished Flying Cross), Henry Rinn (The Baltimore Aero Meet of 1910), Elaine Harmon (Women Airforce Service Pilots, "WASP"), Bill Almquist (Silver Wings Organization), Wendy Carter (Montgomery Co. Airpark, Cluster Channel Wing aircraft) Jane Straughan (Women Airforce Service Pilots, "WASP"), Henry Phipps (Civil Air Patrol), Charles O'Brien and Richard Whistler (World War I aviators), Paul Lebert (Harbor Field & BWI air traffic controller), Maynard Binge (Development and transformation of Camp Springs Air Base and Andrews Air Force Base), Jesse Mitchell (Maryland Air National Guard, Gary Ryan (Westinghouse, development of air traffic control radar systems), Charles Greenslit (Bendix Corporation, development of air weather radar and air traffic control systems), Ferne Virginia Toms and Gayle Barnes (Airplane construction at Fairchild, Janet Lee Simpson and Kathryn Hutchinson James ("The Flying Hutchinsons").

The Middle River Community History Project (1995-1996) sponsored by the Baltimore County Office of Planning, Maryland Historical Trust, and Maryland Humanities Council, this two-year project conducted documentary and oral-history research into a community profoundly affected by the huge Glenn L. Martin aircraft factory in its midst. Among the forty-three people interviewed were pre-1939 residents of Middle River, wartime in-migrant workers (men and women), their children, and African-American Martin workers excluded from living or working in Middle River. Dr. John R. Breihan of Loyola College directed the effort; Jessica Payne and Tom Robertson were the oral historians.

Documentary research and oral histories are combined in more than 150 pages of reports on the Historical and Architectural Resources of Middle River and five of its principal historical structures: the Aero Acres Shopping Center, the Glenn L. Martin Plant No. 1, the Mars Estates housing complex, the Pierce-Cemesto prefabricated houses, and the Victory Villa Community Building. These are filed under the Field and Research Reports (FRR BaCo5) at the library of the Maryland Historical Trust, Crownsville. Thirty-eight cassette tapes containing thirty-two recorded interviews are also at the MHT library, along with full index/logs and partial transcripts.

Interviewees included: Marge Katonka; Evan Brady; Ray and Marge Barhight; James Myers; Minerva Gorden; Virginia Atkinson; Lester Hopkins; Marie Buchanan; Mary Carter; Virginia Flippen; Charles Bader; Edward and Emma Blazek; Olive Richter, Nellie Ruth Ledbetter; Jim Coffman; Andrew Rock; William Hall; Bessie Muenzing; Andrew Poklemba; Carol (Cody) Dick; Rissie Hill; Roy Hill & Phyllis Cunningham; Howard & Ivy Akers; Calvin Tolbert; Sylvia Anderson; Roger & Linda Magsamen; Freda Pollack & Kay Keirn; Barbara Hirsch & Enda Kneavel; Helen Myers; Virginia Preston; Mildred Gardner; Ruby Jankiewicz; Catherine Doehler; Harvey Hodgin; Nora Hall; Gerry Gray; and Julie Kaufman.

Maryland Port Administration: Engineering Department. The June 2000 context report on Baltimore Municipal Airport/Harbor Field (BA-149) lists this department's Dundalk Marine Terminal as source for original drawings of buildings at the former airport; however, inquiries failed to produce the name of a contact person or office.

Maryland State Archives: www.mdarchives.state.md.us; 350 Blvd., Annapolis, Md. 21401; 410-260-6400 (within Maryland: 800-235-4045); The website offers Archives of Maryland On Line, a general search engine, and several specialized ones (the government publications engine is not included in the general engine). The site also provides a general guide to the collection, which includes state and local records, as well as newspapers and special collections. Pertinent items include records of the state aviation regulatory bodies, as well as annual reports and publications issued by them. The on-line search engine of the photograph collection identified about a dozen images of aviation-related subjects, in addition to a large number of aerial views, some of which show airports.

Maryland State Law Library, 362 Rowe Blvd., Annapolis, Md. 21401-1697 (telephone: 410-260-1430; within Maryland, 888-216-8156). The website, www.lawlib.state.md.us, provides an on-line catalogue of the library's collection and other tools such as a search engine for the current Maryland Code. Aids for researching aviation law at the library itself include volumes of the Annotated Code of Maryland, which has an annual supplement and is republished every several years. The library also has the Code of Maryland Regulations (COMAR) since publication began in 1977, and county ordinances dating back into the 1970s. The collection of state publications includes the annual reports of the Maryland Department of Transportation since 1973. Among other holdings are published histories of the state and its regions and counties.

University of Maryland, College Park, Md., 20742-7011; general library number: 301-405-0800. The website, www.umd.edu, includes catalogues for the university's libraries statewide.

At the College Park campus, the Maryland Room (405-9257) is located at the **Hornbake Library**. The Maryland room services both the university's institutional archives and the extensive Marylandia collection of books, periodicals, maps, and state government publications. The manuscripts include a collection on WPA activities that no doubt includes aviation-related information. Much of the Maryland Room's holdings are in the general on-line catalogue, and a page on the website explains what material is and is not included. Other finding aids available at the Maryland Room itself are listed by title on the website.

No finding aid exists for the vertical files, which must be searched by staff members. A preliminary search showed files on the following pertinent topics: Aeronautics; Aberdeen Proving Ground; Airports; Annapolis, general; Andrews AFB; BWI and Friendship; Bendix Corp.; College Park Airport; Fairchild Corp.; Ft. Detrick; Goddard; Patuxent NAS; Westinghouse; US Naval Academy. Also searchable only by the staff are the topical clipping files of the *News American*, a long-standing Baltimore newspaper that closed in 1986.

The most important photographic resource of the Maryland Room is also from the *News American*, a large collection that is mostly from the 1930-80s. These photos may be searched with an electronic finding aid available at the library, but not on the web. The Maryland Room's other photos relate primarily to the university itself, although the Historical Manuscripts Collection includes photos of College Park Airport (301-314-2712). The

Nonprint Media Services Department, also at the Hornbake Library, maintains an extensive collection of films and videotapes that is searchable in the general on-line catalogue.

Other useful libraries on the campus include: the **Engineering and Physical Sciences Library** (301-405-9157) and the **McKeldin Library** (301-405-9075), which has a large general library and a Federal government documents section.

Washington County Free Library, 100 South Potomac St., Hagerstown, Md. 21740. (301-739-3250, ext. 158). The **Western Maryland Room**, in addition to published material, maintains one file drawer of documents and photographs on local aviation. The material in the drawer relates to the Fairchild and Kreider-Reisner companies, including an unpublished manuscript on the latter.

OTHER LIBRARIES

Applied Physics Laboratory, 11100 Johns Hopkins Road, Laurel, MD 20723-6099. website: www.jhuapl.edu. From Washington: 240-228-5000; from Baltimore: 443-778-5000. The library at APL is primarily a technical rather than a historical resource. According to the Naval Historical Center website, however, APL holds 3 linear feet of records relating to the development and production of the radio-proximity VT fuze, 1940-1946.

Johns Hopkins University, Sheridan Libraries, 3400 N. Charles St., Baltimore, Md. 21218; 410-516-8335. The principal element of the Sheridan Libraries is the Eisenhower Library, which has an unusually large collection of published works, as well as a government documents section. All of the library's holdings are searchable through its general on-line catalogue, www.jhu.edu/jhuniverse/libraries. Among its Special Collections are the papers of Hugh L. Dryden, as well as a smaller collection of the papers of Joseph S. Ames. (To view these papers, it is advisable to notify the archivist in advance: 410-516-7202). The Special Collections include some photographs, and the library has a separate Audiovisual Department. The library provides photo reproduction, by permission and for a fee. A preliminary search, however, identified no photos or videos that seemed relevant.

University of Baltimore, Langsdale Library, 1420 Maryland Ave., Baltimore, Md. 21201; 301-625-3135. http://langsdale.ubalt.edu. The Special Collections include records of the Baltimore City Department of Planning that are reported to contain material relating to airport planning and to Civil Aeronautics Board dockets during the era 1955-72.

MUSEUMS

Aberdeen Room Archives and Museum, 18 N Howard St, POB 698, Aberdeen, Md. 21001. Tel. 410-273-6325. www.aberdeenroom.com. In September 2000, the archivist reported that the institution had no artifacts, and only a few records, relevant to aviation history. The archivist forwarded copies of items on local airports and on Aberdeen Proving Ground, which have been added to the project's files, and reported that the collection contained three pertinent photos showing: a 1923 air crash at APG; a related photo of a water

tower; and an early 1950s photo of Aberdeen Airpark. Reproduction is available for a fee.

Airman Memorial Museum, 5211 Auth Rd., Suitland, Md. 20746. Tel: 800-638-0594; 301, 899-3500. website includes a brief description of collection: www.afsahq.org/AMM/amm-htm/mwelcome.htm. The museum focuses on enlisted personnel in the Army's air arm, beginning in 1907, and later in the Air Force. Exhibits include such items as uniforms, medals, equipment and memorabilia. The archives' most notable resource is the personal papers of airmen. Records are organized by the donor's name, airman's name, or by type of artifact. Still photos are filed by collection name (usually that of the donor); reproduction is provided, with permission, for a fee. A separate videotape collection consists primarily of tapes created by the museum itself. None of the records, images, or artifacts are known to pertain directly to Maryland. The usefulness of the museum's holdings for a study of Maryland aviation will depend on researchers' prior identification of airmen from the state.

Baltimore Museum of Industry, 1415 S. Key Highway, Inner Harbor S., Baltimore, Md. 21230; 410-727-4808, archives: ext. 109. The website, www.charm.net/~bmi/, includes detailed lists of the archival and photographic collections. Relevant archival materials include Glenn L. Martin Company papers (three ft.), six flight log books of Martin chief test pilot William K. Ebel, and the Bendix Radio Foundation Collection of records and publications. Vertical files are maintained on the following pertinent topics: aircraft industry; air transportation; BWI Airport; Martin Co.; and Martin Marietta Middle River Aircraft Systems. The photograph collection includes 310 items from the Martin Co., as well as relevant items from the collections of the Baltimore Gas & Electric Co. and the Kopper/Bartett-Hayward Division. The museum arranges for photo reproduction. Other pertinent resources include published books, two videotaped interviews with retired Martin workers, and a videotape on the Dundalk Marine Terminal. The Martin Mini-Mariner test aircraft is on display in the museum, and the "Maryland Milestones" permanent exhibit also features sections on Martin and on Westinghouse.

College Park Aviation Museum, 1985 Cpl. Frank Scott Dr., College Park, Md. 20740; 301-864-6029. The website, www.pgparks.com/places/historic.cpamuseum.html, describes the museum and its collections. In addition to interpreting the history of College Park Airport, the artifacts, library, photographs, and records of the museum include much other material relevant to the broader history of aviation in the state. A detailed list of the subjects covered by the archives, provided by the director, is filed with the material compiled for this inventory project. Among the many topic areas are: the Wright Brothers and their aircraft; early U.S. military aviation and its leaders; civil aviators and aviation companies associated with College Park; other Maryland airports; air mail history; Bureau of Standards research; Emile and Henry Berliner, and their helicopters; the Engineering and Research Corporation (ERCO); women in aviation; the Civil Air Patrol; and aviation history in general.

Glenn L. Martin Maryland Aviation Museum, POB 5024, Middle River, Md. 21220; 410-682-6122. The website, www.

martinstateairport.com/museum/index/htm, describes the museum and its collections, and includes a listing of the Martin papers at the Library of Congress. (Note: the Martin State Airport's main website also offers a brief history of that facility.) Although the museum is expanding its scope to include aviation history statewide, its current collection focuses on the Martin company. The archives includes: several drawers of company records; about 100 boxes of papers and artifacts donated by retired Martin employees; news releases, 1940-61; a complete collection of the *Martin Star* newsletter; design drawings and blueprints; about four linear feet of binders containing news clippings; and several shelves of aircraft technical orders. Martin-produced images include an estimated 40,000 photos, 100,000 negatives, and 2,500 reels of film. The negatives and films are indexed by number, in roughly chronological order, with titles or brief descriptions. The still photos are partially covered by a similar index. The museum also possesses about 125 videotapes copied from the films during production of a "Discovery" television program on seaplanes. Reproduction of images is arranged by the museum, provided that the requester covers the cost and credits the institution. The artifact collection includes a wide variety of items such as production models, memorabilia, and aircraft components. Among the outdoor exhibits are three Martin-built planes: two RB-57A Canberra jets and a 4-O-4 airliner.

Historical Electronics Museum, 1745 West Nursery Rd., Linthicum, Md.; mail: POB 746, MS 4015, Baltimore MD 21203; 410-765-0230 (general number); website: www.erols.com/radarmus/. The museum has an extensive collection of radar and other electronic equipment, including Westinghouse systems manufactured and/or developed in Maryland. The library possesses published books on electronics, many of which are relevant to aviation and space technology. The current catalogue is on a computer in the library. Librarian Tom Ballard is available on Mondays, or by appointment. The archives, which include many company records, are organized by system name and other topical headings. The collection also includes several hundred videotapes, some of which are relevant to Maryland aerospace history. The still photo collection is interspersed with the archives. Reproduction of photos, by permission, must be arranged by the requester.

National Air and Space Museum, Smithsonian Institution, 7th and Independence Ave., SW, Washington, DC 20560: Archives Division: POB 37012, D.C. 20013-7012; library reference desk: 202-633-2320. The NASM website, www.nasm.si.edu, offers a variety of historical information and describes the museum's collection both in general terms and in detail. For example, there are historical summaries on all NASM-owned aircraft, many of which are Maryland products. There are similar listings for selected rocketry- and space-related artifacts, some of which have Maryland associations. The Library and Archives Reading Room is open by appointment. The library's holdings of publications include books, government documents, manuals, journals, and these are searchable through the Smithsonian Libraries' general on-line catalogue, www. siris.si.edu. The Archive Division's collection of personal, professional, and corporate papers are not catalogued online; however, they are described

in the NASM website's guide to aerospace history resources at repositories nationwide. Paper finding aids available at the library for these manuscripts, and also for the Technical Reference Files of documents and photos which have been created by the staff on a broad range of topics. The Technical Reference series includes three general files on Maryland, and an additional files on 15 locations in the state. Visitors may search the large still photograph collection through a disk-based system at the library, and reproductions are provided for a fee. The staff will research and reproduce items from the film archives, also for a fee.

U.S. Army Ordnance Museum: see Aberdeen Proving Ground.

COUNTY HISTORICAL SOCIETIES

The following societies reported that they had no significant material relating to aviation history: Allegany, Calvert, Dorchester, Prince Georges, Queen Anne's, Somerset. No questionnaire reply was received from the following societies: Caroline, Carroll, Charles, Cecil, Howard, Wicomico, and Worcester.

Ann Arrundell County Historical Society, POB 385, Linthicum MD 21090-0385. Street address: 7101 Aviation Blvd. The collection includes about. two and one-half feet of aviation-related vertical file material, including photos. Much of this was compiled for the preparation of John F. R. Scott's *Voyages Into Airy Regions*, which the Society sponsored; however, material has been added since the book's publication in 1984.

Baltimore County Historical Society, 9811 Van Buren Ln., Cockeysville, MD 21030-5022 (410-666-1878. The website, www.baltocounty.org, describes the library's holdings. The Society's collection includes the W. W. Pagon Archives, which contains over 100 photos documenting the construction of Baltimore Municipal Airport/Harbor Field and the Pan American Seaplane Base. Also on hand are published books and articles pertinent to other airports and to the Glenn L. Martin company. Copies of several items were provided to assist the project.

Frederick County, Historical Society of, 24 E Church St. Frederick MD 21701 (301-663-1188). The website, www.fwp.net/hsfc/index.htm, gives a brief overview of the library holdings. Collection includes an airport/airplanes vertical file, as well as three pertinent photos: the first airplane to land in Frederick (1911); Lincoln Beachey making an exhibition flight; and a Civic Club P-51 Mustang.

Garrett County Historical Society, Box 28, Oakland MD 21550. Street address: 107 S Second St. (301-334-3226); website: www.deepcreektimes.com/gchs.html. Collection includes a small number of pertinent items: the log of the county's first licensed pilot, Lawrence Bittinger; a photo of a barnstormer's Waco, c. 1930; an account of a B-17 crash in the county in 1943.

Harford County, Historical Society of, POB 366, Bel Air MD 21014-0366. Street address: 143 N Main St. (410-838-7691). The website, www.harfordhistory.net, briefly describes the archives.

The research files include articles on Phillips Army Airfield and Aldino Airport, as well as a book excerpt on John Wise's 1836 balloon flight to the county from Pennsylvania. There is also at least one photo of early naval aviator John Rodgers with his Wright Flier and his parents in front of their Harford County home, reports librarian Mary E. Henderson.

Kent County, Historical Society of, POB 665, Chestertown MD 21620-0665. Street address: 101 Church Alley (410-778-3499) www.hskcmd.com. Director provided copies of articles and excepts from books concerning local aviators and the county residences of Glenn Martin and Guiseppe Bellanca.

Montgomery County Historical Society, 111 W Montgomery Ave. Rockville MD 20850-4212 (301-340-2825) The website, www.montgomeryhistory.org, gives an overview of the library holdings. In addition to published books, the library has a vertical file on airports, as well as biographical files that include the well-known contemporary aviator, Gustavus McLeod. The photo files include images of Congressional Airport, Montgomery County Airpark, and the Naval Ship Research Center.

St. Mary's County Historical Society, POB 212, Leonardtown, MD 20657-0212. Street address: 41625 Court House Dr. (301-475-2467) www.smchsonline.org. Collection includes newspapers and books pertinent to Naval Air Station Patuxent River, as well as images of the station and of air shows there.

Talbot County, Historical Society of, 25 S. Washington St. Easton MD 21601-3014; 410-822-0773: www.hstc.org. Collections include about 3,000 images of the county taken by pioneer aerial photographer H. Robins Hollyday (copies available for a fee).

Washington County Historical Society, POB 1281, Hagerstown MD 21741-1281 (301-797-8782). In addition to published books, collections include pertinent vertical files entitled: Aircraft Industries; Airport/Hagerstown Regional; Airport/Washington County; Aircraft Industries; Aviation Heritage Museum, Hagerstown; and Fairchild. There are also photo files entitled: Airport, Washington County; and Fairchild. Arrangements may be made with a local photographer for copying photos.

MISCELLANEOUS

Abandoned and Little-Known Airfields (http://members.tripod.com/airfields_freeman/index.htm) by Paul Freeman, copyright 2002, revised October 17, 2002. This website is a pilot's compilation of descriptions, history, and images of selected airfields in fotry-five states. Essays on facilities in Maryland cover seventeen airfields and one Nike missile site.

Aerofiles (www.aerofiles.com) is a non-commercial on-line compilation of data on aviation history, including links to other sites and organizations dealing with various aspects of the topic.

Aerovintage (www.aerovintage.com) is a commercial website by Scott Thompson, an author, bookseller, and Federal Aviation Administration inspector. It includes links to other aviation history sites, and a database that can be used to identify Maryland-made aircraft used by FAA and its predecessors.

American Aviation Historical Society, 2333 Otis St., Santa Ana, Calif. 92704; 714-549-4818. The website, www.aahs-online.org, provides excerpts from AASH Journal issues back to the summer of 2000, and links to various aviation history organizations. All other research services are on a members-only basis.

Aircraft Owners and Pilots Association, 42 Aviation Way, Frederick, Md. 21701; 301-695-2126. AOPA's website, www.aopa.org, provides a brief history of the organization. which moved its headquarters to Maryland in the 1950s, first at Bethesda, later the present location. Its library is open to the public, but catalogue search via the web is restricted to members.

Fairchild Controls Corporation, 540 Highland St., Frederick, Md. 21701; 301-228-3400; 800-695-5378. Spun off from Fairchild Industries in 1994, this Maryland aerospace firm maintains a website, www.fairchildcontrols.com, that includes a brief corporate history (printed out for project files).

Globalsecurity: www.globalsecurity.org, a non-profit website with information that includes descriptions of certain military facilities in Maryland.

Landings: www.landings.com; a commercial "hub" site on aviation that includes links to many aviation museums and history websites.

Lockheed Martin Corporation. The website, www.lockheed-martin.com, includes a chronology of both the Lockheed and Martin companies. The corporation's Naval Electronics and Surveillance Systems-Marine Systems division is located near Martin State Airport at 2323 Eastern Blvd., Baltimore, Md. 21220 The division has its own chronology on its website, http://ness.external.1mco.com/nessb/. It also has a library that maintains newsletters, technical reports, and similar material, most of which dates no earlier than the mid-1960s. The library is not normally open to the public, but the librarian is the contact for inquiries.

The Ninety-Nines, Inc., 7100 Terminal Drive, Box 965, Oklahoma City, Ok., 73159-0965; 800-994-1929; 405-685-7969. Founded in 1929, this organization of women pilots is a possible source of biographical data on Marylanders who may have been members. Its website, www.ninety-nines.org, includes information on the history of women in aviation.

NSS, Annapolis, Maryland: http://members.aol.com/k6dc/nss.html. A website on the history of the now-decommissioned Very Low Frequency transmitter station at Greenbury Point. While the facility was not directly related to aviation, its location near the former air station gives this topic some relevance. Created by Navy veteran Merle Parten, the website was last updated in 1997.

Tuskegee Airmen, Inc.: http://tuskegeeairmen.org; 1501 Lee Highway, Suite 130, Arlington, Va. 22209-1109; 703-522-8590. website includes brief historical information, lists state chapters (D.C. has one, but Maryland does not).

Index